IN MY WILDEST DREAMS

Born in Newport, Monmouthshire, in 1931, Leslie Thomas is the son of a sailor who was lost at sea in 1943. His boyhood in an orphanage is evoked in *This Time Last Week*, published in 1964. At sixteen, he became a reporter before going on to do his national service. He won worldwide acclaim with his bestselling novel *The Virgin Soldiers*. In 2005 he received the OBE for services to literature.

IN MY WILDEST DREAMS

Leslie Thomas

arrow books

Published in the United Kingdom by Arrow Books in 2006

5 7 9 10 8 6 4

Copyright © Leslie Thomas, 1984
Introduction to the 2006 edition © Leslie Thomas, 2006

Leslie Thomas has asserted his right under the Copyright, Designs
and Patents Act, 1988 to be identified as the author of this work.

First published in the United Kingdom in 1984 by Arlington Books

Arrow Books
The Random House Group Limited
20 Vauxhall Bridge Road, London, SW1V 2SA

Random House Australia (Pty) Limited
20 Alfred Street, Milsons Point, Sydney
New South Wales 2061, Australia

Random House New Zealand Limited
18 Poland Road, Glenfield
Auckland 10, New Zealand

Random House (Pty) Limited
Isle of Houghton, Corner of Boundary Road & Carse O'Gowrie
Houghton 2198, South Africa

Random House Group Limited Reg. No. 954009

www.randomhouse.co.uk

A CIP catalogue record for this book
is available from the British Library

Papers used by Random House are natural, recyclable products made
from wood grown in sustainable forests. The manufacturing processes
conform to the environmental regulations of the country of origin

ISBN 9780099499749

Typeset in Baskerville by Palimpsest Book Production Limited,
Polmont, Stirlingshire

Printed and bound in Great Britain by
CPI Antony Rowe, Chippenham, Wiltshire

Foreword: 2006

It has been an odd, perhaps even eerie, experience reading this book again more than twenty years after writing it. Even though it concerns the events of my own life which, goodness knows, ought to be familiar, I discovered it to be both revealing and engrossing as if it were the story of someone I had known quite a long time ago. In fact, once I had started reading the book I could hardly put it down!

This time I felt more concern for the struggles and upheavals of my boy's life than I recall feeling when it was clattering around me. The poignancy of my sick mother having to send away her two sons, knowing that she would never again see them, disturbed me deeply and almost for the first time, as did the shock of two boys abruptly realising they were heading for an orphanage.

But these tragedies were balanced, if only in part, by reliving the optimism I felt when a few years later I found myself firmly on two feet and knowing that I was starting my life again, alone it is true, but confident, even cocky, in knowing that I had a choice of the way ahead. Where I went, what I did, who I *was* even, were up to me. One famously successful man said to me not long ago: 'You had the great advantage of not having parents.'

Not that I go along with this Larkinesque twist entirely but I knew what he meant. I *knew* I had parents until I was twelve and those early years *had happened*. I could rely on the memories, dimming though they are now. What used to be called Dr Barnardo's Homes have produced many successful people but others, in their minds anyway, have never quite left the orphanage. They were always wondering about their roots. I had mine; they were already in place.

When this book was first published I had become a grandfather. Lois, my daughter, gave birth to twins. Charlie and Joe Faulkner are now at university. Joe shows unmistakable signs of becoming a notable writer and Charlie of becoming an agent, which sounds like a useful combination.

My parents had something like twenty brothers and sisters between them so there must be many unknown relatives out there. Mercifully we leave each other alone.

My own sons, Mark, Gareth and Matthew, live not far away. Matthew was married in St Paul's Cathedral on a mellow autumn day last year, a distinction afforded by my being awarded the OBE 'For Services to Literature'. The honour pleased me immensely and I hope showed a sign to those who like to dub themselves The Literary Establishment. Perhaps they did not notice.

For some years I have been a vice-president of Barnardo's (which would seem like taking after-care too far). When I was first elected, Princess Diana was president and there was a famous day (for me anyway) when, sitting beside her, I was to make a speech at the Savoy. This would have been a memorable occassion anyway, even if the outfitters where I purchased my new suit had not shortened the same trouser leg twice.

I counted (I needed to) the list of my novels; up to now they number twenty-nine plus four non-fiction books. I am about to start a thirtieth novel. Writing books is all I can do. Some have been commercially and artistically successful, others less so, but I have survived in the writing game. The advances are less exciting now although I had an excellent run for my money in earlier times. Many of my current readers are regular clients of their local libraries or Oxfam shops.

I did not have to read beyond page one of the original autobiography to find an error. My mother must have had one of her flights of fancy when she claimed I was born in a nursing home on Stow Hill, Newport. It always sounded a bit pricey to me. My birth certificate, which I have since read (after seventy-five years), marks the spot less exaltedly as 'Herbert Street'.

There is, however, some comfort in the knowledge that, as I have told in this story, W.H. Davies, the poet, was born only a few streets away. There was some confusion here too, as I have described, because a plaque commemorating this event, and relying on his own information, was fixed to the wrong house. Newport-born authors are apparently unreliable witnesses.

But, in all, being a writer is a grand life and you can stay at home to do it. My wife Diana, who, when I embarked on *In My Wildest Dreams,* requested that I mentioned her only in passing, has been a warm and interesting companion over more than thirty-five years. We have lived in more houses than some villages contain, we have explored the world in everything from a sailing ship to a Second World War Dakota. But when we get home to our house by the harbour in Lymington, Hampshire, we feel ourselves smile.

The city where I was born, Newport, is still just recognisable. It is an idiosyncratic place, a frontier town between England and Wales. When I was at school the town was geographically in England ('England and Monmouthshire' was the official placing) but its heart was always Welsh. We used to get a half-holiday for St George's Day and St David's Day. The pubs were also open on a Sunday, which meant a Sabbath exodus (religiously observed) from Wales, where they were closed. Now it is placed irrevocably in Wales where it belongs.

There are plans, expansive and expensive, to change the place, but not too much I hope. The River Usk still sidles like a muddy snake below the old girders of the Transporter Bridge which was to me as a child one of the wonders of the world and it is still a landmark. Now there are two motorway bridges spanning the inky river and it was never much good as a bridge anyway. I would not be surprised if somebody called it an icon.

The museum where I used to browse for hours as a boy has moved from Dock Street to John Frost Square (named after one of the Chartist rioters of the nineteenth-century, one of the few perpetrators in Newport of historical unruliness). It houses the marvellously huge ship models that once made me pine to go to sea like my father and brothers.

None of them is now living. My younger brother Roy, who had been closer to me than the others (he could hardly have been more remote), continued his adventurous life, becoming a bosun on a 200,000-ton ore carrier sailing around Australia from Port Kembla, New South Wales. True to the adventurous tenor of his life he finally lost it when he blew himself up. He was in hospital, dying anyway of the emphysema which had dogged him. He was breathing oxygen through a tube and casually lit up a cigarette at the same time. The resulting explosion almost lifted the roof off the ward. He was alive when I telephoned from England. 'I'm all right,' he assured me. 'Except there's not much left of my nose.' He died the next day. I sat down and laughed and cried at the same time.

Maesglas, the last council estate in England or Wales, whichever way you were looking in those days, was a penniless place everybody called Moscow. When it was built in the thirties the winter was of such Soviet severity that the frost-bound workmen gave it the name.

Poor though it was, nobody who ever lived there can today mention its name (which in Welsh means 'Green Fields'), or its Russian nickname, without breaking into a grin. It was a singular collection of streets and people. They have knocked it down now and rebuilt the houses that once half-hid behind the privets.

There was a patch of garden at the front and the back, and they were more spacious than our previous council house on the summit of the hill at Somerton at the other end of the town, where we perched among the Welsh winds. I also made a sentimental journey to that house and discovered that it too had been demolished. But only just. The outline of the brick footings was still to be seen. The only living room seemed so confined, even with the absence of walls. I remembered how my mother had performed the tango, a dance that needs space, across it. It was getting dusk and the same old wind was blowing. Secretly I tried a few tango steps myself in the tight outline of the room. A passer-by stopped to watch me in the dimness and then cautiously moved on.

Mysteries often solve themselves once they become histories. In these pages I have told of the strange 'gas attack' early in the war which had the Maesglas house-wives, snorting through gasmasks, scrubbing down the pavements outside their homes. 'Mysterious White Powder Dropped By Germans' reported the *South Wales Argus* but its purpose was never explained. Recently I discovered that the alarm was occasioned by the overturning of a lorry carrying a cargo of bone-meal powder, which is used in the manufacture of deadly anthrax, presumably meant to combat the expected German invasion, so the emergency was not so unnecessary. There was a factory in Cardiff that processed the bone-meal.

Another discovery I have made is that I might have had a half-sister. As a small child I recall a lively young woman, about the age of my elder brothers, appearing at home. She came from Birmingham and, viewed carefully, I think she may have been the result of my mother's stay in that city. 'You had a sister once,' I remember my mother saying. This lady is only a shadow but even as I have been writing this paragraph I have miraculously remembered her name: Daisy Fern.

After many years I also rediscovered my boyhood

friend Chubber, or he rediscovered me. When we were young and roaming the streets and woods, we used to leave secret messages for each other and at the bottom of the page was a drawing of a dagger dripping blood. Fifty years went past and one day I opened a letter to see that same childish sign. Appropriate to his nickname he became a locksmith and we have since kept in touch, meeting up on occasions. Once he said to me: 'I'm retiring next year. I'm going to finish *my* book then.'

'You're writing a book?' I asked.

'No, I'm reading one.'

Each November I go back to Newport to march in the Merchant Navy memorial parade, organised by another one-time Maesglas boy, Bertie Bale. More merchant seafarers were lost from the town than all the other wartime services put together. My father was one of them and I do it for him, wearing his medals and clanking along the main street. My marching days are limited, though. Last year I could hardly keep up with the mayoress.

The old man would have enjoyed the scene. So many aspects of his life were embroidered with farce – even, so I have discovered, the news of his death at sea. He had written the wrong address on his next-of-kin form before setting off on his final voyage. The message was delivered to another family several streets away and the hapless telegram boy had to trundle his bike around the many Thomas families in Maesglas trying to discover one with a missing-believed-drowned father.

Through the years I have made several sentimental journeys to the rather sombre house on the crest of

Fore Street, Kingsbridge, in the South Hams district of Devon, where two anxious brothers, carrying their sparse belongings, arrived on the day after they had said tearful farewells to their mother. The house seems smaller now as childhood places do when revisited later in life. A housing estate has sprouted in the paddock where I used to ride Pommerse the pony. I used his name for a horse in my novel *Dover Beach*.

Teatimes at Lower Knowle were redolent with peanut butter, a gift from American soldiers; many years later those same Americans provided me with the basis of *The Magic Army*, a book which revealed for the first time the bungling tragedy of more than seven hundred young men who died by German action in one night while they were only *practising* invasion landings off Slapton Sands, Devon.

The success of *The Magic Army* resulted in a summons from the United States, from the Pentagon no less, to receive an award for my part in revealing, years later, the terrible story. In Washington there was an impressive dinner attended by veteran survivors of the ill-starred Exercise Tiger and I was presented with an engraved plaque. But military blunders were not a thing of the past and the framed citation was made out in the wrong name. There were on-the-spot apologies and the right item was forwarded to me when I was back home in Britain.

Barnardo's called their reception homes 'Ever-Open-Doors'. The Kingsbridge home was in the charge of a grey and handsome man who, though not in holy orders, liked to dress in ecclesiastical garb, wearing a clerical collar and preaching in St Edmund's

Church. More than thirty years later I saw his name in a local newspaper at Henley-on-Thames, where Diana and I were living. He had recently died after long being the well-respected vicar of a local church, presumably by then officially ordained.

Since I became a vice-president of Barnardo's I have been called on to assist in various ways. Once I presented a short television film about some disabled toddlers at Harrogate where I could scarcely stem the tears. The day after the film was shown on television I was walking my dogs in Kensington when a hearse, complete with coffin, stopped in the street and the driver alighted.

'Saw your film last night,' he said while the traffic piled up behind the corpse. 'And I want to give you this for Barnardo's.' It was four pounds. 'Somebody gave it to me as beer money.' I thought it might have been 'bier' money – a joke in the undertaking business perhaps.

Cherie Booth is now President. We meet at an event sponsored by Monopoly in aid of Barnardo's. Mindful of the newspaper stories about Mrs Blair allegedly using her position as wife of the Prime Minister to feather her own nest, I warned her: 'Don't let the press photograph you with handfuls of Monopoly money.'

She replied smartly, 'Or the card that says "Go to Jail".'

Barnardo's do not have orphanages these days; their efforts are concentrated on deprived, abused and sick children. In those times they cared, as much as they could, for 8,000 children of various sorts. One of the orphanages was called Babies Castle.

I did cross swords with Barnardo's once about an

advertising campaign that I thought was unacceptable, a baby supposedly photographed injecting heroin, a toddler about to jump from a roof, a man with his head blown apart. I wanted to resign as a vice-president but was dissuaded. An even more grisly set of full-page advertisements appeared the following year and the Advertising Standards Authority banned them.

It is not altogether known that people invited to appear in the famous pages of *Who's Who* are required to compile their own entry. When, to my considerable surprise, my name was added to that illustrious list in 1973 I summed up my career in the armed forces succinctly: 'Army Service 1949–51. Rose to lance-corporal.'

Even that meagre rank was acting, unpaid, and did not last long. I was demoted for failing to arrive on time at a Sunday cricket match for which I had been selected, having had my trousers thrown from a window by a Chinese girl I years later christened Juicy Lucy in my novel, *The Virgin Soldiers*.

This mishap was reprised in the Carl Foreman film of the book and (since she was an eager cinema goer) I often wondered if she had recognised herself, if not her name. Juicy Lucy was, in fact, the nickname of a Chinese airline stewardess I met years later in Hong Kong and I appropriated it for the story. Later still, in America, I discovered that Juicy Lucy had been a jazz tune in the nineteen-twenties and thirties. After *The Virgin Soldiers* was published it passed to yet another generation via a pop group and a popular health food bar in London.

As for the title *The Virgin Soldiers* itself, I will never write three more potent (or profitable!) words. Perhaps in the singular it will be carved on my tombstone. In more than forty years, since I first penned them, they have been quoted by politicians and military men, including Field Marshal Montgomery, in newspapers, on radio, television, and in the sports world.

The novel has scarcely been out of print since first publication in 1966. There have been all sorts of figures quoted for worldwide sales but I don't know how accurate they are. I have lost count. It was the first novel of the twenty-nine, and that simple soldier's story has been a long-lasting blessing to me. The film and its sequel still appear on television (usually after my bedtime) and it has attained, over the years, the odd status of a cult movie and the book has now been dubbed 'a classic'. My ambition had only been to write a story.

But the book and the film gave a hopeful author in his thirties a leg-up which most first novelists could only enjoy in their dreams. It was a lucky try. It was many years before I reread it (most of my books I have never reread) and I had to wonder what all the success had been about; to me it seemed nothing more than a beginner's novel. Today, if I could write it again, it would be three times as long, three times as well written – and probably sell about a third.

One dark afternoon in winter, sitting by a log fire in my house, I decided to try my hand at writing a detective story. By bedtime I had the framework and some of the characters; it was called *Dangerous Davies: The*

Last Detective. He was an amalgam of some of the policemen I knew when I was a young reporter in Willesden, London, the old X Division of the Metropolitan Police. I have a great affection for him.

Willesden was a gritty, working-class, area in those days with many Irish inhabitants. One day I saw two hundred sober and stone-faced Irishmen march towards the Catholic cemetery with a coffin carried at the front of the parade. One of the bearers was a tiny man, much shorter than the others, and he held up the coffin with one muscular extended hand and arm. The lodgings I inhabited, one tight room at the top of a house, had a blackened fireplace where two would-be IRA members had ham-handedly tried to make a bomb. The house became Dangerous Davies's lodgings in the story.

I have now written four books about the hapless Dangerous Davies and his sidekick the philosophical Mod. The unique Bernard Cribbins was the first television Davies and Bill Maynard the elderly muttering Mod. Now, years later, Peter Davison is the latest incarnation of Davies and captures the difficult character perfectly. Mod has been transformed from an old Welshman to a young Irishman, Sean Hughes. It works so successfully that, although I have been encouraged to write a further adventure, I feel that the story has been taken out of my hands. From our family point of view the notable triumph is that our talented son Matthew wrote one of the episodes of the first series and two episodes of the series they are filming as I write. I have had nothing to do with his success (or the series for that matter). It has taken him ten years of hard graft and biting disappointment to find success but he is so fearful of accusations of nepotism that he even refuses to let me see his scripts.

I cannot pretend that the origins of *The Last Detective* lie outside the real murder mystery in my own family, as described in this book, the sordid killing of my fifteen-year-old niece in a field next to a Birmingham fairground. Being the dispersed family that we are I did not realise she was my niece until more than ten years after it happened. As a reporter I even wrote one of the newspaper stories myself from London, unaware of my relationship to the victim. Thomas is a common enough name and there were quotes in the press from the girl's father (who wasn't) and mention of brothers (which she did not have). Her mother had taken up with another man after my brother Harold's death.

The facility which enabled me to think up Dangerous Davies in that afternoon by the winter fireside was, I am sure, something I honed in my newspaper days. At the *Evening News* I wrote articles on myriad subjects to order, often at a couple of hours notice. This has been continued even up to today by an occasional commission from the *Daily Mail* after lunch with fifteen hundred words to be researched, composed and faxed by five o'clock. The fax and the word processor, on which I am working now, are my only forays into modern technology. I tell people I have only just got rid of the carrier pigeons.

Computer matters still confound me. When I had finished my airport novel *Arrivals and Departures* I decided that I did not much like the name of one character – Jack Richardson. So I asked my secretary to tap the instruction that would change all the 'Jacks' to 'Edwards' which resulted in a manuscript which referred to 'the Union Edward' flying at the flag mast and fears that an airliner might be 'hi-Edwarded'.

Keeping my hand in with journalism has always been pleasing and rewarding. The *Evening Standard* once dispatched me to Las Vegas to write what in the trade are called 'colour pieces' about the imminent Mike Tyson versus Frank Bruno world heavyweight fight. I told them I knew nothing about boxing but they sent me anyway. My wife asked me to get both combatants' autographs to be auctioned at a charity event.

The amiable Bruno was easy enough (I had played cricket with him!) but the mean-eyed Tyson was something else. I explained that the autograph would raise a lot of money for disabled children. 'And how do I know you're not going to take the bucks for yourself?' he asked nastily. He is not a particularly tall man and I did not have to look up very far to meet him eye to glinting eye. 'Don't you speak to me like that,' I snapped back. There was an unpleasant pause. I tried not to blink or go pale. At least my death would make the headlines. Tyson grunted and gave me the autograph. At the auction it fetched about a hundred pounds. Hardly worth dying for.

Fleet Street is now vanished. And vanished with it is my generation. Once it was called the Street of Adventure (not to mention Shame) but is now a citadel of banking, insurance and IT, as they call it; the bars serve *cafe latte* for God's sake. All that remains among the blank buildings, modest despite its poetic spire, is the journalists' church (Father forgive them, for they know very well what they do). St Brides in these after-days is often the venue of a memorial service. Men, who laughed coarsely, drank with dedication and knew priceless stories for sale, are only ghosts, staggering slightly as they pass on their way to their spectral upright Underwoods.

Not only men either. There were redoubtable women journalists (what their descendants in the trade now call 'feisty'), like the one who recently died in her seventies. I recall when, as an attractive young woman, she travelled halfway down America in the company of a man who turned out to be a multiple rapist. After he was apprehended the police asked her if she had been assaulted and she answered: 'He'd have to get up early in the morning to rape me.'

The lady who said, 'Just mention me in passing,' when I began the original version of this story repeated her modest request when I embarked on this new intro-duction. She cannot, however, escape responsibility as a co-conspirator in what has been an undeniably nomadic life. In a little under forty years together we have had twenty-six residences, sometimes three concurrently, a house in the country, an apartment in London and a place abroad.

When Diana and I lived in the Close of Salisbury Cathedral, in an exquisite Georgian house with its long, green, garden floating down to the Wiltshire River Avon, we sometimes wondered what a pair like us was doing there. Me, failed working class and she from a terraced house in Leicester. But the residents, some very exalted, were glad to see us and said that we brought a breath of fresh air to that ecclesiastical enclave.

Military and naval neighbours, who included Admiral Teddy Gerlitz, the redoubtable Beach-master of D-Day, were ever kind and tactfully praised the rank of corporal (promoting me at a stroke) as the best in the army. We were once invited to an officers' mess dinner where Lance-Corporal Thomas and his missus sat at the top table, our faces reflected in the regimental silver. In the same barracks I discovered, to my huge amazement, an old comrade from the teenage soldier days in Singapore, who had signed on when the rest of us were heading home, and who was now the Regimental Sergeant-Major – which *is* undoubtedly the best rank in the British army.

The longest we have remained in any location, to date, was our fine house, the Walton Canonry, in the Cathedral Close at Salisbury, where we lived for ten years before we noticed the lease was getting dangerously low. The shortest stay was eighteen months (it was a converted piggery). So far we have spent five years at Lymington, Hampshire, in an enjoyable old house overlooking the harbour and we do not plan another move until I cannot manage the four flights of stairs.

Before we could become owners of the remarkable Walton Canonry at Salisbury Close we had to be vetted by the Dean and Chapter who pronounced us 'eminently suitable'. This suitability included the financial assets sufficient to replace the roof and to refurbish the building. Just to ensure that we had commissioned a good job the cathedral architect would slyly climb to the roof with a magnet to make sure we were using the right kind of nails.

There had been a dwelling on the site since 1198 when the great cathedral was first constructed and we inherited a list of occupants since that time: the first was one William of Cerdstock, who came from Normandy.

The classic Georgian house we had moved into was built in the early seventeen hundreds by Canon Isaac Walton, son of Isaak Walton 'The Compleat Angler'. He died of cholera before he could occupy it and it passed to the titled Eyre family whose coat of arms remained above the huge front door. Me with an escutcheon! Before the Second World War the Canonry was the home of the artist Rex Whistler, who was killed soon after D-Day in Normandy, not far from the place where William of Cerdstock had come.

Edward Heath was the first of our new neighbours to invite us to lunch. As I looked from his window towards the elegant Close and the lofty and lovely cathedral, I said: 'I never thought I would ever live in a place like this. I'm a working-class boy.'

'So am I,' he said truthfully.

To mark his eightieth birthday the BBC filmed a programme and came to Salisbury to interview us. Considerably to my surprise the producer asked bluntly: 'Is Edward Heath gay?'

'No,' I replied immediately. 'He's bloody miserable.'

Actually he was not. I am not a political animal so I took him as I found him, quirkish but often kind. He conducted a village band in 'The Cornish Floral Dance' on our lawn and they never forgot it. He also cleared his crammed diary so he could be chairman at a Foyle's literary lunch, which was given for me in London, attracting a more illustrious top table than I would have ever been able to manage. He made a funny speech and I swear he had never read a word of my book. The venerable Christina Foyle said it was the best lunch since 1931.

As a former prime minister Ted had twenty-four-hour security (and had survived attempts on his life). His armed guards became as much neighbours as he was. It was not unusual to find one of them sitting having coffee in our kitchen with his sub-machine gun parked on the table.

One autumn afternoon I was taking our dog – by this time a sweet-natured Rottweiller called Gipsy – for a walk in the cathedral grounds when she dug into a depression apparently full of leaves and found a body. My artificial hips prevented me getting down to investigate so I returned to my house and rang 999. The Close had a high security rating and as I returned one of Sir Edward's guards was already striding towards me calling, 'Where's the body, Mr Thomas?'

A police car and an ambulance had arrived smartly and as we walked across the grass, the guard with his machine gun and me with the pleased dog, the body sat up. It was a poor wrecked woman clinging to a vodka bottle. The ambulance crew knew her and they assured me I had done the right thing because it was cold and she might have died in that hole.

The split-minute security in the Close saved our house from burning down even before we lived in it. A retired surgeon, practising his golf, spotted a finger of smoke coming from a window. A spark from a workman's blowtorch had smouldered and set fire to some wood shavings. The Salisbury fire brigade was there almost in seconds and prevented the flames spreading to the roof. The builder in charge of the work mentioned that he had insured the house for a million pounds only that day.

There was rarely a dull moment in that holy place. In the cause of ecumenical understanding the bishop once took a delegation to meet the Pope in the Vatican. They were puzzled by the Holy Father addressing them in German. He thought they had come not from Salisbury but from Salzburg.

The inhabitants of the Close were of absorbing interest. There was a dying canon who had the choir from his Oxford college ranged around his bed in Salisbury hospital so they could sing him to heaven. 'He left all his money to them as well,' sniffed the dean.

When I first moved to the Walton Canonry, an angular lady was heard to wail biblically: 'We have a pornographer come among us!' She became a sweet friend and loved to tell stories of her time in the Sudan where her husband had been a district officer. He would go on a tour of his area, about the size of Wales, mounted on a camel but sitting backwards so that he could read a book.

By and large critics have been fair with me, although some do not bother to read the whole book. Certain newspapers either ignore my work entirely or, at the best, are patronising. But, as any writer must admit, it is the bad reviews you remember long after the pleasure of praise has gone. The late Auberon Waugh, a fat man with the expression of a disturbed barn owl, and someone with all the bile and none of the talent of his famous father, made a vicious attack on my second novel *Orange Wednesday* (which was top of the best-sellers) during which he complained that my work always (always? And it was a second novel?) failed to give him any sense of sexual anticipation. I have never since replied to a critic but on this occasion I wrote to the magazine concerned pleading that I was a writer not a faith healer.

Poor Auberon, on one and the same day he had a novel published and two remaindered. My agent, Desmond Elliott, not lacking in bile either, bought some of the remainders and advertised them for sale at one pence each with the catchline: 'Spend a Penny on Auberon Waugh'.

Desmond and I parted company shortly after the publication of the original edition of *In My Wildest Dreams*. The reasons seem trivial now but we never spoke again in twenty years. Urged by Diana and Matthew I had intended to send a reconciling letter to him (although I was assured it would be rejected) but he died in New York before it could be written.

When you write a book you have no idea how many people will read it. Rarely is there any instant reaction either. It is not like scoring a goal or playing Mendelssohn's violin concerto. There is no applause. The book goes off over the horizon and for all you know disappears on the other side.

But then rumours drift back, people mention it.

Sometimes it has even played some significant part in their lives. A lady wrote from a remote place in Cumbria. Her husband had gone to the Carlisle library to collect one of my travel books. 'I never saw him alive again,' she said. 'I found him dead of a heart attack in the car which was in a ditch.' She asked a passing hiker to telephone for assistance. 'Then,' she related. 'I sat beside him in the car, the man who had been my husband for forty years. Your book was on the seat and I opened it and began to read. It got me through the worst half an hour of my life and then through the next week. Thank you.'

An actor once told me that he had married a young dancer, on the spur of the moment. They went off to Spain, in the winter, and before long had run out of conversation. 'It was getting desperate,' he said. 'Then in the village newspaper kiosk we came across a couple of your paperbacks, curled by the sun. We had both read your novels and we took these back to the hotel. We enjoyed them, laughed and discussed them, then we swapped. It would not be too much to say that you saved our marriage.'

There is, of course, the occasional comeuppance. I was giving lectures on the liner *Oriana* and was sitting in the library having just come across my entry in the *Larousse Dictionary of Writers*. I was wallowing in the phrase: 'His writing is unaffected, truthful, funny, often poignant' when I heard two ladies conversing on the other side of a huge bowl of flowers. 'This Leslie Thomas,' one said. 'They say he can write and that he's funny and charming. I can't see it myself.' Her friend replied: 'Nor can I.'

PART ONE

HOME

a throaty Barry Island voice. 'Terrible. Bangs and electric shocks all round the bed.' Another, possibly pregnant, wait. 'And there was me, sitting up, see . . . singing!' I could believe that. She had a faltering Welsh wail. She claimed she had sung 'Rock of Ages' between thunder claps.

Not long ago I went up Stow Hill, a place of elderly large houses crowned by St Woolos Church, now a cathedral, and looked out over the dented roofs of Newport, my homeplace, a frontier town between England and Wales. There is a pub across the road from the churchyard and I wondered, as I sat in the bar, whether my father had drunk there. He probably had. There were few places he had missed.

My parents agreed on little but they would gladly call an armistice to verify each other's tall stories. Like the one about the dog we had who one night came home, pleased enough, with a whole quiver of bones from the St Woolos burial ground. The road was being widened and he had taken advantage of the excavations to do some digging on his own account. In this story they actually *lived* ('in residence' according to my mother) on Stow Hill, possibly to be near the nursing home, but the first domicile of my memory was two rooms in Milner Street down by the murky and mucky River Usk, not far from the Transporter Bridge.

Now there *was* a wonder, the Transporter Bridge. We were told at school that it was one of only two in the country and a Frenchman was brought over specially to build it. I do not doubt that. It must have been the most uneconomic way of ever taking goods, people and vehicles from one side of a river to the other. In recent years the town discovered that it would cost more to demolish it than to keep it; so they kept it. It has two massive steel structures, one on each bank, like the towers you see above Texas oil wells but taller. Between the towers is a Meccano-set bridge and slung below this on cables, a platform pulled by hawsers from one side of the river to the other. For a boy it used to cost a penny to go across.

It was a child's delight to make that journey from bank to muddy bank of the Usk. I used to pretend I was going to another country. It was like travelling in the gondola of an airship, whirring slowly through space, the broad, black-tongued river curling below, little ships lying like dogs against its bank. On one side you could see the other more conventional town bridge and its traffic, the green cupola of the Technical College, with the wharves and warehouses and the stump of the ancient castle. Electric trams travelled in the distance, making sparks on dark days. On the other side of the Transporter, beyond the puffing steel works, the river yawned to the Bristol Channel. Misty miles away it seemed, the gateway, as my father pointed out to me in a scene reminiscent of the Boyhood of Raleigh, to the wide and amazing world. To look directly down below from the moving platform was to experience a delicious terror; snakes of thick water wriggled between slime coated by coaldust drifting from the Welsh valleys. It was legend that people had fallen or jumped and been sucked up by the hungry mud. I used to imagine them lying down deep, engulfed by the stuff . . . *preserved*. When the tide was up the river flowed strongly, but still foul and thick as

5

if its bed were on top. One day, however, we saw a blithe sailing boat with scarlet sails on the moribund water and my mother burst into a loud and embarrassing chorus of a song called 'Red Sails In The Sunset'. I had to ask her to stop and I could have only been four years old.

On another day she made a gallop for the travelling platform moments before its gate slammed, almost dragging me off the ground in her hurry. An avid funeral-spotter she had seen that the bridge's cargo was nothing less than a cortège, the hearse and the two mourners' cars standing dreadly beside a horse and cart and various pedestrians looking decently the other way. No such embarrassment discouraged my mam. We stood holding hands, neither of us being able to take our eyes from the glistening wood and shining handles of the coffin as the platform began its crossing. Unable to restrain herself any longer Mam approached the first mourning car and tapped politely but firmly on the closed window. A distraught and astonished face was framed when the glass had been lowered. 'Who is it?' she enquired in a huge whisper jerking her head towards the hearse. The wind was blowing down the Usk and the platform was swaying.

Hardly able to credit the enquiry the mourner, a man in a black bowler hat, haltingly told her the identity of the deceased. My mam thanked him and whispered: 'There's a pity,' before the window was hurriedly rolled up again. Only a toddler, I witnessed this brazenness with amazement and admiration. She returned to me and once more took hold of my hand. 'Nobody we know,' she confided.

6

The Transporter Bridge straddling the river can now be seen afar from the railway or the motorway like a giant standing over Newport. The borough used to have a nice little Victorian town hall with a big white clock in the main street too, but they knocked that down and built a flat-roofed store instead. You could see the hands of the clock from Stow Hill and, it was rumoured, even further. I remember that town hall well because on the night that Japan surrendered and the war was finally over I went down there dressed as a girl. It was only in fun (the nuances would have been lost on me then) and the boy next door encouraged me. The clothes were his sister's. During the general dancing and celebrations a soldier grabbed me and shouted 'We've won! We've won!' and he kissed me on the lips.

Along the river bank from the Transporter Bridge was a wharf beside the steelworks. One morning in the unemployed nineteen-thirties, my father took me there to act as bait in getting a job aboard a little coaster. 'Suck your cheeks in. Try to look half-starved,' he suggested as we went aboard. It was not difficult. I had seen my mother burst into tears when, having seen the plates put out for tea, I enquired: 'Well, there's the plates – all we want now is something to put on them.'

The skipper of the coaster was presumably impressed by the waif because he not only gave my father the job as a stoker on his weekly boat (so named because it went to Ireland and back in a week) but took us to his cabin where he spread out a hundred or more coins on his polished table. It was like a treasure and my eyes shone. 'Let's see what we can give the boy,' ruminated the captain. He shuffled the wealth about while I trembled with anticipation but eventually decided that every coin was foreign except one, a halfpenny, which he pressed with ceremony into my hand.

During his workless times, and they lasted weeks and months, my father used to look disconsolately for odd jobs ashore, sit at home eating bread and cheese (all he ever ate) or go to the public library to stare at the papers. When he got his dole money my mother would escort him to make sure he did not head for the nearest public bar. Once, the money in his pocket, he abruptly announced that he had been informed in a vision that our house was on fire. Before she could stop him (I was with them and she was holding my hand and that of my young brother) he had loped off into the dusk. He came home at midnight, plastered and penniless, and she threw the chamber pot over his head. Hurt and in a huff he went away and we did not see him again for nearly two years. Then he turned up in the middle of the night. He had been on a ship to Argentina and was dressed in a goucho's outfit and plucking a guitar. He said he thought it would make her laugh.

There was an announcement one day that a free concert was to be given for the children of the unemployed. It was held at an extraordinary Grecian building with white portico and marble columns, which sat incongruously amid the straight streets and was the steel works social institute. My father took me and I sat enthralled by the various acts that attempted to temporarily alleviate the misery of the workless. We sang with feeling a song called 'I Do Like Potatoes And Gravy', a social commentary if ever there was one. One performance thrilled me more than any, a whistler who whistled through his fingers while adopting various poses, on a bicycle, on a chair, and standing on his head. It seemed to me that he whistled better when he was upside down than he did when the right way up. When he had finished the applause shook the Grecian columns. 'Oh, Dad,' I enthused. 'He was good, wasn't he!'

His reply was heartfelt: 'There's too many of them,' he said. Both my parents were born in Barry, Glamorgan, twenty-five miles or so inside Wales, west of Cardiff, a town which managed to combine the difficult functions of being both a seaside resort and a coaling port. More than one hundred years ago, the importance of coal transformed it from a village of fewer than one hundred inhabitants into a major town. I have heard it described as Sin City and the Candyfloss Capital of the Western World.

There was an excellent deep water harbour where the ships would load Welsh steam coal brought down from the valleys, colliers waiting with grey patience out in the Bristol Channel, in Barry Roads, for their turn to berth. This gritty occupation was successfully kept separate from the seaside resort on Barry Island and it was only with a contrary wind that coaldust speckled the ice creams on the beach. Some people thought it was decoration. On the other hand the prevailing breeze often enlivened the dusty environs of the port with the fragrance of ozone and fish and chips.

Barry Island, which boasted (and may still do so for all I know) of being the nearest seaside resort to Birmingham, is not an island at all. A railway embankment and a road stretch out of the resort with its twin beaches, one of sand and one of globular white pebbles, divided by a headland called Cold Knapp. Between the two are the municipal open-air swimming baths where, in the summer the war ended, I entered for the town aquatic gala. I was three months over fourteen and my sole opponent in the 'Over-14s, Under-18s One-hundred-yards Freestyle Race' was a day under eighteen, a fierce Tarzan-like youth whose leopard-skin swimming trunks, tight around his thighs, contrasted vividly with the two pairs I was wearing of plum-coloured, sagging wool; worn in tandem because the holes in one covered the holes in the other.

The event had encouraged a large and festive crowd to the pool. They had a bonus as this white ribbed competitor struck the water a measurable time and distance behind his athletic opponent and as he did so both pairs of trunks fell down. As I gamely struck out in the wake of Tarzan they dangled around my knees, leaving me both handicapped and humiliated. Hoots and exclamations were provoked by my bare bum surfacing. 'That boy's lost his knicks!' I heard someone shout coarsely. Somehow I managed to pull them up around my waist again. Tarzan was now just a splash on the horizon and, in truth, by the time I had completed the course the competitors were already lining up for the next race. Nevertheless, there being only two competitors in mine, I was awarded second prize, a pig-skin hairbrush (the first prize had merely the addition of a comb). Much more important, the results were printed in the local newspaper and my aunt and uncle, with whom I was staying, put it around the town that I was a potential Olympic champion. It was also the first time I had ever seen my name in print.

All that occurred half a century after my grandfather had retired from the adventurous business of rounding Cape Horn on the shrieking deck of a sailing ship. He left the sea, so he said, because he abhorred bad language and one imagines there was a certain degree of that among the calloused crews of those wild waters. It must have been difficult to make a decent comment when you'd just lost a finger. He refused to go to the annual dinners of the Cape Horners for the same reason. 'There is never any excuse for blasphemy,' he used to say to his children.

Back beyond my grandfather was a long tradition of sailors and sea. There were two great-aunts who had voyaged on sailing ships and who, in their eighties, ascended ladders to clean the upper windows of their house in Cardiff and apparently climbed on to the roof itself to get a better view of the Jubilee procession in 1935.

We called the old grandfather Papa, a genteel appellation and apparently we were a family of some substance in Barry in those days. He started a business repairing ships in Barry Dock, later to extend to Cardiff, Newport and ports all around the Bristol Channel. He had the good idea that if he had workmen in all these ports then the vessels would not have to interrupt their coastal voyages while repairs were carried out. He was derisive of steamships, often quoting the sailing man's jibe: 'Wooden ships, men of iron – iron ships, men of wood.' Nevertheless the boilers of the steamships required scaling and it provided additional prosperity. In the eighteen-nineties he was also alleged to have been Harbourmaster of Barry Dock, a boast I have heard many times. His family – there were twelve or thirteen children – lived in a substantial manner. My grandfather was a Liberal candidate in an election in the early years of this century and his election address photograph shows him with a dipping moustache and matching watchchain. Lloyd George knew my grandfather and my grandfather knew Lloyd George and made some attempt to look like him.

Americans like to hear stories more than any other race apart from Arabs, and many years later I spoke about my Grandad during a New York television programme. I was wearing a watchchain across a grey waistcoat and the interviewer concluded, with no great prompting from me, that this was Grandad's. He plainly required me to elaborate, so, to my shame, I said: 'Yes, this was Papa's watch and chain.' I took the bright and bulbous thing from my pocket and dangled it. 'It arrived,' I related, 'in a package in the post with a note which said "I have always wanted you to have this. It was your grandfather's."' There was no signature.' There was no truth either for I had made it up on the spur of the moment and, in fact, the watch was bought by my wife in an antique shop. But I was unable to resist telling them a yarn. They seemed very pleased and interested, too.

My Auntie Kate, who lived with my silver-haired Uncle Jack Roscoe in Barry (although they did not visit the beach – 'The Sands' – for twenty years or more) and with whom I spent holidays at the end of the war, cooked the Christmas pudding that was Papa's ultimate meal. He expired on the afternoon of Christmas Day, 1938, having retired to the red-velvet front room for a nap after lunch. He had been in the habit of going, rather daringly for him, to auctions held every Saturday night and once he came home with a nice wall clock. Auntie Kate alleged that, like the old song, the clock stopped at the very moment he died and never went again.

Auntie Kate was as thin as a vein, with red hair tight in a bun; her greatest achievement was catching flies in flight. She could catch them when she was staring absently out of the window, while she was gossiping, or while she was eating cake. It was remarkable. She had not missed a fly in forty years, or so she told me. She never did it, however, when people came to tea. That, she said, would be showing off. She had even caught flies when she was singing. For she was another Welsh singer. At her most exalted note she went into a locked gargle as if she were drowning. If she could not sleep she would get up and smash out midnight hymns on the piano, howling like a glutton. Neighbours feared these moments but lovely old Uncle Jack Roscoe would wake up and, lying back on the pillows, accompany her from bed. One night he heard a cat howling and after ascertaining that Auntie Kate was innocently snoring at his flank, he threw one of his working boots out of the window and never saw it again.

Of my father's relatives the only ones I knew during

13

my early childhood before the war were this kindly pair. They looked after my grandmother until the old lady died still convinced that Grandad had been elected to Parliament, which was why he did not come home any more. They were simple and childless. 'Children makes you poor,' Kate used to recite a little regretfully. 'Don't go foreign,' was another of her proverbs, warning me against a life at sea. 'Go on the Company', the Company in question being the Great Western Railway. Sometimes she used to cry while laughing as she told me about my father's youth in Barry. How he had ridden the milkman's horse around a field one night so that it was too knackered to pull the milkcart the next morning; how he had once materialised at a roller-skating dance, scattering the participants by zig-zagging between them clad in a bonnet and shawl and with an appropriated perambulator containing a screeching baby. 'Oh, that Jim,' she used to say wistfully, wiping her eyes. 'That Jim Thomas.' And it was nearly half a century before.

These were the few things I gleaned about my father's boyhood because we were not what you would call a close family. I never met any of his other brothers or sisters apart from the youngest, Christopher, who appeared when I was in an orphanage and tried to get me out.

My mother had also fallen out with her family and never saw them although there was a shadowy episode once, just before the war, which was like a short story. She had taken my younger brother Roy and myself to Barry, but instead of going to the beach we went to some gardens overlooking the Bristol Channel. There

14

sat an old man leaning on a stick, staring towards the ships on the flat sea. To our astonishment my mother crept up on this stranger from behind. We had the odd idea she might be going to rob him and we stood expectantly. Instead she curled her arms around his neck and kissed him thoroughly. 'It's me, Dad! Dolly!' she cried. 'Oh, it's you Dolly,' he said calmly. 'Come back have you?' Roy and I were dispatched to the sands but she remained talking to the old man for a long time. When we finally walked away from the place she was quite wet-eyed. 'That,' she said having failed to introduce us, 'was *my* father.' She had not seen him for many years and, as far as I know, she never saw him again.

There were twelve offspring from her parents but, apart from her younger sister, Iris, whose husband was Bert, a soldier who eventually fell into the Newport dry dock, we knew none of them. Once, just after she had ambushed her father, she took us to a street in Barry where one of her sisters lived. She had not seen her since she was a girl. 'Hello, Doll,' said the sister flatly. 'What is it you want?' There was a short conversation, as unfathomable as it was uncomfortable, on the doorstep and we went away, again for ever.

If my mother's relatives remained anonymous then my father's brothers and sisters were familiar only from stories and photographs. There were pictures of Eisteddfod outings by the Barry Choir, each lady in black and wearing a flower, each gentleman throttled by a wide, white collar and topped by a proper hat. That was Auntie Her, that was Uncle Him; each one pointed out and possibly an anecdote related. There

15

were also many pictures of dogs, including some taken over the years of Lady, my Uncle Jack's pet which was like a pig. Hugely obese and horribly pink, it was so engulfed in fat that when it descended to the floor from the sofa it rolled over like dough. Jack loved Lady – whom he inaccurately called his 'pup' – and on occasions took her down to the Institute where he played billiards. He never took Kate because he said that the only females allowed were bitches.

A family photograph that never failed to impress me was of my Uncle Leslie, after whom I was was named. He had been a sportsman, excelling in rugby and cricket (he married a Sussex cricketer's daughter but I don't remember her name and now there is no one to ask) and attained fame as a Welsh schoolboy international soccer goalkeeper. He had thought of turning professional with Cardiff City but instead joined the East African Police Force which my grandfather thought was safer. In the photograph he stands crossed-armed in goalkeeper's jersey at the apex of the Kenya International Team. Every other player is a black man. Leslie died in the late nineteen-thirties of peritonitis somewhere in the African bush. I once met a man on a ship who had known him out there but he could not remember much about him except that he had been good in goal.

There really *is* no one I know to ask, even if I wished to do so. These two large families totalling twenty-five children have vanished. No one ever told anyone anything. Nice old Uncle Jack, a silvery man and decent, spent his waning years working in the Cardiff office of his brother-in-law, Uncle Chris. We were not often in contact but one day I telephoned and during the general conversation asked how Jack was.

'Jack? . . . Oh, Jack, he's *gone*.' I was told.

'But it's only four o'clock,' I said. 'You let him go home early, I suppose.'

'No, not gone *home* . . .' A pause. 'Although I suppose you *could* put it like that.'

An unpleasant notion settled in me. 'Well, where *is* he gone?'

'Just gone . . . you know, well actually he's dead.'

'Dead? Jesus Christ! When?'

'Oh, months ago now. Months . . . let me see, when did Jack die? We must have forgotten to tell you.'

This was not unique in our family. My elder brother Lindon died in hospital in Tokyo while I was staying in the hotel almost next door. I knew nothing about it until a year later when it was passingly mentioned in a rare family letter. My second brother's daughter was brutally murdered and I knew nothing of that either; not for years.

For a long time, I must confess, I have been party to this conspiracy of silent Thomases. I subscribe to it heartily and I truly hope the other unknown aunts, uncles, and what must be a multitude of children, and their children, continue to keep our family secret.

Only with my younger brother Roy have I retained any sort of relationship and contact. When he was nine and I was twelve our parents died within six months of each other and we were uprooted from our poor but secure home and put into the howling corridors of an orphanage. He unknowingly escaped by being lent to foster parents and I lost him for almost two years, having no idea where he had been sent. He had a habit of writing his initials. In the parish church at Long Crendon in Buckinghamshire you can still see the letters he carved in the woodwork while he was supposed to have been pumping the organ. Once, when we were in our early teens, living together again, and I felt responsible for him, I was standing on a railway station and saw his monogram outlined in the soot *underneath* the footbridge. When I upbraided him for this he protested: 'I had to hang by one hand to do that.'

He always wanted to be a sailor and he started by going up and down the Thames on an outings boat. He wrote and told me he was the mate, but it turned out there were only him and the captain aboard. Now he voyages on a different but equally concise course, an eternal circumference around Australia, where he has lived for more than twenty years. Last year I was in Sydney and we arranged to have a night out together. He telephoned my room from the hotel lobby and I told him to come to the fourth floor. The room was directly opposite the lift and seeking to amuse him, for I had not seen him for three years, I stood at the open door wearing a dressing gown and with a tin waste-paper basket over my head. I heard the lift door open and the exclamations of surprise as the passengers got out. My brother, who had paused to get some cigarettes, was not among them.

Quite recently the compiler of one of those odd but apparently fascinating books of lists included my name in a section uncompromisingly headed: 'Ten Famous British Bastards'. The selection was headed by William the Conqueror (who may have been a bastard but was scarcely British) and I was in excellent company throughout. The distinction was, however, undeserved (the researcher, I was told, had mixed up 'orphans' with 'bastards'!) for when I was born on March 22nd, 1931, my parents had been married almost twenty years and had two other sons, Lindon, who was eighteen, and Harold who was fifteen. My younger brother Roy was born two years and eleven months later and his bawling from the open front door of the little brick house in Milner Street provided me with my first graspable memory. I was trundling along the street on my coloured tricycle with a companion called Georgie who enquired about the screams. 'I've got a new baby brother,' I boasted.

'We're going to have a baby soon,' Georgie replied jealously. 'We might even have two.'

'You can't,' I asserted. 'The doctor hasn't got any left.' He looked discomfited and I sought to cheer him up with some sensational information. 'When I was in the doctor's house before I was born,' I confided. 'I looked out of the window and I saw the moon fall down.'

This early foray into fantasy was witnessed by Silvia, the daughter of our landlady, Mrs Jenkins. She returned from the past only a short while ago, a commodious Welsh lady who approached while I was engaged in the hazardous occupation of signing books in a Newport shop. Although I had not seen her since childhood I knew at once who she was. 'Oh Leslie,' she said, full of Welsh accusation and sentiment. 'Why didn't you come and see my mam before she died?'

Fumbling for an excuse, I was taken by surprise when she leaned across the table and embraced me powerfully. We lost our balance, clutched at each other as both we and the stacks of books began to topple. We ended amid the debris of everything I had ever written. We picked the books up together, kissed emotionally again, and I haven't seen her since.

Jinka, the name I gave to Mrs Jenkins, and her daughter, who I called Siv, had taken us in when we had nowhere else to go. Jinka was my godmother and it was in her house that I experienced my first whiff of eroticism when playing houses behind the sofa with a little plump girl who had come to look after me when my mother was out. We had a wonderfully emotive roll around in that warm tight space and I was only three.

In one corner of our room was a loudspeaker from Rediffusion, simply a square piece of plywood with a central panel, presumably an extension from the landlady's wireless set. It played a song called 'Looky, Looky, Looky, Here Comes Cooky', to which I could sing and dance. Sometimes I would stand and stare up at the piece of wood, daring it to play my song.

Jim and Dolly Thomas had gone to live in Newport in the years after the First World War. My father had served in the Royal Artillery and received several wounds, one of them when his own gun carriage ran over his foot. Nobody realised why he was making such a fuss, or perhaps there was a noisy barrage from the German lines, but it was some time before they realised what had happened and backed the horses up to release his toes. The battery was due to move its position in the line and my limping parent was left in charge of a horse which had a like impediment. Off went the other men, horses, and guns into the Flanders dust, leaving Gunner Thomas trudging a great way to the rear. He and the horse limped along together, a picture I can imagine fondly, until eventually they came upon a Frenchman leaning on a gate. My father paused to pass the time of day and the Frenchman admired the horse. He was of the opinion that it might yet recover sufficiently to be useful as transport. Otherwise it would be useful on a plate. A simple bargain was struck and my father continued limping on alone until, at evening, he reached the place where his battery was encamped.

'Where's that horse, Thomas?' demanded the sergeant.

'Gone, sarge, gone for ever,' answered Gunner Thomas. 'I thought you said he was lame?'

'That horse *was* lame.'

'Sarge, there was a German shell landed a hundred and fifty yards away,' related my father sorrowfully. 'And off that horse went. It would have won the Derby.'

'It was a mare,' said the sergeant, loaded with suspicion.

'All right, then,' said the Old Man. 'The Oaks.'

He fought throughout that awful war, then in the Spanish Civil War – on the opposite side to my elder brother – and finally died in the bowels of a torpedoed ship in 1943. When he was in France in 1917 he received the worrying news that his wife had fled Wales and was in Birmingham with a man who played the cello in a picture palace. Father returned home on leave and, with my shocked grandparents, journeyed

21

to the English city where they sat in the cinema watching the man scrape at his cello.

As a serving soldier my father was incensed that, quite apart from anything else, this person was not opposing the Germans in the trenches. His anger was as much martial as marital.

He strode from his seat and put his twin points of view to the cellist. Something of a fracas ensued which I like to think may have been complementary to some silent slapstick fisticuffs on the screen. The reason that the cellist was not on active service became apparent at once because he raised an artificial leg, which he had unstrapped during his work, and struck my father a felling blow on the temple. Gunner Thomas had travelled from the hell of the battlefield to be sorely wounded in the orchestra pit of a Birmingham cinema.

In any event he won back his wife because my mother's recollections of the war were predictably melodramatic. 'When your brother Hally was a tiny, tiny baby,' she recalled by the fireside one night. 'He was screaming his head off in the early hours of the morning. There was I, all alone, your dad away at the fighting, and I couldn't stand it any longer. I threw that baby down the bottom of the bed. Then I saw a vision, yes a *vision*, of Jim Thomas standing straight in his uniform at the foot of the bed, holding up his hand and saying to me: "Steady, Dolly, steady. Don't throw the baby about like that! I'll be coming home soon."'

Generally, however, it was my father who had the visions. They usually occurred shortly after closing time.

*

I have often wondered what those two people, my mother and my father, were really like. Physically, he was thin and I believe quite tall (it is difficult to remember people's heights from your childhood), a spare and sinewy man hardened by a life of shovelling coal into the boilers of ships pitching on the world's oceans. He had low eyebrows, little other hair, and a bit of a hook at the end of his nose, so that I recall him as looking quite fierce. He had a habit of talking out of the corner of his mouth as if passing on confidential information. His hands were like nuts and bolts and he had tattoos hidden among the hair of his forearms. When ashore he wore a trilby hat and a white silk scarf with which my mother several times tried to throttle him.

'You old soak!' she used to shout. For some reason, in my childish manner, I imagined that the scarf was called a 'soak' and I thought so for many years.

Dolly was tiny, with a bird's bright eyes. I have two photographs of her, one taken as a young woman with an elegant profile and a mass of lovely hair done like a cottage loaf; the other is with Roy and me and must have been taken only months before her death. Perhaps she knew it would be the final picture for she had expended the money to go to a photographer's studio in Newport. We two little boys are in our best suits, our mother wearing a flowered blouse stands between us. Her eyes gleam fiercely.

Do I remember them only as caricatures now, plucking from the past only the things they did and said that were noteworthy enough to remain in my boy's memory? Perhaps it is true that you only really

23

get to know your parents when you have grown up and by that time mine were dead. Over the years I have met a good many people who knew my father, mostly men who had sailed with him, and they invariably have some legend to relate. 'Nothing was too hot or too heavy for Jim Thomas to handle,' one old shipmate told me. And as the others always did he smiled at the memory. Apart from my mother I have never found anyone who would say a bad word about him.

She saw him in a lesser light. Sometimes when he rolled home awash with beer she would not let him into the house so he would break some windows and all the neighbours would peer into the street to see what was going on. It was always enjoyable to hear a fight happening somewhere else. During the war when the windows had once more been damaged by Dad, I told my Cub mistress that a small German bomb which had landed in the garden was to blame. Since the windows of the neighbours' houses had remained intact she must have wondered just how small the bomb was. She was a nice young woman. We had to call her Akala but her name was really Miss Rabbit.

Also, I think, my mother must have resented deeply the decline in our social standards from whatever they had been. Even when we moved from the two rented rooms in Milner Street to a council house with a view, boasting a pebbledash façade and a bathroom, she felt the relegation. 'And to think,' she sniffed, 'that we once-upon-a-time had a motorbike and sidecar.'

There were always, of course, the possibilities presented by my father's life insurance for the sea was ever a perilous business. There was one notable false alarm. During the Spanish Civil War he was a member of the crew of a ship which was bombed in Barcelona harbour and sent to the bottom with all hands. It was an unusual thrill to hear 'David James Thomas, Stoker' listed as dead on the wireless. As it turned out he was the only survivor. He had been, unofficially I imagine, ashore when the dive bomber dropped a single high explosive down the funnel of the vessel and blew it to bits. When he came home he told the emotive tale: 'All bits and pieces floating on the water,' he said. 'And there . . . bobbing about among it all was the cabin boy's hat . . . Ah, he was a good lad too . . .'

My brother Lindon, who was also gun-running to one combatant or the other in Spain, returned home trembling from the experience. He had seen his friend killed by soldiers guarding the ship when he and a fellow officer had gone on shore to give some food to famished children. When he and Dad eventually exchanged reminiscences at home it became apparent that something was amiss. What was my father doing in such and such a place in November? After all the other side was occupying it then. Carefully they examined their adventures and concluded they had been running guns and other supplies to opposite sides.

A family of sailors is rarely together. I never remember a time when we were all in one house, which was just as well because there would only have been further arguments. My second brother Harold, known as Hally, was also at sea as an apprentice and Lin was already a junior officer. The old man remained deep in the stokehold.

Our move to the council house had at least given us something at which to look. It was on the eastern side of Newport, on a long-backed hill, with the roofs of the other, lower, streets serrated beneath our very feet and behind us the first green fields of the countryside. There was a lady called Auntie Blodwyn, although she was not truly a relative, who lived at the foot of the hill, next to Newport County football ground. One day her chimney caught fire and brought a match to a standstill. Several of the spectators came and demonstrated outside her gate, but others were quick to offer congratulations and say that it was the best thing that had happened that afternoon. Newport were never very inspiring or even aspiring. Just after the war they lost 13–1 to Newcastle United. My sister-in-law, Mary, told me that she had private information that the goalkeeper was in no way to blame. I remember her saying it because it was the day I nearly killed myself when I demolished her old chimney. It was over a ruined outhouse in her back garden and, aged fourteen then, I stood on the wall and, with a sledge-hammer, knocked the bricks away from under my own feet. The heavy chimney, followed by the whole building, collapsed. Fortunately I fell on top.

Money in the nineteenth-thirties was so scarce as to be a novelty. On my sixth birthday I went to school and rashly boasted that I was having a party. Nobody in those days, in that area, had birthday parties. The eyes of my classmates glowed. The lie, once told, was difficult to retract and with abandon I compounded it by going around the infant class and choosing who was to come to the party and who was not; that fiendish

Not having very much is a great provoker of envy. The boy next door had found sixpence and the story spread with the speed of jealousy around the neighbourhood children. The green eye flickered within me when he showed the little silver coin and told me, and a number of others assembled, how he proposed to expend this wealth. When I next went shopping for my mother, across a muddy quarry to a low street where the crouching corner shop showed its lights, I fell to temptation and shame which I have never forgotten. The shop was kept by a kindly and confused man who would even give credit. My mother once sent me to him with a list of groceries and instructions that the fact that we had no money to pay should be concealed until the ultimate moment, when the purchases were already, so to speak, in the bag. I was very worried about this but I carried out the plan only to be confronted with his aghast face when the credit was suggested. 'I can't do that, sonny,' he said. 'I'd have to ask the missus.' The missus it turned out was in another shop several miles away and I was dispatched there on foot, with a medallion of his as a token to show that I had already seen the husband. I cannot remember whether we got our groceries, to be paid for next week, but whether we did or not the man's kindliness was ill-repaid by the small boy who again approached his crowded counter having just seen that desirable sixpence lying in his neighbour's hand.

As I stood there waiting to be served, while the shopkeeper was getting confused by the demands of half a dozen people, I became aware that on the counter, its milled edge shining at the level of my eyes, was a half-a-crown. It was grand larceny. I had never seen so much stray money, so temptingly close. Before I realised what I was about my hand snaked up and into my pocket thudded the heavy coin. I left the shop, having calmly made my purchases and preserved a criminally straight face while the poor man searched pathetically for the lost money. Mean and triumphant I went home, pausing only to boast to the boy next door that I had found five times as much as his miserable sixpence. The loot sat on my hand, a silver miracle. Like a cat my mother pounced on it.

'Where did you *find* this?' she asked, giving me the credit of having come by it honestly or needing, at least, to keep her own conscience clear.

'In the quarry,' I answered. 'It was just lying there.'

'Oh good,' she breathed. 'That's a prayer answered for a start.' To my chagrin she relieved me of the coin. 'If nobody comes for it,' she said fixing me in the eye, 'I'll give you a penny next week.'

This, it appears, could be labelled the early criminal part of my life, because before long I stole something else. This time it was a vegetable marrow.

On my way to school I had spied this large and lush green object, lurking below its leaves, at the foot of somebody's garden. I had no idea what it was but it looked good enough to eat. After a couple of days I took a kitchen knife to school and on my way home I cut it and staggered the rest of the way, running with it in my arms like a big green baby. My mother, however, was less than pleased. 'I can't cook that!' she protested. 'We don't like it. Where did you get it?'

This time the quarry was out. I confessed. She bore

it back to the owner. After that I had to make a long detour to and from school to avoid the scene of the crime but, even so, I saw the woman waving her fist at me in the distance. I did not steal anything else after that. Nothing large anyway.

As it was, I thought the police had tracked me down. On top of the hill where we lived there was no road, only a footpath so if a policeman appeared then everyone knew that he was on his way to one of the neighbouring houses and observed him spitefully. Shortly after the larceny of the marrow I was digging in the patch of ground next to our front door when a constable appeared, black and lofty on the horizon, and strode purposefully towards our house. Some little girls, who had recently heard me use some bad language and threatened to report me, were playing by the path and the policeman paused and asked them something. Skinny arms went eagerly out and accusing fingers pointed towards me. No, I thought, no . . . surely not . . . not the *police*! All I had said was 'bugger'.

Not daring to look up I counted every footfall as he approached. I could feel my small body shaking. Nearer and nearer . . . and then he turned into *our* house.

'Hello, sonny,' said the policeman. 'Is your mam in?'

Struck speechless, I led him towards the door. Should I make a run for it now? Fancy ruining my life for a marrow . . . Or perhaps it was because of the half-a-crown . . . or the swearing. My guilty past closed in.

'Mrs Thomas?' said the officer when my mother appeared. I stood slightly behind him rolling my eyes and shaking my head to prevent her shopping me.

'Is anyone dead?' she asked with almost dramatic hope. 'An accident is it? An explosion?'

'No, no,' he said, at once both a disappointment and an assurance. 'Not dead, drunk. Your husband, I think.' He looked down at his notebook. 'David James Thomas. Drunk and incapable.' He looked up with some sort of interest. 'Got out of the train at Newport station . . .'

'On the wrong side,' she finished for him. She nodded sad confirmation. 'He's done it before,' she sighed. 'When he came back from burying his father. Where is he now?'

'In the cells,' he replied dramatically. I had heard about the cells. Letting out a toddler's cry of anguish I set off down the hill weeping and shouting. 'My daddy's in the cells! My daddy's in the cells!' Before my mother and the policeman could catch me everybody in the district knew. They would have known anyway because it was in the *South Wales Argus* that night. 'Drunken man fell from train,' it said. The old man cut the piece out and used to keep it in his wallet.

On this occasion I went with my mother to court although all I remember is her having to pay the two shilling fine and muttering 'Bunny rabbits' as she looked for the money in her purse. The kindly court officer collecting the cash enquired what the phrase meant. 'I always say "Bunny rabbits" because it saves me swearing,' my mother explained piously. At that moment my father, ashen-faced, was brought out to freedom. 'Bloody bunny rabbits,' cursed my mother.

The previous time he had left the train on the

31

opposite side to the platform was as my mother had told the policeman, after my grandfather's funeral. On that occasion some concerned people had hauled him up and sent him home in a taxi. I remember him now, standing by my bedside, getting undressed, festooned with long underpants (my mother refused to sleep with him) and looking very bruised and sad.

'Did you cry?' I enquired.

'Oh no,' he boasted thoughtfully. 'Not when I fell out of the train, not at the cemetery either.' His testicles were hanging like prunes from a hole in his pants. 'No, men don't cry, son. Not even over somebody dead. Worry is what men do. Worry.'

Throughout his life he collected a formidable catalogue of injuries and tales through a combination of inebriation and transportation. Not only did he plummet from trains but from other vehicles, and from the platform of a bus that was going over a bridge, ending up strung across the parapet wall, and God knows how many times he had fallen into docks throughout the world. Once he came home plastered, literally, his ribs all caved in and bandages around his shoulders. He took his shirt off and walked around for a bit like this and my mother pretended not to notice. Eventually she said: 'Missed the ship again, did you?' He had. Apparently by several feet.

He was, nevertheless, spontaneously good-hearted. His second weakness was whist drives at which he frequently won prizes. If he were in some port in another part of the country he would send the prizes home. One evening he was in Swansea, just before Christmas, and he won a goose at whist. Full of goodwill and undoubtedly spirits, he wrapped the goose up, took it to the post office and dispatched it home. It arrived several days after the holiday on a bike, stinking to hell, with a green-faced postman propelling it.

It would not be too difficult to deduce that my mother was long-suffering. The uncertainties of her life are endorsed for me in a single cameo. After being for months on the dole and then having, for his customary reason, failed to sail on a ship he was supposed to join, my father finally got himself a berth on a vessel leaving Newport for some place so distant that it even pleased my mother. There was a chance he might be gone for two years. Her anxiety was two-rooted: she wanted him to go away and some money to come in. They had spent a long time rowing miserably, calling each other 'wet-weeks', a recurring insult, a combination of malice and meteorology. Now he was leaving, his kitbag packed, the first week's allotment money only seven days away.

When he left the house she even went so far as to kiss him. She went up to the bathroom and watched him trudging down the hill and up again with his kitbag on his shoulder; like a lookout Indian she observed him waiting at the distant bus stop and eventually boarding the bus. She came down and sat quiet for a long time, studying the clock. Eventually she gave me the final two pennies from her purse, and instructed me to go to Mrs so-and-so's house about a mile away, and ask if they would mind telephoning the dock gates to make sure my father's ship had actually sailed. She explained to me that she was too ashamed to go to the telephone herself. I had the name of the vessel written on a piece of paper and the woman with the telephone, grumbling about the imposition, made the call and told me to tell my mother that the ship *had* left. I returned happily with the news and had just related it to my relieved mother when the smile dropped like a stone from her lips and she pointed in disbelief out of the window. There he was, in the distance, kitbag on his shoulder and on his way home. There had, he said, been some sort of misunderstanding . . .

Despite it all she managed to make a home for us in that boxy council house on the hill. It had an iron boiler in the narrow back kitchen, which was at the front of the house (rumour had it that the builder had read the plans upside down) and in this she used to wash the clothes and cook steamed puddings in pillowcases. We had a wooden three-piece suite with brown corduroy cushions, in the living room, a relic, I imagine, of more affluent days. The settee and two chairs could be transformed into a ship or an outpost when my mother was out. My brother Roy and I played many games in that room, spoiled once when he attempted to make a campfire with some books under the wooden table. We managed to put out the flames before the whole interior was ablaze but there was smoke still pouring from the windows when she got off the remote bus.

Our house on the rise was clearly visible from that bus stop even though, up and down hill, it was a quarter of an hour's walk away. Trouble, in either direction, could be seen from afar, and sometimes the agony and uncertainty seemed far longer than fifteen minutes. The smoke puffing out like a signal was not the first, nor the last, of these distant shocks. Once, in summer, she perceived that we had pitched a white tent at the front of the house and, as she panted home, her suspicions hardened to the certainty that the tent was formed from two Witney blankets, prized possessions, given to her years before and which had never known a bed. In those days good things were often stored away unused.

Roy was more adventurous than me. I would stay at home and read while he set off, in the family manner, to other places. Lin and Hally were away at sea and we rarely saw them. My only memory of Hally from those days was when it was suggested that he should shin up the lamp posts in Milner Street to afix flags and banners during the Silver Jubilee celebrations of King George the Fifth and Queen Mary. Since he was a seafarer, it was calculated that he ought to find it easy, but he made the excuse that he could only climb up things like that when he was at sea and the ship was rocking on the waves. Lin, who was working his way up the decks, had interludes when he returned from voyages, went out to dances and brought girls home. These young ladies often used to make a fuss of me and let me sit on their laps with my head on their chests so I really looked forward to his return from a trip. One of his ex-girlfriends who lived quite near once gave me an old piano, in a spirit of vengeance perhaps. I could only have been seven or eight at the time and I was trying to make arrangements to move it from her house to mine, but my mother found out and told the girl we didn't want it.

Lin used to study with matchsticks on the table, calculating winds and currents for his exams. He had an amiable Latin-looking friend called Guy Hodges, who I can picture clearly even now. He had a concise moustache which he called his 'little bit of dog' and he could draw adventurous pictures of ships and storms and could also play the mandolin. During the war my brother went to visit him and found that both he and his brother Eric had been lost at sea. My brother cried bitterly and I have never forgotten the brothers' names, although I never even met Eric.

When Lin had gone back to sea I would sit studying matchstick winds and currents just as I had seen him do. My mother was both proud and worried. She did not want her younger sons to go away. Then I began to draw sea gulls, sunsets and steamers bedecked with funnels. 'Ah,' she said in an attempt at re-routing my life's course. 'You'll be a *draughtsman* when you grow up. Now that's a *nice* job.'

Thereafter, for some years in fact, I imagined a draughtsman was somebody who poled a raft down a river, a wet and perilous living. I even used to have nightmares about it. When, eventually, I realised that a draughtsman was someone who drew lines on paper, usually in the sanctuary of an office, I found the image more becoming, but at fourteen I went to technical school and quickly discovered it was not my future. My drawing was surrealistically inaccurate and scarred with erasures, my calculations wild; and when it came to practical applications such as brick-laying, mine were the walls which fell down.

So keen was my mother to keep her sons home by

the fireside that she even refused to let us go on one of Campbell's Paddle Steamers that used to sail out of Newport on Bristol Channel pleasure trips. She feared, once we'd got the salt in our noses, we might acquire a taste for the life. So places like the exotic-sounding Weston-super-Mare, of which we heard from our more travelled acquaintances, remained beyond our horizon.

In fact we scarcely went anywhere. The hill of houses, the quarry and its grey-green fields at the back, the cold old pond where we tried to fish and ventured for a muddy paddle in summertime, and occasional trips into the town where the tramcars sizzled along their steel rails, were the stuff of our world. My Sunday school teacher, apparently seized by some temporary missionary zeal, promised to take the class into Newport to show us the sort of blinds and awnings used in the Bible lands, a sort of holy journey. When she failed to fulfil this pledge, and the summer was going by, I asked her when we were actually going and she replied lamely that the blinds of the shop she had been thinking about had caught fire and it was no more. The adventure was off. That night I lay awake with disappointment.

Our great journey of the year was a day at Barry Island. Money was put away in preparation for this trip and the weather became the subject of prayers. Everybody in the street went in what was strangely called a charabanc. Once my mother, having put the fare money into the kitty throughout the year, found when the day dawned, that she did not have another halfpenny to take with us, nothing even for a cup of tea or an ice cream and certainly nothing for a bucket and spade. She went to bed and sulked the night before and she had a good cry the next morning. The shining charabanc arrived for the twenty-mile trip to bliss. The neighbours began to tumble joyfully aboard. 'Dolly Thomas is missing!' somebody shouted. They saw my wistful brother and I watching. 'Where's your mam?' someone demanded. ''Aving an 'owl,' I replied. 'We're not coming.'

Determined neighbours disembarked and a delegation climbed to our front bedroom to plead with my mother who at first hid under the bedclothes. When she emerged they argued that they did not have much money either, although they had more than us. Roy and I had followed the deputation and added our pleas, promising faithfully that we would not ask for impossible dreams like buckets and spades. Reluctantly she got out of bed and made some jam sandwiches. We went to Barry Island and sat on the sand eating the bread and jam. The sun beamed and the fairground blared blatantly behind us. But there was no charge for the sea and the sand so we had quite a good day.

The noise of the sideshow barkers and the music of the roundabouts must have been as thoroughly tantalising for our mother as for us, for she had a dire weakness for fairgrounds. Once, when the August fair was in Newport, in Belle Vue Park, she found the temptation of the airship game too much to withstand. The silvery airship, alight with coloured bulbs, cruised raucously in a long parabola, lighting up various Christian and surnames as it went. If it stopped at Bessie Brown, and you had purchased a ticket with 'Bessie Brown' on it, you were the winner. It was getting towards the end of the evening and mother was almost out of money.

'I *know* "Frank Davies" is going to come up next time,' she informed me. 'I just *know* it.' She challenged me with her bright green eyes. She wanted support.

'How much have we got, Mum?' I enquired.

'Just the bus fares.' Defiance lit her face. 'What do you think?'

'Put it on Frank Davies then.' I shrugged.

She did and we watched the glittering airship float around, finally coming to rest on 'Bertie Jones'. Defeated, downcast, we stumbled from the fairground. She had already transferred the blame and she refused to speak to me. As we reached the road, with a long trudge home ahead of us, it began to rain. It thickened and teemed. Heads down the woman and two little boys ploughed through it.

'It's *your* fault!' she shouted at me, her face streaming. 'You made me do it!' She pointed at Roy, a shivering figure soaked through his skinny clothes. He told me that he had done a wee in his trousers so he was wet both inside and out. 'Look at him!' she bellowed. 'Look – sopping he is. And you *know* he's got a bad chest! I could murder you!'

She gave me a slap on the back of the head which set me bawling. The buses went by tantalisingly, their passengers dry, smug and staring through the yellow windows at the stumbling trio in the downpour. Mother stopped abruptly. 'Les,' she ordered. 'Go and ask the conductor if he'll come up to the house for the fare. I've got some in the teapot. It's not far from the stop, after all.'

'He won't do that . . .' I began to argue. Her streaming face was turned to me again. This time she was all broken up. 'Go on,' she pleaded. 'There's a good boy. Roy will get pneumonia.'

I chased after the bus which was at the stop but it started away again while I was still framing my unusual request to the conductor. I turned back disconsolately. We continued to walk. The rain stopped but the wind seeped through our wet garments. 'You're never going to the fair again,' said my mother darkly. At that moment I was not all that sorry.

Often she was a sweet and loving woman but she needed someone to take, or at least share, blame for the multiplying viscissitudes of her life and I was the obvious choice. One evening my brother and I were playing a game in our small living room which involved jumping over a rope tied between chairs. It was bedtime, but we begged for 'one more go' and the final jump ended with Roy howling on the floor with a broken arm.

A neighbour with a motorbike (the only vehicle in the district) was summoned and he took Roy on his pillion to hospital. They tied him on with a rope and instructed him to hang on with his good arm. It was not far anyhow. My mother, roundly blaming me for the mishap, followed by bus. Tearfully I went to bed and lay awake wondering if you could die from a broken arm (then I'd *really* be for it) until they returned after several hours, all talking quite cheerfully. 'What will be, will be,' quoted the motor-cycling neighbour as he left. Before she went to bed my mother came into the room. I pretended to be tight asleep. She bent over and kissed me and said: 'I'm sorry.'

Roy's plastered arm provided us with a useful excuse for coming home from school early. He had just started at the local infants' department and my mother asked if he could leave early each afternoon to prevent his arm being jostled by the other children. It was agreed and I was given charge of escorting him home. On the first day, having left the classroom ten minutes before the close, we were confronted by the daunting iron gates (the school, notwithstanding, was of wood) which were powerfully locked and were not due to be opened by the caretaker until going-home time. Nothing was going to hinder our privilege, however, and we decided to climb the gates. This was difficult enough for me, for they were high and topped with spikes, but for Roy with his heavy and useless arm, it was much worse. I got halfway and helped him up the initial stage. Then I climbed higher and assisted him again. With difficulty and danger I climbed over the spikes at the top and urged him to do likewise. I half dropped, half fell, but triumphantly landed only to hear a dreadful squawk from above. Roy was dangling there, one of the spikes having gone up the leg of his short trousers and emerged at the seat. His arms, the good one and the plastered one, were waving horribly, his knees pedalling like fury, and his face was a mask of fright. As he wriggled I heard the rip of his trousers.

In a panic I rushed to the caretaker's house and hammered on the door. The man, an indolent person, appeared in his carpet slippers. 'My little brother's hanging on the gates!' I cried.

41

'Let 'im,' replied the man unfeelingly. 'It's not four o'clock yet.'

I went back to Roy. His face was like milk.

'He says he can't get you down until four o'clock,' I called up.

'My trucks is ripping!' he cried.

The man, having been troubled by conscience I suppose, emerged shuffling in his carpet slippers, but wearing his official peaked cap with its Newport Corporation badge. He stared up at the stuck boy.

'Shouldn't be up there in the first place,' he said.

Children were emerging from the school now, rushing shouting to the gate. As if my brother was not impaled overhead, the caretaker unlocked the gate and swung it open, swinging Roy with it. The children were naturally entranced at the spectacle and, as the trousers ripped again, gathered to see what the final outcome might be. Roy was howling dispairingly. The caretaker, at a miserable pace, went for a ladder and, in a scene not unlike the Descent from the Cross, unhooked the sobbing brother and brought him down.

We went home, he with his trousers asunder. My mother said it would be a terrible job to sew them together again.

II

It was rarely that my mother enjoyed the luxury of her problems striking one at a time. In the middle of one sharp winter, with the Welsh wind whistling across the houses and the hills, she found herself with two seriously sick children. When I was eight my legs began aching and have, more or less, gone on doing so ever since. I was stumbling in pain about the room while she tried to coax me to the kitchen with the blatant lie that there was a sixpence lying unattended on the floor. Eventually she was convinced enough to invest five shillings in a doctor who earned his fee by diagnosing rheumatic fever. Roy, who was five, not to be outdone, promptly got pneumonia.

With a siege-like spirit, Dolly Thomas concentrated her resources. Two mattresses were brought down and placed on the floor in the alcoves each side of the fire grate. There my brother and I lay for several winter weeks, with the weather howling outside the iron-framed council house windows, and the coal fire luminous in the grate. It was quite a luxurious way of being ill. We had a battery wireless set and we listened to the daytime programmes, music, talks and the news, and, when we were feeling better, put together our own radio programmes in which I did most things, including the

43

singing. Roy was relegated to reading the weather forecasts and imitating the pips before the six o'clock bulletin. It was amazingly instructive, far better than the infantile lessons at the infants' school where my brother had been rightly offended to have to hang his coat on a peg decorated with a rose ('R is for Rose and R is for Roy'). Mine was a leek.

We learned for the first time of someone troublesome called Hitler and of places called Austria and Danzig. We inserted them in our own news broadcasts, transmitted with the aid of an empty Fry's cocoa tin on a length of cord. Austria we naturally confused with Australia and we interrupted normal programmes to announce the German invasion of the latter. Mr Chamberlain we called Mr Chamberpot, then invariably fell about our beds laughing. My brother tore a page from the *Daily Herald*, which the man next door used to pass on to us when he had finished with it, and fashioned a trumpet to accompany Donald Peers (a thinly disguised me) in song. We heard that Donald Peers, a popular performer, came from Newport and we were astonished and impressed. Radio Luxembourg was awaited keenly, especially Salty Sam the Sailorman who used to extol health salts and tell an acquiescent boy and girl to go and find a pebble and whoever brought the biggest could choose the day's story. In imagination I pictured myself staggering along that mystic beach with a huge boulder on my shoulder, and I often wondered what the little girl was like; me and her on the beach when old Salty Sam had gone home to his cottage or sailed out fishing. There was ample time for fiction in my bed by the fireside.

With this advertisement used to go a ditty: 'I'm Salty Sam the sailorman . . . I sail the ocean blue,' which we would lustily accompany. Roy's pneumonia made him a bit husky at first but his voice got stronger as his health improved. We also used to sing, two pale faces in the flickering firelight: 'We are the Ovaltinees, happy girls and boys.' We were ever optimistic.

It was my mother, I realise now, who *had* to get out of the house. At first she never went beyond the door and, for someone who had known the bright lights of Barry and Birmingham and enjoyed her dreams in the cinema, it must have been an imprisonment. Eventually she broke. She shouted at us for something and then her expression fell as she saw our apologetic faces one each side of the grate. That afternoon she got a girl to come in for a couple of hours and just went for a walk around Newport, not a voluptuous occupation. She promised to bring presents back for us and she did. Lack of funds limited the nature of the gifts but she had been touring Newport market and returned with a dozen old copies of Enid Blyton's *Sunny Stories* periodical which she gave to my brother and a huge, wonderful glossy book of unending interest which was for me. It was called 'The Littlewood's Catalogue'. I remember the sleek feel of its great bulk as she laid it on the bed. It was like a large woman wearing silk. The catalogue was a couple of years old, she explained, but you could still buy the same things by paying so much a week. Its glossy cover glowed in the firelight. I opened the pages and was lost to the world.

Ever since I could read, I had been prey to the desire evoked by advertisements in the *People*, the only newspaper we took regularly and that on account of the astrological assertions of Edward Lyndoe, who unfailingly forecast an improved future for my mother, which, considering her usual circumstances, was not difficult. She always referred to him as 'old Lyndoe' as if he were a friend, which I suppose he was in a way. I always felt her faith misplaced because none of the promises seemed to happen. Indeed, my mother recorded a distinct loss when prompted by Mr Lyndoe's forecast: 'There will be no war – the stars are against it.' She made instant bets of several shillings to this effect. The date was Sunday, September 3rd, 1939, the day war was declared.

The advertisements in the *People*, however, enslaved me with their fair words. Double your strength in three weeks; Grow your own raspberries; Make costly jewellery AT HOME; There is BIG money in pigeons; and other such pledges, some promising YOUR Money RETURNED if not satisfied. Imagine someone not being satisfied with his pigeons or his raspberries. There were also drawings of mighty ladies clamped in corsets, looking like the armoured horses of medieval knights. Sunday was a day of guilty thrills.

Now there was placed before me this compendium. It was as if someone had revealed the secrets of life. You could have anything, absolutely *anything*, it appeared, and pay for it at two shillings a week, or even less. It was not merely the pages that opened in my rheumaticky fingers, it was a whole new, bright and patently attainable world.

It was not only the glistening toys, red kiddie-cars, triangles with bells, fire engines, soldiers in forts, animals on wooden farms, skates, guns, scale models

46

and jigsaws, but a far wider enchantment. Lawn mowers, green and powerful, hunched on the verdant frontages of long lush houses with red roofs; a real working, squirting hose, with a pond and statue in the background; picnic hampers cluttered with pies, thermos flasks for instant refreshment, collapsible ironing boards, electric fires, comfortably folded blankets and sheets, unending carpets, plush chairs, kitchen gadgets, and . . . oh, my God, there she was again . . . in her *corsets*! Not only her, but several softly coloured pages of her wanton sisters, posing in their peachy bloomers, elastic straining at waist and knee, or garments open to upward draughts and enticingly called French knickers. What did *Directoire* mean? And what of those things like tureens which well-fed looking ladies had strapped to their chests? That was intriguing because our mother was thin all the way down, but I had noticed that other boys' mams were bulging above the waist. Petticoats there were also, hemmed with looping lace and those corsets again, some bent like tin around the thighs, some, locked with a spanner it seemed, from which the female form might explode at any moment. Guiltily I wished that my mother was a bigger woman. There were so many things I wanted to know. How did these amazing Amazons go to the lav? Did they creak as they crouched?

'What you looking at?' enquired my brother from across the fireplace after I had been studying the catalogue for several days. He had finished *Sunny Stories*.

'Nothing for you,' I said with the brusqueness of the secret sinner.

'That book's got bloomers,' he confided archly.

'With ladies inside them. I had a decko when you was asleep. They're not as good as our mam's, though.'

Indeed they were not. For someone who had hardly two pennies to make a clink, Dolly Thomas had the most wonderful silks and fripperies, drawers full of them in the palest of hues with lavish lace and unscrupulous fancy embroidery. She had long lovely nighties and silk pyjamas with flopping leg bottoms, negligees that might have graced a window in Paris. And she wore them, too. Where they had originated is anyone's guess – perhaps from her flappier days in Birmingham. All I know is this thin, anxious, hard-pressed, emotional, loving and impoverished lady went to her solitary bed in our council house each night, with all the allure of a favoured duchess.

On the back cover of our blue school exercise books was a map of the entire known world. Arranged about its edges were the words: Fifty Miles Around Newport. The circumference of my home town was the first geographical fact that ever impressed itself upon me. It encompassed a good deal more than my entire world. The rest of the earth was merely composed of wriggly and possibly untrustworthy lines on the flap of the book. Cardiff was distant, Bristol beyond the sea; London might as well have been Babylon.

The fifty-mile circle encompassed a gritty town, no stranger to distress, whose history included notable Chartist Riots but little else to excite mankind. Its major son of fame (apart from Donald Peers) was W.H. Davies, who composed the lines: 'Ah, but this life's so full of care, we have not time to stand and stare.' No one seemed quite sure where he was born, least of all himself. They found the street but Davies, when asked, was uncertain of the house. When he died they put a plaque on the wall recording his birth but it turned out to be the wrong place.

Coal travelled from the Welsh valleys to be loaded aboard ships at the docks, which ran along a district called Pill. The ships sailed away and then eagerly returned for more. Coaldust lay in ledges and littered the narrow streets. Smoke from the steel works, the other great employer, billowed gloomily over the dead-eyed river.

Pill was a forbidden city to us. My mother said we must never venture there for it was mysterious, full of nameless alarms and, what was more, rough. Pill sounded short and threatening, especially to my mother with her past social standing and her hopes for the future. 'It's wicked,' she warned. 'Never go down there.'

She was apt to deliver one-sentence sermons which somehow left their message. When I came home from school one day and said: 'Oh, fuck', she took on a stunned aspect and said: 'That is the Devil's *personal* word—you could drop dead!' I never said it again until I was in the army.

Pill seemed almost orientally attractive but, being timid, I more or less obeyed her, although I have no doubt my more daring younger brother knew its ways fairly well. Once, impetuously, I ventured into this casbah wearing my Wolf Cub uniform and hiked right through its sin-strewn streets without anything untoward happening to me. One of its major lures was a cinema called the Gem where the entrance price was a penny. The combination of excitement and economy was powerful. Clutching my brother's hand I took him there, or more probably he took me. We sat on splinter-ridden benches while the silent doings featured in *The Mark of Zorro* flickered like bats across the well-darned screen. There were several fights among attending children, and a full-grown woman stood up shouting filth at the pounding pianist and violently hoofed the door as she went out. Eventually a patently important man in a bow tie and frock coat imposed himself between the projector and the screen. Throwing his arms sideways he bawled: 'Stop pictures! Stop orchestra!' The pianist, glancing around to see who else might be playing, stopped in mid-clatter. 'Right-o,' volleyed the man. 'It 'as come to the management's notice that you kids 'ave been bringing fleas into the Gem. I'm up 'ere to tell you that you bring the buggers in – then you'll take the buggers out!'

After this brief and obviously heartfelt decision the pianist began to wobble again on the keys and Zorro rode again across the stretched and grubby sheet. A man wrote to me recently from the same building. It is now an office block.

My mother was mortified when she heard of our visit to Pill, but hygiene quickly replaced wrath and she avidly searched our heads. She loved the cinema especially films featuring Edward G. Robinson of the rubber scowl. She went to see *Brother Orchid* four times. After our adventure at the Gem she announced that a new picture palace was opening in Newport, the

Maindee *Supper* Cinema, a sophisticated place where, she asserted, you could eat off trays during the performance. Unfortunately, she had misread it. It was only the Maindee Super Cinema.

When I was eight I was allowed to go on the bus to the Odeon Saturday Morning Club, a hell-on-earth of screaming, rampaging kids where I relished every moment. The first film I believe I ever saw was a Popeye cartoon and one of its images kept itself locked in my memory for years. Popeye and Olive Oyl were walking down a street of mean houses, he just like my father, whom he somewhat resembled, holding his sailor's kitbag. At the bottom of the street, a poetic detail in the corner of the screen, some matchstick children were playing ring-a-roses around a lamp post, its circular light beaming down upon them. I recently passed a television shop and there, on a screen in the window, was that same scene. I remembered it perfectly.

Sometimes on Saturday afternoons my mother would take Roy and me to the cinema. We usually had to see what she wanted to see, which often meant some weepy love story or, yet again, Edward G. Robinson, who like Popeye had an odd, squashed likeness to my father. The images that come from those remote after-noons at the pictures are, however, not always those from the screen. They are of leaving, at five o'clock in winter, to the lights of the town reflected on rainy roads, of tram cars clanking and of the prospect of going home to tea.

There were times, although they became fewer, when my parents declared some sort of armistice and we briefly became the sort of family that I read about

51

in 'Sunny Stories'. They were so unusual as to be noteworthy.

My mother was one day at her washing board, looking out the misted window over the rooftops to the town beyond, wistfully, perhaps, or it may have just been the vapour from the steaming tub. One of my playmates had acquired a set of miniature blue dungarees, bib and brace, brass buckles and all, and I wanted a similar set. To my surprised satisfaction my mother did not come back with the usual riposte that we did not have enough money. Yes, I would have them. Just like that! Yes, my father was coming home from sea and he would buy me a pair of dungarees on his return. He was due in dock on the following day. And – on Friday night we would be going to the Empire and on Saturday to Barry Island.

The Empire! Barry Island! My cup was full. Even now I can see us, all four holding hands, at the bus stop waiting to go on the first part of that magic journey. I stand there, hugging myself with happiness, for I loved the stage lights, the funny men and even the singers and dancers at the Empire. And tomorrow . . . tomorrow . . .

We sat in the gods, gazing down at the iridescent stage. The number of the act used to go up formed by light bulbs at the wings, in the interval a curtain, thick as a wall, would descend, hung with advertisements for the attractions and businesses of Newport. It is hard to describe that delight. I cannot now recall what variety of acts were on stage that night, although this may have been the occasion when, to my guilt, surprise and pleasure, a lady standing at the back of a finale tableaux suddenly allowed the gauze covering her front to fall and reveal two marble-white and marble-hard objects which I thought for a moment might be spinning tops. It was only when the curtain had dropped, and the vision vanished, that I realised that I had glimpsed something that was to hold a lasting interest for me.

It must have been at this same period of their armistice when my parents went dancing together and took us with them. We went to a place which had the sniff of romance, the Newport Labour Hall. Roy and I sat on hoop-backed chairs, our eyes becoming clotted with chalk dust, as the dancers swooped and skidded around the floor in a swirling anti-clockwise haze. The fact that my mother was being flung backwards (it was the era of the Argentinian tango) by an utter stranger disturbed me a little. My father, meanwhile, swooped pan-faced across the boards with the dash of a marauder.

'Why is our dad doing it by himself?' enquired my brother. Like me, he must have thought dancing was an odd way to spend an evening, especially since the entrance fee was ninepence.

We had a good back view of our distant parent. Apparently alone, he was flicking his feet this way and that, sending up puffs of chalk, bending almost to the floor. Eventually he spun, kicked sideways, and zoomed towards us, clutching to him one of the smallest women I had ever seen, or have seen to this day. Whether he sought to impress his sons, I do not know, but as the appropriate beat of the tango occurred he arrived in our proximity, threw her backwards across his knee and her head tipped, like someone slaughtered. Then with a devilish grin he whirled her away.

'I could see right down inside her,' sniffed my brother.

The news that war had been declared was given to me by a boy with a stutter. 'W . . . w . . . w . . . ar,' he said as I was going up the street. We had moved in the spring of 1939 to a district called Maesglas, at the Welsh end of Newport, bordering on the ebony River Ebbw and rising meadows. Maesglas means 'green fields', but to its inhabitants and those in other council estates, it was known as Moscow.

On that first Sunday morning in September I had been sent, in the crucial few minutes before the fateful eleven o'clock speech of Neville Chamberlain, to the greengrocer's shop at the bottom of the street. My mother, as convinced as Edward Lyndoe that there would be no war, had decided that life should go on as usual, so I was sent for the vegetables. While the man was putting the muddy potatoes and carrots in a bag, so the announcement of hostilities was coming over the wireless in the back room of his shop. I could not hear what was being said but the greengrocer was clearly disturbed. 'We're for it now,' he confided in me. He turned to weigh the potatoes. Believing firmly in Lyndoe, I remained unworried and stood whistling through my teeth as any eight-year-old boy can and does. Abruptly, the anguished greengrocer turned and gave me the most frightful whack around the ear with an earth-bound potato. 'Stop that whistling, boy!' he shouted into my upset face. 'I can't stand you whistling, boy! It will all have to stop soon!'

He was right, in a way, because one of the first edicts to come from the British Government at the outset of the noisiest period in history was the banning of noises. There were to be no whistles, hooters nor, eventually, tolling bells, either.

After the boy with the stutter had filled in the details of the Prime Minister's speech for me in the street, I went into our end-terrace house, with its pebble-dash, red bricks and lingering single dog rose over the path and found my mother more disgusted with Edward Lyndoe than with Hitler. Her soothsayer, blindly believed every week in the pages of the *People* newspaper, had been found to be a false prophet. At first, she was inclined to put the blame on Chamberlain rather than Lyndoe. But in the end it sank in; not only had she lost faith and face, but also her housekeeping money, because she had backed his forecast with the same misplaced intuition that had led her to wager on Frank Davies on the fairground airship. Somewhere there was a streak of recklessness.

The war, contrary to most expectations, brought few immediate sensations. In fact there was a widespread feeling of being short-changed. Most people had forecast heavy bombing, and possibly a gas attack, within hours. My father returned from sea a few nights after the declaration, this being a time of truce for my parents. The final truce, as it happened, because they soon launched into a period of bitter hostility that made the first year of the greater conflict appear even more placid. My mother, looking quite mystic, carried a candle because the blackout curtains were not drawn across the window when my father arrived. Within a moment a policeman and an officious air raid warden were pounding at the door demanding to know why we were signalling to enemy bombers. There were none within several hundred miles at that time and, seeing that my father was a sailor home from the sea, they said they would not press charges but that we would have to blow the candle out. When they had fussed off, my father, holding forth in the dark while my mother hoisted the blackout blinds, announced that, if he had only had two white feathers on him, he would have presented one each to the policeman and the air raid warden.

He was ever caustic about what he considered to be the cowardice of the civilian services, particularly the police force, for which he had little time, although its members sometimes had time for him. His own activities ashore during the first two years of the war were, perhaps needless to say, not without drama. After being torpedoed twice in the open sea and surviving in a lifeboat, he returned home one black night, breathing bravery and brandy. Deciding that my mother might think twice about letting him into the house, he chose to drop into the air raid shelter in the garden to await daylight. There were four feet of water in the shelter and, stepping into the void beyond the door, he plunged right into it. After cheating the Atlantic he came close to drowning on dry land. There was also a period when he worked ashore, on Newport Docks, although it was brief. He wept openly with other men at being rendered virtually homeless by the destruction of the Dock Hotel by German bombers. 'Wanton,' he muttered, damp-faced as he viewed the wreckage. 'Wanton.'

One night when he was working on the docks he somehow came into possession of a couple of dozen kippers and bore these home at dawn as a triumphant addition to our rations. My mother, for once, was pleased, but worried about the police. To spread the good fortune, or perhaps the evidence, she distributed some of the fish to neighbours. At teatime that day she watched trembling from the window as a constable slowly strode the length of Maesglas Avenue, sniffing the aroma of grilling and frying kippers. But no arrests were made.

During this early wartime period, my father also provided sacks to be used as sandbags for bolstering the defences of our air raid shelter. He did nothing, despite my mother's scolding, to help fill them with earth. That was left to me.

Not that I minded. The air raid shelter was my pride. In my eagerness to get on with the fight against Nazism, I had dug a hole fifteen yards from the back door at the bottom of our garden, by the boarded fence that divided us from the Great Western Railway engine repair sheds. My mother told me where to dig because she had read in the paper that Anderson shelters, corrugated iron huts half-interred in the earth, were to be situated fifteen yards from the place of exit from the house. It was a warm autumn and I was only eight. Nevertheless, I was very determined and I dug and dug until I had a suitable hole. Every afternoon when I returned from school, and every Saturday and

Sunday, I made that hole wider and bigger. Eagerly I awaited the arrival of the air raid shelter. We would be the best-protected family in Maesglas. Hitler could do his worst.

When the men arrived with the curved and shining metal panels that were to be bolted together to form our refuge, they said that the hole was in the wrong place. My mother had mixed it up. The shelter had to be established fifteen *feet*, not yards, from the back door. I set about digging another hole.

Some workmen arrived to complete the job but I still had to fill in the first hole. Then came the satisfaction of piling earth on the naked corrugated iron shelter, filling the flour sacks that my father magicked from the docks, fitting the floorboards and witnessing the delivery of the wood and wire bunks. We had a little table and an oil lamp, a ladder to step down and a wooden door, like a bastion, to pull over the hole. It was wonderful, a home from home, deep in the ground; on fine nights my brother and I camped out in there.

Whether the sight of my labour, or my mother's scorn, was too much for him, I do not know, but my father quickly returned to the sea. His excuse was that his chest ached on land and he breathed better in the stokehold. I missed hearing the wheezings, gurglings and hissings within his body as he lay next to me in bed at night. Sometimes, if you listened carefully, you could imagine they were playing a tune.

On our air raid shelter I planted vegetables and flowers, a multiple achievement since it provided us with produce and decoration and camouflaged our hide-out from German reconnaisance aircraft. Mr Coles next door had a wonderful shelter, all lined and padded, with proper beds and even folding chairs and a *wireless set*. His son, who was called Flare, used to boast about their air raid shelter (which was fifteen *yards* from the back door at the bottom of the garden near the fence with the engine sheds). I was jealous, but pleased when Mr Coles gave me some strawberry plants and I put them on top of the shelter. In the hot summer of 1940, while Britain stood alone and aeroplanes battled in the sky, we had a splendid crop of strawberries.

Enthusiastically horticultural, I dug the entire back garden to grow potatoes, lettuces, carrots and onions. Somehow I felt that the injunction to 'Dig For Victory' on the Government advertisement hoardings was addressed specifically to me. I even set to work on the patch of front garden behind our ragged but sweet-smelling privet hedge, trimming the dog rose and cosseting the irises, which were our only flowers. I dug a rectangular flower bed at the centre of the patchy grass and was very proud of it until Mrs Holtom, a local fortune-teller, walked past and pronounced that it looked like a grave. She told my mother to instruct me to make it a different shape. I did. The resulting cross was apparently even less acceptable, and I could not manage a circle. 'You'll have a death in the family,' warned Mrs Holtom, looking grimly over the gate. 'Just mark my words.'

I don't know how accurate her prognostications were as a rule, but this time she was right. Twice.

III

Although the red-roofed houses of Maesglas were tightly regimented around its streets, pastures were visible enough in the distance, lying aslant the hill that led up to a better class of district called the Gaer. My mother had taken a job cleaning one of the houses there and, by standing on the summit of our air raid shelter, I could see her walking home, come down over the fields in her red coat, bright as a ladybird.

The countryside was at our doorstep, beyond the inky River Ebbw that curled through Tredegar Park; vales and big trees, a handsome enough landscape that I appreciate today on occasions when I drive through it. Predictably, though, our world ended at the bottom of the street. Our games, our gossip, our hearth and our homes were all contained in that space. Our rural activities were confined to the Woods, a small unkempt valley with a few gritty trees and a tangled, smelly pond. In winter this froze thickly and in summer became a bottle-green cauldron of newts, tadpoles and, in due time, frogs. Every child in the district used it as a tom-tiddler's ground and was familiar with every inch of its rough covering. Yet I remember saying to my best friend, Chubber, at the start of the August holidays: 'Let's spend all the time exploring the Woods, so's we know every bit of it.' Our horizons, like our ambitions, were not large. At its western boundary Maesglas was half-circled by the River Ebbw which descended almost solid with coaldust from the colleries in Ebbw Vale. The damp powder lay in heavy layers lining the river's banks, the texture of sand, its particles glistening like diamonds in sunshine. Sometimes we would collect a bucketful of Ebbw coal, as it was known, for the fire, drying it into blocks first or just sprinkling it over the heavier coal. Occasionally men with barrows would sell it around the streets and there was a near-deadly rivalry between the several families who made their living this way. Fights with fists and weapons took place on the jet banks of the river, men and boys rolling fiercely in the coaldust over which they fought.

South of the district, unrolling straight and flat to the Bristol Channel, was a vivid green marsh, cut with ditches and drainage channels that we called reens. A cobbled road led from the working men's institute, the last outpost of Maesglas, down towards Newport Docks. Directly across the bright marsh you could see big ships looking as if they were afloat on grass.

At the other extreme of our street the main road went towards Cardiff. There was a line of shops, which once provided fortuitous pickings when most of their windows were blown out by a German landmine in 1940. People went there in the early hours of the morning to inspect the damage and came back laden with all sorts of groceries, cigarettes and bottled beer which they had found lying around. They said they had just been tidying up. A little apart from this shopping parade, across the road, like a stronghold set on a small hillock, was Shepherd's Fish and Chips, where the juvenile population each evening formed a struggling mass in the narrow alley outside its doors, waiting for the moment when Mr Shepherd would open them and let the howling mob in. You had to take your own newspaper because it was in short supply and there was little fish to be had once the war had really got under way. Most of the children in that area were brought up on Shepherd's chips. The shop was still there when I last looked.

So, also, was the doctor. Only a year or two ago, Dr Galloway Smith was still practising from his surgery on the end of the shops, as he had been forty years before. In those former days he was looked upon with awe for he was the only man for miles around who had a car. His surgery was the last place to which I went in Maesglas – with my brother for a quick medical before we were sent off to Dr Barnardo's Homes. Although to us he had seemed a stern and forbidding man, people respected him and even loved him because he had served them so long.

On that recent return I walked up Maesglas Avenue, where we had lived at Number 39. The old houses had been demolished to make way for new. (The next day I found that the houses at Somerton, at the far end of Newport, were also knocked down; Newport Council was pulverising my memories.) Across the street from the site of our former home, in one of the new, neat houses, was Fred Martin, a lovely white-haired man in his eighties. Very Welsh and very articulate, with a great gentleness about him that I remembered from long ago, he told me how the houses had been demolished.

'I sat at the window,' he related, 'watching them, the demolition gang. Waiting for the moment when our old castle would go. We'd lived in that house since 1927 and I wanted to see it fall down. They were going along the street with a big metal ball on a crane banging every house to the ground. I waited until they got to ours, *watching*, see. Then Beryl called me from the back kitchen and I went out to see what she wanted, just for a minute. When I came back they'd done it! It was vanished!'

He had been a docker and part-time fireman in the war. He was also a bit of a poet. He told me that once when my elder brother and his wife had quarrelled, and Mary was staying in our house, Lindon used to sleep in *his* house next door, lying, unknown to his wife, a six-inch wall away from her. 'People don't know what romance is these days,' said Fred, shaking his head.

At the centre of Maesglas in the nineteen-forties was a large grubby farmhouse which had once been the only building for miles. It was used as a junior school – the Farm School, as it was known – and it was there that I continued what never turned out to be an extensive education.

The previous school, where my brother had become impaled on the gate, left little memory, except of a headmistress who had haircut like a cooking pot and wore a pin-striped suit. I remember her as being of particularly nasty disposition, smacking the red, bare knees of her charges with alarming force and frequency. Very recently a man called Terry Underwood, who composed a splendid volume of old photographs called *Yesterday's Newport*, and still lives in the town, told me that he had attended the same infants' school and suffered the same indignities. We are the same age so we must have been classmates. 'Remember Miss So-and-So?' he reminisced. 'The way she used to go for your knees?'

This fierce lady took a particular interest in me. She would stop me at random in the school playground and painfully peer in my ears. Apparently she did not think that I washed or blew my nose enough. On the very last day at the school, when I was eight, she had me circling the asphalt yard while continuously blowing my nose. As I came around for each new circuit, with this ogre standing like a ringmaster urging me to trot and blow faster, I could see the removals van standing in front of my house. On my last moment in the school I dropped my snotty handkerchief through her letter box and ran.

At Maesglas, the Farm School was a cronky old building that leaned perilously to one side. As the robust children rushed and bustled inside, it creaked and swayed and there appeared to be a race between the building of a new junior school and this one tumbling on our heads. Across a playing field was a newly built senior establishment, to which I transferred, where the patriotic headmaster, urged on by wartime Government posters, decided to enlist every pupil in a gardening campaign. Each one was to invest a shilling in a limited company and the profits from the produce we grew would be distributed accordingly. This was not welcome news to me for I was weary enough after my own efforts at digging-for-victory at home, not to mention the fatiguing hours spent working on the air raid shelter. Now I had to take up the spade at school as well. For a skinny boy I had biceps like a navvy. Sometimes my brother would bring his friends to the house to see them. Nobody would fight a boy with muscles like that and I became the lightweight champion of Maesglas without ever having a contest. At least the school, with its shilling-a-head capital, provided proper gardening implements. At home my own tool was a garden fork with one of the outside prongs broken. Any shovelling, including the filling of the sacks so freely provided by my father, had to be accomplished with the hand coal shovel from our fireside. Once my mother heard me shouting and rushed to the back of the house to see the garden fork apparently impaling my foot. Actually it was the broken prong merely resting on the toecap of my shoe. Thinking I was pinned to the ground, she screamed and pulled the fork out, staring in relief and then fury when she realised that she had been tricked. Her hand came around my ear again and again and I ran out into the street shouting: 'Can't you take a joke?'

Whatever his plans for helping the war effort, the headmaster of the Maesglas school was ill-prepared when the Germans eventually attacked. There were no air raid shelters provided and his instructions were to send the children home at the first howl of the air raid siren; not, in retrospect, very clever advice. One day a German plane was crossing at only five hundred feet while we were galloping home below. The local anti-aircraft guns were firing and missing jubilantly. Their deadly shrapnel, however, was showering all around us as we ran unprotected down the middle of the street. I was running with my brother, slapping our hips, pretending to be cavalry. The firing was directly overhead and jagged metal clattered all around. All the boys were enthusiastic collectors of war souvenirs and when a huge lump of shrapnel bounced in the gutter almost at our feet Roy and I both made a grab for it, pushing at each other for the prize, the battle above of no importance. I picked it up. It was red hot. A woman howled from a neighbouring doorway for us to take cover in her house and, realising at last that we were in dire danger, we ran for shelter. When the firing was done, there was a mad rush from safety by all the children seeking to claim the shining shrapnel. The big lump was still hot but my brother and I both made for it. We reached it simultaneously and there was another battle, in the middle of the road this time, over who should have it.

Like many brothers Roy and I were rarely on close terms, although I was often protective towards him if he were threatened by other older boys. He had a gift for being injured. He broke his arm (again) tumbling from our fence. In a street fight in which missiles were thrown, he was hit by an edge-on roof slate. It split him spectacularly above the mouth and he had to go to hospital for stitching. When the wound was almost healed, he was trying to climb on the local dustcart, to retrieve some treasure, when the vehicle stopped suddenly and he collided with it. His face looked like the end of an exploding cigar. Some years ago I had a letter from the one-time urchin who had thrown the slate, a most erudite note, quoting the classics and full of wisdom and humour. I could never imagine him writing like that. He also apologised for damaging my brother.

Because of the everyday dramas of the real war, the children of my generation went in for a military type of violence. Maesglas was often like a citadel – Moscow indeed – roamed and patrolled by armies of boys bearing arms. Bows and arrows, spears, catapults and cudgels were used in imitation wars with armies from other districts. Each street also had its own gang which might be at war with the next street or those living a few rows of chimneys away. Within the street were even smaller echelons waging brisk civil wars until called upon by the street or the district itself to form part of a larger force.

These battles, or charges as we called them, were frequently injurious. One boy plummeted on his head from a railway water tower while dropping housebricks on the heads of a horde from the Gaer invading across the railway line.

This aerial bombardment was itself an extension of the pastime of dropping bricks aimed from a bridge into the funnels of passing steam trains. If you scored a direct hit down the funnel the brick came back like a cannonball. The Gaer army made an armoured car from a perambulator festooned with dustbin lids. I personally countered this weapon by inventing a giant catapult of a cycle inner tube fixed to the back framework of an upright wooden chair. Anchored strongly, it could project a half brick at great velocity, and the

67

brilliant innovation of a horizontal cycle wheel as a base gave it a circular field of fire. Our first shot drilled a jagged hole through the perambulator armoured car and almost through the lad crouched within. Our giant catapult also sank a raft being paddled across the pond at the Woods during another raid by the Gaer gang. It was so successful, in fact, that I had definite thoughts of using it against the Germans if they ever mounted their threatened invasion. Our Moscow would have been defended with all the devotion and ardour of the real one.

Unless called upon for the larger wars, I belonged to the smallest gang in the street. There were only two of us, Chubber and I, but we were lithe and mobile, we told ourselves, able to strike and vanish in a way that the larger echelons found impossible. We also had a knife, an air rifle and a real revolver.

Chubber Helmich was my only real friend. He was an india-rubber boy who could duck, feint and fold up like a concertina, so that hitting him was next to impossible. His father, a Belgian, adored his little son. If we were playing in his house his parent would gaze at him and at regular intervals murmur: 'Howya, boy?' and Chubber would blush but dutifully reply: 'Howya, Dad?' I found this very odd and I told my mother but she was thoughtful about it and eventually said that it happened because the man loved his boy so deeply.

Chubber's father bought him a wonderful box of tools, a real carpenter's chest, and I was consumed with envy. I had begun collecting bits and pieces for carpentry (I don't know where the urge or the skill, if any, vanished, for today I am incapable of putting a picture on a wall without the area looking as if it's had the attention of a firing squad). Chubber's tools were magnificent – planes and saws and many sizes of chisels and screwdrivers; measuring implements of precision and beauty – all housed in a handsome wooden box. My mother vowed to help me to get a similar kit together and bought me a saw for my birthday. It was, however, a strange, narrow saw; it could only be used for cutting keyholes so its use was limited. Even when I cut some new keyholes in our own doors it did not work out successfully. In fact they became extremely large and my mother hid them from the rent collector in case he reported us to the council.

I did, however, have the revolver. This was an unequalled possession. A genuine Colt service revolver 'as used in the battle of Madagascar', according to my elder brother Lin, who came home after taking part in that skirmish against the Vichy French. I had made a wooden gun and Lin's baby son, Graham, had cried so much to have it that Lin offered to make an exchange – the real weapon for my wooden fake.

'Say he goes and shoots somebody?' my mother said anxiously after my undelayed acceptance. And an unusual understatement: 'He could get into trouble.'

There was no ammunition with the weapon and my brother had removed one or two essential parts. Nevertheless, it was a *real* gun. I would stride through the streets of Moscow with the huge revolver stuck in my snake belt and Chubber ranging alongside with his scout knife and Diana air rifle. A formidable pair.

We had a secret sign, leaving messages in niches known only to us, signed off with a drawing of a dagger dripping blood. One day Chubber was taken to hospital where he nearly died of peritonitis. My mother was also ill and I cried in bed at night. After several weeks Chubber had recovered enough to send me a letter – signed with a shaky, dripping dagger. I knew then he would be all right. Forty years later, opening a letter I saw again the sign of the blooded dagger. I had forgotten it.

There were sporadic outbreaks of fighting at the Sunday school where Roy and I were sent by our mother while she went to bed with a cup of tea and the *People*. We each had a penny for the collection plate which we spent on sweets. When sweets vanished in the war they were curiously replaced by carrots and we spent our collection money on them instead. I still have perfect teeth.

There were agitators at Sunday school who caused trouble, and one afternoon I was leaving the corrugated iron church clutching my Bible text card when I was set upon by a jealous rival. I fought with my bony fists and elbows and we ended up in a pool of mud. An angular Sunday school teacher rescued me and my text and insisted on accompanying me home. I could not understand why she did this. My assailant had vanished, vanquished, and my clothes were only wet and muddy. I could have done all the necessary explaining myself. She probably had an urge to take the gospel into someone's home and she chose mine. I was annoyed when she insisted on coming with me and I strode off on the wet Sunday pavements, with the zealous lady lagging behind. Indoors my mother was fluttering the pages of the *People* with gentle snores. I waited, half-hiding, hoping the Sunday school lady had changed her mind.

She had not. She puffed to the front door and knocked evangelically. My befuddled mother was brought down to face a prolonged monologue. It was not all religious for the visitor's ploy was to obtain conversion by conversation, by discussing the children, perhaps, or the victim's hobbies.

My mother's hobby, apart from going to bed with the *People* on Sunday afternoons, was knitting and eventually, to get rid of the garrulous woman, my mother promised to knit some clothes for the Sunday school nativity play.

We had ample wool because my father when returning from a voyage would bring home sweaters, scarves, gloves, balaclava helmets and suchlike, knitted by patriotic ladies and sent to the armed forces and the Merchant Navy. The garments were in service colours; air force blue, navy blue and khaki. Roy and I would go to school on sharp mornings wrapped up like whalers. We could wear a different colour balaclava each day. The sweaters were huge but Mum swiftly unravelled the wool and made something else. She even knitted us woollen drawers to wear under our short trousers, but these itched and, since it was the debagging season, the risk of being found with our loins encased in RAF blue was too great. We stopped wearing them.

As promised, my mother set about making the costumes for the nativity play; a cloak for the Virgin Mary, a coat for Joseph and some swaddling clothes for the baby in the manger. It was undoubtedly one of the few occasions when the infant Jesus has been seen wearing khaki.

War at once brought to Maesglas a great deal more excitement and novelty than to most places in Britain. Elsewhere in the country, very little actually happened in the early days and there was relief as well as disappointment. But for us it was different. What appeared to be most of the British army tramped and trundled down our street on its way to France to face the foe.

Tredegar Park, a mile away, had overnight become an enthralling place of camouflaged tents, drilling soldiers, horses and vehicles which swerved in clouds of summer dust. Sentries with long bayonets and uncertain expressions were posted at the familiar iron gates. What had been our commonplace playground was transformed into a fortress. The swings and the see-saw were cordoned off. Nothing so thrilling had happened in the park since Kenny Griffiths, a thin boy from Maesglas Avenue, got his head scrunched under the moving roundabout and had to be rushed to the Royal Gwent Hospital to have it straightened. Now all the local children went to the railings, their faces pressed between the bars in zoo-like attitudes, witnessing the might of the British Expeditionary Force assemble and flex its muscles.

There was much lining up, and orders echoed over the tents. We saw a private soldier arrested for letting a couple of girls go into the park and having a lark with them on the playground swings. A fearsome sergeant-major in a flat hat arrived and bawled at the man who was led, head hanging, away. My brother said he had heard he was later shot.

Every day and on many nights the soldiers marched and their vehicles rumbled down Maesglas Avenue on their way to Newport Docks and the troopships. Thousands of men clumped past our house, some blatantly singing, some with bands, some with heads set straight ahead. When the first rank of the day was spotted at the end of the street, we and our neighbours would leave our houses. People used to throw cigarettes and fruit and sweets to the soldiers who caught them on the march, or sometimes in the face. One young private was injured by an apple which hit him in the eye. He had to sit on the pavement outside our front garden for quite a time before continuing on his journey to the war. Sometimes my mother would stand at our gate and sing with the passing soldiers. Although the doomed prophecy of 'We're going to hang out the washing on the Siegfried Line' was popular, they also sang songs from the campaigns of another generation. My mother liked 'Goodbye Dolly I must leave you' because her name was Dolly. Army lorries and platoon trucks and ominous ambulances rolled up the little street, and, most thrillingly, small tanks, Bren-gun carriers and armoured cars. In the middle of the night I would wake and rush to the window when I heard them coming. They passed in the darkness like metal ghosts. There were also horses pulling field guns. After thousands of years the horse was at last being excused man's battles and there were now only a few which my mother said was as it should be. My father, perhaps recalling his profitable deal with the French farmer, one war ago, was of the opinion that they would never be satisfactorily replaced. 'In an emergency,' he said, 'you could always eat your horse. You can't eat a tank.'

We had a family interest in the army's embarkation, for my Uncle Bert was a regular soldier and was in camp in the park, waiting to go to France. He was the husband of the only sister to whom my mother ever spoke, Auntie Iris who lived in Maesglas Crescent. She was younger and they had kept in contact when mother had abandoned, or been abandoned by, the rest of her family. (In writing this, I have just recalled that when I went into Barnardo's I 'gave' my aunt to another inmate, a boy called Stephenson who had no relations. He was very pleased to get letters from her, although she must have been somewhat puzzled because she had intended to write to me. My attitude also seemed rather lofty in the circumstances.)

Although Sergeant Bert Lucas had been in the Royal Engineers since the First World War, his wife was wracked with anxiety. I had orders to watch out for him passing by and, if possible, get a message to Iris, two streets away, so she could run and kiss him on the march. The tender moment, however, was not to be. He suddenly appeared, mixed in with hundreds of others, and was abreast of our house before we realised. My mother got to the gate and Bert broke ranks and scampered over to give her a kiss. I ran like mad, beating my imaginary horse along the pavements, alongside the troops, but by the time I reached Iris's house it was too late. The formation had tramped on.

Uncle Bert served through the early months in France but was then injured when he fell from his bicycle after a shell had landed in the vicinity. He was sent home and invalided out of the service. He went to work in the port where he fell into the empty dry dock and was killed.

Between the moving regiments, on a Sunday, came a kilted pipe band, with drums and busby hats, and a leader who tossed a silver mace. They were nothing to do with the military but were regular visitors. 'It's the Scotchilanders!' the children would shout and rush out into the road to watch them and perhaps put a penny in the proferred hat. Then, amazingly, we read in the *South Wales Argus* that they had been arrested as suspected IRA men. My mother said she had guessed all the time. 'Did you notice,' she said, her eyes narrowing, 'how that one in the front, the one with the stick, used to look down the side of our house every time they passed? Spying out the engine sheds, see. Planning to blow them up I expect.'

We had other familiar itinerants. Nocka, the ice cream man, whose full name was Nockavelli. He was Italian, we all thought, until Italy entered the war against us. Harmless Neopolitan cafés had their windows smashed in Newport and frightened Italian people were rounded up by the police. Nocka appeared as usual on the Sunday in his curly-painted van with the words 'Maltese Nationality. Loyal British Subject' large upon its sides.

There was also a man who sold greengrocery from a cart drawn by a dozy horse. The man was very lively and popular and when Pill, where he lived, was

75

bombed, the story came back that he had been killed. An immediate collection was made around the houses and the money dispatched to his widow. Then, it transpired, that there had been some misinformation. It was his *horse* who was blown up. The man was all right. He kept the money, though, and said it was to help him buy another horse.

Although the dock area was thoroughly bombed the remainder of Newport escaped comparatively lightly from the German air raids of 1940 and '41. My mother – who had been to Birmingham on a mysterious visit – graphically described the terrible scenes there and said they were pumping lime down into the debris because some of the corpses would never be brought up. She had been to Birmingham once or twice before the war on anonymous visits and on one occasion an unexplained lady, about the age of my elder brothers, appeared to stay with us for a few days. We called her Auntie Daisy. I often wondered who she was.

One night the Germans dropped some landmines on Newport. They drifted down lightly on parachutes and then exploded resoundingly. Hally, my second brother, was home from sea, where, God knows, it was dangerous enough, but the air raids unnerved him. Roy and I lay on the air raid shelter bunks, peering over the edges with wonder, while our elder brother lay flat on the floor with his hands clamped over the back of his head, which, he explained breathlessly between detonations, was the prescribed way to lie while under attack. This was an attractive novelty and we were eager to try it. There was, however, only room on the floor for him, and he told us to get back in our bunks. I don't know where my mother was on this occasion, possibly making a cup of tea, or doing her make-up so she would look decent in death. She was particular about such things.

Hally, in fairness, had been under weeks of stress at sea. He had been bombed and torpedoed and was then discharged as unfit and told to get a civilian job ashore. So, in the midst of a war that was growing more violent and threatening by the day, he found himself as a door-to-door salesman of Kleen-e-zee brushes.

He used to bring home samples, brushes of every use and size; brushes for cleaning shoes and sinks, for brushing your hair or your clothes; thin, flat, wide and fat; some hard as a bed of nails, some soft as our cat. We had more brushes for things than anyone in Newport. He became embarrassed by this peaceful occupation, and, in the end, he just disappeared, vanished, true to the family tradition. No more was heard until the postman brought an inauspicious parcel containing his clothes. There was no note, no explanation whatever. My mother thought he was dead and somebody had kindly sent his trousers home. Eventually Hally himself arrived in Royal Air Force uniform. That, as far as I recall, did not last long either. Knowing he was an experienced sailor they put him on a rescue launch used to pick up ditched airmen from the sea. The first time he went out on a mission a loitering enemy fighter machine-gunned the boat. After that he went to live in Birmingham.

One night German planes over Newport scattered

a pointless white powder. At dawn it looked as if there had been an out-of-season snow-storm. The authorities were convinced initially that it was a poison gas attack and everyone had to wear their gasmasks. Then a van with a loudspeaker came up the street giving orders that housewives had to scrub down the pavement outside their houses. It was a curious sight, my mother and all her neighbours right to the far end of Maesglas Avenue, swishing with water and brushing brooms. They made jokes and laughed about it, especially when one simple woman came out to do the job still wearing her gasmask.

Then there was a tragedy that touched many of us. At the top of Dock Street was a stamp dealer's shop owned by a family called Phillips. We went there with our pennies and twopences to buy British Colonials or the new issues of Free France and Free Holland or stamps with President Roosevelt or Hitler on the front. One night a German bomber, disabled by anti-aircraft fire and losing height, fouled the wire of a barrage balloon and fell to the ground. It landed on top of the house where the Phillips family lived on a hill and set fire to it. The husband and wife escaped by the traditional method of climbing down from their bedroom on a sheet. The young son went back into the blazing building to find his sister and both died. A rumour went around that the garden was littered with foreign stamps and there was a rush of boys to see if it was true. All that could be seen was the blackened shell of the house and the pathetic sheet hanging from the window.

IV

Season followed season in those boyhood streets. Our Moscow had its own enclosed calendar of dates, times for certain things and times for others. After the army had marched through and the main bombing had finished, the war seemed only to flicker on the skyline of a world governed by days off from school (we had a holiday for Empire Day and for both St George's and St David's Days, straddled as we were between England and Wales or, as some would have it, in Occupied Wales); by the ripening of conkers; by Christmas, a season commenced as early as we dared, even in November, when we would go to front doors, pipe out the first line of 'While Shepherds Watched' and bang demandingly on the knocker; by the summer holidays, long and seemingly ever sunlit. Bonfire night had been extinguished by the war. I can never recall, either at school or out of it, playing organised sports. In a land of rugby I knew only that it was performed with a wedge-shaped ball; my brother Hally bought me a soccer ball and with the first wild kick I smashed one of our windows. Any boxing was done with bare fists behind the school lavs, and although my mother bought us what she called 'cricket shirts' I had no notion of how the game was played.

Our games were street games. Gritty nights chasing around lamp posts, cowboys and Indians and occasionally English and Germans. We stalked newts and frogs, lying on our bellies by the turgid pond, and sometimes a child would acquire a tortoise and everyone would troop to stare at its tardy but majestic progress across the street. There were few motor vehicles, but if a car or a van, or better still something substantial like a coal lorry, did come up Maesglas Avenue, we would sit in hushed, engrossed lines along the gutter as the tortoise negotiated a perilous journey.

There was also a season for roller skates, which my mother discouraged after a neighbour's boy called Sidney broke his leg outside our gate; and there was a marbles season. Is there anything so memorable from boyhood as the coloured lights and glassy, globular feel of a marble? We called the pastime 'alleys' and it gave me the first of the several nicknames of my life – Fudge. We had just moved to Maesglas, that very day, and Flare, the boy next door, was playing alleys with Chubber in the gutter when I came from our gate and alleged that Flare was 'fudging' – cheating by moving his hand forward to gain distance. To 'fudge' had been the local verb on the far side of the town, but provoked instant hilarity here and it thereafter became my appellation. I was Fudge Thomas and my brother was Little Fudge.

For a few weeks every year, in early summer, the rage of the street was 'Fota-a-go'. The fota in question was a photo, a cigarette card, showing some notable person, event, invention or butterfly. A lick down the sticky back meant that they could be fixed in coarse-papered albums obtainable from Craven 'A' or Capstan or the manufacturers of Woodbines, the most popular smoke in the district. My mother disdained smoking Woodbines, preferring the select-sounding, but equally economical, Park Drive. The loose cigarette cards were used as currency during the 'Fota-a-go' season. Along the pavements were chalked areas, like small hop-scotch patterns, each square bearing a number. The proprietor of the stall, marked out in front of his own house, would sit in the gutter shouting 'Fota-a-go . . . Your mother won't know!' Within each square was placed some minor treasure, a pencil, a tin whistle, a small toy, a book, a comic paper, or even a penny, and, on payment of a cigarette card to the stallholder, the gambler could try and push a flat stone or a disc of some sort into the square, thus gaining a prize. The appendage 'Your mother won't know' was often apt since, to boost their stall's attraction, the proprietors frequently used to purloin the personal property of parents to be used as prizes. (Another fragmentary cry, like the beginning of a fairground ditty, comes to mind: 'Ask your mother for ninepence to see the lady bare!')

One dusty day my mother appeared unexpectedly to find that my brother, who had a rival establishment to mine, had on offer as prizes most of the contents of her meagre jewel box, together with a pair of colourful garters which might well have been able to tell an exotic story.

These stalls were a singular sight, stretching the length of Maesglas Avenue, with just as many in neighbouring streets, each with its wailing stallholders touting for custom. Since almost every child had an enterprise, they had to become each other's clients, leaving their own ventures in charge of a brother or sister and strolling along, as though in some bazaar, to see what wares others were risking. If something particularly sought after, or illicitly gained, was on display then there would be a rush of would-be players to that particular stall. When cigarette cards became scarce because of wartime paper restrictions, an added commercial element was introduced and the stake became a half-penny or a penny. Naturally the value of the prizes had to be increased accordingly and a large, coal-faced docker once knocked on our door demanding the return of his watch. My brother, howling that he had won it fair and square, had to surrender it.

Life was narrow, but we did not know it was narrow and neither did we care. Our days seemed full enough. We had the comfort, comedy and companionship that only street-livers know. My son, Matthew, has lived the thirteen years of his life in country houses, with all the neighbours beyond trees or fields. I have often thought how much he would have enjoyed my child-hood; the knocking on doors and running away, the games of tag in the dusk, the swapping of comics, running the gauntlet of an evening of swishing rain to a house up the street. By this time the comics of my father's day, the *Gem* and the *Magnet*, had given way to the coloured lures of the *Dandy*, the '*Beano*', the *Knock-out* and the hilarious *Chips Own*. Pansy Potter, the Strongman's Daughter, Our Ernie (whose father always said 'Daft I call it') and Desperate Dan (known to us as 'Desperated Dan') were our weekly compan-ions. I was reading Desperate Dan while walking from

Sunday school one afternoon in 1941 when a boy told me that the Germans had invaded Russia.

This must have been a rare lapse on my part (not to mention on Hitler's) for I had heard nothing about it and yet I retained a keen interest in the news of the distant war. Indeed, I had changed my weekly comic for *War Illustrated*, a red-black-and-white journal notable for heralding forthcoming military triumphs which turned out to be crushing defeats. Less than a month before Dunkirk, its cover photograph featured British troops disembarking in France, displaying the traditional optimistic thumbs and announcing that they were on their way to Victory. Four issues later those same troops were shown being ferried back to England, beaten and bewildered but still with that everlasting thumb in the air. Many years after, while I was researching for my novel *The Dearest and the Best*, I was astonished to find a complete set of *War Illustrated* covering 1939 to 1940 in the second-hand bookshop that quaintly part-occupies the buffet at Yeovil Junction station in Somerset. I bought the lot. Some of the covers I recognised. The magazine even smelled the same. *In The Dearest and the Best* I made use of my thoughts on the thumbs-up habit of the British servicemen (Churchill is persuaded to outmode it by raising two fingers in a Victory-V sign), as I had done previously in my first novel *The Virgin Soldiers*:

Why did they do it always? Off they went again in the next war, those proud, confident, mistaken digits. Thumbs up on the troopships, thumbs up in the tail turret of the

bomber, thumbs up on the Arctic convoy. That's right,
lads, just show we're not down-hearted. Come on now,
you on the stretchers, thumbs up all those who've still got
'em. Thumbs up! Thumbs up!

Avid listening to the wireless meant that I usually
knew what was happening in the war rather better
than my mother. One night, whistles began blowing
among the houses.

'Fire-bombs,' I said when she woke me to ask what
they meant. We opened the curtains to see the wooden
fence along the backs of the gardens blazing red and
yellow. Fred Martin from next door and some other
men put sandbags on the sizzling bombs and put the
flames out with stirrup pumps. One night, in
December 1941, I was again awakened by my mother
calling up the stairs that it was on the wireless that
Japan had bombed American ships and the United
States was at war.

'It means we're going to win,' I remember replying.
Many years later I read that Churchill's comment had
been the same.

Now and again my father would come home from sea
with gifts. By this time he and my mother were legally
separated and I suppose the presents were in the hope
that she would soften and allow him to stay. A Chinese
coffee set and a Japanese tea set were already deli-
cately in place in our Welsh dresser, alongside the
family library which consisted of *Murder in the Mews*,
a lachrymose story called *Wops the Waif* and *Old Moore's*

Almanac. To these gifts was added a many-coloured Egyptian table cloth, its camels and palms lending an exotic air to the council house's small room, and my mother's pride, its new three-piece suite. I was sitting on this table cloth when my father came home one day. (My brother and I habitually sat on the table. I would often squat, cross-legged under the single central bulb, to read my library books, and there we did our cutting-out-and-sticking-into-scrapbooks and played with my lead soldiers.) For days my mother had been busy instilling into us the necessity of our best behaviour when the old man returned from his voyage, presumably so that he could see that we were being properly brought up. We were, however, still permitted to sit on the table while he told us of his aventures in the exposed Atlantic and the icy perils of the Arctic convoys. In the middle of his narrative I let off. I quickly apologised. 'What did you do?' asked my mother who had not heard. 'I'm sorry,' I repeated in what I imagined was a well-behaved voice. 'I've just flarted.'

My father's gifts were always keenly awaited. He brought a tin machine-gun for me from America and a tank for Roy, then a pocket-watch which I used to show off at school and which, in the absence of a chain, dangled from a bootlace. Some presents were less easy to accommodate. He took us to Newport market after returning from one trip and recklessly purchased six newly born chicks. With much excitement we bore these home in a cardboard box. My mother liked them but was worried about feeding and the fact that we did not have a hen.

85

One by one the chicks died. The last one went while she tried to warm it in her own bed.

It was *Wops the Waif* followed by *Murder in the Mews* that began my life of reading, indeed my education, for I have had little other. Even today I find anything but the most basic mathematics beyond me, I know no sciences, nor any languages, and it was years before I was relatively certain what an adverb was.

Wops was a pathetic little fellow who dragged himself around the darkness and dirt of London's Victorian East End. He was always good for a cry. My mother and I had dampened many of the book's pages. Roy was persuaded to try it, but after a couple of minutes he closed the covers and said it was too miserable for him and embarked on a journey to the lighthouse, six miles distant, somewhere I had never ventured. He has, in latter years, when perhaps we have both imbibed a little too much, been heard to accuse me of having all the advantages of education. He, as a sailor, has continued his connection with lighthouses. 'If only I'd read that Wops book,' he once bemoaned as we sat in a bar. 'There's no knowing what I might have done.'

Murder in the Mews terrified me. I sat by our fire, in one of the armchairs of the three-piece suite – with Tussy our black and white puffy cat on my lap, daring myself to go on for another page as though physically creeping through the murderous mews itself, squinting at the shadows of our familiar room.

My mother's taste in literature and music was

'anything light', which included, oddly, murder mysteries and Handel's *Messiah*.

'Something light for my Mam,' I would tell the library lady when I went to change my books. Usually she would send me home with Ethel M. Dell or someone similarly romantic but once, perhaps as a joke, she gave me *Das Kapital* which my mother said she couldn't understand for the life of her. The Newport library was in Dock Street, a sooty stone building that also housed the town museum and reading room. In the days of unemployment I had gone there with my father and hung about aimlessly while he stood up and read the newspapers. They were arranged around the wall so that the men, and they were only read by men, would have to stand and would not get too comfortable and spend all day in there. Once when I was six or seven, and getting restive, the old man had the brainwave of taking me upstairs to the museum. At once I was spellbound. Right inside the door was a stuffed eagle, so fierce of eye, bent of beak and wide of wing that he looked set to fly straight out into Dock Street. He had a rabbit in his talons, a drama in a glass case. From that day I used to stand and study him for hours, sometimes fancying I saw him move. One night I had a dream in which the eagle let go of the rabbit with one claw and scratched his head.

I had never seen a real live wild animal in my life (even the rabbits of my experience were dead and bloody and selling at ninepence in the market). Once at Barry Island my father had taken me to view a dead whale which was being exhibited. My old man tapped it, put his ear close as if he expected an echo and concluded it was made of wood, and I was inclined to agree with him.

In the Newport Museum there were also other stuffed and encased animals, with lambent eyes and bared teeth; foxes and otters and a nice badger whose stuffing was bulging out at the back. There were also beautiful model ships with miniature lifeboats, ropes, rigging and crewmen. In one corner there was a statue of the Boy David showing all he had.

On one visit I went to view these familiar wonders on the upper floor while my father was propped up reading the newspapers in the ranks of leaning men. I had never been to the 'gents' by myself but decided that it was time to attempt the adventure. The lavatory was on the upper floor and I timidly pushed open the polished door. There was no one there. After wrestling valiantly but unavailingly with my buttons for some time, I decided that I ought to come back alone when I was older. Out onto the landing of the hushed place I went and, leaning over the ornate balustrade, called loudly: 'Dadda! Dadda!' My small voice echoed about the creamy ceilings, heads poked out and a lady librarian told me to 'Hush!'

Eventually the old man's concerned countenance appeared. 'Dadda!' I called in an echoing whisper. The other faces remained looking up at me. 'Dadda, I can't find my winkle anywhere!'

My father said it was the most embarrassing thing that had ever happened to him when sober, worse even than the occasion when a teaspoon, which I had quietly dropped down the back of his shirt, fell out of his trouser leg in the street.

When I was old enough to belong to the library a new world opened for me. I read my first 'William' book and went around for days wearing a bemused grin because I had discovered something wonderful. After that I read them all. I would go home clutching the book preciously, peeping into it on the bus or walking along the street. In the house I would wriggle deeply into the armchair and enjoy the luxury of beginning. I imagined myself with the urchin William, Henry, Douglas and Ginger, roaming an idyllic boys' countryside populated with tramps and hay ricks, with Jumble the dog and occasionally Violet Elizabeth Bott, who always threatened to be sick. Many years later, when I was a journalist, I went to see Richmal Crompton, who wrote the stories, a frail and dreamy old lady, who gave me a cup of tea and sent me away with copies of her books for my own children. Whether they read them I don't know. Times had moved. Perhaps the enchantment had grown cold.

One day my mother brought a pile of Sexton Blake detective magazines back from the house where she worked as a cleaner. She had been engrossed in one of them as she came home over the sloping fields and had tripped, hurting her leg. She limped the rest of the way, still reading. I was supposed to be deep in extra studies for the entrance examination for Belle Vue Central School. But the lure of Sexton Blake proved irresistible and I spent a furtive evening immediately before the exam reading the adventures, my homework put aside. When, pessimistically, I opened the English examination paper the next morning the first sentence I saw was: 'Write a Detective Story'. Never having heard of plagiarism, I invented my own detective and lent to him an abbreviated form of the mystery which I had read the previous evening. I passed the examination and started at the Belle Vue School in the following September.

My new status delighted my mother for I had to wear a *cap*. And I was going to learn *French*! 'There's posh!' she enthused. 'Now there's something to tell.' She did. Every neighbour and anyone else who was unguarded enough to let her begin. When they first took her off to hospital she told the ambulance men all about it.

Because of the war the original Belle Vue had become a fire station and its pupils and staff moved to join another school on Stow Hill close by where I was, according to legend, born. The work was difficult and the staff heavy-handed. Anyone who was late was automatically caned. Standing in a long line of outstretched hands was an almost daily experience for me after my mother became ill, because I used to get up, make her a cup of tea, get Roy's breakfast and my own, light the fire and then miss the bus.

French I enjoyed, partly because of the plump, perfumed lady who taught it. She wore brown suits, vividly tight around the bum, and had a handsome, wobbling bosom, encased in silk and smelling like heaven. I was so besotted with her that on one occasion I failed to close my eyes when reciting a verb, and my glazed devotion was rewarded by a bang around the ear from a hand like a piece of wood.

My entanglement with the language has remained primitive. For six seaside summers in the nineteen-seventies we lived as a family at Barcares, near Perpignan in south-western France. My exotic French was accepted by the Catalan people of that corner, whose version of the language, fortunately, differs considerably from the rest of France. Some of them thought I was from Britanny.

In that region was a Frenchman called Clovis whose use of my native language was as battered as mine of his. Some evenings beside the harbour we would drink a pastis or so and, when the time was ripe, he would invariably reveal that he was a leader of the Resistance during the war. After a third or fourth pastis I was content to sit back in the warm dusk and listen to his oft-repeated exploits. The Resistance members, he said, still kept in touch and helped each other in all manner of ways.

I was taking my children on the night-sleeper to Paris from Narbonne and I mentioned this to Clovis. He puffed his cheeks out over the cloudy liquid in his glass. 'If you 'ave trouble,' he said. 'Etienne is the master of the station. Etienne was a member of Group X. The Resistance, you know.' We raised a glass to Etienne, Group X and the Resistance. Clovis looked over one shoulder and then the other in that deeply furtive way only Frenchmen can achieve. 'I will tell you, because you are my friend,' he whispered. We had another pastis and he told me. 'If there is trouble, you go to Etienne and you say – The moon is high tonight.'

I was aware of my eyebrows rising. But pastis is a

wonderful aid to belief. 'The moon is high,' I repeated also looking over both shoulders.

'*La lune est haute*,' he recited and I whispered it several times.

'Etienne will reply – The sea is quiet,' promised Clovis.

I swallowed. 'The sea is quiet.'

'*La mer est calme*.'

'*La mer est calme*.' We raised our glasses.

On the following evening I took the children to Narbonne. The car was being temperamental and we were further delayed by a small landslide en route, so we were late arriving at the station. To my dismay I saw that the entire station car park had been dug up and there was a dormant yellow bulldozer poised ready to take a further bite the following morning. I had to park at once or we would miss the train. The minutes were going by. I was very agitated. A man with a peaked cap strolled from the station. Etienne! Yes, monsieur, he said, he was indeed Etienne.

'*La lune est haute*,' I suggested timidly.

He stared and looked over each shoulder. '*La mer est calme*,' he replied. 'Group X?'

'Clovis,' I nodded.

'*Bon, bon*. What can I do for you, mon ami?'

In a moment the car was parked in his private lay-by, the train was delayed long enough for us to climb comfortably aboard and find our sleepers. Etienne saluted from the platform as we chuffed away. Long live the Resistance!

*

Newport, however, was a long way in distance and in time from Narbonne. Roy and I had to eat ignominious free school dinners while others paid fivepence for theirs. Then a doctor decided that I was too thin and needed more fresh air. I was therefore, a further indignity, sent to the Open Air School in Tredegar Park, where lessons were informal and in the afternoon the pupils lay on camp beds in the sunshine alongside the sooty River Ebbw. The soldiers had all gone (in fact they had been to France and returned home defeated) and were replaced by a jovial barrage balloon tended by some air force men and women who seemed to live a life of private domesticity in the park. They were always laughing and having cups of tea, their balloon either tethered to the ground like some giant pet or on duty up in the sky. When I lay on my camp bed in the afternoons I could watch the silver balloon floating far up in the Welsh firmament.

In the summer of 1940, when every man was needed in the defence of his country, there was still unemployment and men were hanging around outside pubs and lined up in the library reading room. But as the demand for munitions was harnessed, so jobs became more available and Dolly Thomas found herself in the blue overalls and jaunty cap of a Royal Ordnance Factory.

This was the last happy time of her life. Through the years she had attempted all sorts of employment in a brave effort to supplement a sparse and uncertain income. She had polished people's homes and she had cleaned the local school at Maesglas. Roy and I would stay behind after lessons and help her put the chairs on top of the desks in the classrooms. We had unauthorised peeps into the staff room and into the headmaster's office. Roy wanted to hide his cane but I said that he would soon realise who had done it. We persuaded our classmates to put their chairs on the desks before leaving, until a malicious teacher vetoed the idea by saying that it was the charwoman's job to do that.

After cleaning the school from end to end during one holiday, our mother tottered home exhausted and coated with chalk dust. She dropped into a chair and announced that she was finished. From now on she would make toffee apples.

This seemed to us a brilliant idea. The ingredients were bought (it must have been in the days before sugar rationing) and our back kitchen was piled with green apples and redolent with sticky odours.

At first it seemed as if the venture would be blessed with success. Saucepans wobbled on the gas cooker and the boiler (which she also used for washing the clothes) steamed energetically, the toffee jelled and Roy and I helped by splitting up bits of wood and using them as sticks for the toffee apples. Children congregated at the back door clutching their pennies. It was our part of the operation which scuppered it. Some child complained of a mouthful of splinters and then a man with a stern sort of cap and an official black book appeared and told my mother she mustn't do it. She had broken more regulations than Hitler.

Downcast she dowsed the gas and the boiler and let the last consignment of toffee apples go free. The remainder we ate. With a thin sigh, Mum sat down but she was not defeated for long. She went back to cleaning the school until the Christmas holidays and then she became a postman.

Throughout her life I doubt if she ever weighed more than seven and a half stone, but the festive season saw her humping a bulging brown bag of letters and parcels along our street. It was fortunate that she had contrived to get herself consigned to home territory for the neighbours gave her cups of tea and she was able to dash into our house to give us a quick meal between deliveries. On Christmas Day as she walked her round she was given a drink at almost every house. Before she was halfway up Maesglas Avenue, she was staggering about on her spindly legs giving away letters and parcels indiscriminately. Neighbours were going up and down the street exchanging misdirected mail in the most friendly and seasonal manner. Dolly Thomas came home, cooked the Christmas chicken with the giblets still inside and then fell asleep in the armchair.

She tried taking lodgers. A small bald man and a large flowery woman arrived and Roy and I were put on our best behaviour. At the end of the week they left and I cried because I thought we had let the side down. It turned out that they were not married and had only come for a dirty holiday anyway. My mother was quite glad to have her bed back.

In the following spring came the job at the munitions factory. She was only sweeping up the metal filings but the money was more than she had ever dreamed of earning. She worked seven days a week, finishing at four on Sundays, sometimes transferring to night shift. (We were lodged with a family down the road who had a monkey-puzzle tree in their front garden. They also had a pretty daughter of my own age and each night we used to go and get chips from Shepherd's shop. One evening, after we had finished eating them from the paper she kissed me with lips perfumed by vinegar.)

Perhaps needless to say, within a week of employment at the Ordnance Factory my mother was telling everybody how to run it. Half those shells, she averred, would never fit a gun, half those guns would never find a shell to fit them. She had her photograph taken with a jaunty crew of fellow munitions ladies and she brought home a handsome poker for our fire which had been made in somebody's spare time from apparently surplus war material. She wore blue dungarees and had a badge in her beret showing a cannon and cannon balls. She also fell in love.

Love, I suppose it was. Her last time.

It was a Sunday, her early day, in summer and I had gone to the bottom of the street in the afternoon to meet her from the bus. The bus arrived but she did not. Then a car pulled up and out she got. My mother riding in a *car*! I was thrilled and flabbergasted. I could not see who was driving but she told me it was a gentleman friend from the factory and I was not to mention a word about him because he was on secret war work.

This man, as later revealed, was about fifty, tall and powerful in a flabby sort of way and given to wearing hairy sports jackets with matching caps. His face was rubbery and he had blue eyes in a florid skin. His name was Jim and we did not like each other. I thought he had wicked eyes and he thought I was a nuisance.

He was, however, my mother's last chance and he *did* have a car. Where he obtained the petrol – then rationed – I could not imagine, unless it was on account of his secret work. We had never known anyone with a car before. Sometimes he could not avoid taking Roy and me along with them and once we maliciously persuaded him to drive us down the Lighthouse Road, a restricted military area during those days of threatened invasion. There were barbed wire and red warnings everywhere but we persuaded our mother, and him through her, that we knew lots of people who had gone down the road with impunity. He pressed on grumpily until we were caught in an area of tank traps and wire entanglements that barred further progress. Nor could he turn the car around. A threatening-looking soldier appeared and we were enthralled when he pushed a tommy gun through the window, right at Jim's throat. 'Where d'you think you're going?' enquired the soldier.

'The lighthouse,' muttered Jim while we squirmed with pleasure. Our mother told us to keep quiet and still.

'Didn't you see the notices?' demanded the sentry. 'They're plain-a-bloody-nough.'

'Yes,' mumbled Jim. 'But I . . . I . . . heard it would be all right.' He turned his frozen blue eyes on me.

'Another twenty yards and you would have been in a minefield,' said the soldier. 'You'd better back up, mister.' He looked at the car and us inside it. 'I'd like to know where you get the petrol anyway,' he said. 'There's supposed to be a war on, you know.'

Jim had gone even plummier than his normal shade. Fiercely he backed the car, sending it directly into a mesh of wire entanglements. With delight we heard the barbs scratching into the paintwork as he tried to get out. Then the wheels went into an anti-tank ditch and eventually a whole glut of cat-calling troops had to be mobilised to push us out. All the way to the bottom of our street Jim was grim and silent. For us it had been a really worthwhile outing.

There were bonuses from this association, however, for in the summer of 1941 my mother announced that we were going on a holiday on a farm. A *holiday*! A *farm*!

It transpired that only Roy and I were going. She was remaining behind to help her friend with his war effort. We were excited enough, however, to be deposited at a staunch stone house a few miles up the valley from Newport, which might have as well been a different country. It was owned by a couple, elderly and miserly, who obviously viewed two young lads as a welcome addition to both their income and their work force. We were set cleaning out pigsties and cowsheds and, more painfully, picking thorns and this-tles out of cut corn, peeling vegetables and sweeping out the local church where the farmer's wife changed the altar flowers. One day we all went to try and sell all the potatoes that the farmer had been ordered to grow by the Government and we could not find a taker. In the end they were more or less given away to a fish and chip shop at Bedwas Colliery. On the way back the farmer and his wife went into a house and had supper with the people there. We were left outside sitting with the horse and cart for about three hours. On another occasion they parked me with the horse outside a public house, and when they came out to feed the horse they forgot all about me. Roy was climbing about inside a barn when a huge wooden beam fell on his head, knocking him cold; another day he had to be transported to the doctor's because he had eaten so many apples. Jim, who was without doubt financing the holiday, must have laughed the special laugh of those who have taken revenge.

He turned up at the farm with our mother and we went for a walk up the local green mountain. They left us sitting in the ferns and the sun and walked off, far far away, up the next slope, arms about each other.

'Look at that!' my brother said with indignant astonishment. 'He'll be trying to kiss her next!'

We watched minutely and saw the two distant, but distinct, figures slip down into the heather. 'He's got her down!' said my brother hoarsely. 'He's got our mam down!' He started up. 'We'd better go and get her.'

But I was older. 'Maybe she won't want to,' I said sullenly.

How long the affair went on, I don't know. I think it was about eighteen months.

Then our mother became ill. It dragged on over two years, gradually diminishing the already spare woman. One day, Mrs Vokes, a fat and jovial neighbour, looked in at our back kitchen window when mother was having a strip wash at the sink. 'There's not much of you, Dolly, is there!' she bellowed through the pane. Well, soon there was even less. When she was within a few months of her death she arranged to meet her lover Jim but then was too weak to keep the appointment. She sent me instead to their trysting place, near the bridge across the Ebbw, but I couldn't find him. Later lying white on the sofa in our sitting room, she sent me with a note. 'He gets on the bus behind Newport Station,' she instructed. She told me the number of the bus and the time to be there. Presumably by now his petrol supply had run out. When I got to the place and saw that he had already boarded the bus, I stood on the pavement and waved the envelope at him. He stared for a moment, then with a curl of his fleshy red lip he turned away and opened out his newspaper to block me from his view. I waited until the bus had gone; then I went home and told my mother. She seemed very upset in a thoughtful way.

Things come back over the years, like strange birds flying home; there are threads and coincidences, and my life has been woven with them. One summer's afternoon many years later I was playing in a cricket match just outside London. I was fielding and during one of those intervals which cricket affords, I fell to conversing with the umpire. He had a rich Welsh accent and I discovered that he came from the same valley village as my mother's gentleman Jim of long before. I had remembered the man's surname (I still do) and I asked the umpire if he knew the family. He knew them well, especially Jim, who was late and un-lamented. 'A real old bastard,' was the umpire's verdict. 'Absolute swine with the women, too.'

*

In the spring of 1943 my father returned from sea for the last time. In his hideously optimistic way he attempted to gain entry into the barred family home by playing on my mother's sympathies. He brought a homeless cabin boy with him by night and calling up operatically pleaded that neither of them had anywhere to go. 'Go and find somewhere then!' shouted my mother before slamming her window.

They trooped away. He found lodgings by the docks and returned most days during this leave with tales of chickens running loose in the house, an outbreak of Oriental plague and finally the harrowing death of the cabin boy, none of which my mother believed for a moment.

Now I find it very difficult to understand how she could be so hard to him. True, he had been no great husband, but few men are. He had drunk and gone to whist drives (once hunting for our non-existent money boxes to do so) and he was a gifted liar. But he was the same age as I am now, as I write this in my house; he had no home to which he could go. At sea he faced the most awful of dangers. German submarines were sinking flocks of helpless merchant ships, not to mention the normal hardships of the life, and when he came back he had nowhere. I find this very difficult to understand, although now it does not matter.

On this final leave there was some sort of half-reconciliation and she promised that after the next voyage she would think seriously about having him back. I remember even now the clumsy wetness of his last kiss, so beery that it made us turn our faces away, before he went out, his kitbag over his shoulder.

He sent a letter from Freetown, Sierra Leone, and a week later – the worst week of the war for merchant shipping losses – his vessel, the *Empire Whale*, was torpedoed in the Atlantic and he was drowned. On the Merchant Navy Memorial at Tower Hill in London, among the many thousands of others, his name is on the list of fifty men, from master to apprentice, who went down on that vessel. I have taken each of my children to see it for that is all there is left.

I first suspected his death when the local soothsayer (the lady who had warned about the 'grave' in the front garden) came to the house and had whispers with my mother. 'Illness or Hitler?' she enquired dramatically.

That evening when Roy and I were in bed my mother came into the room and said curiously: 'I've got some bad news for you, Les. Your father has been lost at sea. The ship was sunk.' My first reaction was annoyance that she should have thought that only *I* would be sorry. What about my brother? We had both been brought up to regard our father as a devil who turned up between voyages. When I was not much younger I had recited an evening prayer: 'God bless Mam, God bless Roy, God bless me, God bless the cat, and everybody else – and make Dad's ship sink.'

It horrifies me now but it *was* my prayer and on that day in March 1943 it was answered in full. The following morning the insurance man was around early and counting out bank notes across the Egyptian table cloth. There was over a hundred pounds. I sat on the table with my brother and touched the notes. We had never seen so much money in our lives. My mother seemed to think it was a fair exchange for a husband.

To me, at twelve, my life appeared both secure and happy. Number 39 Maesglas Avenue was a small council-built fortress keeping at bay the perils and ills of the world. A little more money was available now, my father having proved a better source of income dead than alive. There was a war widow's pension, my mother was working and the marvellous insurance money was banked against a rainy day. We bought a two-bar electric fire and a whistling kettle. The fire was placed on the table, with the wire running down from the central and only light, and we would sit on the Egyptian cloth and warm ourselves by it. We also cooked toast on its red bars. To my mother's immense satisfaction the kettle whistled so loudly that all the immediate neighbours could hear it.

Roy had begun his war work. At the bottom of the street, lined along the shops on the Cardiff road, appeared a convoy of ugly vehicles, each with a great oily boiler and chimney on its back. Their function was to provide a smokescreen for the engine sheds at the back of our houses and each evening at dusk they spewed out wide spasms of oily smoke. They were operated by permanently black-faced soldiers and my brother's war work was to run and get relays of fish and chips for these men. He used to come home worn out, with his face like a minstrel, eyes bright in the black and with a pocket full of pennies.

Apart from games with Chubber, riding our

imaginary horses around the Woods (whose pond had been fortuitously enlarged by the addition of a crater from a German landmine), I spent much time at home. I read books and newspapers and listened avidly to the radio. 'Monday night and eight o'clock, oh can't you hear the chimes?' went the chorus. I can hear them, now. 'Settle by the fireside, look at your *Radio Times*. For *Monday Night at Eight* is on the air.' Would I be able to spot the week's deliberate mistake? Another favourite was introduced by the sound of rushing vehicles, the calling of a newsvendor . . . 'In Town Tonight . . . In Town Tonight.' The important voice of the announcer would say: 'Once more we stop the mighty roar of London's traffic to bring you some of the interesting people who are – In Town Tonight!' And on would come a fisherman or a clockmaker or a man who had once been to Tibet, or perhaps someone who could play the spoons. Simple magic, but magic just the same. I imagined that they actually stopped the traffic for each programme.

Every variety act I knew because *Music Hall* was broadcast on Saturdays. There was Afrique who did impersonations, many of which, of course, you could not fully appreciate because you couldn't see him. There was Suzzette Tarri, a gentle and gossipy comédienne, and Jeanne de Casalis, Mrs Feather as she was called, who was posher. Two Ton Tessie O'Shea was another, and Ethel Revnell and Gracie West. Whatever happened to funny ladies?

The funniest lady to me was a man, Arthur Lucan, the knobby, bulbous-nosed Old Mother Riley, whose daughter Kitty was his real-life wife. 'Oh Mrs

Stonochy!' Mother Riley used to howl, rolling up her sleeves preparing for an Irish fight. When they came to the Empire in Newport the street and those around were besieged with people trying to get into the theatre.

My mother, who sat the other side of the fireplace on those nights of radio entertainment (we shared the cat, passing it to each other at intervals), preferred the singers, Ann Ziegler, Webster Booth ('When I'm calling you . . . ooo . . . ooo'), Richard Tauber and a roving tenor called the Vagabond Lover who not only sang but managed to give the impression of travelling throughout some rural and peaceful country. He sang: 'I'm only a roving vagabond, so goodnight pretty maiden goodnight . . .' We once had an argument across the fireplace as to why he was called 'glover' a mishearing on our part. My mother said it was his name, like V. Glover, and I said it was a man who travelled about making gloves. We had a sudden and squally row about it. She said that I thought I knew everything, just because I always had my head in a book. She was so angry that she got up from the chair and threw the cat at me.

It was astonishing that this set life, so ordinary and so seemingly secure, should have ended so abruptly. But it did. In the space of twenty-four hours all was changed. My mother had been ill for over a year, not desperately, but with spasms of pain, days in bed and two operations. After the second surgery I lied about my age and managed to get into the hospital to see her. She was lying, like a corpse already, but she whispered proudly to me that they had put five hundred pounds worth of radium into her. She was ever impressed by money.

After three years in the Wolf Cubs (rising to senior sixer, the highest rank I have ever achieved in anything) I transferred to the Boy Scouts. My departure from the cubs was marred by an occurrence at the home of the Cub mistress. Her name was Miss Rabbit and she had a parrot (although it may have been Miss Parrot and she had a rabbit), and she also had a monkey. One day she took the Cub pack to her house to visit the monkey and it bit me. In my anguish I gave it a kick up the arse and all bedlam broke loose. I was stripped of my stripes and went into the Scouts with no great regrets.

At my first Scout meeting, I stood at the back behind the veterans, as we lustily sang: 'We're the Seventh Newport Scouting Boys, From the town of Newport Mon!'

It was a stirring boast to the tune of the US Marines song 'To the Shores of Tripoli'. Joy flowed through me when a weekend camp was announced. A camp! I had never camped in anything but our air raid shelter. I rushed home, clutching a list of required equipment including an axe and my personal food rations. My mother was lying on our sofa. If I had not been so excited, or perhaps if I had been a little older, I might have seen that she was wasting away. She scarcely had the strength to prop herself up on her elbows. She looked at the list of rations – a square of butter, a piece of cheese, a few ounces of sugar –

and she sent me with my ration book to the shops to get these.

I took one of my father's old chipping hammers instead of an axe. These hammers had two edges to the head, each shaped like the bow of a ship. Their function was to chip away deposits from the inside of marine boilers. He would never need to use one again. I took also some ship's biscuits which he had brought me home; square and solid as rock, they were intended as provisions for lifeboats. Even with strong teeth it would take up to one hour to eat one biscuit. Sometimes we used to smash them up with the chipping hammer.

On the Saturday morning I set out with the rest of the Scouts for the camping ground. It could not have been too distant because we walked, pulling a trek cart loaded with tents and other equipment, singing our brave Marine song as we marched. There seemed to be lots of hills and the cart was heavy to heave. Then it came on to rain. Apart from me everyone had some protection. With clever thinking, the Scoutmaster halted the march and instructed me to sit under the trek cart, where I remained until the shower finished. Unfortunately I had sat on a patch of wet tar and as I rose it tore the seat out of my flimsy trousers. They managed to unstick this from the road and the resourceful Scoutmaster sewed the piece on again, at least after a fashion, before we proceeded.

The camp was memorable because during the night there was an air raid on Newport (by this time, 1943, a fairly rare occurrence) and we stood by our tents on the hilly field and watched the fireworks over the distant town, the searchlights, the exploding guns and the fire glowing over the roofs. I began to wonder if my mother was all right.

She was not, although it had nothing to do with the air raid. When I returned on the Sunday evening, a strange man was sitting by the couch talking earnestly to her. My first reaction was that the CID had caught up with my brother on account of an incident in which he and a friend had removed a baby from a pram, removed the pram from its wheels, and used the wheels as a plaything. This was not, however, the case. When the man had gone my mother explained carefully that she would have to go back into hospital for a while and that this man had come to tell her about a wonderful school in the country – in distant and romantic-sounding Devon – where we could go until she was better. We would all be together again by Christmas.

She must have been purposely vague about it because at first I imagined that this adventure was to be some obscure time in the future. It sounded exciting, a holiday to some place of which I had only read. 'The masters play soldiers with the boys in the woods,' she told us. She said it again and again, reassuring us, and herself.

We went to bed, Roy and I, discussing this unusual prospect. The following morning I woke and heard her crying in the next room. We both went into her and weeping she clasped us to her. 'You might be going today,' she sobbed. Today! We were dumbstruck. Now, right away, instantly. She told us to go and put on our best blue suits and then the same man who had been sitting on the couch turned up and took us down to Dr Galloway Smith's for a medical examination. On the way we met Gwyneth, a girl with whom I had been in love for some time, and I smirked and was glad I was wearing my blue suit. 'We're off to Devon,' I boasted.

Everything happened so quickly then. All this, our street, our friends, our very life – was changed in less than a day. We went home from the surgery and once more went up to our mother's room. She tidied our hair from her bed, hardly strong enough to lift the brush. 'Be good boys,' she said. 'See you at Christmas.' We believed her; we could not imagine that it might be for ever. She could not help crying again and I remember going outside the room and having a howl against the passage wall, marking the green distemper with my tears.

Then the man came back and told us it was time to go. We went in and embraced her once more. She was wearing one of her posh silk nighties but her bones showed through. We all had another cry and promised we would be back for Christmas and we went out of the room and house. I'm not sure how old our mother was; about forty-eight, I think. We never saw her again.

PART TWO

THE HOMES

so concerned on the couch had told her all the tales about the school in Devon where the masters played soldiers in the woods with the boys, just to get us away from her. Dr Barnardo's probably collected children from all over the place with this disgraceful ruse. The train whistled along the banks of the River Ebbw and I saw some boys I knew playing on the coaldust. 'Look,' I said to my brother. 'There's ole Fatty Turner and Ben.' We waved but the boys did not look up from what they were doing. In a moment some trees blocked the view, they were gone, and we were gone too.

Almost immediately, although I find it difficult to credit now, I began to get interested in the scenery. The sense of adventure caught me. The bright marshy fields ran away down to the Bristol Channel. We were going for one night, the man told us, to Cardiff, only twelve miles away but somewhere I had never visited, except when the annual summer charabanc threaded through it on its journey to Barry Island. It was my first taste of that anticipation which comes even now, a great many cities later, on journeying to a strange place. On the following day, the man told us, we would have to go back the way we had come, through Newport, and then change trains at Bristol and Exeter and Newton Abbot on our way to south Devon. Bristol! Exeter! *Newton Abbot*! Suddenly the world was opening up. And *south* Devon. That had a touch of the exotic about it. I could picture it lounging and lush in warm climes. And it was only going to be until Christmas. That had been her promise.

We reached Cardiff Central, a cavern of steam, and then out into the strange city, onto a foreign-looking brown and cream bus, through streets of unfamiliar shops and faces. We arrived outside a large house with a notice on its gate: 'Dr Barnardo's Homes. Cardiff Home.' The gate opened onto a new life.

That night they put my brother to bed early and I went down to the front gate and watched the traffic running by on the main road, the route to Newport. It occurred to me that Roy and I might make a dash for it, board one of the lorries and easily return to Maesglas. We could get off at the bottom of our street. What that sick, solitary woman would have done had we abruptly reappeared I cannot think. I dismissed the idea and it was just as well.

On the following morning with a woman bundled up in an overcoat as an escort, Roy and I embarked on the longest journey of our lives, a journey that, in time, was to prove very long indeed. The train retraced our route of the previous day and once more we stared from the window at the river, the engine sheds and the houses. There was no smoke coming from our chimney. Then, as if to compound the irony, we passed, on the other extreme of the town, the hilly street where we had previously lived, with the houses perched against the September sky, the cut of the quarry and the familiar grey pond. But it all quickly vanished as we travelled east, below the mysterious blackness of the Severn Tunnel and into England.

At Bristol, our first pause, we waited on the platform. What strange voices the people had, with red faces and rolling walks. One station porter shouted to another that the war would soon be over now. It was September 9th, 1943, and the newspaper placards announced in big letters that Italy had surrendered.

All the way down to Exeter I was pressed to the window, watching the fields of Somerset and Devon. Pleasant hills began and the earth became a red-brown. My brother read comics, a parting gift from a boy in Maesglas, but when we got beyond Exeter he joined me at the window and examined the foreign landscape. 'It's a long way, ain't it,' he said. 'It'll be a long way to get back.'

We changed again at Newton Abbot and it was drawing on to evening by the time the puffy local train reached Kingsbridge, in the district called the South Hams.

The old stone town, unlike anything we had ever known, spread up a steep hill with a wide creek at the bottom of its main street. It was brimming with evening quiet, late sun falling through the gaps between the grey buildings as we trudged up the incline of Fore Street with the bulky and morose woman. Our luggage was minimal. Roy had his comics and I had half a dozen William books. I cannot remember now where I obtained them (they may have been unreturned to Newport library, although half a dozen does seem rather a large haul) but they remained my most treasured, in fact almost my only, personal possessions throughout the next two years.

As we neared the crest of Fore Street my foreboding increased. Roy nudged me and said he already wanted to go home. I thought he was going to make a run for it. The place where we were bound, however, was a reassuring surprise; a sedate period house on the brow of the hill, with wide white windows and an impressive blue door with a brass knocker. The lady who answered the knock was tweedy with the sort of English voice I had only heard on the radio or at the pictures. She seemed glad to see us and said that we could have some food after we had been bathed.

Been *bathed*! Roy and I glanced at each other in panic.

'She ain't bathing me,' said my brother. 'No bugger is.'

She did, however, stripping off our best suits and throwing them into a pile. I was more offended about the suits than the treatment. We had been quite proud of them and now they were being tossed aside like rough rags. What is more it was the last we saw of them. When I enquired, some weeks later, what had happened to our suits I was told they had been burned, which upset me even more.

It was a memorable evening. Two girls, sisters of our age, had also just arrived and were efficiently undressed and bathed with us, in and out of the bath in blushing rotation. Trying not to look at their naked-ness we asked their names and where they were from. The younger one began to howl. The lady who did the bathing, scrubbing us all without expression, said there was nothing to cry about but the little girl carried on just the same.

Afterwards when we were in bed, in odd, hard pyjamas that smelled of ironing and mothballs, with four or five others in the dormitory, Roy leaned over to me and whispered: ''Night, Les.'

''Night, kid.'

Silence, then: 'What about them girls then?'

I opened a concerned eye. 'What about them?' I asked.

'Well, you know. Did you see anything?'

'Not much.'

'I couldn't either. But I had a good look.' A pause. 'I hope our mam's better soon.'

'So do I. Better not talk any more. 'Night.'

''Night, Les. Never seen one with no clothes before, have you?'

'No. Go to sleep.'

'All right. 'Night.'

It must have been that there was an odd day before the end of the week so we were not sent immediately to school with the other children. Instead we were permitted to go out for a walk. We bought some bright yellow September apples from a basket displayed outside a greengrocery shop. We walked through the inclined town, quiet in that wartime autumn, and down to the ribbed waters of the tidal creek.

Sitting on a seat by the creek I wrote an urgent letter to our mother asking her to send for us at once as we had decided we did not like the place. We bought a stamp and posted it, one of a succession of notes over the next few weeks, but I don't suppose she ever read them. I hope not. After the post office we walked along the water bank and then had a paddle. Roy, always the more adventurous, ventured further out and became stuck in the mud. His pale horrified face turned towards me. Both his legs sank unstoppably into the slime. The water lapped the bottoms of his short trousers and he began to cry. I stood on the bank giving instructions: 'Lift that leg, now lift that. *Don't* lean backwards.' He tried it. 'I'm still stuck,' he said heartrendingly. 'Les, I reckon I'm sinking!'

An old man came along and suggested wisely that if Roy leaned forward we might be able to reach his hands and tug him out. The mud was well up to his knees now and there was no doubt he was going down. With a terrible squelching he managed to lean towards us and we caught his hands. He very nearly pulled the old chap head first into the creek but in the end we triumphed, hauling him black-legged to the bank. We thanked the man and asked him the time. He pulled a watch from his waistcoat. 'Always carry my old turnip,' he said. It was one o'clock and we had instructions to be back by twelve-thirty.

Roy was still encased in mud to the knees, his shoes oozing, as we hurried up through the town and presented ourselves at the back door of the home. One of the staff, a jolly young woman called Nurse Nelly, saw us and burst out laughing. Back into the bath we went.

Lower Knowle, as the house was named, was far from being an unkindly place. It was a reception house, an Ever-Open-Door as Barnardo's called them, using the Victorian doctor's own phrase for his first shelter for homeless children in the grim and gritty East End of London of the eighteen-seventies.

It had been the home of a kindly Mrs Patterson, who had lent it to Barnardo's for the duration of the war. When I was grown up I went back there and stood on the pavement outside. An elderly lady approached and asked why I was looking at it.

I told her I had once lived there. She was pleased. 'It's my house,' she explained. 'During the war I kept thinking of those poor children in Barnardo's at Plymouth with the bombs falling all round them. So I offered Lower Knowle so they could be safe.'

She invited me in. As such places always are, it seemed much smaller now, but I remembered well the rooms; the long, stone-flagged dining room with the French doors out onto the garden, the staircase, curved like a feather in the elegant front hall, the bedroom where I used to lie and hear the American tanks trundle down the street.

It was on that visit, and on subsequent occasions in Kingsbridge, today a lively holiday centre, that I came to thinking about the occupation of part of south Devon by the American armies rehearsing for D-Day. Thirty thousand acres, including six villages, to the north-east of Kingsbridge were cleared of their people and for eight months the soldiers practised their beach landings to the accompaniment of live artillery bombardments. More than seven hundred Americans died one night only a few weeks before the invasion of Normandy in 1944 when a flotilla of German torpedo boats crept out of Cherbourg and ambushed a landing exercise. The story – the civilian evacuation, the American soldiers and the tragedy of those who died before they had ever seen a German – I used as the basis for a novel *The Magic Army*.

The Americans arrived in south Devon only a month after the two boys from South Wales. The wide exercise area was cordoned off but there were mishaps. When I was researching for *The Magic Army* I saw in the 1944 files of the *Kingsbridge Gazette* that two of my schoolmates had been killed by a mislaid hand grenade. It happened two weeks after I had left for London.

There were happier stories. The girls, or 'maids' as they were called in that region, accustomed to the awkward courtship of rural lads, fell easily and whole-heartedly for the young American newcomers whose uniforms and talk were both so smooth. They were ever-generous and resourceful. They raised money for a church by charging a penny a time to *see* a pineapple and a banana, unknown fruits in wartime. As for us, at the orphanage, they sent us barrels of peanut butter.

We had peanut butter every night for tea for six months, so much so, I have never eaten it since. Roy said it looked like sheep shit.

There were only about sixteen children at Lower Knowle. We had our photograph taken and it appeared in the Barnardo magazine under the caption: 'Steps!' It was apt for we stood in a line, from a home-less toddler called Winston at the front to a strong boy named John Mills at the end, with me next to him. My brother was somewhere in the middle.

The home was in the charge of a handsome man with silver hair who had a propensity for dressing as a vicar. He was not ordained and that, together with some other irregularities, later led him into trouble, but I knew nothing of this. After I had gone away from Kingsbridge I sent him and his wife a Christmas present, a book which I can still remember cost six shillings, a sum which must have taken me a consid-erable time to save. It was *The Way Of All Flesh* which, considering the trouble that came upon him, was not altogether inappropriate.

Young lady members of the staff worked under the pseudonyms of Auntie Sally, Auntie Judy, Nurse Nelly and Nanny. In the main, they were kind and jolly. One of them fell backwards into the churchyard while coping with a local fireman on the wall. She used to embrace me at times and I looked forward to it because it was my first close contact with a large bosom. There was also a pink-faced youth who filled the function of an assistant master. One evening, just at dusk, he said to me: 'Do you feel like having a wrestle?'

He was not much bigger than me and I said all right and we went out onto the stepped lawn and grappled for about half an hour. He rolled on top of me and jumped up and down and then I sat astride him and jumped up and down. We were both red-faced and sweating by the time we had finished and it seemed to me, at the time, to be an odd way for a grown man to spend an evening.

Perhaps, thin and pale as I was, I was a natural victim because soon afterwards in the churchyard of St Edmunds, after Sunday evensong, I was savagely beaten up by a gang of choirboys still wearing their cassocks. It was then that I began to have my doubts about religion.

After we had been about a month in Kingsbridge, and I was wondering at the absence of replies to my letters, our mother died. The grey-haired super-intendent softened the blow as much as he could by breaking the news in instalments. On a Friday he told me that she was very ill with cancer and on the Monday he said she had died and was out of the pain. He gave me his stamp album to look at and went out of the room so that I could have a cry in private.

Strangely I did not shed my tears for very long. The superintendent came back with a letter from an uncle of whom, until then, I had no knowledge, my father's brother Chris. My mother had called him to her hospital bed and asked him to look after us. He was the only one of the family with any money, having a thriving ship-repairing business (the descendant of that founded by my grandfather) in South Wales. Inside the envelope was a folded pound note which was more money that I had ever possessed in my life. While still sniffling over my mother I put it gratefully in my pocket.

No one had told Roy. He was taken suddenly ill and it was decided to keep the news from him until he was better. When I went to bed that night he was sweating in his sleep. For the first and only time in my life I kissed him. He grunted. The following day he was taken to hospital with appendicitis and this was followed by diphtheria.

The following day I went to school and the bespectacled headmaster put his arm about me and told me he had been told my bad news and advised me to keep a stiff upper lip. We were in the school vegetable garden and I was digging again. He said he was casting me as a cavalier in the school play and if I would like to go to the storeroom with him he would fix me up with a costume. This he did, suggesting that I took my trousers off so that he could see if the costume fitted.

123

It apparently did not, so he gave my winkle a flick with his hand, transferring it from one side of the cavalier's trousers to the other. 'That's better,' he said, beaming happily.

At the home of one of the aunties, a fruity fat girl not much older than me said she was sorry to hear my news. 'That's all right,' I assured her brazenly. 'I treat life as one big joke.' I must have read it somewhere.

Soon there was someone else's misfortune to share. The big lad John Mills, who used to help the grumbly old gardener to shovel coke into the hot water boiler (called by the old man 'that incinerator'), had become my firm friend. We had joined the local youth club and he taught me the rudiments of football and cricket. He had a younger brother, a happy boy, called George, and one day I found them sobbing in each other's arms. Their father, who was in the navy and whom they adored and talked about all the time, what he did, his jokes, his letters, was missing presumed drowned at sea.

'Don't cry, George,' I remember saying, sitting in the inglenook fireplace of the dining room. 'My mam's just died as well, but I didn't tell anybody because of Roy.' His round, tear-streaked face turned towards me. 'That's right,' confirmed Nurse Nelly, adding to the dubious theory that two sorrows are better than one. 'Leslie hasn't got anybody either.'

John and George's mother had already died and that night, when John and I went down the gloomy path to shut up the chicken house, our regular task, he said: 'I can't believe it. I can't believe he's dead.

Not our dad. It was like I just saw him today. I don't
know what we'll do now.'

If the natural resilience of children enables them to
play in the rubble of their own houses, as they were
doing in many parts of the world at that time, then
the same optimism helped me, if not to play at least
to sit quietly, in the rubble of my early life. It surprises
me to recall it now, but I started to weigh up the situation quite coolly and with logic while walking to
school one day soon after my mother's death. It was
raining on the steep streets and the water gurgled down
the gutters and drains. We progressed in a crocodile
with John Mills in charge, over two hills and up the
side of another. Head down against the downpour I
watched it run over the pavement slabs and sluice down
the gratings. When we reached the school I stood
under corrugated iron shelter with the other boys and
maids (some of whom had just been deprived of their
homes by the Americans) and with the rain drumming
and the children chattering, continued to think out the
situation.

I was twelve years of age, my parents were gone,
my small brother was in a Plymouth hospital, my elder
brothers were somewhere anonymous, Lin probably
at sea, Harold perhaps in Birmingham. Harold did
eventually write ('My advice is, money talks. But it's
always said "goodbye" to me') and he also sent a tin
of toffees, but that was months later. As far as I can
recall I never received a letter from Lin. On the other
hand, I had gained an uncle and an aunt and a cousin,

all previously unknown to me. Uncle Chris continued to write, his handwriting the most polished I had ever seen, certainly in our family. He told me about himself and his family and promised they would visit me as soon as they could. He and his wife Nance even made some attempt to discover whether they could reclaim Roy and me from Barnardo's – being 'restored' as it was called among the boys in the homes, for most of whom it was a constant but hopeless dream. Apparently our mother had legally 'signed us over' to Barnardo's but, nevertheless, someone was sent from the Homes head office to visit Chris and Nance at their home in Barry. The house, as I came to know, was comfortably middle class; they owned a car and a cocktail cabinet and it was the cocktail cabinet that scuppered us. The amiable Chris offered the visitor a gin and tonic. I do not need to have seen this person to guess what he was like, for sobriety and religion were the cornerstones of the homes. He must have left the house with a shocked expression and that was that. We would be in Barnardo's for the rest of our childhood.

My more immediate world, viewed that day in the school playground shelter, oddly felt secure. The house where I lived was comfortable, the food, despite the eternal peanut butter, filling, and if love was missing then affection was the next best thing. We had a fine garden and a large paddock; there was a pony called Pommerse, which I was learning to ride bareback, and three friendly dogs. I also had my first long-trousered suit.

This was my 'bundle-suit', part of a scheduled

126

bundle that appeared in a bulky blue bag a few weeks after my arrival. I no longer had to sleep in camphor-smelling pyjamas and go to school in somebody's discarded coat or shoes. The bundle contained a completely new outfit; shirts, socks, underwear, a tie and the long-trousered suit. Already, I was deeply in love with a girl in my class and I wore my long trousers to impress her. Strictly the suit was for best but I was allowed to wear it to school. Not that it did anything to enslave her. Her nose always travelled past me as though suspended on a cord. At Christmas I bought a National Savings Christmas Card, with half-a-crown's worth of savings stamps on it, and sent it to her. She never mentioned it when school began again in January but she kept the stamps just the same.

For the first time in my life I was enjoying lessons. I was put into a class with children two years older than my age group (one of my self-delusions about my beloved was that I was too young for her). We worked under the cheerful and robust regime of a teacher called Mr Casely, who, I am glad to say, is still living down in Devon. A few weeks ago, when I was taking my son Matthew to a pantomime in London, a man and his wife boarded the underground train and sat opposite. He leaned forward. 'You're Leslie Thomas, aren't you?' he said in a pleased sort of way. 'I was a teacher at Kingsbridge School when you were there. I've heard you talk about it on television.' He beamed. 'But I don't remember you at all.'

Few people would. But I remember them. The Luscombes and the Steers and the Hannafords. When I have walked in later years up Fore Street in

Kingsbridge and read those same names over the shops and businesses, I have seen them again in the school playground or at their wooden desks, with the wintry Devon rain dropping outside the window. I went to evening classes for woodwork and made some toys for my brother, a steamroller and a jaunty tugboat and barges. There were also evening lectures on psychology, bird migration and local history which I never missed. The church in Kingsbridge held a series of mid-week talks in its shadowy chancel, Aspects of Christian Thinking, I believe it was, and I did not miss one of these either. I suppose I was trying to educate myself.

For the first time, also, I began to realise there was something called sport. We played rugby and hockey at school, although I was so wispy that I was useless at the former and at hockey the big Devon girls could easily knock my feet from under me, and did. The one I adored so much seemed to take real pleasure in striking me around the thin knees with her stick, or in trampling over me when I was winded and prostrate. It was the only contact we had. On Christmas Eve, however, there was to be a hockey match and, glory, glory, I was selected as linesman and possible *reserve player*. I left the home, without permission, and muddily ran up and down the boundary waving a windy handkerchief. My elation was quickly shattered for when I returned to Lower Knowle I was summarily put to bed. I lay there, on Christmas Eve, feeling fairly sorry for myself. At midnight they needed somebody to help pump the organ at the church service and all was at once forgiven. This organ was pumped with a wheel, to which was attached a wooden handle, like an old-fashioned clothes mangle. John Mills pushed it from one side and I caught the handle and pushed it back to him. I needed to stand on a box or a stool to operate the system and on this holy night, with the congregation carolling how the shepherds saw a star, I saw a number of stars because I slipped forward and the handle caught me under the chin. I woke up groaning and out of wind, the same condition as the organ.

With March the light evenings drifted in and the early western springtime arrived. On St David's Day I wore a daffodil to denote my Welshness although by then I must have already been losing my Newport accent, the sounds that had caused much hilarity among the Devon children when Roy and I first arrived. Voices, I think, change according to the age at which one moves from one environment to another. There are people who have left Wales as adults and never lose their native sound, but twelve is an age of change. Going to live in Devon, among the broad vowels, then to London, and eventually to Norfolk, made my voice an unusual compound. Once I heard a BBC producer describe it quietly as a 'bastard accent' and I suppose it is.

In the pale evenings we began to play cricket; someone fashioned a bat from a piece of cherrywood and we played in the garden. From the first moment I made contact with the ball was born a love affair and it has lasted all my life. Not that I was any good. At school, stiff with pads and lifting a heavy bat, I proved an awkward performer. So often did I miss the ball that a secondary batsman was placed behind me

129

during practice sessions, hitting the many deliveries with which I had so miserably failed to make contact. Also the hard leather ball kept hitting me in the testicles and knocking the breath out of me. Someone said solicitously that I should get myself a box and, not realising that this was the term for a protector, I stuffed an egg box down the front of my pants in the hope of buffering the blows.

In March my brother returned. He had been in hospital from the previous October so he must have been seriously ill, although I did not realise it then. Appendicitis followed by diphtheria – from which in those days children died quite easily – was a formidable combination. He came back to Lower Knowle even thinner and whiter than he had been. I remember sitting on the floor with him showing him the tugboat and the steamroller I had made for him. He seemed very pleased. Then he said casually, as he pulled the boat and its barges along: 'How's our mam?'

Nobody had told him and I could not gather the courage to do so. 'She's still ill,' I mumbled. 'But she's getting better.'

'We'll be going home soon then,' he said brightening. 'I want to go home to Mam now I'm all right.'

The next day we were told we were going to London.

VI

London had always seemed far, far, beyond any horizon, but as beckoning as Shangri-La. Roy and I went around Kingsbridge smugly telling everyone where we were bound. None of our schoolmates and few of the staff had ever been there. The headmaster led me out onto the steps outside his office and said that in the school play I had looked superb in the cavalier's trousers. He put his arm around my waist and said, with an ambiguity that only occurs to me now, that in London I should watch out for peculiar men.

Roy and I said farewell to the cosy house at Lower Knowle and went towards the outside world. Once more the local train puffed us to Newton Abbot, then on to Exeter, where we boarded the express for London. Below the netting of the luggage racks in the compartment were framed photographs of places served by the Great Western Railway, their hue as brown as the livery colours of the company itself. Roy sat opposite me and above his head was a picture of the Transporter Bridge at Newport.

My eyes scarcely left the window through the whole journey. I witnessed the landscape change before my eyes, the red and spring-green fields of Devon giving way to the chalky uplands of Wessex; then the flat country before London, our first glimpse of the Thames in Berkshire, and finally the spread and sprawl of London's outer towns and suburbs. I knew exactly where we were because I had borrowed books from the Kingsbridge library and had charted our course in an exercise book noting each landmark – a pleasure that is still very much mine before going on a distant expedition. The armchair travelling is as rewarding as the real journey.

We arrived at Paddington, steam and echoes rising to the bomb-broken roof, crowds of travellers, fat cheery porters in waistcoats, anachronistic taxis, and one ambulance. That was for us.

Roy, it was true, had been acutely ill, but we were both embarrassed having to get into an ambulance. Ambulances were bad news. We used to touch wood when we saw one and in our street in Newport sick people requested them to come after dark because they did not want the neighbours to see them carried away. My mother insisted when she first went to hospital that she should be taken under cover of night, although, naturally in the event, a whole crowd of wellwishers turned out to see her off.

It was frustrating being in London, the most exciting place I had ever visited, and having to view it through the meagre slit near the roof. I saw only a thin panorama of the magic city, bits of buildings, top windows of houses, the upper decks of buses and strange trolleybuses with their arms stretched above them in attitudes of perpetual amazement. Many of the buildings were ragged as old teeth, bleakly standing as a reminder of German bombs; there were lamp standards, long blind because of the blackout and segments of advertisement hoardings. One of these, realistically representing a brick wall, was scrawled with rough white-painted words: 'What We Want Is Watneys!' With my enlarged imagination about what London might be like I thought this must be some slogan of revolution or, at least, politics. I asked the dumb-faced woman who accompanied us, sitting hunched like a bag of forgotten washing on the other side of the ambulance. She sneered: 'It's *beer*. You mustn't have anything to do with that. Not *beer*.'

That, I think, was the sole observation she made throughout the journey. She fell back into blankness, her hands wringing, her mouth chewing some private cud. Her chin had whiskers.

She was no exception among the staff of Barnardo's in those days. It would not be too much to say that many of the people employed to look after the children needed a home at least as much as the children themselves. They were given a room, food and a doubtlessly minimal wage, and they went about their work wrapped in a blue overall and a formidable expression.

It has to be remembered, of course, that this was wartime and there was a shortage of everything, including people. Nor would I include all the Barnardo staff in this doleful company for there were some who worked with faith and enlightenment. There was, however, a sadly sized collection of these grim and inadequate persons, of little cheer and ready to resort to the back of the hand when in doubt. They would not be tolerated today.

133

The shuffling, sniffling woman who finally led us from the ambulance at the Village Homes at Woodford Bridge in Essex made, I remember, some sort of flapping gestures with her chapped hands. I was to get out and Roy was to remain in the ambulance. When I said I was not leaving my brother she said: 'You'll 'ave to.' She glanced at me and lied: 'You'll see him tomorrow.'

The tomorrow was almost two years away.

In the Royal Borough of Kingston-upon-Thames, on the hill towards London, is a street today called Galsworthy Road. It was renamed in recent times following the showing of the *Forsyte Saga* on television and the realisation that the author of the novel, John Galsworthy, had lived there. I remember it as Gloucester Road (still the name of the far end of it) and it was on its corner with Kingston Hill that there stood a dire building with a yellow brick tower. Across its impoverished front, in oddly golden letters, were the words: 'The Dalziel of Wooller Memorial Home. Dr Barnardo's Homes.' It was a test of daring on the part of the young inmates to climb outside the building at the third-floor level and clamber along the gleaming letters.

I arrived at this ominous place on a streaming March morning just after my thirteenth birthday. With two other boys I had trudged with yet another spectral escort, this one with a limp, from the local station and we stood, all of us carrying our blue bundles of clothes across our shoulders, like some juvenile postmen, outside the main gate. I also had a parcel containing my William books. The silent man was puffing behind and in the interval it took him to catch up we were able to take in the awful façade of our new home.

'Bloody 'ell,' said one of my companions, John Brice, who was my friend until some time later he knocked me cold in a fight. 'It's just like a prison.'

The other lad was freckled, podgy and ginger-haired with staring glasses. He had confided to us during the train journey that his father had been killed in the *First* World War, which would have made him at least twenty-six. He began to cry and had to wipe his glasses on his clothes bundle. The man caught up, berating us for leaving him behind. 'Come on then,' he ordered. 'Stop staring. There's nothing to stare at.'

As was to be expected, he was unperceptive. There was a lot of be stared at. And we did not like the look of it. The place sprawled before us, across the horizon of a tended garden, with a moon-shaped drive going to its glowering front door. For what purpose it had been built is a mystery, although it had once been an orphanage for girls. It was the tower which, at once, both caught and repelled the eye. It rose two storeys higher than the rest of the pile, capped with a sloping roof under which was lodged a huge water tank. A German flying bomb missed this by inches a few months later. Had it struck, everyone beneath would have become, apart from other injuries, very wet.

We were ushered to the front door by our escort, stumping along behind, urging like a cowherd. The knocker, the central door knob and the bell smiled inclement smiles.

The door was opened by an urchin in an indescribably filthy blue jersey. He regarded us suspiciously as if we might have arrived to take something from him. Then, possibly thinking he ought to make an attempt to clean himself up, he wiped his nose on his streaked sleeve. 'I'll go and get the Gaffer,' he said.

He left us standing on the step. Muttering, our escort pushed open the door and we stepped into a place redolent with floor polish and echoing with remote voices. There was a short flight of red steps leading to a lobby which soared up into the central tower, the tower itself lined with a staircase that diminished into lofty dimness. Over the iron balustrades on the several landings pale faces looked down like moons from the sky. The cosy days were over. This was a real orphanage.

'New kids!' the shouts bounced about the landings above and more faces appeared. One boy, apparently to impress us, did perilous gymnastics on the iron bars fifty feet over our heads. Then, to our left, we heard shouts and the door opened to reveal two scraggy boys pushing another, smaller, boy with a seraphic expression and bottle-thick glasses, over a glistening linoleum floor on a square of blanket. They propelled him from one end of the room to another. On the back wall was a blue table and a wooden cross. This was the chapel and this was the method of polishing the floor.

'We're Ronuking,' shouted one of the boys. 'Don't it pong!'

Stony footfalls sounded and a man of ominous aspect appeared. He was gaunt and grey, with a steely jawline and well-scattered teeth. He wore a hairy green suit and sharp rimless spectacles. His name was Ernest Gardener, feared by all boys and known as the Gaffer.

As I came to know him, over the years I was there, I realised that here was someone from another time. He was like an ancient sergeant-major, a narrow man of Victorian thought and values, in charge of a hundred and fifty hard-cased urchins who varied from the sly to the rumbustious to the downright criminal. His attitudes had scarcely shifted an inch in forty years. At the end of the road for us, he was confident, was only Hellfire. One day he announced in chapel that all our brains would be turned to milk because of the filthy things we did in the night. He had some kindness but it was well buried. He ended his days alone in a Barnardo-provided cottage eating his food straight from a tin.

There was no way back. I realised that as soon as I stepped into that place. It would need to be my home and I would have to make the best of it. They took me to a big hollow dormitory, where thirty other boys slept in three long rows. Each bed had its blue and white counterpane, folded and tucked to a certain ritual at the foot. Each bed had a scarred wooden locker. Large areas of the long windows were stuffed with cardboard and plywood because they had been blown out in the bombing of 1940 and had not been replaced. Wearily I put my bundle on the bed, my William books underneath it, and sat and stared around. I felt very unhappy and wondered where my brother was.

It was not, however, a place for dwelling on your sorrows. Everyone was there for some misfortune and some had experienced more than others. The boys had hardened themselves into a tough but resilient mob. There were more laughs than tears. Each one had his own bedspace which was guarded jealously. 'Get out of my bedspace, Breadcrumb,' I heard one boy shout at another. Breadcrumb was the nickname of a lad who gathered the last crumbs from the table and rammed them in his mouth. Everyone had nicknames. I had only just arrived when I was dubbed Monkey. I had a brisk fight with the inmate who first gave me this appellation, rolling between the dormitory beds, and I won resoundingly, but it made no difference; they still called me Monkey and it remained my name while I was there.

It was in those early days that I learned the singular power of the story-teller. Existence in the home was in layers of violence; certain boys could overcome others with their fists, and they in turn were subordinate to others who were bigger or punched more swiftly. It was a basic law and there seemed no escape from it. When I arrived I found myself very much in the middle strata, being able to lord it over half the boys, while trying to keep one step ahead of the other half. There were fights every day and I had plenty. If I won then I ascended one place on the fisticuffs ladder. If I lost I went down a place. Then came the miracle that removed me from attrition entirely – I found I could tell stories.

Each night, in the dormitory, with the lights doused and the blackout curtains giving only a little extra protection from the winds and rains that knocked on the makeshift windows, there was a time set aside for what was called 'spinning up'. The dormitory matron, who had a pokey room at the end like that of a barrack room corporal in the army, would leave us, heads projected from bedclothes, with the words: 'You can spin up for half an hour – and that's all.'

Although this might conjure an intriguing picture of pyjama clad lads bounding on bedsteads like trampolines and whirling like tops in the air, it was nothing more than the enjoyment of a bedtime story. For the first few nights I lay and listened and realised that the standard was not high. Whoever was telling the tale usually related the plot of some film he had seen or occasionally a story from a book. It was rarely they were accepted with appreciation and sometimes brief but violent criticisms flung across the darkened room would result in a quick foray from a bed and a shadowy beating-up of someone in the dimness. It was to stop the boy in the next bed being slaughtered by someone much bigger that I first offered to make up a story.

'All right, Monkey,' agreed the aggressor, giving the victim a dismissive push. 'Let's 'ear it then. If it ain't any good you'll get bashed up as well.'

So I began to spin up. It was a yarn, I remember, about a group of horsemen in the hills of some German-occupied country in Europe, who carried out guerilla warfare on their oppressors by abruptly appearing over the horizon and swooping on convoys and patrols. Even now it does not sound a bad plot. I made it up as I went along and before long I realised that the room had fallen into an enclosed silence. When the end of the half-hour arrived and the dormitory matron, Miss Robinson, a tall angular lady known to her charges as Chuck, came from her room to tell us spinning-up time was over, there were pleas for 'just another five minutes, Miss, Monkey ain't quite finished'.

She was adamant that the session was over and after quelling beneath-the-bedclothes grumbles she went back to her den. 'Come on, Monkey,' demanded a sibilant voice. 'Whisper it.'

Every night after that it was demanded that I spin up. Older boys, who were permitted to stay up later, began voluntarily to go to bed early so as to hear the next instalment of some serial I was desperately cobbling together. The denizens of other dormitories crept in on all fours, some of them lying concealed beneath the occupied beds to listen. I will never have a more attentive or appreciative audience.

'You ought to 'ear the new kid spinning up,' the word went around the home. Any threat to my person made during the everyday warfare was met with a counter-promise by me that if I were bashed up there would be no story that night. Immediately the bigger boys moved in and defused the menace. The only trouble was that, like Sheherazade, I had to keep thinking up tales. Any shortfall was likely to result in immediate difficulty so I always managed to scrape up some idea, although I don't think it went on for quite a thousand and one nights.

The gardens and wide-windowed houses of what is called an executive estate (such as the one I wrote about in *Tropic of Ruislip*) are now spread over the two or three acres once occupied by the Kingston home. Barnardo's sold the site in the nineteen-sixties, and when the demolition men were at work knocking down the mouldy old building, I took part in a television programme filmed while the place was tumbling around me. The men and the bulldozers were taking chunks out of the walls and piles of wood were burning like funeral pyres. At the request of the director I was posed, like the boy on the burning deck, high above the flames and the crumbling bricks, ostensibly looking out over my past. The story very nearly finished then on a less than triumphant note because, fifty or sixty feet up, the floor began to give way beneath my feet. Gratefully I reached safety. It would have been ironic to have met a dramatic end in that of all places. And on television.

That day to be walking about among the ruins was an odd experience. Generations of homeless boys had passed through that institution since I finally went out of the front gate; times changed, as well they might have done. In the dining hall, under the baronial spread of stags' horns, and with a dusty bust of someone in marble standing guard over the door, we survived during the final two years of the war on the most meagre of rations. Breakfast would be two slices of bread and beef dripping and a cup of unsweetened cocoa; tea was two slices of bread and margarine or bread and jam and a mug of tea. Anything extra was a treat. On your birthday you were given, with some ceremony, a boiled egg. When I arrived first, I had just had – if not actually celebrated – my thirteenth birthday. Boz, Gerry Bosley, a doughy lad who became one of my great friends in the place, consoled me: 'Pity it's gone. You've missed your egg, Monkey.'

Fortunately we went outside the fence to school, to St Luke's elementary school, down Kingston Hill and into the outsiders' streets. Midday meals were provided, and while they may not have been every child's idea of plenty, they were most certainly ours. We ate every scrap and anything outsiders left as well.

It was the others, be it noted, who were the outsiders – those children who went home to fires and food and parents every day punctually at four-thirty. We had neatly, if unconsciously, reversed the social order. The Dickie boys, as we were widely known (the home, for some incomprehensible reason, was called Dickies) with our patched blue jerseys and robust independence, were not the ones beyond the pale.

On the other hand it was difficult for me, who, unlike many of the other inmates, had known a home and a mother, not to envy those free children. We had a few friends among them, for we were always a clan apart, but on one occasion I went to a boy's house in Kingston after school. The room, the furniture, the cat, the fire, all brought back a heartful of young nostalgia and regret.

By a coincidence, the daughter of the Martin family, our neighbours in Newport, lived in Kingston and on a Sunday afternoon (when, if we had not misbehaved, we were allowed out for a walk) I went to her house for tea. It was cosy and wonderful and I regretted having to leave. The lady's husband, a cheery sort of man called Billy, gave me a cigar to take back to the Gaffer.

142

I had not asked permission to go to visit them but I took the cigar back and hid it in my locker. There it was discovered. Smoking, next to thieving and masturbation, was the most heinous of crimes and here was I found with not merely a dog-end but a whole cigar! The Gaffer sniffed at it. 'And where did you steal this from?' he enquired ominously. The cracks in his gnarled face seemed to get deeper.

'I didn't steal it, sir,' I trembled. 'I went to somebody's house for tea and the man gave me a cigar for *you.*'

That did it. Going out to unauthorised teas was another crime and he was outraged. 'Which people?' he demanded. 'Who are they?'

'Friends,' I explained. 'Friends of my mum from Newport.'

'Friends of your mum! Listen, sonny, you don't go to people's houses without asking me. Don't go again!' He gave me a smart clip around the ear and sent me off. He kept the cigar, however, and later the same day I saw the old devil smoking it.

Crime was not unknown, of course, and he was always on the lookout for it. He would creep about like some old grey preying eagle. Once a boy aptly called Hands, who was a skilful burglar, was apprehended helping himself from the oddments lodged in the office safe. 'Just putting it back, sir!' he howled desperately.

A kindly dentist lent some of the boys his prize stamp collection while they were in his waiting room. When he came to look at the albums again he found several valuable exhibits missing, including a set of

Victorian penny blacks. The Gaffer, wearing his ancient smile, crafty and cracked, announced benignly in the chapel that night that there was to be a competition to see who had the best stamp collection in the home. First prize would be a whole pound note. Eagerly the Dickie boys hurried off to get their albums and very soon someone was standing boastfully displaying a page of penny blacks. He said he had bought them in a stamp shop when the owner's wife, who was nearly blind and liable to error, was in charge. The Gaffer did not believe him.

It was a wonder any inmate had money to buy *anything*, let alone stamps, although postal orders received from relatives were put in a 'bank' and could be drawn upon before the recipient was allowed liberty on a Saturday afternoon. Otherwise pocket money ranged from threepence a week to a shilling, depending on age, and it took three weeks of threepences to buy a cinema seat. The largesse might also be stopped at a moment's notice on account of theft, a minor riot or, as it was rumoured in a rhyme, if Brentford Football Club, said to be the Gaffer's favourite, was having a bad run. The couplet went:

> Digs, the boss,
> Brentford lost,
> Dickie's get no pay.

In Dickie-boy language 'digs' meant 'watch out', the equivalent of the public schoolboy's 'cave!'. By a fractional change in emphasis it also meant 'excuse me' or 'get out of the way'. 'Digs-I, you kids' meant

'Look out, I'm coming through' as you pushed your way through a crowd crouched like crows on the hot water pipes. A boy with a face of rubbery exuberance, called Porky, invented an entirely new language of his own including words like 'renze' and 'loom' accompanied by running his knuckles across your ear ('renzing'). He spoke this language alone, with some of us repeating the occasional word. Even when he was angry, tearful or in an argument he still used it. It was, I suppose, his way of remaining an individual. There was a general internal language: dush was money, tuck was sweets. When the Gaffer 'dushed-up' he gave you your pocket money (in my case fourpence) with one hand. If you wanted 'tuck' he took it back with the other hand and gave you your ration of confectionery.

I enjoyed sweets as much as anyone but I was able to resist them. In my locker was still half a tin of toffees, half of a gift from my brother Harold. I was keeping them for when I again met my younger brother and, although the temptation was sometimes sharp, I never availed myself of his share. Once I had clutched my fourpence at dushing-up time I used to walk out quickly. My uncle continued to write to me and to send me occasional postal orders, and I would go down into the town to the cinema or, better still, sit in the gods in the Empire on Saturday afternoon, forever entranced by comedians, singers, jugglers and magicians. My heart lifted when I saw that Old Mother Riley and Her Daughter Kitty were to top the bill. I could scarcely wait until Saturday, but when it arrived some misdemeanour had been committed in the home

145

and no one was allowed out. This time I made a break for it, climbing over the fence and haring down Kingston Hill. I sat up in the dimness, next to the cherubs carved on the roof of the Empire, watching my music hall idols and engulfed with guilty pleasure. I was not caught, either.

Hard though he was, stern his face, bitter his tongue and swift his hand, I cannot now think of the Gaffer without some measure of affection. There was a constant warfare between him and one hundred and fifty urchins (for much of the time he had no male assistant) and both sides took advantage of every ploy and counter-ploy. It would be difficult to assess him by today's standards: narrow, scarcely bending, bigoted beyond belief (he despised the Welsh, including me; something to do with their attitude to Winston Churchill; the Irish were unmentionable). He was a lonely, beleaguered man who believed implicitly in Victorian morals and standards. Nothing less would do.

He was blind in two directions. The first was in the matter of his wife who, though entitled 'matron', played little useful part in running the home. She was a little bun of a woman, with bright glasses, a fat waddle and an incandescent religious mania which never managed to spill over into anything approaching practical Christianity. Once a week when Korky, the sickroom matron, had a half day, she would take over the sickroom duties. I once saw a small boy with his hands tied to the iron bedhead 'to stop him picking the sores on his face'. She also took Bible class on Sunday afternoons and could be moved to tears while

146

telling us how she was almost sure that the Lord Jesus had visited Cornwall. Apart from those two weekly manifestations, she remained entrenched in her cottage, a brick house set apart from the main pile of the place, eating her way enthusiastically into our sweet ration. There was nothing for her to do in her house; she had two boys to do all the cleaning, serve at table and do the washing-up, in itself a privileged post since it enabled the incumbent to eat the scraps from matron's table. These 'cottage boys', as they were curiously called, were made aware of their choice position. A lad called Peter Lott, who had been my friend, when selected for these duties was told by matron that, if he wanted to keep the job and its culinary perks, he must have nothing more to do with me. Apparently I was a bad lot; a liar and a thief.

I may, indeed, have dispensed a few untruths; it was one of the ways to survival, but there was not a lot to steal, except the odd slice of bread and margarine when one attained the duty of 'spreading'. This was another much-sought-after task which involved cutting the bread and spreading on the margarine or dripping for each day's breakfast or tea. Indeed, I had been much more sinned against than sinning, for my precious William books had disappeared from my locker. It turned out that the Gaffer, while snooping around, had purloined them and given them to another boy at Christmas. I was so outraged that I braved a protest. 'You must have stolen them from somewhere,' retorted the Gaffer.

The Gaffer adored the matron. He led her by the arm as she rolled towards the chapel on her weekly mission; everyone, staff and boys, had to stand when she waddled over the horizon. He ignored the sweet-jars full of our sugar which were carried to the cottage for her unending cups of tea, and when her budgerigar was assassinated he was so anxious to cover up the crime that he did not even punish the culprit.

This was a gangling Suffolk lad called Cyril Thorne (now a chimney sweep who became gloriously drunk after appearing from my past on the *This Is Your Life* programme). Thistle, as he was known, killed the budgie accidentally while using it as target practice for his catapult. There was the budgie, lying legs stiff in the air at the bottom of the cage. For the first and only time in anyone's memory, the Gaffer panicked. 'We've got to get another!' he cried. 'Before matron gets back.'

Matron was away in Cornwall looking for Jesus and when she returned there was a budgie sitting in the cage in her sitting room. 'Joey! Joey!' she twittered, eyeing it suspiciously, for it was a good deal bigger than the original, a bruiser of a budgie. 'Caw, Caw!' it answered. 'Bugger off!'

This outmoded couple, in charge of a battalion of lost boys in the midst of war, had a son, an army chaplain who served with courage in Italy and eventually came home wearing the Military Cross. He was an extraordinarily handsome fellow in his uniform and dog collar, and we felt it was only his proper due when he married a lovely, rosy girl. Any of the urchins in Dickies would have been delirious with happiness to take his place. I recall a day when I was working in the front garden and she walked by. I dared not look up at her. All I knew was that a heavenly perfume floated by on the Kingston Hill air.

One day in the nineteen-sixties I received a letter from this lady asking if she could come and see me and, puzzled, I agreed. She came through the door of my office in Fleet Street and there it was again, that fragrance from long ago. She was almost blind now and she had come because she had heard me talking about my Barnardo days on a radio programme. It was a remarkable tale she had to tell.

Predictably, she had always been resented by her husband's mother, the woman we knew as matron, but once demobilised from the army her husband had become vicar of a prosperous parish and she settled down happily to the life it afforded, the church and its various activities. She ran the Mothers' Union and the Sunday school. There were three daughters growing up and everything was contentment until *the day the Gaffer died*, the old matron having gone before. 'On that day,' said the lady, 'my husband came home raving drunk. And with two women of the lowest sort. I was so horrified I ran from the house. Never before had I known him touch a drink but after that day he never stopped. He drank all our money away, the house was full of undesirables, the church congregation dwindled. One day he fell out of the pulpit.'

She went to see the bishop but he did not believe her. However, there were confirming reports and eventually the vicar was defrocked.

'One day,' she related, 'he told me he was coming to kill you.'

'Me!' I almost fell from the chair. 'Why me?'

'Because of the way you described his mother in *This Time Next Week*,' she said. 'He was coming to kill you with a sword, a sabre, which we used as a fire poker in the vicarage. He had already terrorised us with it.'

I was glad to tell her that I had seen no sign of a vicar advancing on me with a sabre. 'I don't know where he is now,' she sighed. 'We are divorced and he has vanished. The last time I heard of him he was working in a factory somewhere.'

Why had she sought me out? She had never spoken to me before. I was just one of a hundred and fifty boys.

'You are the only person I know who remembers those days,' she said simply and sadly. 'I would like to know *why* all this happened. Do you have any idea?'

Since I had been a mere inmate of the orphanage, this might at first seem a tall order. But, as we talked, we came to the same conclusion. Here was a man who had seen all the horrors of war and who had returned with his faith demolished. For the sake of his parents he kept up the pretence until they were dead. Then there was no need to pretend any longer.

The tale had a sequel. A year later when I was living in Surrey, there came a knock on the door one Sunday afternoon. My wife Diana went to answer it and there standing in the streaming rain was a woebegone figure in a ponderous overcoat. 'Is this where Leslie Thomas lives?' he asked. She let him in. He needed a strong cup of coffee. Diana went to make it, and I took his soaked coat and asked him to sit down. His face was drawn and he had only one tooth. 'Do you know who

150

I am?' he asked. 'The last time you saw me I was wearing a dog collar.'

There we were, the boy from the Homes, now at long last settled and happy, and the man who seemed to have had everything and yet had somehow lost it. Unfortunately the Gaffer's son then became abusive, demanding money and behaving in a wild way. I picked up his coat and propelled him to the door. Firmly I pushed him out into the rain. Diana was all for calling him back, but I knew that once we did we would never have been rid of him. We saw him pitifully struggling into his overcoat in the deluge outside. It must have taken him three or four minutes.

The second blind spot in the Gaffer's make-up was that he, with an eagle eye which could pin-point a boy throwing a stone at two hundred yards, who knew every trick his charges could perpetrate, failed to understand that we had both resident and visiting pederasts.

In my four years as a member of that primitive community I can never remember any sign or talk of homosexual associations between the boys. It may have been an acknowledged part of public school life, but it was not of ours. Perhaps we were not sophisticated enough. We had inmates ranging in age from eight to sixteen or seventeen and, although there was a practising masturbation society, nothing remotely like a homosexual association ever became apparent. But that was between the boys. The masters and the visitors were different.

Two gentlemen, always welcomed by the Gaffer and matron, shared a house in the town and asked boys there for tea on Sundays. More than tea and cakes were involved, however. I went to the house only once (the host's aged mother was blindly knitting while it all went on around her) and left quickly through a window when I could not dodge around the rooms any longer. Others described how they had made similar getaways. One of these genial householders used to come to our home to play the piano for hymns on a Sunday evening, and he later attained high civic office and sat as a magistrate.

Within the home we had a succession of murky masters, one of whom used to stride around in Scout's trousers, blowing a whistle. He had a 'room boy', a pearl-faced oggle-eyed lad, who was supposed to make the man's bed and generally to skivvy, but who rarely seemed to leave the small bedroom at all. One day one of the dormitory matrons came upon a scene which sent her running, ashen-faced, to the Gaffer. At least the old man believed *her*. The transgressor was thrown out abruptly, with scarcely time to pack his medicaments, but by then he had been in residence two years.

This same man once told me that there was to be a special competition for a stage play, to be written by a boy and to be performed in the professional theatre. It seems an unlikely story now but, at a trusting fifteen, I believed him. Yes, I would like to enter. And he was going to help me! Oh, good!

I wrote the play and handed it to him. He said it was wonderful and later gave me the encouraging news that whoever was running the competition thought so too. It needed some polishing, however. He suggested that, as I was then of an age to stay up later than the other boys, I should go to the room at the top of the tower where he, another master and our two jolly visiting gentlemen would perhaps be able to give me some help. Clutching my script, I mounted the big shadowy staircase late that night and then up the small stairs into the highest room in the place. The four men sat there, wearing strained expressions. I sat down and there was a curious hiatus, as though no one knew what to say or how to start. A few desultory remarks were made about the plot, but mostly there remained an uncomfortable silence. Suddenly I became apprehensive. Saying it was my bedtime, I got up and went out of the door, almost falling down the stairs. Nothing more was ever mentioned about the play. It was a very strange and ominous interlude.

Fortunately there were also kindness, belief and understanding. Spinsterish though they were, the majority of the dormitory matrons tried their best and one or two younger women were lively and attractive. Towards the end of the war a new generation of masters appeared. The Gaffer, who had frequently been in sole charge, had known some strange helpers during the war years, including one religious soul, now a Nonconformist minister, who recently wrote to ask me if I minded sending him two thousand pounds to give his daughter a nice wedding.

A decent man and his wife appeared, Mr and Mrs Pamelly, who once called me from a cricket match and, to my everlasting gratitude, took me to hear my first performance of Handel's *Messiah*. There was Marlow, a handsome man whose real name was Marshall, a civilised person who became a rural dean, and Jim Guertin, a returned prisoner of war, who was good at sports and married one of the younger and prettier dormitory matrons. Then there was the man who first encouraged me to write.

His name was Wally Brampton and to us he was known as the Walrus. He was a large Lewis Carroll figure with a moustache, a waistcoat and a pipe. Back from the war, he proved a gentle character and the Dickie boys were swift to take advantage. He began to institute the miracle of suppers, scrounging any extra food that might be going and appearing beaming with it at eight o'clock in the evening. To children who never had a morsel to eat after five-thirty, this was a matter of some excitement. The story went down in legend of how he obtained a big tray full of suet pudding one evening and benevolently bore it to the dining hall. The Gaffer had given his grudging approval for this luxury on condition that grace was properly annunciated before it was consumed. Wally closed his eyes and recited grace. When he opened them again every crumbling crumb of pudding was missing, grabbed from under his praying hands by the boys who quickly wriggled away to hiding places only they knew.

It was this kindly person who one day came to see me when I was shut away in the billiards room because I had chicken pox. It seems astonishing that Dickies, where everything was so threadbare, where necessities were thinly spread, should have something so grand as a *billiards* room, but it did. It was behind the chapel and housed a full-sized billiard table. There were no balls, however, and no cues. I was sent there because the sickbay lacked an isolation room. Spread with spots I sat in a bed in the corner and began to try to write. I composed a story, which must have owed a fair amount to Henry Williamson, called 'Sleek the Otter'. The opening sentence ran: 'Sleek the Otter, ears and eyes alert, lay on a grassy bank beside the stream . . .' The Walrus came in and I showed the story to him. He read it carefully. 'That's very good, son,' he nodded. 'Very good indeed.' He went to his room and brought me some of his own books to read – *Stalky and Co.* was one. Then he took my story and showed it to the Gaffer. The old man grunted and said: 'Good. Since he's so clever he can write my report for the *Barnardo Magazine*.'

Thus I had my first work published. It was a description of Bonfire Night 1946, the first after the wartime blackout. I still have the cutting.

When I had read *Stalky and Co.*, I sat down and wrote out what I considered to be my targets in life. Kipling's schoolboys can scarcely have given anyone more inspiration. I cannot remember what those juvenile objectives were now, but they included a provision that although I intended to be a good Christian I was not going to be the goody-goody type because 'Those sort of people are not to be trusted.' The document completed, I folded it away in a ragged photograph album into which I had put my two pictures of my mother and some coloured postcards of Newport, Mon. One day, when I was staying briefly in the

Liverpool Barnardo's (en route for a camp in the Isle of Man), I found one of the young nurses in tears. She was holding this juvenile deposition of hopes. 'I shouldn't have done it,' she sniffled. 'But I was nosing through your things. I found this and read it.' She began to boo copiously. 'I think it is the most beautiful thing I have ever read,' she wailed. 'And I'm so sorry for being so nosy. I just had to tell you.' I was a little embarrassed, but grateful that a few sentences of my modest hopes should have such an effect. And now I've forgotten what they were.

Wally Brampton continued to encourage me, a help I regret to say I did not always appreciate, because I was as ready as any of the others to rag this gentle man. A year or so ago, thirty-five years after he had read my story about the otter, I was told that he had remained on the staff of Barnardo's and was about to retire. At that time a television company wanted to produce a programme about various people and their schoolmasters, and I was asked to take part. I knew that none of my schoolmasters would remember me, but I suggested Mr Brampton, who had so profoundly influenced my first efforts to write. He was living, newly retired, in the Midlands, at Kingswinford where he had once played rugby football, and although in poor health he agreed to appear on the programme. Then it was decided that he really did not fit the format and he and I were both written out. Disappointed, I wrote to him and in return he sent me a marvellous letter, full of reminiscence, full of the decency and understanding he had shown me all those years ago.

As I read it, a memory returned of a day when,

folded in the big Bible at Dickies, I discovered an unsent letter. It was to Barnardo's headquarters at Stepney, in east London, and it was from the Gaffer. It was asking for Wally Brampton's removal because matron disliked, among other things, his foul-smelling pipe. Fortunately the letter had not been sent or, if a another had, it was ignored. Now, these years later, Wally wrote to me: 'We had the Gaffer at my Barnardo home during his retirement years. He lived in one of the cottages. He used to ask me to get him American tinned food and he used to eat it straight out of the tin.'

I have never been either an enthusiastic 'visitor' nor a conscientious correspondent; I rarely write personal letters and, apart from a few near friends, I hate the notion of 'dropping in' on people. But I dearly wanted to see the Walrus again and, in my reply to his long and wonderful letter, I said that the next time I drove through the Midlands I would love to visit him. Less than a week later I had a telephone call from his son. 'My mother has passed your letter on to me,' he said sadly. 'It arrived the day after my father died.'

VII

For the next three years, until I was sixteen, the pile on Kingston Hill, with its cold corridors, its threadbare dormitories, and its lively inmates, was my home. There was an interval, however, when for six months we were sent, wonderfully and at a moment's notice, to the wide countryside of Norfolk, where we lived in an old rectory.

This occurred in the summer of 1944 when, just as everyone believed the war as good as won, with the Allied invasion armies ashore and advancing through Europe, there came the rude and dangerous interruption of the German flying-bombs. These robots, with their grunting engines appeared over southern England in July. For three years air raid warnings had sounded only sporadically but on this pale summer night we were hurried from our beds, in my own case in memorable fashion. I was in the sickroom, an enjoyable situation since it was comfortable and had a radio set. The matron in charge, however, a lady with button eyes and whiskers, known as Korky the Cat, had her own ideas of treating patients. In my case, because I was only half awake and enquiring dreamily what was going on, the remedy was a tremendous smack across the face which sent me tumbling over the bed but had the desired effect of rousing me.

Everywhere the Dickie boys were heading for the air raid shelters, with some going off at a sharp, sly tangent because it was discovered that someone had left the food store unlocked. Eventually we crouched in the dank earthen sanctuaries, in darkness except for a few torch beams, munching illicit grub and listening to the eerie and threatening engines in the night above our heads.

Over the next few days and nights we learned to play the game that the pilotless bombs provided, to listen for the engine cut-out and then count slowly until they exploded on striking the ground. We were on the direct route to London and, since the weapons fell at random, a great number blew up in the immediate surroundings. On the first Saturday afternoon, one robot shied off at the last moment and missed Dickies prominent tower by inches. It detonated only two hundred yards away, bringing down the ceilings and raising the dust of ages from the floorboards. Crouching below one of the dining room tables I felt the impact shudder my bones. Another bomb struck the hospital a short distance down the hill. Clearly it was time to move away.

Initially some boys, myself included, were evacuated to Hertfordshire, to a Barnardo technical school, which was still not out of the danger zone. There the air raid shelters were waterlogged so the instruction was that on the approach of a flying-bomb a watcher on the roof would sound the fire alarm and then everyone was to *put their heads under their pillows*. On the night following this adroit advice the jolting jangle of the fire alarms awoke us and we lay listening to the robot, grunting like a pig as it neared. It cut out, as we knew it would, and every head went under every pillow. Fortunately, after a long and frightening pause, it came to earth some distance away in open country.

This appeared to be a classic case of frying pan to fire and we were briskly dispatched to Norfolk to join the rest of the Dickie boys in two old houses, at Narborough and at neighbouring Marham. There we lived in rural bliss until the next January.

I had only known the countryside in spasms; the fields at the bottom of our road in Newport might as well have been stage scenery. Even at Kingsbridge it had been a small-town rather than a rural life. That apart, there was only the brief holiday on the Welsh farm.

Now I found myself basking in what seemed an unending summer of warm boundless skies and flat fields, bright with buttercups, living on the fringe of a village scarcely altered since the Middle Ages. For weeks there was no school. There was a great expanse of parkland in front of the house, more fields and woods to explore and a hidden lake where we swam and paddled a boat which some airmen had fashioned from the fuel tank of a crashed plane. For the first time I became acquainted with animals, moles, rabbits, foxes; I watched fish loitering slyly in a stream; lying, as I often did, on my back, I began to study clouds.

We had with us a whole library and I read a book every day, relishing especially the public school stories and telling myself that really the lives and activities of those privileged boys were not unlike those which we knew.

Walking through the village to church, or eventually to school, it was possible to stare right into the front rooms of the cottages in the single street. One always attracted me, for the window framed a scene of armchairs, a wireless set and, when the autumn came, a red fire eyeing me from the grate. There was a girl who lived there, a girl with dark ringlets and blackberry eyes, and she became my sweetheart. Each night I would creep from the house, my hair plastered down with purloined margarine. She would be at our rendezvous and, after one innocent kiss, we would walk along the dim road with our arms around each other's waists. We would go to her cottage where her mother would give me home-made cake and I could settle back before the fire, their dog at my feet, listening to Tommy Handley on the radio.

When we eventually went to school it caused problems in the single classroom. We were an unruly bunch, regarded with awe by the village children. Only a curtain separated us from them and our behaviour was so monstrous that the village teacher often used to march her charges into the playground rather than have them infected by our rowdyism.

When winter came they would push their little blue noses against the windows, pleading with us to be good so that they could return to the warmth of the schoolroom.

Our teacher had voluntarily come from the school at Kingston, a poor panic-prone woman who found it impossible to control us. Her name was Maggie and she rode a bicycle as big as a bedstead which, on occasions, we would dismantle when she was otherwise engaged. She tried valiantly to interest this rude mob in nature walks, in local history and in the Bible. She was a hapless person trying her best. If she only succeeded in teaching one lesson in her entire career, then I was the one who benefited. One morning she instructed me to read the daily excerpt from the Bible and, with the rest of the boys cat-calling, smirking, and munching stolen sugar beet, I realised like a vision how poetic were the words I was reciting. 'For lo the winter is past, the rain is over and gone, the flowers appear on the earth, the time of the singing of the birds is come, and the voice of the turtle is heard in our land . . .'

After school I asked her what sort of voice a turtle might have. When she realised that, for once, I was not being supercilious, she promised to find out for me. She asked the vicar and the next day she told me he had looked up the reference especially. 'The turtle in *The Song of Solomon*,' she said, 'is really a turtle dove.'

After that I began to look at words and language in a different way. The meek, and Maggie was of that kind, may never inherit the earth for it's too late now; but in some places where they have laid a kind hand the touch has been deep and lasting.

It was through Maggie, also, that I earned my first money by writing. In her enthusiasm for the past she planned to take a group of the more controllable boys to Norwich, and the Gaffer, who liked to encourage anything he saw as a glimmer of interest in education, offered a half-a-crown prize for the best essay to be written about the visit. I won despite the fact that my effort was entitled: *Exertion to Norwich*. I don't think anyone else bothered to write anything.

In winter the bitter North Sea winds swept across the flat country. Christmas Day was heavy with hoar frost, lying like snow and clogging the iron branches of the trees. At sunset the whole landscape turned pink.

We had been taken to an American air force base for Christmas Dinner, an amazing mixture of turkey and sweetcorn and candied carrots, with as much ice cream as we could eat. I could hardly remember the taste. There was glistening holly and a starry Christmas tree and decorations such as we had never seen. Out on the white airfield, like skeletons in the mist, were two bombers which had crashed the day before on returning from a raid on Germany. No one mentioned them.

A lofty officer took charge of some of our party for the day. His name was Oscar H. Scarf. He was immediately popular and another group of boys joined us, deserting another young man who looked hurt and disgusted. 'Aw, go to hell,' he muttered and sloped away. A few months later when we were back at Kingston, Oscar called at Dickies and took *thirteen* of us to the cinema in the town. 'One full ticket and thirteen half tickets,' he said to the bemused cashier.

Shortly after New Year we had boarded the train at Narborough and Pentney Station and with a mixture of sadness and relief the people of the village said goodbye to us. My girlfriend Mary was waving to me and holding up her dog so I could see it. Later she wrote a letter to me which began: 'Dear Leslie, I've still got the same dog . . .'

Our return to Dickies, marching like a junior army down Gloucester Road, had a touch of comedy. The home, its grim façade now embellished with battle-scars, had been occupied by Irishmen working on emergency repairs to the town's hospital and houses.

The Gaffer was aware of their presence and had

decided on a pre-emptive strike to reoccupy the place. Two of the Irishmen, peering from a window, almost fell out when the column of one hundred and fifty boys led, as though by some warrior general, by the Gaffer advanced up the drive. The Gaffer simply marched us into the building and succeeded in occupying half of it before anyone in authority could intervene. We had four dormitories back but had to share the dining room with the robust Paddies. Before they left for their day's work, they lined up for a steaming hot breakfast of sausages, bacon and eggs and fried bread, and it was not long before the Dickie boys, nostrils twisting, crept down the stairs and helped themselves also. The Gaffer, whose distrust of the Irish was every bit as deep as his solemn dislike of the Welsh (the Scots he absolved because his wife had Scots blood), assembled us and warned direly that there must be no fraternisation with 'these filthy and foul-mouthed men'. But sausage, bacon, eggs and fried bread were thicker than warnings and they became our allies and friends until the time when they were found other billets and we were left in sole occupation of Dickies again.

I still had no idea what had happened to my brother. It seems extraordinary now that two children could be so casually separated and, being already bereft of parents, each should then have no knowledge of where the other had gone. With hindsight, I suppose that I could have demanded to know where he had been taken after that abrupt and careless parting in the ambulance, but I was only a boy and it was difficult to approach anybody, and particularly the Gaffer, on matters like that. Once or twice, when he was in one of his occasional benign moods, sitting in the chapel before the assembled inmates, making humorous guesses about what he imagined our homes had been like or what was to become of us in the future, I mentioned that I did not know where my brother was. But, because I failed to put it in a forthright way, he had passed it off as a joke, asking around the room: 'Anyone seen Thomas's brother?' and pretending to search under the benches.

He was not as monstrous as he sounds but he had moments that made him seem very close to it. He once ridiculed a boy to tears by saying that some people who had visited him had 'smelled to high heaven'. All the others, of course, had smirked and turned their faces on the unfortunate lad. 'Doesn't anybody have a bath where you come from?' he demanded. Then there was a running joke that one inmate had lived in a hovel in Chapel Alley, Brentford, a location which the Gaffer alleged he knew well. Everyone always laughed at this familiar patter, including the boy. Another pathetic youngster, called Willy, was always weeping and demanding to 'go home to my mum'. The Gaffer, and in truth the boys as well, picked up the phrase as a taunt. Well, eventually Willy tried to go home to his mum and ended up electrocuted on the Southern Railway near Waterloo.

The situation sounds disgraceful, writing it in this age, yet none of us at that time thought it was cruel or unjust. When my Uncle Chris and Aunt Nance eventually appeared from South Wales to take me to visit the London Zoo, they arrived looking prosperous

165

and in one of their two cars. The Gaffer entertained them in his cottage but later, when all the boys were assembled in the chapel, he ribbed me unmercifully about my relatives. Later Chris told me he had given the Old Man five pounds to put towards the 'funds'. 'Thanks very much,' the Gaffer had replied blithely, thrusting the fiver deep into his pocket. 'He didn't give me a receipt or anything,' said my puzzled uncle.

This eccentric man had some memorable ideas. Once, patriotically seeking to help the fight against Hitler, he bought two goats for ten shillings each, having some notion of mating them and starting a small goat farm. The passage in *This Time Next Week* about the goats has brought me hundreds of letters from children who have read the book, which is set for school examinations:

Three of us he sent to collect his goats. I've never worked it out yet why he wanted the wretches. Probably because he was intensely patriotic, he imagined that if they had kids (as if he didn't have enough) he would be able to raise a goat herd and thus help the national war effort.

There was Grandpa, a melancholy youth with spinneys of hair cropping his face, and Frank Knights and myself.

We claimed the goats from a piggery somewhere beyond the river and Kingston Bridge. The three of us saw the animals for the first time and knew we were buying trouble. One was fawn and white and the other white. Both had pink, sleazy eyes and sniggering expressions. I have never looked upon two more debauched creatures. Unfortunately for the Gaffer's ambitions they never got around to having kids. They were both billies.

'We oughta brought the cart,' said Grandpa, dolefully regarding the animals. 'We'll never get 'em back.'

The cart referred to was a sturdy hand-barrow which nominally belonged to the Kingston cleansing department and was supposed to be used by road-sweepers. The Gaffer had borrowed it years before and had never got around to giving it back.

'We'll walk 'em – like dogs,' said Frank, who was one of the brainy kids in the home. 'Let's get some string.'

The crook who sold us the goats gave us the string and looked as though he was tempted to charge us for it. We tied it around the stiff hair of their necks and set off on the return journey.

At first it seemed that it was going to be smelly but non-violent. The putrid pair trotted along willingly.

'It's going to be simple as anything,' I said.

'Yerse,' muttered Grandpa. 'They're too shagged out to cause any bovver. Look at 'em.'

The bother came immediately they saw a trolleybus. It was going at a spanking pace and the white goat tried to get underneath it. It pulled Frank with a swift and decisive tug. He gallantly held the string, but the goat was going to do battle with the low snout of the trolley, and nothing was going to stop him.

Fortunately the bus driver had good reflexes. He hit his brakes ferociously; the ungainly vehicle skidded and stopped. When it stopped, the goat, horns down, vile glint in the eye, was three inches from death. Frank was only a fraction further away. The conductor of the bus had fallen from the platform onto the road.

There was huge confusion. Traffic squealing, bus driver in a near faint, conductor rubbing his backside, passers-by giving advice and trying to tug the goat away from the trolleybus. In the middle of it all the goat I was holding, and which had remained placid, had a hearty pee all over my boots. So interested was I in the animated scene that my first awareness of this disgusting act was when the warm water trickled through the lace-holes and soaked my socks.

I cried out in horror and Grandpa, who was tugging the string of the other goat with Frank, turned and shouted: 'Wot you standing there for? Come and 'elp us.'

'I can't,' I bellowed. 'The thing's just pissed all over my boots.'

A man who had been laughing on the pavement sat down on the kerb and began to howl into his crossed arms. Everybody started laughing and Frank's goat, with two little jerky frisks, escaped and galloped away in the direction of Kingston Bridge. A whooping posse followed it, with the elongated Frank galloping bonily in the lead. At the bridge the goat stopped and looked around mildly as if wondering who was causing all the confusion. Frank regained the string, Grandpa held it with him, and I splashed up with my goat which until that time had been more insanitary than violent.

But there was time. At the centre of the bridge my goat tried to jump the parapet. There was a small stack of concrete tank traps, the sort that were hurriedly mounted everywhere during the invasion threat. They were piled like steps on the pavement, offering an ideal scamper for this goat who must have had mountain ancestors. The creature ended up straddling the stone coping, forelegs over the river, hind legs over the pavement. In a red panic I released the string and grabbed two handfuls of the scrubby, stiff hairs on its back.

Frank and Grandpa, who were a few paces ahead, turned. 'It's trying to get into the river!' I cried.

'Let it,' said Grandpa stonily. 'Best place for the soddin' thing.'

Frank left Grandpa with the first goat and came to my aid. So did half a dozen passers-by, several of whom had followed us from the last performance. A soldier got hold of the goat's tail and the animal began to bleat horribly. A gnome-like lady put down her shopping basket and began tweeting humane instructions, an action which she later regretted since immediately we got the goat down it put one of its back legs into her basket.

People on the river and along the bank below, accustomed to seeing human heads peeping over, did a double-take when they observed this one.

Eventually we got it back and having had its moment of glory it seemed satiated and content to be led along. So did the other goat, apart from an abrupt and momentarily terrifying charge at a nun, and we triumphantly led them into Dickies.

The advent of this pair began a reign of terror. The Gaffer had them set free at first in the fenced-off, grassy area beyond the mud patch. But he knew more about boys than goats. The following day one was discovered truculently challenging the traffic in the middle of Kingston Hill and was returned by a policeman who said it could have caused a messy accident and should be tethered.

So the Gaffer had the goats tethered. They apparently liked their tethers because they ate them to the last strand and were next found pottering around the grounds of Kingston Hospital.

Chains were the next deterrent and they were more

successful. But by industrious and secret tugging both animals were able to remove the stakes from the ground. Then they would break through, or go around, the fence and fly in fury across the mudpatch, over the playground, through the rooms and corridors scattering boys and staff.

'The goats are out!' the cry would ring. The Bulls of Pamplona caused no more scattering than this. Shrieks and shouts and tumblings. Down the Death Row passage they plunged once, with half a dozen boys just in front of their seeking horns and a hundred more shouting encouragement from behind. The pursued boys fled through the kitchen and gallant Mrs Mac tried to defend her territory with her ladle. But her bravery was brushed aside by the twin terrors who charged around and around the big table like tribal devils.

One of them – the white one – found a cloth in which some Dickies pudding had been steamed. It gobbled up the cloth and within the hour it was dead.

Boz, who had been on kitchen duties and had witnessed the entire drama, related it in the dormitory that night.

'After it 'et the puddin' cloth,' he said with relish, 'it laid down and sort of swelled up. We thought it was going to go off bang. Then it just conked out.'

'Fancy being killed by a Dickies pudding cloth,' I remarked.

'It weren't the cloth,' said Boz scornfully. 'It was the bits of pudding that was sticking on it.'

The other goat lived for years. Its escapades continued after its partner's going, although it steered clear of the kitchen. In later years it became an embarrassment to a neighbour who would telephone and say: 'Your ruddy goat is in my outside lavatory again.' The goat one afternoon

cover, his guarantors. All the sports gear had to go back except a football which was hurriedly and sufficiently kicked to ensure that it was left with us. The fraud was eventually caught but we wished him no evil. The memory of the Gaffer praying for him and singing 'Waltzing Matilda' was something we savoured.

The boys who were my companions in this place have reappeared over the years. Some have wanted no memory of it. One boy, who was my close friend, changed his name and vanished. Occasionally I see his younger brother and he has been unable to trace him. The inimitable Boz, cheery as ever, reappeared providently after thirty-five years and helped me get over the sad weekend when my dog had died. Some of the others organised a Dickie boys reunion and later trooped into the television limelight when I was the subject of *This Is Your Life*. The first get-together, held in a Kingston public house next to the church where we once howled hymns, was an occasion viewed with some apprehension by me. Reunions are notoriously prone to disappointment. But when I entered the room there were so many there who were instantly recognisable although years had vanished. Wives and girlfriends were ranged, passive and puzzled, around the wall and the Dickie boys were in a bunch in the middle. They all looked and sounded the same as ever; the laughs, the jokes, the same rough optimism that had kept us going. The only difference was that we were drinking beer and wearing long trousers. That night we sang the remembered songs, including the dubious versions of 'The Jolly Blacksmith' and 'Jesus Wants Me For A Sunbeam' ('And a bloody fine sunbeam, I'll be'), and finished with the chorus that we had once echoed as a piece of hope that was unlikely to be fulfilled:

> This time next week,
> Where shall I be?
> Sitting by the fireside,
> Eating my tea . . .

It was my brother who found me in the end. I was in the bathroom, up to my neck in the murky water which had seen the ablutions of several other urchins, when a letter was tossed in my direction. I failed to catch it and it fell into the water but I managed to rescue it before the words were obliterated.

Roy had spent some time in the hospital at Woodford Bridge where he was visited by the kindly Martin family from Newport who told him that his mother was dead. His letter now told me that he was then sent to foster parents, a homely thatcher and his wife, who lived in the Buckinghamshire village of Long Crendon. Apart from changing his name from Roy to George (his correct first name) they had helped him to live a happy village life. He became part of their family.

At once I wrote back and then a plan began to form to 'do-a-bunk' and go to see him. Doing-a-bunk had a long tradition at Dickies. There were some who were bunkers, who ran away regularly, and others who only did it when a need or crisis arose. Some enterprising bunkers had a sort of circuit, spending days making their way through towns and countryside, always giving themselves up at carefully selected police stations of an early evening. The time was important because it guaranteed a friendly supper, a decent bed, even if it were only in a cell, and a full and satisfying breakfast, before being returned to retribution. Some survival experts were able to remain at large for a long time and others escaped to far distances. One boy, it was rumoured, got to Yorkshire on the buffers of a train.

I was not a natural bunker. From the start I had fashioned a personal defence, tucking myself away in a corner, preferably on some hot water pipes, and getting my head in a book. Once I did conceive a plan to hide in the loft on the dormitory landing, coming down at night to scavenge food, perhaps having obtained a duplicate key to the bread room. I aimed to remain in the loft for two weeks until the hue and cry had died down and then slip quietly away. The loft, however, I found to be icy, hard and running with mice, so I abandoned the scheme.

When I did abscond I planned it minutely, working out a route to Long Crendon, a distance I calculated of about fifty miles. I took provisions and I had a map. I also carried the half a tin of sweets my brother Harold had sent long before. It was a good time of the year for hiking and I suffered little physical discomfort. One night, when it rained, I slept on the towpath under the river bridge at Marlow, within sight of a house I now have. The last few miles were the most trying. Wearily I turned onto the final stretch of road wondering if I would make it before nightfall. Then I spotted a bicycle in the yard of a police house. I purloined this and rode the rest of the way in wobbling triumph.

By a poetic chance I actually saw my brother coming

across a field as I pedalled into Long Crendon. I shouted to him and he shouted back. The bike skidded and I fell sideways. We ran towards each other and stopped. Boys that we were, there did not seem much to say.

''Lo, Les,' he said.

''Lo, Roy,' I replied. Then: 'I've got some sweets for you. Hally sent them. I've eaten my half.'

*

Things began to change, as they well might. The Gaffer retired and strode off straight-backed in the direction of Cornwall, with matron waddling at his side. It was after she died a few years later that he returned to Barnardo's in need of a home. The couple were replaced by a stocky man with a grin like a slice of orange peel. His name was Vernon Paul and he was a bachelor. The new matron was a sweet, gentle and hard-working person called Miss Blott. Dickies was all the better for them.

Vernon Paul had been a Barnardo boy himself, although he was for some reason reluctant to talk about it. When, years later, I interviewed him for the BBC he refused to say anything about his days in the homes and asked me not to even mention it.

Before he went on his upright way the Gaffer left me with one more memory. I was now fifteen and determined to become a writer. At the time I was at a technical school in Kingston, trying to solve the mysteries of plumbing and building brick walls which collapsed with a sigh. The work open to Barnardo boys in those days was limited. A carpenter, a rail-wayman or, at the poshest, a clerk in an insurance office seemed to be the best that could be achieved. No one had ever announced that they wanted to be a writer.

The scene had a touch of *Oliver Twist*. The boys were in the chapel, waiting for the Gaffer to release them into the playground, and he was showing no inclination to do so. He sat at the front, nodding at his *Surrey Comet* and chain-smoking (his one indulgence although he occasionally went alone to the cinema). This was the moment I decided to state my case and I stood up at the back and walked tentatively down the Ronuked central aisle.

'What do you want, son?' he enquired, not unkindly but without looking away from his paper.

This was it. I took a deep breath. 'Sir,' I said perhaps not as firmly as I might, 'I want to be a writer.'

He had grown a trifle deaf with age and it was some moments before he revolved from his newspaper. But he always encouraged ambition. 'Good,' he said eventually. 'Well done. I'll see you're a waiter in a good restaurant.'

The only waiting I did in those days was for girls who never turned up. I was very romantic, and still am, about women. Certainly the women of my boyhood dreams were always pink-cheeked, with a parasol and possibly surrounded by a bower of roses. Humiliation, perhaps not surprisingly, was to be my lot throughout my boyhood and into my teens. At one time I thought I must be close to holding the world record for waiting under clocks.

I confided in Frank Knights, the oldest boy in the home, that I had made a date with a deliciously pretty girl from Surbiton High School. Frank, who was known as Nightshirt and was worldly-wise, enquired if she had a similarly beautiful friend. It turned out she had and we arranged to meet them under the clock at Kingston bus station. Brushed and clean we hung about for an hour and a half but they did not show up so we went and spent the money on egg and chips in a café. It was the first time in my life that I had been out to dine.

There occurred another far more mortifying experience with a girl who did keep the appointment. She was a snooty, thin thing I met at evening classes (in pursuit of my dream, I was learning shorthand and typing after drawing inaccurate lines, building bad walls and defacing pieces of wood during the day). We began to talk about music and, in a moment of extravagance, I invited her to a concert at the Albert Hall. To my ecstasy and horror she accepted. She would telephone me to fix the day.

Now she did not know I was in an orphanage and I did not want her to know. This was when Mr Paul had become Superintendent and I was able to haunt the office on the Saturday, waiting for the phone to ring. It would never do for someone to pick it up and say: 'Dr Barnardo's.' Fortunately she called at more or less the arranged time and I was swift to the receiver. I can still remember the number. 'Kingson 0232,' I responded in my poshest voice. Matron put her head in the door and went out again. 'Sorry,' I said and, to explain the pause, truthfully added: 'It was just one of the staff.' Now she thought we had servants too.

The assignation was arranged. She rang off,

saying thrillingly that she was looking forward to seeing me again. Now I had the problem of obtaining money. As a senior boy I was getting half-a-crown a week pocket money and I worked out I could just manage the train fare and the lowest-priced tickets for a total of ten shillings. The sporting Mr Paul advanced me a month's pocket money on account of some fiction I related. On the day, shaking and shining, I went up to London on the train and then by bus to the Albert Hall. *There she was.* Waiting – for *me*! As though I took women out every night, I kissed her on the cheek.

Difficulties then began. She grumbled that we had to go and sit up in the highest *gods*, clumping and complaining up the endless stairs. When Cedric had taken her, she moaned, they had sat in the *front* stalls, just behind the conductor.

'You don't hear the music properly down there,' I argued with inspiration. We sat down. It was like peering into the mouth of a volcano. 'Up here the music floats to you.'

She kept muttering through the first half of the concert and then horrified me in the interval by announcing that she really *would* like a drink. Dumbstruck I mentally counted the money in my pocket. 'Please, dear,' she said archly. 'A gin and ton.'

A gin and ton! Christ, how much was a gin and ton? Trembling, I went towards the bar. 'And *might* we have a programme,' she called after me. 'We ought to have bought the programme before *surely*.'

Sod the programme, I thought. But there was no escaping the gin and ton. I approached the bar. I had never bought a drink in my life. 'Gin and ton, please,' I mumbled.

The lady had a suspicious eye and I had a sudden hope that she would refuse to serve me. It would, on the other hand, be a humiliation to have to admit that I had been turned away as being under-age. But that gin and tonic would mean that I would not have enough to buy her a ticket on the train home. I gritted my teeth while the bar lady hesitated.

She made up her mind and said: 'All right then. How many? Two?'

'*One*!' I bellowed. She fell back shocked. 'One, please, just one,' I whispered.

It left me with only enough money for the bus fare to Waterloo and my own return ticket. I would have to give her that. Jesus Christ, a gin and ton, if you please.

'Aren't you having one?' enquired the girl loftily when I returned.

'Me? Oh no. I'm in training, see. For football, I've had to cut out drink. Especially gin and ton.'

She sniffed. 'Did you get a programme? I'd like to know what they're playing even if we are a long way up.'

'Sold out,' I said desperately. 'All gone. Anyway I think it's more fun guessing, don't you?'

'Not really,' she said. 'I feel quite giddy up here, you know.'

I was glad when it was over. We silently boarded the bus and she stared out of the window all the way to

Waterloo. She took out a gold case and selected a cigarette which I tremblingly lit for her with her own box of Swan Vestas. I was so miserable.

At the station I felt for my return ticket and prepared to hand it to her, planning to announce at the same time that, although it was eleven-thirty at night, I had remembered a sudden urgent appointment in the City. To my overwhelming relief she produced a season ticket from her bag. I wouldn't have to walk after all.

At the other end she gave me a peck like a hen on the cheek before heading for home. So much for romance. I brightened when I was walking up Gloucester Road, though. I woke Nightshirt and told him how wonderful it had all been, the Albert Hall, the inspiring music, the gins and tonics. He stirred in the dormitory moonlight. 'That must have set you back a packet,' he mentioned.

'Oh, it did,' I said, getting into my iron bed. 'But it was worth it. She's terrific.'

Nightshirt sniffed over the blankets. 'That's the trouble with women,' he said wisely. 'It's the bloody expense.'

Ever the romantic, my other early experiences with girls were not fulfilling. In the summer of 1945, the first of peacetime, I went for a holiday to my uncle's house in South Wales. Both my uncle and aunt and my cousin Adrian worked in Cardiff all day and some-times stayed long into the evening. I went to their office on Cardiff Docks, Tiger Bay as it was called, and one day Adrian, who was two years older than me, took me to a café where he appeared to be on lascivious terms with a lush-looking girl with a flower in her hair. I could only gape as they clutched each other at the table. God, what would I have given for a girl with a flower in her hair.

Most of that holiday I was left in the charge of the beautiful and benevolent granny – my aunt's mother – who realised I was lonely and several times took me to the pictures although I am sure she did not want to see either *Hellzapoppin* or *The Picture of Dorian Gray*. Emerging from the cinema on the latter occasion we agreed that neither of us had understood what had happened.

To keep me occupied during my unaccompanied days my uncle bought an Eskimo canoe, a wood-and-canvas kayak. The beach was two miles away but I optimistically bought some pram wheels and dragged it there one evening, took my clothes off, stowed them and the wheels in the bow of the tenuous craft, and eventually launched out into the leaden Bristol Channel. I had no idea what I was doing but merely paddled the slim boat straight out to sea, intending to round the rocky headland of Cold Knapp and land on the pebble beach on the distant side. Out and out I went. The waves became morose and choppy and water began to slop over the side. While I kept the kayak's head into the sea it was not so bad but once I tried to turn the Knapp – which I now know has currents so notorious that even experienced boatmen shun it – I knew I was in danger. The boat began to fill with water. Desperately I paddled, trying to round the cape, looking for help towards the shore. Nothing moved in the lessening light. Not for the first time I was on my own. Eventually, battered, wet and weary, I made it and the ingoing waves carried me side-on to the stony beach. Tumbling from the boat, I managed to drag it clear of the waterline, and collapsed face down on the pebbles. It was late evening and I attracted no attention. Eventually I sat up and, shivering, managed to get my clothes on and go to the top of the beach where there was a telephone. No one was in my uncle's house. Unbelievably, I then decided I would have to get the boat back to the house. It proved impossible to fit the wheels so I picked up the craft and put it on my shoulder and set out to walk the two uphill miles. About halfway there I was staggering about all over the road when some youths came along, rough kids, smoking and joking. They took the boat from me and carried it to my uncle's front door. I was very grateful.

It was during that August they had the swimming gala in the open-air baths which I have already described – when I came second in a two-boy race because my two swimming costumes had fallen off in the water. As I was proudly looking at my second prize and the local reporter was noting my name for his column a pretty little girl in a brown swimming suit came up to me and smiled: 'Hard luck.' That is all she said; they were the only words she ever spoke to me, but at once I was in love again.

The following day I went back to the baths but she was not there. She had been sitting with her family outside one of the private chalets and, by dint of sly enquiries which augured well for my future as a reporter, I discovered the family's name and their address. That evening I loitered in the rain at a bus stop just opposite the house. Buses stopped and the conductors could not understand why I did not get on. I was there for hours waiting for her to emerge. 'Oh!' I would exclaim with many-times-rehearsed surprise. 'Fancy seeing you again!' When I was about to give up she came out. It was almost dark but I was sure it was her. She was with another girl and they ran chattering to another house across the road, so quickly that I had no time to arch my eyebrows or utter a syllable of my speech. I pulled up the collar of my coat and went moodily home. I suppose I was simply lonely.

After four weeks at my uncle's comfortable house I was glad to get back to the rough familiarity of Dickies. There, at least, I knew where I was and I was never alone. We had a concert during which Boz and I performed a lusty song called 'Dear Old Donegal', not you might think the ideal choice for a blatant Yorkshireman and a boy from Newport. Two of the visiting audience, a pair of cosy sisters in their late twenties, invited us to tea at their house at Kingston. We jumped at it and on the following Sunday had a splendid time with lots to eat followed by singing at the piano. One sister played and the other put her arms about each of our shoulders while we chorused, pressing us close as she sang so that we were each aware of a large warm breast. Later they took me to hear the *Messiah* at the Albert Hall and I paid several visits to their house. I was harbouring hope that they might have similar designs as some of our slinking male visitors but, unfortunately, nothing improper ever occurred. My run of ill luck with women was continuing.

There was one further humiliation and it was again associated with swimming. (There is doubtless some Freudian interpretation.) We had gone camping on the Isle of Man – life was now much more free and enjoyable – and there I met a lovely dark girl, with long eyelashes, who was called Isa Luny. Determined to impress her I swam out one evening from the beach, out, out, far out, to where cormorants were diving. I turned onto my back and saw her miniature figure waiting on the shore. She must have been a mile away and I turned and began to return. It was cold and darkening now with the shore becoming indistinct; it was much harder swimming back. Eventually, out of strength, out of breath, I staggered up the sharp shingle. White, thin and shivering, water running down my long nose and my hair stuck on my forehead, I stumbled on. My beloved was waiting. 'You know,' she remarked thoughtfully, closely studying the sight. 'You look just like a crow.'

Having told the story on a television programme, and mentioning the little girl's rememberable name and where she had lived, I had a charming letter from her. Thirty-eight years on, Isa Luny confessed she could neither recall me nor the incident, but she felt very sorry about it.

Crow or not, I doubt if I was much to see, although we were being fed properly now and I was playing football and cricket, both at home and at school. Indeed I cut a fine figure, I thought, when I was a ball boy at the first Wimbledon tennis tournament after the war. Barnardo's traditionally provided the ball boys and it lent us a touch of glamour that was otherwise far beyond our reach. Seeking the limelight, perhaps, I one afternoon strayed onto the court when Colin Long, an Australian, was serving. The ball hit me in the seat of my shorts. Afterwards the player apologised and I apologised to him for spoiling the service. 'Kid,' he said. 'When that upsets me, then it's time I packed up.' I wonder what reaction it might have provoked today?

Sheila Summers, a golden South African, and Kay Menzies, the British champion, played in that first post-war Wimbledon. Predictably I could not make up my mind with which one, the fair or the dark, I should get involved. Every day I turned up looking my smartest and one day when a door opened accidentally, I actually viewed Miss Summers in her brassiere, her sunbathed skin under the white straps. Oh God, I thought, nothing else matters now.

There was a men's doubles couple called Cohen and Tallart and during one of their matches a spectator leaned into the court and asked me where they were from. 'They're Jews,' I replied confidentially. 'I suppose they're from Jerusalem.' I wondered why the man and everyone in earshot laughed uproariously.

My efforts to be handsome, to prowl rather than walk, to stand my quiff on end (I prominently wore white gloves while fielding the tennis balls) were abruptly wrecked by a bump like an onion which blossomed on my forehead.

This was the aftermath of a breakfast-time fight

with John Brice, usually a friend, the boy who had first arrived with me at Dickies door. The battle ended with him delivering a well-directed left-hander to the side of my head, knocking me down. The bruise was bad enough but, I realised with gradual horror, it showed no signs of diminishing. A lump remained. An ugly lump that, even as I surveyed it in the mirror, seemed to be growing by the moment.

In Kingston there was a man who sold newspapers who had an even bigger bump in the same place. A purple knob over his eye. He was obviously the one to ask, so I asked him. 'It's a cyst, son,' he informed me obligingly. He fingered it familiarly. 'Won't ever go down now. Not till I'm dead.'

Horrified I went away, hands to my own bump. God, it was enormous! What was I to do? Without telling anyone I went to a local doctor. He was very doddery, so elderly he would have retired but for the war. 'Oh yes,' he said looking at the projection with interest. 'I think that will have to come off.'

After all the other patients had gone I lay on his couch while he gave me a local anaesthetic and proceeded to saw and chisel into my head with obvious enjoyment. He went at it with such endeavour that he cut the main artery.

Blood hit the ceiling, blood sprayed the wall. It was everywhere. Belatedly a nurse, not much younger than the doctor, came in and fell down in a dead faint on the floor. The ancient physician was clamping clips to the side of my head in an attempt to stop the flow. He kept muttering. 'I just can't find it. Ah, there it is. No, it's not.'

186

I was the calmest person there. It occurred to me that there was a good chance I might bleed to death at this rate and I lay thinking over the few years of my life and coming to the astonishingly bland conclusion that I had experienced a pretty good time. My shirt, my trousers, and my new tartan tie, of which I was very proud, were soaked and scarlet. 'I think you'd better call an ambulance, nurse,' suggested the doctor, not before time. She had pulled herself together and went out of the room like an old rocket. Then, to general relief, he managed to get the clips on the right bits and I was carried to the ambulance with so many piece of metal on my head (he was not sure which ones had done the successful job) that I looked like a stuck bull transported from the ring.

The ambulanceman who sat in the back with us eyed me moodily. The doctor, trying to be bright, said: 'I've been asked to give a lecture on haemorrhaging next week.'

The ambulanceman grunted: 'I should take 'im along with you.'

To the end of my days at the Technical School I was never capable of building a wall that did not tumble down. They fell with all the readiness of those of Jericho, but without a trumpet. They were badly put together and the mortar was too wet or too dry. I was even less competent at metalwork and there was an uncomfortable incident due to my cavalier use of a blow torch and the vicinity of the instructor's backside.

Few of my lines executed at the drawing board

187

managed to proceed neatly on the intended course. Any form of mathematics left me thwarted. I would never have made a draughtsman. My mother's dream of long before came to naught.

In the woodwork class I shared the dunces' bench with a resourceful and well-spoken chap called Harry Futerman, who became a London solicitor. The tight woodworking joints we were required to fashion tended to rattle like castanets, the gluepot was called for and often spread itself over bench, tools and pupils. Futerman and I were set the elementary task of planing the top of an ill-fitting door on the school canteen. Our passions were football and cricket and our conversation was directed on these subjects to the detriment of the job in hand. We planed away happily, a little bit more here and a little there, just a shade here to balance that bit where we seemed to have taken off too much . . . At the conclusion of the task a boy, or small man, could have slid through the aperture and that is exactly what happened, for the canteen was burgled that night and some buns and loose change stolen.

In an attempt to carve out something more artistic than the required mortise and tenon joints I devoted a lot of secret time to an elegant miniature tombstone embossed with the slogan 'RIP', followed by the name of the woodwork master. This was discovered by the instructor himself who thought it in poor taste and hustled me to the office of a particularly obnoxious man, the deputy headmaster, who sported both a monocle and a sneer. His hair was always plastered down from a middle parting, like some antiquated upstaged actor. He wore pin-striped suits and spoke with a voice that squeezed from his nose. He was not a nice individual.

'After this,' he pronounced, having been told of my crime, 'I shall never again denote a penny to Barnardo's.'

This outraged me. 'If it's only a penny then you'd better keep it,' I answered. 'We don't depend on people like you.' Whereupon he hit me around the ear.

There were others who were more sympathetic. The man who taught us plumbing was a companionable chap who liked me even if I never conquered the mystique of wiping joints or bending lead. When I had first attended the school he had set each of us the task of drawing a plan of the water system of our own house. For the majority of pupils this was reasonably simple. At Dickies, however, with its sixty rooms, passages and towers, the water system was on an heroic scale. I asked Bosky, a cross-eyed teenager who stoked the home's boiler.

'I'm *not* a Dickie boy,' he used to philosophise while squatting on the coke pile. 'And I'm not a master either. I'm a sort of in-between.' Inspiration would light his coaly face. 'I'm the *boiler-master*, see.' Bosky had no notion of how the water worked. He just shovelled the coke, quite often everywhere but through the door of the furnace. So I had asked the Gaffer who, liking to encourage knowledge, immediately showed me the plan of the water pipes from the tank in the tower through the labyrinth of curves and corners. It looked like the map of the London Underground. I copied this faithfully and handed it in with the more prosaic plans of suburban houses as offered by my school-mates. The plumbing master mentioned that I seemed to live in a mansion and I explained where and what it was. After that he was always kind. One day when I had made a particularly monstrous mangle of a basic pipe circuit he sighed: 'What do you want to do as a job, Thomas?'

'I want to be a writer, sir,' I replied promptly.

'Good,' he said. 'Just as long as it's not a plumber.'

I was better at some things. At the end of the two years I emerged with distinctions in English, History and Geography, coming last or next to Futerman, in all the other subjects. The *Daily Mirror* was running a series of very brief fiction called 'Story to Read in the Train' and I submitted one, tenously typed on the old Dickies Underwood. It was not published but I had, in return, a wonderfully encouraging letter from a man called C.E.T. Field who was in the *Mirror* features department. It was very good, he said, but I was competing against professional writers. I must keep writing, and reading . . . write something every day . . . read something every day . . . I still have the letter.

Futerman used to run a racket in the free bus tickets which some boys were permitted. Bartering, selling, exchanging these tickets, was a daily trade. My involve-ment meant a considerable difference in my pocket money, enabling me to buy both the *News Chronicle* in the morning and the *Evening News* (from my acquain-tance with the cyst) at night. The first English cricket team since the war was visiting Australia, and Boz, my friend from Dickies (who was at the same school), and I would race to see what the scores were. Recently I found myself sitting next to Alex Bedser at a dinner and I told him how I remembered the excitement of learning that he had taken a catch to dismiss one of the Australian, opening batsmen in the first of the post-war Test matches. Even now I can see Boz, red face gleaming, reciting the words of the cricket correspondent E.M. Wellings. 'And Bedser, because of 'is great 'ight was able to knock t'ball opp and catch it as it dropped.'

Futerman, who had considerable style, opted to skip school and attend the Derby in 1946, and he invited me to accompany him. On the suspect bus tickets we made our way to Epsom where we saw Airborne score a memorable victory. Well, we saw its legs go by our noses as we crouched in the crowd at the edge of the rails. Futerman had been running the book at school and had lost heavily, so much so that winnings would have to be paid out in free bus tickets. We began to walk back but it was a long way so we got on a bus. 'Somebody,' pronounced Futerman, 'will have to wait for their winnings.'

VIII

It seems now that I occupied at this period a dispro-
portionate amount of time listening to ladies who sang
at the piano. The jolly sisters at Kingston were
succeeded by another hostess, of good intention but
limited scale, who would attempt notes well beyond her
reach. Her eyes would go up as her voice vanished, as
if she were trying to see where it had gone. I found
that my eyes were ascending searchingly also. She did,
however, make excellent chocolate cake and was far
from mean with it. Delving into my half-a-crown pocket
money I myself had set out on a musical career. For
ninepence a week an incredibly rheumy old dear taught
me scales, a piece called 'Merry Bells' and Rubinstein's
'Melody in F' on a piano with a keyboard like a mouth
of bad teeth. Notes were missing wholesale and when
nothing but a wooden mallet sound came out she would
la-la it. A firm press on the hard pedal (the other one
didn't work) would sometimes set off the journey of a
Guinness bottle, rolling bumpily across the floor.

Given the limitations of professional player and
piano, Rubinstein would have been excused not
detecting his 'Melody in F' (La-la-la, clunk, la-la clunk,
la-la clunk) and my repertoire never advanced beyond
it.

However, by one of those almost mystic moments of fortune, it led the way to the furtherance of my dream of being a writer. I was practising on the piano in the chapel one evening when a visitor to the home came and stood behind me.

'Rubinstein,' he murmured.

Pleased, even astonished, that anyone should have recognised it, I went back to the beginning and treated him to 'Merry Bells' as well. The following week I found myself sitting in a huge chair, in a sumptuous apartment, while the man's wife, an opera singer, performed an aria at a white piano. My benefactor's name was Charles Mitchell and he was a journalist and an author. I related my ambitions and soon after he took me to lunch at the Authors' Club in London.

Curiously, being in Barnardo's had always provided a reason and a means of social elevation. We orphans were taken to tea and circuses by wealthy and influential people who hired buses or even taxis to transport us into an enriched world. We became quite familiar with it, particularly at Christmas time, when there was an embarrassment of outings from which we could take our pick. At times we became quite choosy.

Now, here was I, from Maesglas, Newport, Mon, and at sixteen, having lunch, at a club in Northumberland Avenue with authors and writers all around, eating, drinking and talking about their books and travels. It was thrilling and I dreamed of the day I might sit there and discuss *my* work and *my* journeys. I never did. That visit was my first and last.

It was on the kindly Charles Mitchell's advice to Barnardo's that I was sent to a college in Walthamstow, London, to start a course in journalism. I was to live in a hostel, a bus ride away, in one of two adjoining houses run by the Homes for older boys waiting for jobs.

One of the houses was a tall, pale Victorian pile called 'Staffa' and the other a neat modern place with a bow window called 'Iona'. They shared a pleasant, and mysteriously unkempt garden and, wonder of wonders, I was given a room of my own.

It is easy for me to remember, even at this distance: walking in, putting down my suitcase and closing the door. It was on the ground floor with a French window opening out on the rear garden. There was a bed, a wardrobe and a chest. After hanging my jacket in the wardrobe, I arranged my few books on the top of the chest and then sat down on the bed, looking about me, realising with joy what a turn for the better my life had taken.

An ex-RAF man and his wife were in charge – the Wellbeloveds (a name I was to borrow for a sergeant in *The Virgin Soldiers*). There was another adult resident, a dusty fellow who went out to work in some capacity for Barnardo's and lived in the house called Staffa. His hobbies were boxing (during which he was fiercely pummelled by all the boys and appeared to relish it) and chasing the same lads around the bathroom with a syringe loaded with soapsuds. We were in no doubt as to what were his aims with this weapon but we made sure he was never able to implement them. If he got too close we would gang up on him and give him another pummelling, leaving him propped up in a corner with a smile on his face.

At the college, a giant brick building with a Grecian pillared front, I discovered that I was the only male in a class of students studying shorthand and typing. Even with this plethora of riches, however, my achievements with girls continued to disappoint. We had regular ballroom dancing lessons at lunchtime and I learned to tango and foxtrot with the best. Three times a week there were midday 'gram-dances' and we would whirl about the floor to the wonderful rhythms of 'Skyliner', 'American Patrol' and 'Twelfth Street Rag'. I remember distinctly the first time I asked a girl to dance. Having newly mastered the one-two-three of the slow waltz I ventured to the Saturday night extravaganza, bursting in my best suit, and stood on the sidelines trying to remember the steps and gain the courage. A young man called Michael, who was hardly over twenty and had returned from the war minus his legs, had bravely staggered around on his metal substitutes, and I thought my task was a good deal less demanding than that.

A waltz was announced from the bandstand and I strode stiff-legged, teeth gritted into a dog-like smile, up to the most voluptuous young woman in the college. There was no merit in starting at the bottom. She had a great round of black hair like a Michelin tyre behind her dark and sensuous face. Her eyes were large and dreamy. She wore tight clothes, sweaters which bulged with pulchritude and promise. Her name was Babs.

She was a sporting girl and, to my mixed terror and delight, she accepted my invitation to waltz. I was

195

shorter than her and my head slotted almost exactly between her breasts, nose pressed into that perfumed escarpment. The dance took us around the outside of the floor. We never revolved an inch, just one-two-three, one-two-three, in a straight line, an awkward turn at the corner and then off on an unvarying course again, one-two-three, one-two-three. I held her as if I feared she might topple over. I could not, of course, keep this miracle to myself and as we cruised by the ranked faces at the fringe of the floor my eyes were seeking desperately for a friend, or even an acquaintance, at whom I could roll them to demonstrate my ecstasy. Each time I turned my head in search of approval or better still, envy, the end of my nose brushed the slopes of her bosom and I apologised, red-faced. She must have been a composed young lady because I remember her reply: 'Don't worry about them. They do get in the way.'

This temporary triumph was offset, however, by a continuing trail of real failures. One Saturday I decided to knock them cold by wearing a spotted bow tie to the dance. Only a stiff collar could be properly worn with this, I thought, and went on the train to Leytonstone to buy one. When I got it back to my room it was patently too loose. The clip-on bow hung like a boat about to capsize. Back on the train I went, the one stop to Leytonstone and the shop. The assistant accepted the crumpled collar in exchange for a size smaller. On the train once again I went and to my room where I stood puce-faced in front of the mirror while the collar garrotted me. Once more to the station and to the outfitters. This collar was distinctly sweaty but the man very decently changed it and I returned to the room where, delighted, I found that the third one fitted and the bow tie, with its spots and pointed ends, looked dazzling.

It seemed to work brilliantly. A girl with whom I performed the final waltz smiled agreement when I suggested I should see her home. The motive behind her ready acceptance became apparent when we stepped outside the college. Everywhere was thick with fog, the buses had stopped; we would have to get a taxi. There came a point where the routes to our homes diverged. There was nothing for it but to get out, pay for her journey, and walk the rest. As I alighted from the cab the lady broke off a flirtatious conversation with the driver to give me a passing kiss. 'Never wear that bow tie again,' she warned darkly. 'It makes you look like a skull and crossbones.'

This may, or may not, have been better than looking like a crow but generally in matters of romance the situation was neither encouraging nor improving. Even when I did eventually meet a fair-faced girl who might easily have held a parasol beneath a rose bower, those twin evils disaster and humiliation were waiting, glee-fully rubbing their hands.

Her name was Ann. She was small and shy, given to whispers and blushes. She sang in the church choir, looking like an angel in her cassock. Already I had fitted her into a scene. Here was the girl, I told myself, for the rowing boat on the lake, even if it was March. I recall the month because it was my birthday and, at seventeen, I thought it was time I became more deeply involved with women which, surveying my dismal record until then, could not have been diffi-cult. The sweet Ann, however, seemed to have gleaned some rumour that I was of bad amorous reputation; one who needed to be carefully watched for the first sign of a trick. She agreed, however, to let me take her rowing on the lake, Connaught Water, near Woodford.

It was an encouragingly sunny day causing us, in playing the idyll, to be singularly ill-dressed for the real season. I was wearing a sports jacket and open-necked shirt and she had a flowered summer dress with a knitted cardigan over her slight shoulders. Gallantly I helped her into the hired rowing boat while the atten-dant pocketed what must have been the first shilling of the season. She sat one end and I sat the other. Once clear of land and the sheltering collar of trees the breeze was keen. She pulled her cardigan closer and looked worried.

'I love Mendelssohn,' I declared as I tugged the oars. We had already discussed music. 'Wouldn't you love to see Fingal's Cave?'

Not a bad opening from a lad of seventeen, you might think. Then I saw she was gazing at me with growing alarm. 'Fingal's Cave?' she muttered.

I looked down to where her eyes were pinned. Oh, God, all my fly buttons were open! My legs were wide apart and as I stretched to pull the oars so the terrible aperture gaped. There was nothing I could do. She was right in front of me, a truly captive audience, and my hands were fully occupied with the oars.

She was convinced it was a trap. 'Take me back, please,' she trembled. 'I want to go back.'

Ahead was a small lump of scrub-covered mud projecting from the lake. 'An island!' I exclaimed with high-pitched brightness. 'Look, an island! We'll land there.'

She was glad of any port in a storm I suppose. Still staring at the gaping mystery in my trousers, she nodded agreement. I headed for the landfall.

What took place next has been repeated in many film comedies, but I still find it difficult to appreciate. After helping her ashore I found myself trapped in that familiar farce – the boat began to move away from the bank. I had one foot on the island and one in the boat. My fly was gaping wider than ever. Something had to give. I made a pathetic penguin-like attempt to gain the shore and fell backwards into the icy water. The girl began to scream uncontrollably.

She continued to scream until the attendant came out from the shore to retrieve us and his drifting rowboat. Later she told her friends that she thought the whole scenario was some ruse which would enable me to remove my trousers.

This story reached me and, properly distressed, I wrote a lovely letter to her saying that I felt for her so deeply that nothing was further from my mind. I even concluded it with a little poem.

On the following Sunday the choir boys and girls in church were seized with fits of giggling. Every face turned to me in the front pew where I sat to gaze at my adored. My love letter and my private sentimental rhyme were being passed secretly around during the sermon. The following week I was in love again with another girl who actually took me to her house where she was to cook a meal. On this occasion the pressure cooker blew up. It seemed I was doomed to a life of celibacy, dreams and regret.

From the widespread windows of the college library I could look out over Forest Road to a single bulky building outside of which, spelled vertically, was a sign in red lights which said 'Guardian'. It was the local newspaper, the *Walthamstow Guardian*, and the legend beckoned me like a long, nail-varnished, enticing finger. Since I was the solitary student taking the journalism course, which was in fact merely an adapted commerce curriculum, I spent much time in the library; for mathematics and business practice were outside its scope, and mine also. Sitting at a self-imposed thesis on Mendelssohn on dim winter afternoons my eyes would drift across the greasy road to the lit windows of the building and I would imagine the activity within. The editor in his book-lined office, the bowed and dedicated sub-editors, the urgent reporters coming in with the news from the streets, perhaps from as far afield as Chingford and Epping. Sometimes I saw a car hurrying off and I wondered where that lucky man was going in search of adventure and sensation. Mendelssohn seemed to have happened a long time ago.

At last I was getting the feel of Pitman's shorthand, its world of grammalogues and diphthongs, even beginning to think in it, which I still often do, although my typing was woefully uncoordinated. We learned the touch technique by placing a shield over the keyboard and typing out sets and systems of letters to the accompaniment of martial music. The tutor would wind the gramophone and the stout sounds of the Colonel Bogey march would crackle out. Sitting there among all the girls I would be several bars behind and fully aware that I was once more committing some sort of Assyrian cryptogram to paper. Sometimes I tapped between the keys and the whole basket of the machine fell in on itself. You could, however, sing under your breath to the march:

> Be kind to your web-footed friends,
> For a duck may be somebody's brother.
> They live in the fens and the swamp,
> Where the weather is cold and damp.

Charles Mitchell continued to encourage me. Barnardo's had given me a typewriter in a wooden box and I sat at home slowly composing articles and short stories for newspapers and magazines that were returned so punctually that I marvelled at the speed of the post. He knew that I was fretting at my lectures and wanted to get onto a local newspaper in any capacity. One day he sent a thrilling message to say that he had arranged for me to have a trial on a group of papers whose printing press was only a walk around the corner from the hostel where I was living.

It was evening in late spring when I first walked up the truncated road called Voluntary Place, Wanstead. Wedged between the houses was a corrugated building, a large shed, every wall of which was trembling as if the whole flimsy structure was in the grip of a spasm.

You could hear the ponderous thumping of machinery from halfway down the street and the pungent and beautiful smell of printing ink drifted on the late air. Even after years I never ceased to thrill to that oily smell, although in most places now it has drifted away for ever.

The place was more like an engineering shop than a newspaper office. There was a trapdoor set in a bigger door and, as I stood uncertainly outside, it opened and a man in oily overalls, his thin face streaked black, emerged, sat on an upturned box and muttered: 'Bugger me.'

However, he appeared to have pulled himself together after a while and I approached him timidly. Yes, he confirmed, this was the place. 'I wouldn't go in that 'ell 'ole, if I was you, mate,' he mentioned. 'Anyone wot takes up this life is off their bleedin' rocker.'

I thanked him for the warning and, turning up my overcoat collar to give at least the impression that I was a newshound, I climbed through the small entrance.

It was like Alice stepping through her tiny door into an amazing world. The main floor space was occupied by the huge and pounding printing press. It seemed to be struggling like a captured elephant to be free. Men stood around it regarding its tantrums with anxiety. One was holding a pathetically diminutive oil can. 'Don't come through here, son,' he warned, not taking his eyes from the monster. 'This sod's likely to go through the roof any minute.'

I retreated outside and the blackened man, still

sitting and wiping his face with a rag, merely said: ''ad enough already 'ave you.'

I enquired about taking another route to the executive offices. This provoked a croaky explosion of laughter. 'Executive offices!' he howled. He looked frantically around as if he wanted to spot someone he could tell. There was no one, only a dog which came into the yard to pee. 'Those bloody pits!' he chortled. 'Executive offices! That's a good one, I must say. That's a good one!'

Only a little discouraged I went around the yard at the side. Among piles of scrap metal and waste paper stood a grubby caravan from which issued an insipid light. Through the open door I could see two young men sitting at a table. One was reading aloud from a piece of paper while the other checked a printed proof. I asked them the way and when they had told me, determined not to be overawed by the splendour and excitement, I said knowledgeably: 'Checking the galleys, are you?' They stared at me in disbelief. Eventually one, a tall, thin fair-haired youth with rimless glasses, answered: 'No, it's our bloody football pools, mate.'

I discovered an alternative door and entered into another yellow-lit mayhem. Further machines grunted and wheezed, each one it seemed watched by an attendant who looked ready to flee at any moment. The air was thick with fumes. Through the centre the only calm figure in the scene wandered about the chaos, wearing a pin-striped suit and smoking a pipe. This was clearly someone in charge. Tugging my collar about my neck I took a long breath and advanced on him.

'Ah,' he puffed unhurriedly when I had introduced myself. 'Just the chap we need.'

My God, I thought. Luck at last.

'If you want to be a newspaperman, you could start right away,' he said. Another globe of smoke went to join the general fumes.

Even over the thumping machines I could hear my heart. 'Now, sir?' I said. 'Yes, please. Of course. Anything.' Perhaps it was a murder, a train crash, a missing film star. 'What do I have to do?'

'Fold them,' he replied laconically.

The machine folding the *Wickford Times*, one of the umpteen small journals published by the company, had broken down. Each of the three thousand copies had to be folded by hand. I was instructed to take off my coat, then a piece of metal was pressed into my hand and I was positioned alongside two other perspiring individuals who were taking the pages from the press and folding them by running the metal along the intended crease. Thus began my career in journalism.

One of the other folders was a young, amusing and owlish fellow called Evans who became a great friend. The other was the fusspot chief, and only reporter of the *Wickford Times*, who was anxious to ensure that every crease was straight. It must have been a hundred degrees in that sweatshop. We folded and perspired. Someone brought us each a pint of cider which we drank greedily. When we had finished in the early hours of the morning, they gave us another pint. Reg Evans and I walked out into the dark cooling air and were spectacularly sick in the gutter of Voluntary Place.

It was three o'clock by the time I got back to the hostel. Every muscle and bone in my body groaned and I was coated with grease. But I rolled aching into bed with a joyous feeling. I was a newspaperman.

Among its former employees, now spread throughout the writing trade in every part of the world, the stories of the press at Voluntary Place are still told with the relish that time gives to hardship. Its location was not inappropriate, since we were pressed into volunteering for all manner of tasks and conditions, which today would send even the least dedicated union man howling for a strike. I, for one, worked for several weeks without wages.

It transpired that the organisation, which published something like twenty-five newspapers ranging from Southend in Essex, to Brentford in Middlesex – the two outer extremes of the London region – all on a shoestring, did not believe in encouraging young trainees overmuch by giving them money. On my second visit to the press I was taken to see the editor, a Mr Cyril, a tall balding person with staring blue eyes and shining skin. His ears were transparent. Each of the brothers who controlled this Heath Robinson empire was known by his Christian name. The one with the pipe who had set me folding was Mr Leonard. There was also a thin, nervy, beleaguered man, called Mr Harold, although this was his surname, and he was not related to the owners. He ran the entire empire from a partitioned office the size of a lavatory. He had a cynical humour and a terrible fatalism. One Friday, which was the quiet day of the week, I found him head in hands at the oilclothed bench which served as his desk. 'Look at bloody that,' he demanded. 'Look at it!' Amazed that he should inform me, the most junior of the staff, of his troubles, I stared at the proffered front page of the *Chingford Times*, which had hit the streets that day. 'Council Abandon Annual Ball' howled the headline and underneath, 'Two few tickets sold.'

'You would think somebody in this fucking place,' he sobbed. 'Would know the difference between TWO and TOO, wouldn't you?'

He could afford to be nice to nobody but he is recalled with laughter and affection by the veterans of those times. One of these, Maurice Romilly, a distinguished parliamentary correspondent, attempted a few years ago to mark this fondness by organising a dinner with Mr Harold at the head of the table and all who knew and suffered under and with him ranged down the sides. My enthusiasm for this project, and the willing support of many others, was not, however, reciprocated by the intended chief participant. The papers had folded and, predictably, this lifelong servant had been discarded shabbily. When Romilly telephoned him about the proposed event he said: 'Son, I don't want anything to do with any sod who had anything to do with those papers.' Then he put the phone down.

Each of the newspapers had its own district office, some less opulent than others. The one at Willesden, in north-west London, I was eventually to discover, had naked clay beneath the linoleum in the reporters' room. They were all printed on the fairly elderly machinery at Voluntary Place, where the journalists were expected to travel once a week to put their own paper to bed, to read proofs and to assemble the make-up. These operations were accomplished in a single cubicle jammed between that of Mr Harold and that of another senior sub-editor, a handsome man called Rashbrook, plus the caravan I had first visited, and a room in a neighbouring garage. The garage had been acquired with an eye to installing another rotary printing press there. When purchased this took six months to assemble. On the first night it ran the house next door fell down, and its operations were suspended.

It is difficult to believe such a conglomerate existed. To publish all those journals, spread through the Home Counties, was some feat in itself. With a sparse staff, sparser facilities and faltering machinery it was nothing less than miraculous.

My first day as a reporter was a Saturday. I had rather hoped that I would be dispatched to write some action-loaded prose about the football match at Clapton Orient or at least at Walthamstow Avenue. Instead I was given the doleful assignment of visiting undertakers in Leytonstone to note who had recently died, and to visit their homes to discover whether they had ever achieved anything in their lives which might merit a few lines in the paper.

Reporters these days doubtless do not have to under-take such lugubrious assignments, certainly not as a speculative thing. Unhappily, I set out drooping with a long black Barnardo overcoat which on future visits to the homes of deceased caused me to be mistaken for the undertaker's assistant ('Come to measure up, have you?') or more cheerfully the insurance man ('Have you got it in cash?') and on one occasion as a long-lost relative.

There had been no mention about the money I was to earn and indeed nothing was said for weeks. I worked myself into the ground, tramping the streets in the wake of the mortician, having nightmares, and drawing only expenses, which were limited to bus fares between corpses. On that first Saturday I approached my first undertakers' with much misgiving, finally raising enough courage to enter to a bell that chimed like a knell. The smell, and I can smell it now, was pungent; French polish, flowers with a whiff of formaldyhyde. There was a coffin on a trestle just inside the door and a little man who was bending over it shut it as he might have shut a book he was reading.

His immediate breeziness once I had told him who I represented overcame the proximity of death. 'Oh yes, my lad. Got one or two good ones for you,' he assured. 'Let's get the book. Should be a good tussle down at Orient this afternoon, don't you think?'

He produced his book and read out some names and former addresses. When he got to one name he nodded at the coffin. 'He's in there at the moment,' he mentioned as if the man might later be available for an interview. I looked about for somewhere to rest my new notebook and he again nodded to the coffin. I laid it on the sweet-polished lid and took down the list of the dead.

Then I had to go out and face the difficult part, to enquire if there was anything of interest about the loved one who had passed on. My first call, at a terrace house in a Walthamstow back street, has remained forever in my mind. Timidly I knocked and was breathing a sigh of relief at the absence of a response when the door was pulled open with some difficulty and standing there was a little girl, four or five years old, wearing a grubby nightdress. We stood staring at each other. I could think of nothing to say. Eventually I managed to enquire if there was anyone else at home and she summoned her brother, who was at the most seven. He was in pyjamas with jam all down the front. He saved me further embarrassment. ''Ave you come to see our mum?' he enquired. He opened the door and let me into the small front room where their mother was lying in an open casket. I almost fainted. They were in the house by themselves. It taught me, at the opening moment of my career as a reporter and indeed a writer, that knock on any door and behind that door is a story. If you can bring yourself to write it.

This funeral procession continued for some weeks. My eyes became hollow from being awake at night and from the miles I tramped in search of interesting anecdotes about the dead. There came a point when I was exchanging backchat with morticians. It started to get me down. I went to see Mr Cyril in his cubicle and he noted how black-eyed and despondent I was. When I told him the reason he clucked in sympathy and asked how much I was earning. 'Nothing, sir,' I replied. 'Just bus fares.'

'I expect you walk most of the way,' he mentioned. I thought it was goodbye to bus fares too.

'Well,' he said. 'I think we ought to start paying you. Let's say a pound a week, for a start. And perhaps we ought to move you to Woodford. You can do a few dancing displays and flower shows, that sort of thing. And people don't die quite so much there. It's a much better area altogether.'

Among the characters who made up the staffs of the various journals in the group was a man who was the most accomplished romantic liar I have ever encountered. He was short, youngish, and pugnacious, a distress to many, including his wife. He was our chief reporter, someone who lived by stories. When there were not enough true stories to go around he simply made them up.

One Wednesday the newspaper on which he worked showed no sign of finding a report strong enough to make the front page headline, and in those latitudes it did not have to be particularly sensational for that. He went thoughtfully to the pub at lunchtime and returned with a thrilling yarn about an old man he had met who carried with him a suitcase full of banknotes. This man had returned after many years in Australia to find his long lost love, the girl to whom he had been engaged fifty years before. Our chief reporter, whom we shall call Phibbs, had even obtained a photograph of the girl from the hoary traveller. 'I've told him to stay in the pub,' Phibbs announced. 'We've got to get a photographer around there and quick.'

The cameraman was dispatched but returned saying that the pub was shut and there was no sign of an old man with a case full of banknotes. Undeterred, Phibbs wrote the story and even quoted some local ancients who felt sure they remembered him from back in misty time. Across the front page the romantic legend was spread – with the faded picture of the long lost love the traveller had come to find.

Naturally the national newspapers became interested in this human drama and sent out reporters and photographers to find the returned suitor. No one ever traced him. Someone alleged that the girl in the picture looked very much like a photograph of his father's great-aunt which had appeared in our periodical many years before. Was he sure there had been no mistake? Phibbs dismissed the doubt. He was mystified but not daunted. The following week's issue was led with the headline: 'Millionaire Lover Vanishes'.

He also organised a running-backwards race which had the contenders trotting rear first up the main street of the borough. As they came in this curious fashion, Tom Merrin, now of the *Daily Mirror*, observed them with a sinking heart. 'I knew they were something to do with Phibbs, who was nowhere to be found,' he recalled. 'They came backwards through the office door and began claiming prizes.'

Some trusting soul at the local greyhound stadium commissioned Phibbs to organise a gala night which Phibbs promised would include the personal appearance of a famous and voluptuous film actress. Two hours before the event, with bands preparing to parade, flowers and champagne all ready, Phibbs still had no idea from whence his star was to come. Then the unexpected piece of luck, for which he had been waiting confidently, arrived with the casual mention by a local policeman that he had a pretty foreign girl, a friend of his daughter, staying at his house. In no time the young beauty, who spoke little English, found herself being fêted at the dog track, carted around on an open float to the cheers of the punters who were in no doubt they were viewing a Scandinavian film actress. The young lady, having enjoyed it immensely, merely wondered why it had happened.

These fantasies sometimes affected the personal lives of Phibbs's colleagues. One Sunday afternoon while he was walking with his wife and baby (who had recently – according to Phibbs – survived as a kidnap victim), I happened to be playing soccer and they paused to watch. At half-time Phibbs, who apart from being in the American Airborne Forces and MI5 simultaneously, had played soccer for several first division teams and cricket for Yorkshire, approached and said it was obvious to him that I had star quality. I believed every word and was overcome with delight when he promised he would arrange a trial for me with Clapton Orient, now Leyton Orient, the local professional side. I dubbined my boots, had my kit washed, and could hardly sleep while I waited. Nothing happened and after a week I jogged his memory. 'Tuesday,' he said without hesitation. 'It's all fixed. Be at the ground by four for a trial.'

I had always harboured a hidden dream that one day I might be a footballer and cricketer as well as a writer (just like Phibbs) and on the Tuesday I turned up at the stadium to find it deserted except for an old man sweeping the terraces. 'Help me sweep up and I'll give you a trial,' he promised after I'd told him why I was there. Although this sounded dubious I was ready to try anything. After half an hour of sweeping and picking up debris he went into the dressing room and appeared with a football. He placed himself between the goalposts and I kicked the football at him. When it was almost dark he picked up the ball and walked towards the dressing room. 'You'll never do,' he sniffed. 'Got no left foot, 'ave you.'

It was Phibbs who announced to the junior reporters one day that he was concerned for the well-being of a number of foreign students and workers in the area. 'They don't seem to have a social life at all,' he complained, while we wondered what the catch was. 'I think we ought to give them a chance to meet some local people, have a get-together, and help them make friends.'

Knowing him as we did, we dispersed with doubt-hung faces. Later, predictably and cheerfully, he announced that he had arranged a social evening and if we would just contribute as little as half-a-crown a head each then the whole enjoyable idea could go forward.

To some of us this was a sizeable slice from our wages, but we glumly put the money into the hat and Phibbs took immediate charge of it. He revealed a sudden friend in the wines and spirits business on the far side of London, who would provide the drinks at half price. Phibbs would personally drive the consignment to the social.

On the night of the 'Overseas Friends Evening', as it was heralded in our paper, a good number of French students, former German and Italian prisoners of war, and Indian restaurant waiters turned up. Unfortunately Phibbs did not. We waited with grim, growing certainty. The sandwiches hardened with our hearts. There was not a drink in the room. In the end the foreigners began to get a bit awkward and we had to send out for some crates of beer. The guests eventually went off into the Walthamstow night grumbling at British promises which had gone unfulfilled. One of the Germans told me that he had always thought that Englishmen kept their word. He had been under the impression that some sort of Bacchanalian feast was to be provided. All he had been offered was a curly cheese roll, a bottle of brown ale which he could not open and a couple of songs he did not know. There had also been a decided shortage of likeable women.

Phibbs turned up the next day swathed in splints and bandages.

'The bloody car,' he said throatily, looking from his dressings like a man peering from prison. 'Turned right over. Smashed every bottle. Nearly finished me, I can tell you.'

The location of this tragedy was never firmly identified, except it was many miles distant. Even when a paragraph appeared in our paper headed: 'Reporter's Narrow Escape', the geographical information was vague. Phibbs said it was in the Middlesex area but confidential telephone enquiries to several police stations and hospitals in the region failed to establish the occurrence. Also, considering the scale of his wounds, Phibbs emerged from his bandages somewhat quickly. Several years later I saw him staggering along Fleet Street with identical injuries.

Woodford was a leafy place compared to the gritty streets which I had been trudging. It had a wide green, a lilied pond with frogs below and a willow above, canopies of trees over its housetops, and open country stretching to Epping Forest. The local member of Parliament was the venerable Sir Winston Churchill and while I was there a powerful statue of the famous man was unveiled. The office of the *Woodford Times* was across the road from the green where I played cricket on a Saturday. There was a good homely café which provided thick-lipped cups of tea and doorsteps of bread and margarine, where the lady liked me and told me of her many hours on the operating table. It was spring and I took to the place with a smile.

Also, coincidentally, the district included Woodford Bridge and the Dr Barnardo Home where I had, five years before, been separated from my brother. It was part of my duties to make an occasional call at the home in search of news and one day they whispered in my ear that Princess Margaret was to make a visit. I hurried away and wrote the story. Thus Barnardo's provided me with my first scoop and my first front page headline; an odd instance of after care.

Unfortunately, the big day was a Thursday, when the *Woodford Times* was actually going to press. For the first time, but by no means the last, I had to imagine

what would happen and compiled a graphic description of the bunting and the crowds, the pleased staff
and the thrilled children, with details (gleaned from
my friendly contact) of what the Princess was wearing
with her smile. The whole thing was set and the paper
was ready to be printed. Then Her Royal Highness
failed to turn up.

She had been taken mildly ill and at the last moment
the event was cancelled. The distress of the Barnardo
authorities was nothing to mine. Panic-stricken,
knowing that even now the details of the event that
did not happen were being fed into the rollers of the
printing press, I got to the telephone, fiercely ejected
a nun who was jabbering to someone in Ireland, and
called Mr Harold at Voluntary Place. 'Oh blimey!' I
heard him howl. I could hear him running to stop the
presses, which he managed to do. He returned to the
telephone. I could hear him trembling. 'You've got
three and a half minutes to write the story,' he said.
'You'd better start now.'

I managed to piece it together as I went along,
something I learned to do as a matter of course in
time to follow, and I got my front page headline after
all.

In that suburban village sensations were rare. There
was the exclusive story that Mrs Renée Dubois, a local
celebrity, did not believe in God and Canon Wansey,
the rural dean, did. I managed to get them together
in the village hall on a Tuesday night and the debate
was a sell-out. But mostly life was peaceful. A circuit
of rural police stations, undertaken once a week, rarely
yielded sensation, although country crime sometimes

tends to the exotic. A drunk drove a steam roller he had found parked into the River Roding; a man alleged that someone dressed like Robin Hood had fired an arrow at him in the forest; what was said to be a human hand found buried among trees turned out at the post-mortem to be the paw of a bear, how it came to be there we never solved.

It is a continuing tradition. A friend told me in lugubrious earnest that he had suffered a major loss, all his garden gnomes had been stolen during the night. 'Twenty-one assorted gnomes, pixies, elves and trolls,' he reported deeply. 'And the windmill.'

The police, he added, said, 'It wasn't malicious.' The gnomes, pixies, elves and trolls were later found lined up at a country bus stop, but he never got the windmill back.

My daily round in Woodford, now undertaken by bicycle, included the required calls on undertakers and the subsequent usually sad and often embarrassing calls to bereaved homes. Once a widow actually clutched me as she wept because there was no one else to clutch. It was an unhappy task gathering memories for publication but the final shame was the instruction that the reporter, having garnered all the information about the bowling club, war service, the love of his garden or her interest in knitting, would then be required to ask for three shillings and sixpence for the insertion of an official notice, separate from the news report, in the Deaths column. I managed to do this a couple of times but it stuck in my throat. Fortunately there was a rider to the instruction which said that if the bereaved family refused to part with three and sixpence then the reporter was to insert the death notice anyway, free, the idea being to make the rival newspaper think we were carrying more advertising than we actually were. I, and most of the others who had this indignity forced upon them, simply wrote the notice without asking for the money and said that the family had refused to pay up. It was such a miserable subterfuge.

One afternoon, calling at a cottage where an old lady had died, I was astonished to see, as the door was opened, not one but *two* coffins in the tight front room. As sometimes happens, the death of one lifelong partner resulted in the quick following of the other. Then I discovered that the deceased woman's sister had dropped dead on hearing the news and the deceased man's brother had done likewise. Naturally I told this to one of the senior reporters and it appeared the next day in all the national newspapers. He pocketed the proceeds.

I was, however, becoming aware of the bounty called linage, the journalist's perk of adding to his income by transmitting local stories of sufficient interest to Fleet Street newspapers. On November the Fifth I was on a bus and I saw Woodford Council workmen dismantling Guy Fawkes bonfires which had taken children many hours to build. Getting off the bus I asked the men why this was happening and was informed that the bonfires were in unauthorised places. I telephoned the London *Evening News* and they sent a proper reporter to Woodford and the topical story appeared on the front page that evening. I received one guinea for my tip. When I showed it to one of the boys at the hostel he said: 'Don't you feel like a common informer?'

The trouble was that I did.

Naturally I was deeply in love again; now with a laughing woman reporter called Sybil who was in her twenties and never caught so much as a sniff of my devotion; her unawareness was such that she went off and married another journalist called Fred who roared around on a motorbike. Fortunately a fresh girl with blonde ringlets joined as a junior and within a few days I had charmed her to having coffee at the Kardomah and taken her to the ballet at the People's Palace in the Mile End Road.

Since I had now been a reporter for several months I was able to impress her considerably. When no one else was looking I would turn my collar up, speak out of the corner of my mouth and wear a pencil behind my ear. I lent her a book about journalism and, keeping to my scenario, I inserted a creased piece of paper between its pages as if it were some overlooked message. It read something like: 'Thomas – re. the Smithson murder story. I think you're right. The police won't listen. Keep digging.' It was prosaically signed 'Miss Rose', who was my chief reporter on the *Woodford Times*. I had folded the paper – the rough toilet-roll variety upon which we wrote our reports – and abbreviated some of the words so that it looked authentic. Reality, however, was somewhat less breathless; a round of dancing displays, Conservative whist drives, flower shows, rabbit club meetings, and amateur theatricals, with the odd funeral to add drama.

Possibly because I had no real home to which I could return in the evenings, I came in for a great many of these assignments, which few others welcomed. Rotary Club functions replenished my repertoire of jokes and I drank chummy half-pints of brown ale with the elite of the Chamber of Commerce. Dancing school displays were graphically described, as was *See How They Run* performed energetically at the parish hall. I took an interest in people's angora rabbits and King Edward potatoes. Pleased organisations wrote appreciative letters to the editor and I was given another ten shillings a week. At sports meetings I noted the winning times for the egg-and-spoon race ('A new record was set at Woodford Green on Saturday . . .') and if at weekends I made a few runs or scored a goal on my own behalf I made sure it was well reported. Once I was playing football on a Sunday and we lost 14–1. My report failed to mention by name any of the numerous goal scorers on the victorious side, indeed their blitzkrieg was mentioned only in passing, but the construction and final execution of my brilliantly worked, though lonely goal, was recounted in detail. It appeared with the headline: 'Fine Goal by Thomas'.

Part of my mid-week duties was to visit vicars and ministers and to keep a finger on the pulsating world of Women's Institutes, Mothers' Meetings, as well as the Folk Dance Society, the Model Engine Club and the Woodcraft Folk. A mechanical Methodist minister used to whirl me around his parish on the back of his powerful and terrifying motor cycle. Once I was so frightened that I bellowed over his shoulder that even if he were ready for Heaven I was not. One day we went to a district gathering of a wives' and mothers' organisation. About a hundred of them were sitting around the wooden walls of a large hall, facing inwards, slapping their thighs and singing: 'Thousands have been here, thousands more to come . . .'

Another job handed to me was to write a weekly précis of the films coming up at the local cinema in Wanstead. This only involved collecting the publicity material from the manager, roughly working out the story and compiling the column. It assured me of a free seat at the pictures twice a week, although the manager made it clear that if I took anyone else they would have to pay and I was accountable for such accessories as ice cream.

From my thirty shillings a week and what I could add to my expenses, I had to pay fifteen shillings for my keep at the hostel. Next door lived a nice wealthy couple called Hensher – he was a furniture manufacturer – who, wanting to encourage me on my way through life, told me that if I ever needed anything, but *anything*, I was to go to them. Many years later I met with widowed Mrs Hensher on a cruise liner and she recalled that the only imposition I made on their generosity was on the night immediately following their offer. 'We wondered what you wanted,' she laughed. 'You came to the door and reminded us that we offered to help you in any way – and then asked if we had anything you could use to go to a fancy dress ball. We gave you a table cloth and you went as an Arab.'

221

I recall the ball well because the reporter assigned to cover it for the paper, a handsome lad with a well-rehearsed enigmatic smile and a trilby, put a card saying 'Press' in his hat brim and won a prize as a reporter. Walking home with Tom Merrin, we found a horse with a bowed head wandering towards us through the gloom. It had a forlorn halter around its neck and Tom suggested that we should tie it to somebody's door knocker. There was a small cottage nearby and we coaxed the horse down the garden path and hitched him to the brass knocker. As he moved about the knocker began to knock and an old lady wearing a nightie who came to the door had a terrible fright when the horse walked in.

With my pocket money I began buying books. Neville Cardus's *Autobiography* was the first and *How to be a Sporting Journalist* followed, and then *The English Counties in Pictures* and *The Poems of Rupert Brooke*. A girl I had taken to a few dances gave me a *Bedside Shakespeare*, which was the nearest we ever got to any bedside. These books are on my shelves today, each with the square-lettered inscription: 'L.J. Thomas, Iona House, Hollybush Hill, Snaresbrook, London, E. 11.'

My life on the paper was enjoyable although every week at Voluntary Place was an unending frenzy. When so many editions were produced in such a rush on such machinery and with such facilities, mistakes did creep in. There was a libel action when a court report stated that a man had cruelly burned his wife with a *red*-hot poker. The poker had not been red, but white. The man's defence was that he did not realise it was hot. Then someone in error consulted a year-old calendar and all the various twenty-five papers announced that summer time would begin (or end) on the Sunday night. It was a week early. People missed appointments, children were sent to bed at the wrong time, and a bus company was in chaos. Somehow the extraordinary monster croaked on.

When Christmas came it seemed quite logical that I should go back to Dickies. Unfortunately, on the usual basis that I was the one without family commitments, I was assigned to cover a football match at Ilford on Christmas morning. In those days there was a Christmas Day train service and at the final whistle I hared down the street to Newbury Park Station and arrived at Kingston, on the extreme opposite side of London, at three in the afternoon, just in time for the plum pudding.

One day to my astonishment my brother turned up at the hostel. We had kept conscientiously in touch since our reunion but I was quite unprepared for his arrival. Barnardo's had again overlooked telling me. After a long six years we were to live together again. It was not easy. He was a roamer, a law unto himself, who liked to wander off with the milkman, and have me searching the streets for him as we had once done in faraway Newport.

He left his mark in various places, which included the incident of his initials carved in the soot underneath the local railway bridge. Last year I was being interviewed by a woman writer and I mentioned the death of my elder brother in Tokyo. When this appeared in print the word 'elder' was omitted and I had a letter from a boyhood friend of Roy's sympathising with me on his departure, and recalling that his initials were cut deep into the organ loft at Long Crendon in Buckinghamshire where he spent his years with his foster parents.

On the very day my brother arrived at the hostel, however, something else occurred. When I returned from work there was an important-looking letter waiting for me. On His Majesty's Service, it said, and instructed me to report to Devizes Barracks, Wiltshire, where they were going to make me into a soldier. Or try.

PART THREE

THE VIRGIN SOLDIER

IX

No bright-eyed, patriotic volunteer of the Great War ever looked forward to being recruited into the army more keenly than I did. At one point, between my registering for national service and receiving my reporting orders, I actually marched into the local Ministry of Labour office and demanded to know exactly *when* I was to be called up. I thought they had forgotten me. This eagerness to get into the army was only matched, after a short period in uniform, by my eagerness to get out again.

I decided that if I were to play my full part in the forces of my country then I ought to be posted to the Army News Service, which produced magazines and handled press and public relations. To this end I wrote to the War Office (on notepaper potently headed the *Woodford Times*) and informed them of the luck that was about to come their way. Since the primary thing that military life achieves in a conscript is to blunt ambition, this aim was at once thwarted. Its attainment was initially and lastingly damaged, I was later to realise, by my first interview with the civil servant to whom I reported for national service registration, some three months before my actual call-up.

'What is your profession?' he enquired over his

glasses and the counter. Then, as if he thought the words might be too difficult: 'What do you do for a living?'

'I'm a journalist,' I replied, pulling my collar up and striking an attitude which looked as if I might start asking a few questions myself.

He sighed ill-temperedly and laid down his pen. 'Aw, come on, son,' he said. 'I haven't got all day. I'm fed up with you kids coming here and telling me you've got fancy jobs. You can't all be ruddy field marshals.'

'I'm a journalist,' I repeated firmly. I fiddled in my pocket for my union card.

'What sort?' he grunted. Then sarcastically, 'Editor of *The Times* are you?'

'Not yet,' I replied modestly. 'I'm a junior reporter.'

He wrote: 'Junior *porter*'. I did not see my records until many months later and I was shocked at the libel. In the event, I suppose, I was very lucky I did not spend my army time carrying loads around on my head.

One of the motives behind my eagerness to serve the King was my desire to cut for good the bonds that still held me to Barnardo's. After all I was eighteen, a trifle old for an orphan. In the event, of course, all I was doing was moving from one institution to another. For me the army was nothing new; I was back in a dormitory again. Another aspect of my military ambition was that it might enable me to travel overseas and meet a lower class of woman. I was weary and frustrated with the Saturday dances; with walking hand in hand, the cumbersome kissing on doorsteps and the long lonely treks home after the last bus had vanished.

228

Nothing ever *happened*. Once, with trembling hand, I had touched a girl's nipple and as if I had pressed some activating button she burst into tears. This was no way for a lusty young chap to live.

So truly a Virgin Soldier, I boarded the train to Devizes, Wiltshire, to commence the great adventure. My calling-up papers had disappointed me in one way, in that I was not joining a famous regiment. The War Office had blundered. It also remained indifferent to my pointed suggestions about the Army News Service. I was joining the Royal Army Pay Corps. They were going to train me to be a clerk.

Reluctantly I cast aside the thoughts of putting through a telephone call to Whitehall protesting that I could scarcely add up my expenses let alone the army's, or demanding at least to be conscripted into my father's old regiment, the Royal Artillery, or into the Royal Engineers like my Uncle Bert who had fallen so fatally into Newport dry dock.

My complaint, of course, had firm foundations, for in the British Army it was commonplace knowledge that if you desired to be a parachutist then you applied for a posting as a cook. Equally any men with culinary skills found themselves dangling on strings in the sky. It seemed to me illogical that, at some expense, the Government was going to keep me for eighteen months doing something for which I had no aptitude whatever. Even when I eventually settled to the dull and drearsome life in the Pay Office in Singapore, I had good shorthand speed and I could type, but these jobs were allotted to civilians while I tried to make sense of army accounting.

My entry in *Who's Who* sums up succinctly the resulting period of my life. It says: 'Army service 1949–51. Rose to lance-corporal.'

At first, however, it was almost as brisk and interesting as I had hoped, even if I continued not meeting women. Basic training, the nightmare of so many writers who have described it, I found to be enervating. It was July and the Wiltshire weather was fine. We pounded up and down the barrack square, shouting out the time of the movements like chorus girls; our feet emerging with howling blisters from boots stiff as tombstones. On the firing range I discovered that I could not close my left eye independently to sight my shots and so I either had to fire the 303 service rifle left-handed or somehow block out the vision of my non-aiming eye. We were among the last soldiers to use the elongated weapons, for they were phased out quickly after that, and the monster proved impossible to aim and control with the wrong hand. The first time I tried, the kick jolted it sideways, to the extreme anxiety of the recruit in the next firing position.

'Right, Thomas,' bellowed the sergeant-instructor. 'If you are not to inflict widespread and nasty casualties on your own side, you 'ad better block up your left mince pie with somatt.'

Thus I had to fix a handkerchief under my beret or steel helmet, hold the other end tight between my teeth, thus cutting out the vision of the contrary eye. 'Good lad, Thomas,' approved the instructor on inspecting the white device. 'When you want to surrender – wave it.'

For the first few days we went around like cardboard men in the new, stiff, ill-fitting, battledress. Some big youths had to embarrassingly march up and down the square in their own clothes and shoes until outsize supplies arrived. There were twenty or so men to a barrack hut, the buildings arranged in what were known as 'spiders', each section of huts being linked by corridors. A good-natured Scots corporal slept in a room at the end of ours and there was a similarly humorous NCO in the neighbouring barrack room, a big, blue-chinned Cockney whose shouted orders could be heard in distant Devizes on market day. The platoon sergeant was a small springy individual, a little action-man, full of bullshit as sergeants were thought and ought to be. Bullshit was a word we began to use with energy; also fuck and fucking. I had never used this oath since my mother warned me that it was the Devil's private word and I could drop dead on the spot, but now I renewed the acquaintanceship with enthusiasm, and I've been using it on and off ever since. Apart from 'bollocks' there were few other swearwords. The ones we used were designed to fit each and every occasion.

My years in Dickies had prepared me better than most for the army life. I was accustomed to hearing twenty different rhythms of breathing in a long, moonlit room. One night I heard one of the youths sobbing under his sheets. 'Don't worry,' I advised with the voice of experience. 'It's only for eighteen months.' At that he cried even louder.

Dollops of bromide were put in our tea, it was said to reduce our sexual urges, and there was plenty of

231

shinning up ropes, running across fields while shouting, lying in ambush among red ants, marching and counter-marching and charging into a room full of tear gas (for what purpose I never discovered). There were lectures on the cleaning of rifles with a pull-through, oil bottle and a magic piece of material called four-by-two. And, of course, there was bayonet practice.

Nothing about military days has ever had so much note from writers as bayonet practice. To anyone of any sensibility it was the most revulsive and haunting part of training. Firing bullets at distant targets was a remote pretence, even though the holes they gouged out of the earth were ominously wide, but to thrust a bayonet was something more personal and proximate.

'Them channels, down the side of the weapon,' mentioned the action-man sergeant with anticipatory enjoyment. 'What are they for? Anyone?'

The squad regarded him dumbly, no one liking to mention it. The bayonets gleamed in the Devizes sun. 'Blood!' he would bark at us, running his finger pleasurably down the groove. 'For the blood of your enemy, the one what you have just slaughtered. Now, let's see how you can use them.'

A line of sand-stuffed sacks, already hanging like executed men, were the targets of this barbaric rite. It has become a familiar scene in books, plays and films, and for me, as for many, it never loses its personal horror. In Carl Foreman's film of *The Virgin Soldiers* two twee privates (one played by the ballet dancer Wayne Sleep, then unknown, as were others in the cast who subsequently became famous) are required to charge at the sacks. As they do they emit

the traditional howl: 'Stick it in – twist it – pull it out.'
One of them faints.

It was very near the truth. In the unlikely event of
the Royal Army Pay Corps having to charge 'over the
top', steel pointing towards enemy torsos, then I'm
afraid there were more than a few, myself included,
who would have been unable to bring themselves to
make the final deadly thrust and would have doubtless known the consequences.

What was extraordinary, however, considering that
most of the recruits had been conscripted very much
against their will, was the way we began to think and
act like regimental robots. There was a barrack room
competition with points awarded for the cleanest coal
bucket, the neatest beds and for the smartest man on
nightly guard duty. He would be 'stick-man', be
dismissed from the duty and return to his comrades
in triumph with another ten brownie points on the
total. The eventual prize was an extra day's leave.

Such was the enthusiasm to get the man detailed
for guard as shining as possible, that almost surrealistic rituals were observed. To send him unblemished
to the parade was everything. Everyone in the barrack
room would take a hand with the preparations. No
virgin ever went to a marriage bed more enhanced.
His uniform was ironed until the creases cut, his
buttons and buckles were burnished as gold, lead
weights inserted into his trousers ensured that they
hung symmetrically over his balanced gaiters. Spit,
blacking and other mystic and unmentionable combin-
ations, steeped in army lore, went into the lustre of
his boots. His hair was cut, his nose was blown, the

interior barrel of his rifle reflected the probing human eye. At the end he was arrayed in his panoply and *carried*, yes *carried*, on a litter to the guard parade, so that no speck of dust would dull him.

The litter carriers, having deposited this khaki peacock, would then repair to the barrack room, for it was considered bad luck to remain watching the guard parade while the chosen soldier was drilled and inspected by the orderly officer. If he returned to the room, having been dismissed from the guard, there followed scenes of rejoicing. Often he did not return, for competition was keen, and we would wait with gradually descending spirits. Once our champion, having failed, returned during his four hours off-duty, and burst into remorseful tears. Admittedly it was the youth I had heard crying in the night, an emotional individual with the unfortunate surname Bandy, but it was an emotive moment. We had sent him out spick and shining and he had failed the officer's survey.

'I farted,' he wailed. 'I couldn't help it. I just farted.'

Weekend leave came after a month in camp during which our social activities were confined to drinking cider at the NAAFI and having Sunday breakfast in the Church Army canteen. Our first freedom was greatly anticipated and on the Friday night there was a queue to use the barrack room ironing board. I had to admit to myself, as I stared into the full length mirror provided at the gate guardhouse (to make sure you looked smart as you left camp), that the vision presented was somewhat less than the conquering hero. My uniform remained as stiff as sandpaper except at the knees and elbows. I wore the insignia of the

Aldershot District on my arm, crossed searchlights which looked reasonably martial, but the words Royal Army Pay Corps bowed across each shoulder in blue and yellow did nothing but diminish the warrior image. Some of the old hands wore shoulder flashes which merely said 'RAPC'. Enquiring girls in pubs and dance halls could then be told that it was the Royal Army Parachute Corps ('Tomorrow could be my last day') and quite a lot of them believed it.

If the aspect of a non-combatant was something I wished to avoid then my beret betrayed me even more than the shoulder flashes. It was of the old-fashioned khaki variety, unyielding and ridiculous, squatting on my head like a squashed brown cardboard box. I had tried sleeping on it, stamping on it, soaking it overnight, throwing it against the barrack room wall, but it retained its stiff groteque shape, and my embarrassment. Few men have ever looked less soldierlike than the narrow youth topped with the ill-shaped hat who boarded the train for London on that August day. A kindly lady enquired whether the bristly khaki was very hot to wear and her husband grunted: 'He's too skinny to sweat, ain't you son.' My cap badge was a sturdy lion surmounted by a crown, below it a scroll with the words *Fide et Fiducia*. Faith and Confidence. Sitting in the corner seat looking at 'Royal Army Pay Corps' reflected in the window I had very little of either.

My leave was spent in the only home I knew – Dickies. Old boys strolled back regularly now that Vernon Paul had taken over as Superintendent. They went back, sometimes having only left the previous week, and sauntered about the terrible old pile with a proprietorial air and hands in pockets, something that the Gaffer had never allowed even on the most shivering of mornings when we were lined up in the open in our vests waiting for our turn in the wash-house.

Many of my generation were now doing national service and they strutted about more than most, telling the little kids how tough the home was in their day and relating unlikely adventures of their careers in the army or air force. One boy, Tom Chaffey, had joined the Royal Marines for *twenty-five* years, and he had a splendid and well-deserved dark blue dress uniform.

'Nightshirt', my old dormitory mate Frank Knights, was on leave in his uniform of the Royal Electrical and Mechanical Engineers. He blanched when he saw my shoulder flashes. 'The Pay Corps,' he said caustically. 'The Pay Corps!' He regarded my sparse khaki figure as perhaps an officer of the Household Cavalry might have done. 'I should do something about that,' he advised. 'And quick.'

'What can I do?' I demanded miserably.

'Why don't you desert?' he suggested.

Back in the barracks it was explained to us that wicked women could send us blind, eventually that is, and that we ought to have pride in our regiment. After all Napoleon had said that an army marched on its stomach, and he might easily have added that it went into battle on its pay packet. Soldiers who were not paid, were soldiers who did not care to fight. It was also necessary for the man going into action to know that his wife and family were receiving their proper allowances. I felt better about it after that.

That summer of 1949 was only four years after the

war had ended, and yet they were talking about the start of another one.

'Wait till the balloon goes up!' our action-man sergeant used to exclaim happily, banging his small tight boots on the square. 'The Ruskies will have you lot for breakfast!'

I felt vaguely cheated. After all we had been told and all we had expected, there was every sign that we were going to have to fight again. Only yesterday, it seemed, we were collecting money to buy weapons for Russia. And this time I would be old enough. Nevertheless military training was at least open-air activity and it was a fine summer. Charging across corn stubble, burning realistically as if some scorched earth policy was being pursued, made me feel quite warlike although my enthusiasm would have doubtless waned perceptibly if a Stalin tank had appeared on the next hill.

With the second part of the basic training course came four weeks of technical instruction in army accounts. My heart plunged into my boots and stayed there. We sat in hot huts, with the September sun pouring down on the countryside outside the windows, and endured the most boring month of my life. Not only did I not understand the work, I had no urge to understand it. I wrote a private letter to the War Office, explaining what was happening to the ace reporter of the *Woodford Times* – what potential they were over-looking. Someone wrote back and, in a sentence, said it was hard luck.

The month ended with the Passing-Out Parade, the climax of the whole ten weeks' training. We had further drilling rehearsals in the evenings, after putting the damned ledgers away for the day, and our action-man sergeant, eyes and chest bulging, voice squeaky with emotion, promised every punishment in hell if we did not win the award for the best platoon on the day. And we really *wanted* to win; for ourselves and for our sergeant. But, on the night before the big parade, tragedy struck. Something terrible happened to Farrell.

Farrell was a tall, thickly spectacled youth with a galaxy of pimples. At that time there was a radio comedy team called Forsyth, Seaman and Farrell, and our Farrell, staring tall and blindly from the ranks, was known to the drill instructor, the good-natured blue-chinned Cockney, as: 'Forsyth, Seaman and Fucking Farrell' when there was reason to bawl in his direction, which was often.

Farrell, however, had a gift. He possessed a loud whisper. We had been taught to drill by numbers, each movement accompanied by the timing of one-one-two-three, and sometimes even four. At first, in our early days, we had all bellowed these numbers as we raised our knees and stamped our feet, wheeled, whirled, presented arms, thrust out legs and marched. In the more advanced stages, however, only one time-keeper was designated and this was Farrell. From his height his loud whisper would hiss across the heads of the squad, unheard by anyone at the distance of a saluting base, and we would perform the movements accordingly. He was the mainspring of the platoon. Then, on the night before the Passing-Out Parade, Farrell, possibly through sheer fright, lost his voice. He came into the barrack room mouthing things that no one could hear. At first we thought he was joking and told him sternly not to make fun about things like that. Then we realised he was not. He was rushed to the latrines and made to gargle with everything anyone could think of from cough mixture to whisky. Someone tried to scrub his tonsils with a toothbrush while the rest of us held him down. He was theatrically sick but his voice stayed resolutely absent.

Even before this disaster our barrack room had not been thick with confidence over the outcome of the Passing-Out Parade. We were lagging in the points table and now our opportunity for glory and an extra twenty-four hours' leave seemed doomed. No one else wanted the job of whispering. It was not a difficult task but one fundamental error could throw the whole squad into disarray and disgrace. The onus was placed on the nervous shoulders of Private Bandy.

'Me! I *can't* do it!' he moaned. 'I'll muck it up, honest I will!' It appeared he was declining into one of his sobbing fits. Brusquely he was told that there was no backing out. If persuasion were needed then his bed could be hauled with him in it to the rafters of the hut. It had been done before and he had tumbled out onto the hard floor below. With a defeated sob he nodded agreement.

Everything went wrong the next day. The inspecting senior officer arrived from Aldershot and the barrier at the gate became stuck and could not be raised to admit his staff car, so everyone was on edge from the start. Action-man stomped onto the square, muttering little orders as we marched. Other platoons went through their drill, heads cocked, arms straight, boots hitting the parade ground like mallets. We watched with lowering spirits.

When our turn came we stiffened our resolve, and managed to march correctly into position. The initial drill movements were negotiated safely. No one dropped their rifle and Bandy's whispered timing was audible if not convincing. Then, as we began the marching and counter-marching, his nerve cracked. Hesitation entered the hisses. Some we failed to hear at all, although he afterwards swore he uttered them. Action-man detected at once that all was not going well. The responses to his bark and his stamping feet became a matter of conjecture. Then, with a wild alteration of whispering in the middle of an about turn and a quick wheel left, the ranks faltered, fell out of time and step and finally panicked. Comrades collided with each other, half the platoon continued in one direction and the other stamped off at a tangent. Eyes swivelled. Men in the separating vanguards began to perform a curious knock-kneed side-stepping movement, not seen in the drill manual, in an attempt to join up again. When action-man finally and emotionally barked us to a halt we were spread like a posse over half the parade ground. Somebody started laughing on the sidelines. Action-man's eyes dilated. 'I'll kill 'em, bloody kill 'em,' we heard him incanting. The inspecting officer slapped his cane on his thigh impatiently and soon strode off to lunch. We clattered crushed to the barrack room.

Sitting on our beds, waiting for him, we said nothing. We could not even look at each other. Private Bandy was shaking so much his bedside locker was rattling. Action-man stamped in, his countenance like a bright, tight plum.

'I'm disgraced! Finished! Fucking finished!' he bawled as we sprang to our feet. He bounced in front of us. 'You 'orrible fucking shower, all of you.' He made for Bandy. 'As for you, son! I'm going to fucking well *kill* you.'

Private Bandy burst into tears.

The following week, gladly, we dispersed throughout the country to the various units to which we had been posted. There was a barracks concert the night before departure. I had to stand at the side of the stage with a blackboard upon which were written the Regimental Sergeant-Major's jokes. His eyes would swivel towards me and I would point to the key-word for the next joke in the list. During the course of doing this I managed to wipe half his repertoire off the board with my sleeve and he was none too pleased. I was quite glad to get away from the place in the end.

In the early morning after the concert, immediately before we left, I had to take some props to action-man's married quarters. I stood in his army sitting room and through a door I could see his wife humped in their bed. He came out, much smaller in pyjamas, and smiled a sickly smile as he took the props from me. 'You're a good lad, you are,' he whispered. Then he attempted to embrace me.

I got out of the quarters as quickly as I knew how, running back towards the barracks. His voice followed me, the old familiar bawl. 'That's right, Thomas! At the double, lad! At the double!'

*

During the following weeks something happened that became the root of a family tragedy, its bleak and unhappy echoes occurring over the years. It came out of the past and has continued into the future.

My posting had taken me to the Regimental Pay Office at Whitchurch in Hampshire where, to my relief, I was directed to the orderly room where my short-hand and typing were of use and life was very congenial when compared to the pen-scraping boredom of the accounts sections.

The army took on an unhurried almost domestic pace, a weekly routine of work and sports, pay parade, the ironing of uniforms in preparation for weekend leave. Virtually the only drill was the short march and salute at the pay table on Thursdays. Then, thrilled, I saw that 22157741 Private THOMAS L. was on a draft which was scheduled to sail for Singapore in December. The orderly room sergeant told me that I did not *have* to go if I did not feel inclined; after all a Communist terrorist war had broken out in Malaya. It might even be dangerous. I could easily be removed from the list if I wished to spend the rest of my eighteen months service in the cosy confines of the office. I begged him not to do it. Singapore! The mystic Orient! Wicked women!

Two weeks before I was due to sail, I received a letter from Chris, my uncle in Wales, a sort of anchor man for my dispersed and generally disinterested family, telling me that my elder brother Harold – Hally of whom I had not heard since he had, years before, sent me the tin of sweets – was dangerously ill in Birmingham.

242

Since I was about to be posted overseas I was granted compassionate leave and a rail warrant to Birmingham. There I was met by a sister-in-law I did not know existed. She was a gaunt girl, inarticulate and full of worry. My brother was in hospital she said nervously, and was in danger of dying. When I asked what the illness was she answered miserably: 'He's gone mad.'

They had four little daughters, all under six, and lived in a confined and noxious slum, a crumbling house in one of four terraces around a square at the centre of which were communal lavatories.

We went to visit him in hospital the next day. The poor girl trembled with nervousness and shame as we were led through corridor after corridor. Great locks were undone and bars rattled away until eventually we went into a ward where my brother Hally was sitting up cheerfully in bed. He showed no sign of surprise that I had turned up. He was not even sure who I was. I was in my army uniform and he imagined I had come to recruit him to fight somewhere.

'I can sing,' he suddenly announced and launched into a baritone ballad. 'I play rugby for Newport, you know,' he boasted. Wasted and white, he sat in the bed. 'And,' he whispered, 'I've lived with the Trappist monks.' He nodded to the man in the next bed and winked. 'He's barmy, he is,' he confided. 'Off his rocker.'

Stunned I led his tearful wife out of the ward. I was only eighteen but I had more confidence and logic than she could summon, poor lady. I sought out a doctor whom I finally traced to the hospital dance. A

243

band was playing and a lot of people were waltzing around the floor. 'Everyone seems to be having a good time,' I ventured after I had told him who I was. A woman suddenly began whooping and jumping up and down. 'That's matron,' he nodded.

'Your brother,' he told me. 'Has general paralysis of the insane, GPI we call it. We are treating him as best as we can but there is no hope that he will ever recover. It's caused by untreated syphilis, you know. He's like that for life.'

It was early in the Christmas season. On the following day I took the four little girls, the youngest under two, to Lewis's store in the city to see Santa Claus.

The weather was icy and I wore a civilian overcoat – my brother's probably – over my army khaki and I worried in case I encountered any military police.

On the following day their mother accompanied me to the station and this stranger, who was my brother's wife, kissed me on the cheek and lent me half-a-crown because I had hardly any money. As soon as I got my first pay packet on my return to camp I wrote to her and enclosed a postal order in repayment of the loan. After that, when I reached Singapore, I sent her several letters but I never received a reply. The Thomas family had withdrawn into its isolation again. I was not to know for many years of the terrible thing that was to happen.

December of that year saw some spectacularly raging weather around the British shores. Dented ships limped into Liverpool and you could almost hear them sigh with relief as they berthed. We, however, were sailing out.

Marching from Lime Street Station to the dockside was hard enough, for the wind battered against us as we pressed forward in our widespread greatcoats and our bulky kit. We marched bent forward and as we did so the gale was shredded by a sleet storm. In the stoic tradition of the British Tommy we tried to sing in fractured voices. Not many people were about the streets in that awful weather but some who paused to see us march by were treated to one or other of the traditional digital salutes of the British soldier, the thumb or the two fingers up.

'Thank God we've got a navy,' taunted a building site labourer, sheltering and idle. I bent forward with the rest, imagining I was being heroic, perhaps even leading the retreat from Moscow. My military ambitions were confined to fantasy, however; not that I minded the wind and sleet. After all I was off to Singapore.

The troopship's white hull almost merged with the clay-coloured sky. We tramped up the gangway in the sleety wind. No band played. No one was there to see us off, nor did we expect there to be. Before the ship cast off it was announced that there were postal officials aboard who would accept what were somewhat ominously classed as 'last messages to the next of kin'. I had no idea who my next of kin might be but, perhaps to show myself as much as anyone else that I belonged to someone in the world, I queued with the others and sent a telegram to the plump girl

I had met the previous evening at a dance in Slough. She made Mars Bars for a living, at a chocolate factory just along the road from the transit camp where we had been posted to await the troopship. Romantically I had walked her home, the soldier on his last night before going to a distant war, and we had shared a fumbling cuddle at her gate. She had given me a chaste kiss and a free Mars Bar, which I munched on my way back to camp. Now I sent her the dramatic message: 'Sailing troopship *Orbita*, Liverpool, today. Goodbye. Love Les.'

I don't know whether she ever received it because I never saw her again. My sense of petty drama often obstructed more practical things; on the voyage I wrote to my Auntie Kate in Wales heading the notepaper: 'Somewhere in the Indian Ocean' and she simply replied to that address. I had appended my Singapore address but she ignored that. The letter took ten months to find me, having been presumably floating around in tropical waters until then. This grasping onto people, casual acquaintances and scarcely known relatives, seems banal now that I have my own family. But in those days, I suppose, I needed to feel I had known *someone*, *anyone*, long enough to send them a telegram even if I had only met them the previous night. When the ship reached Port Said I paid ten shillings to a bumboatman for an aromatic toilet case, splitting at the seams and loaded with bottles of sordid liquid. You could smell it from the deck. This I kept for my Mars Bar love as well. At least initially. When she stopped writing (she met a boy in the coconut department) I reserved it for the lucky girl, whoever she was, who might take her place. For the whole eighteen months I was in Singapore I kept it. When all the contents of my barrack room locker were stolen, just before I was due to return home, the thief left it behind. By then it had so fallen to pieces that it was hardly worthwhile stealing anyway and in the end I dropped it in a rubbish bin just before sailing. A waste of ten shillings if there ever was.

Despite the December tempests, and the forecasts of more and worse to follow, the SS *Orbita* cast off on time and proceeded up the murky Mersey. We were sitting in the messroom, at the midday eating shift, when the BBC News, being broadcast over our heads from loudspeakers, and retelling the terrible storm, announced: 'The troopship *Orbita*, with a thousand men for the Far East, was unable to sail from Liverpool this morning because of the bad weather.' Everyone cheered this travesty. At that moment we felt the bow begin to dip.

I had never been to sea, apart from crossing to the Isle of Man on the ferry, also from Liverpool, but my father's and my grandfather's blood must have been there in my veins because I found I enjoyed it; I watched the Liver Birds disappear into the ragged sky and then turned and sniffed the raw ocean. Outward bound, I whispered to myself, I was outward bound. That day, and for three days after, it was raw indeed. Black waves, with sharp white edges, lumbered from the horizon and battered the large ship, throwing her this way and that and sometimes in both directions at once. The sky shrieked, the rain deluged, landward lighthouses flashed distantly. Sheltering in a companionway hatch I watched the drama spill across the sea.

My face was wet with salt, my hair felt as if it would be torn off by the gale. Hanging onto a stanchion or a rope I let myself sway and dip with the deck. Sometimes I hummed 'Fingal's Cave'.

For most of the time I was up there alone, apart from the crew who were largely unenthusiastic about my poetic feelings. A friendly chap from the galley who came up for a breath of air now and again, confessed that the only thing he really liked about the sea was when the Liver Birds again appeared over the horizon and he knew he would soon be paid off and home. He had been everywhere but seen nothing but a few bars. Like my father he could scarcely pronounce some of the romantic names. He was content to spend his time below in the dry.

Every now and then I would go to the lower decks myself and walk among what appeared to be the dead and the dying. There was a unit of the Coldstream Guards aboard and they had never looked so small. Soldiers lay groaning everywhere. When I reported at mealtimes and ate heartily, I was one of only a dozen who managed to get to the table and these valiant few would invariably be diminished by the end of the sausage and mash or fatty pork fillet.

My own close comrades scarcely rose from the horizontal by day or night although such inducements as bingo, dance-band rehearsals, and a quiz were dangled tantalisingly. One fellow, a professional corporal, who complained more bitterly than any conscript about the army sending him abroad, kept muttering dark poetry to me: 'Can you still see England? Is the land in sight?' Perhaps he had thoughts of making a swim for it.

We sighted no other vessels except the famous

German training barque *Pamir* with her crew of boys, plunging and rolling through the great grey storm. She sank only shortly after; all the youthful sailors being lost.

After two days of this wayward voyage I saw from the framed chart that we were about to leave the last outriders of England. Going out to the port side of the ship, with the oily smoke from the funnels flying around me, I looked over broken ocean to the Isles of Scilly. They lay low like whales against the horizon, the light from the Bishop Rock winked a last goodbye. The deep sky had broken for a while and above the islands fell pale fingers of wintry sunlight. I thought I could see a white smudge, perhaps a house on the shore. At that moment I felt very sad in my heart for it came to me that I was truly leaving, that the last land would disappear out of sight and that my life would again change. Islands, even then, were very attractive to me and I would have been glad to be going there instead of some unknown far country. As it was, I went below and told the morose regular soldier that indeed England was slipping away. He made the prophecy that he would never return alive, but he did. On the voyage he found a medical book and studied it carefully. Within a few weeks of arriving in Singapore he was given a discharge on the grounds of chronic ill-health and went happily home.

While the storms persisted the Jonahs, those of them who could actually raise themselves on their elbows and speak, forecast that worse was to come, for before us was the dreaded Bay of Biscay. We slept on crowded troop decks, in bunks layered one above the other, although these were an improvement on some troop-ships where the other ranks also had their meals in the same cramped space, an uncongenial experience in a turbulent sea.

When we entered the notorious bay, however, it sat quietly waiting for us, sunshine soft as a smile upon its face. The ship eased her rolling and the soldiers began to appear, blinking in the light, pacing the deck and pointing out the European mainland to each other. Other ranks had to keep to one area of the ship and were not allowed to pass into the officers' accommo-dation. It was possible, however, for a conscript to crane his neck out and peep into the forward saloon where lieutenants only our age lounged about in what seemed acres of room sipping drinks and talking to *women*. These were service wives going out to join their husbands in the Far East. And the officers had them to themselves.

In the army, however, there are always ways. There was a call for volunteers for a concert party, an *all-ranks'* concert party. Those who wished to take part should report to the purser's office, in the *forward* saloon. Swiftly I was over the barrier with my reper-toire of songs and stories learned at Rotary dinners, added to which I had a good stock of army jokes stolen from the Regimental Sergeant-Major's blackboard at Devizes.

About twenty other ranks were assembled and we were given chairs and tea. Not beer, because it was apparently thought that it might set us on a rampage.

This, however, was more like it. I took a good look at the women and they looked back, doubtless through curiosity, at the army's lower members. Lounging back in the padded chair, sipping my tea, I wondered why I could not have been an officer.

The concert was to be held on the open deck once the ship had rounded Gibraltar and was sailing through the Mediterranean. During rehearsals I began to converse with an attractive lady soprano. Each time the producer dismissed us and I had to return over the divide to the mob on the troop deck, she would accompany me to the barrier and say goodnight. Her husband was in the air force police in Singapore and was captain of the combined services' water polo team. If there was going to be an affair then it would have to be reasonably soon.

She sang beautifully and I stood, speared by romance, in the wings while she stood on the hatch-cover stage causing soldiers' eyes to dampen with 'We'll Meet Again'. Unusually for me, I almost missed my entrance.

My jokes went down well, I thought, although the act did go on rather a long time and some stories that had been suitable for smoking nights at Woodford did not meet with the full approval of a colonel's wife. This became clear when her husband eventually stood up, strode out purposefully and dragged me bodily from the stage. There was a roar of booing from the non-commissioned ranks at this, and the crew standing around the rails joined in. 'See,' said the Colonel, trying to excuse his action. 'They're booing you.'

The crew were trouble. Not to me or my fellow

conscripts, because they treated us like the boys we were. But as the voyage went on they became more rebellious and on Christmas Eve, in humid Aden, open mutiny was close. The sailors' leader was a giant New Zealander, a man like a side of beef who looked even more like one when the ship reached the sunshine because, stripped to a mass of waist, he went red, then purple, then the tone of a leather armchair. He also had a curl in his eye and he rolled around, amiably threatening, and swinging a length of knotted rope.

On Christmas Eve, after returning from Aden where we had been maudlin through Yuletide memories over warm beer in the NAAFI, we joined the passengers around the forward hatch and sang carols under the Arabian stars. Religiously waiting for the conclusion of 'Silent Night', the huge New Zealander then mounted the stage holding his knotted rope and tried to enlist our sympathy, even physical support, in the mutiny that was about to break out. 'The captain of this ship,' he bellowed, 'is a right bastard! He's refused to let us have a single bottle of drink on board to celebrate the birth of baby Jesus. Now I ask you, what fucking justice is there in that?'

It took seven military policemen, and one or two of his own shipmates who thought he had gone too far, to get him from the stage. He was put in a place of safety (from the passengers' point of view, that is) but a few days later was about the decks again. In the heat of the Red Sea there came a confrontation which we young conscripts watched with some appetite. A human barrier of Coldstream Guards was placed across the deck with a violent and vocal sergeant,

252

whereupon the grumbling crew, under their beefy leader, came one by one from a forward hatch and advanced with barefooted threat. The rank of young guardsmen looked straight ahead as the sailors advanced. At the time I personally thought that it would have been a better strategy to disable the mutineers as they emerged from the hatch, one by one, but no one asked my advice. The hairy-browed, axe-handle-swinging, rope-dangling crew neared the rank of unarmed, inexperienced but upright soldiers. At the final tense moment, with the two parties stationary and facing each other only six feet apart, the sergeant snapped an order, or rather a series of orders, managing to give the impression that he had only been trying to remember the words. 'Guard . . . stand at ease . . . Stand easy . . . Guard *dismiss*.' With sighs of relief all around (although with a certain feeling of disappointment on our part) the crew walked through. One of the guardsmen told me afterwards that they were saving their fighting for the Communist bandits in Malaya.

All was calm, at least as far as we could ascertain, until Colombo. There a naval party and civilian police (who arrived with an elephant) came to the ship and, after some negotiation, several members of the crew were transferred ashore. Later, it transpired that one of them was charged with a murder committed shortly before at a cinema in Liverpool.

Now the SS *Orbita*, in sunny seas, sailed on towards the Orient. A further call for volunteers was made, this time for Welshmen. I had not had sufficient service experience to know that you never volunteer for anything. Since the summons was for those of Welsh birth I imagined that we were required for singing but instead I found myself with a dozen others in a hold where the temperature was about a hundred degrees – skinning leeks, our national emblem.

Predictably my love affair had not come to very much. We waltzed on the deck during the all-ranks' dances and we stood at the rail and observed the ocean scuttling by. 'I want to go home,' she said moonily one night. 'This ship is going the wrong way for me.' She laid her head on my shoulder and wept: 'Please, please, take me home.'

It was a tallish order for a class three private in the Pay Corps, earning a pound a week, and being himself carried off he knew not where by forces beyond his control. 'I'll try,' I promised wildly. 'I'll think of something.'

The bravado must have been less than convincing because she afterwards transferred her devotions to a bathroom steward who had walked in while she was having a shower. He was obviously a far more worldly man than I (he had been aboard when the *Orbita* took Australian war brides to Sydney, six hundred of them, and had sailed into harbour with a pair of knickers flying at the mainmast). However, getting the ship turned around for her was also beyond him and the last he or I saw of her was when she disembarked in Singapore and fell into the arms of her husband – one of the biggest and fittest-looking RAF police water polo players I have ever seen.

For once I was not distressed. Looking out from the deck over the grey-clouded, steaming city, I knew that adventure lay there in plenty and that some portion of it might be concerned with women. With any luck my days as a virgin were numbered.

As we waited to disembark it commenced to rain, warm and soupily, and it scarcely ceased during the next thirty-seven days. I remember the total precisely because when the weather did at last clear the *Straits Times* headline proclaimed: 'Old Sol Shines Again'. It had been the longest time without sunshine that even the most ancient of Chinese could remember.

Looking down at the cluttered dockside I observed that the Europeans had iodine tans, almost yellow as if they were sick with fever. The rain rattled the palm trees and coolies cantered about with sacks over their heads. Viewed from above the warehouse roofs the city looked like a hot Newport, Mon.

As my unit clattered down the steep gangway, hung as we were with rifles and equipment, there at the bottom was a newsreel camera crew, whirring away while we raised a cheer and a few expected thumbs. It was twenty-five years before I saw that piece of film. The well-known newspaper correspondent, turned novelist, Noel Barber, wrote a book about the Malaya Emergency called *The War of the Running Dogs* and this was adapted for a television documentary. Having written *The Virgin Soldiers*, a private's eye view of that segment of history, I was interviewed as part of the programme. When I saw the entire film for the first time there was a sequence of newsreel, culled from some archive, showing national servicemen leaving a troopship in Singapore. It was us. My half-forgotten comrades were clearly recognisable and there was a moment when my head poked out from behind some-body's pack. My first appearance before the camera!

On the journey from the port to the barracks at Nee Soon, about ten miles from the city, our truck knocked over a village dog. The driver laughed and drove on. One of us newcomers protested loudly: 'No wonder they hate us out here, knocking their pets over like that!' We had much to learn. Indeed there were designated 'dog-days' when an open vehicle from each garrison drove around, with eager marskmen in the back shooting every dog in sight which did not have the benefit of a collar. Sometimes they presented such a good target that the collar was never noticed until the dog was dead. Then it was taken off and quietly thrown away.

X

Nee Soon was a broad, tropics garrison, four three-storeyed concrete barrack blocks around one square and the same pattern repeated a quarter of a mile lower down the hill. They had been planned, intended for Indian troops, in the early days of the war and had been completed conveniently in time for the Japanese occupation of Singapore. The Japanese fenced them around with wire and allied prisoners were herded into the confines, hundreds of lost souls living in appalling conditions, made to stand for hours on the open square in the fierce sun. Many died and indeed they had little to live for. The military police guard dogs of my day were struck with fear when they passed some of the buildings and refused to enter, snapping at their handlers and with their hackles raised. Bodies were discovered buried in the sports field.

These deeds were only five years old when I first arrived there in January 1950. I was never aware of any ghosts although the place was bad enough without them. We had taken thirty-five days on the journey from England. Calculating that another thirty-five days might be required to get home again and taking into account disembarkation leave and the process of demobilisation we would probably only serve ten months in Singapore. Just enough to have a good time, perhaps; something of a holiday. Or so we thought.

As soon as we arrived, handed our rifles into the armoury and left our kit within our allotted bed-space, we were taken to the mess hall. A lugubrious corporal with both a limp and warts accompanied us.

'What's the food like?' I enquired as we queued.

'Terrible,' he said solemnly. 'Fucking terrible.'

'I suppose you can always fill up with fruit,' I suggested optimistically. 'Plenty of that about.'

'Never see it,' he answered. 'Not unless you want to climb fucking trees for fucking coconuts.'

'Go into Singapore much?' I persisted. 'Do you get to mix with the Chinese at all?'

His eyes started watering. 'Never go down there,' he said. 'The Chinese 'ave all got the pox. I'm saving up to go 'Ome. That's the only place I want to go, mucker. 'Ome wiv a capital H.'

Most of the soldiers did. In fact homesickness was endemic, not only among the national servicemen, who had been plucked from familiar streets, jobs and families, but the regulars who were presumably in the service as a career.

'Get your knees brown,' was the ritual jibe directed at anyone newly arrived. 'I'm peachy!' was the boast of the soldier about to board the troopship for home. It was like Barnardo's all over again.

The man whose bed I took over, whom I met for only a few minutes before he joyfully boarded the truck which had brought us and headed towards the docks and the troopship, was a reporter I had known in my first days on the papers at Voluntary Place. I took over

258

his bed and he went home, took over one of my failed girlfriends, and married her.

After all the anticipation of tropical adventure, Singapore, or at least the piece in my immediate view, proved a dire disappointment. It was the hapless boredom of our daily military routine that primarily made it so. If I had been given a task which, even occasionally, glimmered with interest I could have enjoyed it and might even have been of some positive use. In fairness to the army in general, it could have been scarcely aware of this.

Nee Soon, as so many barracks are in whatever part of the world and whichever army is occupying them, was a sort of ghetto. We mostly lived, worked, slept and entertained ourselves within its confines and those of the adjoining village. The city was a bus journey away and we had little money to spend when we reached it. You could go there to the services club and tango with especially selected partners, who were all good girls; you could sprawl out like a nabob in Oriental wicker chairs lined up in the NAAFI lounge, or trudge around and take photographs. That was the way I, and the others, saw it. Very soon all we wanted to do was go home.

Naturally today this attitude embarrasses me. But at eighteen (especially eighteen as it was *then*) you do not know and appreciate the things that come later in life. In eighteen months in the Far East, for example, I never once sampled Chinese food. Years later I returned to the city with my wife Diana to take part in a television commercial. On arrival we were told that the film would concentrate on the delights of eating in Singapore, which puzzled me since the original contract was for some quite different aspect. The advertising agent explained that the man they had brought out to promote their food on television turned out to be a vegetarian. It was only then, years later, that I discovered the noodle paradise of Albert Street.

In 1950, however, my culinary demands were confined to egg and chips and yellow Tiger Beer in Nee Soon village. There was also real steak, when you could afford it, something I had never seen before. In Britain the mean hand of rationing was still on the land but in Singapore meat (mostly from Australia) was plentiful.

Our barrack rooms were lofty and cool. There were forty beds to a room, a radio loudspeaker in one corner, a balcony overlooking the parade ground at the front and the latrines at the back. We were issued with mosquito nets, but malaria had been eliminated in Singapore Island and we hardly ever used them unless we wanted privacy; a curious but effective way of shutting yourself off from the army and the world. The net would be hooked over the head of the bed and tucked in at the bottom and the sides. Sometimes, on a Tuesday when I did not even have the price of a beer or a camp cinema seat, I would put it up like a green sail and sit in bed reading, the life of the barrack room kept outside its confines. If anyone wanted to speak to you they had to tap on the outside like knocking at a door. It was the only privacy we had and was respected by all.

Each morning, in our billowing green shorts and baggy bush jackets, we would troop from the barracks to the offices which were reached by a wooden bridge over a ravine. The bridge was still there when I was last in Singapore, now tramped by the smaller but

civilians also worked in the office with us. On the transfers section we had two, Mr Wee and Mr Lee. Mr Wee was a dear doddery old chap who managed to get everything wrong but still somehow clung onto his job. Accounts of troops far up in the Malay jungle would mysteriously turn up at Warley Barracks in Essex and the finger would eventually point to Mr Wee. He stayed because he often bought the tea. Mr Lee was younger and neater. He was also an exceedingly kind little man. On my nineteenth birthday, knowing my writing ambitions, he gave me a present of a *Roget's Thesaurus*. He was the only one in the world who remembered it was my birthday and I was overcome with gratitude. I took the book back to the barrack room, hoisted the mosquito net, and began to look through its unending pages of words. It lies on the desk before me as I write this, thirty-four years later.

The operation of the transfers section was scarcely arduous and I began to think I could undertake some work of my own if only I could get away from the gaze, often as bored as mine, of the officer in charge, a bald amiable Welshman, Lieutenant Williams, or the huge sweating Cockney sergeant, a gentle elephant called Darby. We plodded on while the fans whirled eternally. Tea and cakes came and went. Lunchtime saw us clanking over the bridge again, then enduring three hot hours in the afternoon office before trudging back to the barrack room to flop on our beds, or wanking chariots as they were called, until it was time for the evening meal. Where, I used to wonder, had the mystic East gone?

In one corner, distant from the general section, so cosseted that he even had a little plant in a pot on the window sill, was a young sergeant dealing with something ominously called Death Cases. One day he mentioned that it was getting him down, dealing with the final finances of dead soldiers, and he was applying for a transfer. Reasoning that handling Death Cases could not be more demoralising than traipsing around undertakers and bereaved homes as a reporter, I applied for the job and they gladly thrust it at me. At first the Adjutant was a little dubious; after all, the work had previously been accomplished by a *sergeant*. Did I think I could manage it? I said I thought I could and I did. It took me about an hour and a half each day. I was pleased with this for, in my out-of-the-way niche, I could get my official work done and then concentrate on industry of my own. No one ever suggested that since I was doing a sergeant's work I might at least be promoted to lance-corporal but, although I would have welcomed the extra pay, I did not mind very much about this. The army, bless its heart, had provided me with time to write.

More cheerfully now, I would march each morning over the bridge with the reluctant clerks and, after watering the plant on the window sill, I would go through the post and do some work on outstanding matters. Then, leaving a voluminous file open on the desk in front of me, I would insert some scrap paper and, while apparently wrestling with funds and figures, give myself to composing some article or short story. I am afraid that some of my earliest published work was fashioned on the last accounting of some moribund soldier.

My one-man department also dealt with local releases, soldiers who had completed their service and had married Chinese or Eurasian girls or for some other motive had decided to stay in the Far East and make a civil career. It even crossed my mind to take advantage of this facility myself. An England cricket team was going to Australia about the time when my service would be coming to its end and I wrote to the MCC authorities at Lords suggesting that they might like me to accompany them on tour as a baggage man, secretary and general factotum. I guaranteed to find my own passage to Sydney (how, I knew not) but the offer was politely refused in a letter which pointed out that they already had a baggage man. I was, however, fairly pleased with the letter headed 'Marylebone Cricket Club' and I pinned it on the inside of my locker in the barrack room.

My daily job, by its very definition, had its sad and sometimes grisly aspects. Up-country, in the Ulu as we called it, across the causeway spanning the Straits of Johore, which kept Singapore immune from their activities, Communist guerillas were waging a deadly and often successful campaign.

Almost daily there were jungle ambushes and casualties. I would read about them in the *Straits Times* or hear the news on the barrack room radio; then, after a few days, the paybooks and the personal financial documents, letters written in round uneducated hands, would arrive on my desk. It was my task to finalise these money matters and I did it conscientiously and sadly. One morning a patrol of the Royal West Kents, all national servicemen under a regular sergeant, were caught in a trap on a rubber plantation only a few miles from where we sat at our figures. They were slaughtered and some had their teeth cut out as trophies by the jungle bandits. (The Communists were not alone in barbarity. The British-enlisted Dyak trackers from North Borneo not infrequently appeared from the trees grinning and transporting severed heads.) The Royal West Kents had been camping around our barrack square when they first arrived and we had got to know some of them. One young fellow, taking fright while on night guard duty, began spraying everywhere with Sten gun bullets, until he was calmed and told that this was a *safe* place; danger was some miles away. They soon found it because they had scarcely been posted up-country when they fell into the deathly ambush. Eventually the documents reached me. They included a paybook so soaked with its owner's blood that it had to be prised open. I almost threw up as I did it. It was against King's Regulations to carry the paybook on active duty but this poor young fellow must have forgotten. Then I saw his army number. He had joined up *after* me; he was three months younger.

This episode was dramatised in the film *The Virgin Soldiers* and shortly afterwards I was signing books in a store in the Midlands when a man approached and asked if the incident had been based on the Royal West Kent ambush. I said it had. I even remembered the sergeant's name. It was Rowley. 'Yes,' he muttered. 'It's a long time ago now, isn't it. Years. But I still remember like it was yesterday.' With tears beginning to run down his cheeks he turned and walked away.

Standing there that distant morning the steamy sunlight coming through the window with that bloody paybook in my hands, I looked around at the safe domesticity of the office, the fans, the scratching pens, the murmurs, the mugs of tea and the munched cakes, and thought that it was not such a bad place to be after all. Few of the regular soldiers at Nee Soon would have been fit for active service anyway. Many suffered minor disabilities; limps, dim eyesight, obesity, and deafness. Some were left-overs from the war, serving out their time in this torpid territory, the army their hearth and home, their life. Again, in its way, it was like Barnardo's.

The conscripts were, in the main, in better condition, although some were far from soldierlike. One had the opposite to a hunched back, a hunched front, his chest rearing like the bill of a pelican under his chin. Another, with faint eyes, spent hours in the chemically laden swimming pool, hoping to infect them badly enough to be sent home. When he was almost blind he was discharged on account of deafness. Judging by photographs of those days I was scarcely a warlike specimen either, thin and little with sunken eyes, like an undersized skeleton.

Each Saturday morning we left the pens and ledgers and played soldiers. We were required to fire our rifles on the range, attend lectures, or take part in military exercises such as riot control. Sometimes the Chinese from the village used to stand on the road watching us and spoil it all by laughing, and it takes quite a lot to make a Chinese laugh.

During one of these manoeuvres half the platoon were sent off over an area of fairly open ground and the other half had to cover their eyes while they hid. The soldiers on the road turned their backs to the hiders and after counting up to fifty they turned around and tried to spot them. I was in the spotting party and we soon picked them out. Then it was our turn to hide. Instead of going off into the distance I merely dropped into a shallow scrub-hidden ditch almost at the feet of the watchers. I crouched there, within a few feet, and they peered beyond me and pointed out the others. They failed to detect me and in the end they gave up because it was NAAFI break. They called me to come out and I emerged from under their noses. Some of my comrades were quite miffed, alleging unfair play. The officer in charge, however, was really impressed by this demonstration of initiative in camouflage. 'Good chap, Thomas,' he enthused. 'We ought to think about transferring you to an infantry mob up-country.'

I never did it again.

My military aspirations were nil, although my free-lance journalism, undertaken under the cover of dead men's files, was showing promise. I had composed an article about Chinese lanterns and another on the traditional Dragon Festival and these I sent to Charles Mitchell in London where, among his other writing activities, he ran a features agency. The Dragon article was published in the *Liverpool Post* and the one about lanterns in the *Leicester Evening Mercury*. Proudly I pinned the cut-out pieces inside the door of my locker and people came to read them. I was paid a guinea for each.

Someone must have mentioned my extramural activities to authority because I was summoned before the Adjutant. Yes, I admitted, I had been contributing to newspapers in Britain. Fortunately he did not ask in whose time the articles were composed.

'Do they contain military information?' the

Adjutant asked, consulting the thick volume of King's Regulations.

'No sir,' I replied convincingly. 'I don't know any.'

'Not necessarily *secret* information, Thomas, *any* information. We have to be jolly careful out here, you know.'

'Nothing like that, sir. All I wrote about were lanterns and dragons.'

He regarded me steadily from behind the desk. 'Oh, I see,' he said eventually. 'Lanterns and dragons.' He had another deep look at the book. 'Well, that seems to be all right. How much did you get?'

'Ten shillings each,' I lied. I thought the army might want half.

'That's good money,' he nodded. 'Well, all right. There's nothing in King's Regulations to stop you, apparently. But you will have to show the Regimental Sergeant-Major what you write, so he can check it over, just to make sure you're not divulging military secrets. All right?'

'Yes sir,' I readily agreed.

'And Thomas . . .'

'Sir?'

'Write a bit for the regimental magazine, will you, there's a good chap. Anything you like. They want me to do it and I can't think of a damned thing to say.'

I wrote the article for him just as I had written as a ghost for the Gaffer a few years before. Its heading was: 'First Impressions of Singapore'. It did not appear under my name but the Adjutant later told me privately that he had received lots of compliments about it.

The articles I continued to write for provincial

papers in Britain – 'Secrets of the Opium Smugglers', 'Sacred Snakes of the East', and other grippers were typed out during guard duty. During the four-hour breaks when I was not required to be standing with a fixed bayonet, staring out into the cricket-clicking night, I was busy tapping away in the deserted orderly room.

The office block, with its financial secrets, was always under armed guard through the hours of darkness. Standing on the dog-watch stage, from four to six, the damp, warm night about you, trudging up and down, watching the dawn nose over the crab-like palm trees, was the time you thought of home.

By some outlandish, and admittedly unofficial, logic the armoury guard, which was intended to keep secure the store of garrison weapons, was manned by a detail who traditionally went to sleep. All of them. After eleven o'clock the six-man guard and the corporal in charge would get tucked into camp beds, wish each other goodnight, and snore away sweetly until dawn. This state of affairs shocked a newly arrived officer who marched in at midnight to make sure that everyone was alert. I was guarding the armory that night engulfed, as were my comrades, in dreams when the new broom arrived. Angry and amazed he threw us out of our beds and told the corporal he would be put on a disciplinary charge, at which the corporal burst into tears and protested that the armoury guard always went to sleep. It was a traditional perk. That, however, was the last time.

Every month there was an additional guard duty we were obliged to perform at a major ammunition dump in the far north of the island. This was a serious matter for, only a boat trip across the narrow Straits of Johore, were the bandit camps in the jungles of Malaya. We were let into a barbed wire compound and stood nervously through the night watching for invaders. In our off-duty time we used to bet on bull-frog races. No Communists came across the strait while I was there. But a tiger did.

Disturbed by the rude aerial bombing of its natural home – the RAF used to fly sorties and try to attack hidden Communist camps – it decided to opt for peace and quiet and swam the channel to Singapore. No one had seen a real tiger loose in Singapore since the legendary one appeared in the billiards room of the Raffles Hotel many years previously. That tiger (although it does tend to spoil the story) had escaped from a circus. This swimming tiger, however, was the genuine wild thing and it roamed bravely about for several days, giving us goose pimples on guard and keeping the women and children of service families behind locked doors. The poor animal was finally shot dead at the RAF base at Seletar. Perhaps it had gone to find the chap who had bombed its home.

Our drills, guard duties, our field games and the occasional hilarious rehearsals for dealing with revolting natives were the only army activities which disturbed our domestic garrison lives. Until one night I found a shocked platoon grouped around the notice board on which were pinned the Company Orders. There was a list of soldiers required for active duty in Malaya. My name was one of them. That bloodied paybook floated before my eyes again. I thought I was going to faint.

XI

To send a small army of pen-pushers into the green
dangers of a jungle harbouring lethal bands of
guerillas was the bright scheme of someone at General
Headquarters. It was not endorsed by the personnel
of the Pay Office, both those who were going and
those who were not. The Commanding Officer grumbled about essential work being left behind and senior
NCOs, some of whom had seen action in that jungle
during the war, looked at us with extreme dubiety.

'God, fancy sending you lot,' was our barrack room
sergeant's parting blessing as twenty of us sloped off,
bowed under full packs and carrying rifles, towards
the truck which was to take us away from the safe
boredom of Nee Soon. One of our conscript
comrades, an emotional Welshman, waved us goodbye
with a broken expression and the words: 'Don't worry,
boys, I expect you'll get back all right.'

The rest of the company, shaking their heads,
watched from the balcony and they turned away one
by one, as though they could stand it no longer. Once
we were in the truck and on our way, tightly holding
our rifles in the darkness, the accompanying NCO, a
doleful corporal, reminded us that there was a section
for the soldier's last will and testament in the army

paybook and that it might be as well for us to study it when we had a moment.

The risk of dispatching such novices up-country had apparently not been entirely ignored at headquarters for it had been decided not to send us along the winding and ambush-prone roads of Johore. We were to go by sea, aboard a landing craft, just like the real soldiers who invaded coastlines during the real war.

I have to confess that I, for one, cheered considerably at this prospect. Not only did it eliminate the very-present peril of being machine-gunned from the roadside undergrowth as we travelled north but, neatly, it also lent a more warlike appearance to the whole operation. As we boarded the landing craft our rubber jungle boots padded on the steel deck, there was a clatter of rifle butts, a shifting of equipment, the grunts of the soldiers in the dark. It was just like being in a film.

We set sail with a boatload of nondescript conscripts. Men from workshops and stores, from cook-houses and offices all over Singapore Island were there. They grumbled about being taken away from essential military tasks to go and play at war. Who would change the wheels? Who would issue the rations? Who would cook them? Who would make out the invoices? There appeared to be a danger of the entire military life of the island coming to a standstill.

Through the warm night we sailed among the out-islands and turned north into the China Sea up the coast of Johore. I was enjoying the romance of this part and, crouching, half-sleeping, remembered innumerable Robert Mitchums, Errol Flynns and other handsome heroes I had seen sailing through such nights on deadly missions. The Oriental sun came up abruptly and in a wash of brilliance. We were lolling along a mile or so off the coast. We could see palm trees, beaches and rising mountains lipped with morning clouds.

The landing craft was long and low, not unlike a Chinese junk; the crew lived in a little house at the back. There was a bridge from which the commanding officer commanded and a soldier steered, and beneath that were the living quarters. They did their own laundry and hung it to dry from a line slung between two masts. It transpired that all the crew and the commander were occupying their national service time by sailing up and down like this and I wondered, not for the first time, how it was that the more attractive aspects of army life had passed me by.

We lined up for tea, poured from a bucket into our mess tins. We were closer inshore now and we could hear monkeys screaming. A squaddie, a stranger to me, standing alongside on the deck, pointed landward. 'Ulu,' he said. 'That's what it is. Ulu – jungle.' He grinned at me to see if I was impressed. I was only slightly. 'Mucken,' he said. 'Means grub. Dinner. Bint is a bit of nooky.'

I thanked him for this information. Later I was able to add to my vocabulary the Malay words for trousers and belt. I knew that the Muslim Malay had the word 'bin' in the middle of his name, thus Abdul bin Malik. We had a garbage collector we nicknamed Dust bin Lid. The Malay's wife was binte, hence the traditional and coarse army slang for a lady. Later I learned to count by listening to the head porter summoning the chauffeurs outside the Raffles Hotel in Singapore. I also memorised the names of the Malay states and their main towns and I later learned the word for death. But that was my sum total knowledge of the language.

Everything about the operation seemed to be going well. The sun came up, clear and hot, as it rarely did in Singapore. There were fishing villages on stilts in the sea. Fishermen were out in skinny boats and they waved as we went by. 'Spies,' reckoned the squaddie who had taught me Malay. 'Soon as we've gone, they'll scarper and tell the bleeding bandits.'

The first hitch came when it was discovered that almost every scrap of food on board was contained in cans and between two hundred of us there was only one tin opener and that belonged to the crew. This was also a private tin opener, not army property, and its owner, after lending it out a few times, became mercenary and thereafter charged twenty-five cents per usage. He made a fortune before breakfast.

The deck became baking and we lay sprawled on it like cruise passengers soaking up the sun until about noon when the engine nodded and we saw that we were turning into a beautiful bay with islands off-shore and a shining white strand decked with palms. There were tents visible through the trees and soldiers, baked brown, on the beach waiting for us. The place was called Mersing.

The romance of the adventure was accentuated when we were ordered to wade ashore with our equipment. Through the limp water we trudged with rifles and packs. On the beach an enterprising corporal was taking snapshots of us as we waded ashore like commandos and he, like the owner of the tin opener, added considerably to his wealth by selling off the prints.

Mersing camp was set in a place something like paradise but beyond it was the thick and dangerous jungle. 'A bandit gang of about two hundred – all killers – is operating this area,' announced the Commandant with brisk and, I thought, untoward enthusiasm, as soon as we were assembled on the sand. 'We're jolly lucky we'll have the opportunity of screening the region and turfing the blighters out. That's *something* we've got to look forward to.'

To me, and judging by the expressions on the faces of my newly arrived companions, the expectation was his alone. Our eyes ticked around at the green barriers beyond the camp perimeter. High trees through which hundreds of monkeys swung and screamed. 'There's a good-sized swamp to the west,' the officer breezed on. 'And there are only a few tracks through that swamp. We'll perhaps be able to set up some useful ambushes in that area.'

I had my own anxiety about who was going to ambush whom and this quickly accumulated when, hardly before I had dropped my belongings in one of the tents, I was picked out to go to the neighbouring village to collect the mail and milk. Detailed with me were two Malay soldiers and this at first gave me some reassurance. At least they would know what they were doing. Their native eyes would spot ambushes and be quick to react. I resolved to trust them.

As soon as the open platoon truck left the guard-post at the edge of the camp and began twisting along the close track towards Mersing village, five miles distant, these two Malays lay flat on the floor of the vehicle, closed their eyes tightly and began to moan. Over and over they whispered the word: 'Mati, mati,' as they trembled.

Too embarrassed to lie down with them, I completed the journey at a painful crouch, like a runner kept too long at the start of a race. When we reached the village and the driver and his mate got out to go to the post office and the milk shop, I asked the Malays what 'Mati' meant. Their eyes rolled like black marbles. Then one ran his finger across his throat and said, 'It mean dead.' The other nodded. 'Dead,' he confirmed.

Unfortunately, thereafter this pessimistic pair seemed to haunt me; whatever duty I was required to perform they seemed to be there also, their Amos and Andy faces throbbing with fear and the words 'Mati, mati', never far from their lips.

Every other night we had to do guard duty, keeping watch over the stores, over the ammunition and arms dump, and patrolling the tenuous perimeter of the tents. Each time I seemed somehow to find myself in the vicinity of the two Malays. Their eyes would appear through the night like glow-worms, seeming to be around the back of every tree and hiding in every hole in the ground.

Once I saw them sitting back to back each with his hands over his eyes, like the croucher monkeys who squatted in the trees in this posture, apparently, as the ostrich in the sand, believing that if they could not see you then neither could you see them. Soldiers never shot at a croucher monkey because, the legend said, if you killed one you would never leave Malaya alive.

We were deep on unenthusiastic patrol in the swamp one morning when a single burst of fire erupted some way ahead and lying flat in the mire I found my involuntary companions curled in terror beside me. One was murmuring their fated word, 'Mati, mati,' and the other was blowing little bubbles of fear across a muddy pool. Then they began *touching me for luck* and I realised that this is why they always appeared in times of anxiety. To them I was some sort of mascot! God, I needed a mascot myself. On this occasion the luck held because the alarm turned out to be a nervous burst of fire from one of our own men at the front of the patrol.

Almost everyone in the camp was jittery, although some of the officers adopted a daredevil pose, swashbuckling around in a jeep and rising early to go out into the jungle and shoot wild pig with their Sten guns; a disturbance that never failed to cause panic in our tent. A conscript who ventured to the latrines in the middle of the mysterious night and sat there, Sten-gun across knees, saw lights in the trees. At once he presumed they were ambushing bandits and tried to bring his Sten into the firing position while sitting on the bog, attempting to pull his trousers up at the same time. The result was that the weapon became wedged in his trousers and shattered them when it went off with resounding staccato. He was lucky he did not shoot off his own feet, or worse.

At night the camp presented an almost surrealistic spectacle. Lights glowed in the tents and in the beer hut, while music was relayed over a loudspeaker, Sinatra, Count Basie, Doris Day or the Andrews Sisters harmonising 'Boogie Woogie Bugler Boy', filling the jungle air with their voices. I swear the monkeys used to sit in the branches and listen. Outside the boundary an Indian, devoted to commerce, had set up a rough wooden shop where he sold everyday necessities such as toothpaste, tins of Peak Frean biscuits and packs of cards. Each night he slept on his counter apparently unworried by the peril of the concealed Communists. From our guard positions we used to look out at his heaped form and wonder why nobody ever attacked and robbed him. In the absence of any attempt by the bandits several of my comrades considered doing it themselves.

For soldiers accustomed to the sedentary life of an office in a secure garrison, the requirements of active service were often sapping. Every other night was guard duty, two hours on, two off, lying sprawled on the ground when not prowling tentatively around the camp or sidling among the palm trees in the hot darkness. The guard tent used to become very sweaty and I decided that the only place to rest when I was not keeping watch was on the sacking and tarpaulin spread over the ammunition pit. It was dangerous but cosy and very private. Had anyone with nefarious intentions slunk into the camp and lobbed a well-placed grenade into my bower the sleep would have been more protracted than I expected.

As it was I came within an inch of being shot dead. The man who fired the gun was on our side. It happens very easily. I had just completed my regulation creep around the camp perimeter and had returned to the guard tent when a regular NCO approached me chattily and, as he did so, pulled back the bolt of his rifle, ejecting the round from the breech. Then, disobeying a basic rule, he slammed the bolt home, thus effectively loading the weapon again and, idiotically holding the muzzle towards me, pressed the trigger. I felt the explosion in my face. We stared at each other. Then I slowly revolved and saw the hole in the tent a fraction from my ear. We continued to regard each other dumbly, the colour gone from both our faces. He did not even say sorry. All around were snoring Malay troops, not one of whom even stirred. The sergeant-major, however, had heard it. He rushed into the tent, Sten-gun cocked. For a moment I thought *he* was going to shoot me, thinking in the dim lantern light that I was a raider.

'Did you hear a shot?' he demanded. The NCO, still trembling, rolled his eyes at me and shook his head. The sergeant-major nodded briskly at my own wan expression. I was conscious of the little hole in the tent just behind my head, like a winking eye in the canvas wall. 'What about you, lad?' he asked. 'Didn't you hear it?' It was a cleft stick. If I said I had heard nothing and was found to be lying, then I would be in the mire as deeply as the other man. On the other hand I did not want him court-martialled because of me. I managed the non-committal. 'I've just come in, sir,' I said. 'I've just been around the perimeter.'

For some reason that satisfied him and he went mumbling back to bed. I can't remember the NCO either thanking me or even saying he was sorry but I remember his name. You do when someone almost shoots you dead. Many years later the same man telephoned Columbia Pictures, the day before the première of *The Virgin Soldiers*, and demanded a seat on account of the fact that he was the original Sergeant Driscoll, the tough and heroic NCO of the book. He was not.

We had further, equally accidental, brushes with death. No guerillas appeared from the jungle and we intimated, once we had returned to the defences of Singapore, that they were pretty wise to keep away. Nonetheless there were dramas enough. Every day we were paraded on the beach for physical training and in our free time we played football on the firm sand and swam in the limp sea. Someone noticed a series of strange bumps in the sand and after further investigation a Royal Engineers officer was called. 'Mines,' he said with a big sniff. 'Anti-personnel mines. Very unpleasant. Blow the lot of you to God, they would.'

It was not the Communists who had laid them. The mines were British, left over from 1942 when the Japanese were invading Malaya. A bomb-disposal team appeared and detonated the booby traps with a roar that shook the trees for miles.

Not being of a very courageous, or even a very military, nature I was ever conscious of the potential danger around us. There was an ambush on a road only three miles away and several civilians were killed. These attacks occurred daily. Not even the highest were safe. A newly appointed High Commissioner for Malaya was shot dead when his car drove into an ambush in the supposedly terrorist-free Cameron

Highlands area. One day we had sent out a patrol which failed to return at the appointed time. Dusk dropped and there was still no sign. Random men were chosen to form a search party and, unfortunately standing there, the finger pointed at me. As we were about to set off into the darkening jungle the lost patrol appeared in the other direction. So abruptly did we chance on each other that we almost opened fire before the mistake was realised.

One day we were led across the swamp and into a Malay kampong, the houses on stilts around a haphazard circle. The people, simple-faced children, ancient women, and a few mothers (the men were out working), regarded us without expression. Intrusions like this happened regularly over the past few years. First the British Army, then the Japanese, now the British again and the Communists too who came to cruelly take food and money from them. The poor people were caught between the factions. We 'screened' the village (our sergeant thought it strange that all the men were absent), pushing our way into their houses and overturning their belongings. I felt very ashamed.

From the kampong we continued far into the jungle. I had volunteered to be getaway man, a double-edged position, at the rear of the patrol. The getaway man, twenty or thirty yards behind, had a duty to *run away* in the event of an attack so that he could summon assistance. The attraction of this early exit, however, was countered by the fact that the straggler was frequently, and for good and obvious reasons, the first to be shot. Ever unsoldierlike, I was holding my snub-nosed rifle at the incorrect angle and I contrived to push it, snout-first, into a looming ant-hill, made of damp earth. The muzzle sank into the wall and when I pulled it out the barrel was stuffed solid. I dared not clean it out then but as I stumbled on I could not help wondering what would happen if I was required to pull the trigger. Would there have merely been a sludgy sound with the bullet dropping softly out of the end like something from a slot machine? I was told later that I would have blown my own head off.

My personal appearance in the jungle was a trifle irregular. Being unable to close the left eye independently I had needed to resort to the handkerchief stuffed under my hat. In the event of ambush I would have needed to pull this down over my eye and grip the loose end between my teeth. By that time I would probably have been dead anyway.

Trudging, thus ill-fitted, through the close and muttering jungle we once came to a stream about fifty feet wide, the water thick as chocolate. The lieutenant at the head of the column was a keen young fellow, eager, yes *eager*, to make contact with the Communists. He decided that we must cross the river, and, in his phrase, forget the crocodiles. Crocodiles! We stood looking down at the ominous water. A rope was brought up and one of our men went a little upstream where there was a perfectly good wooden bridge crossing from one Malay village to another. He then walked down the opposite bank and secured the rope to a tree before throwing the loose end back. I was tempted to mention that I had a long history of rheumatism and a longer aversion to the crocodile but the officer was too busy playing soldiers.

There was no reason, other than this military madness, why we should not all have crossed the stream without getting soaked and possibly eaten by using the bridge like the natives. One by one we dropped into the rusty, warm-flowing water, hand over hand on the rope, our rifles around our necks. Most could just touch the bottom, where there were stones, by standing on tip-toe. I could not reach. Reg Wilcocks, the national serv-iceman suspended behind me, told me more than thirty years later that my head actually went under the surface and he caught my hat as it floated away. My rifle was awash, and then, I still don't know how, my bayonet slipped and dropped to the bottom of the brown river. 'That, sonny,' said the officer when I owned up after we had gained the other bank (he could not have been much older than me), 'that is a court-martial offence.'

On our last day at Mersing, before gratefully embarking on the landing ship again, I saw to my astonishment a luminous blue Cadillac bump down the track from the village. It pulled up in the camp and out got a bronzed and breezy fellow accompanied by two stunning young women. We stood, as green and virgin as ever young men were, gaping at this man and his twin visions. We heard later he was a famous war correspondent. That, I thought, is the job for me.

Before I could set out on the path I had charted for myself to glamour, glory and girls, there was the matter of my pending court martial. For some reason I had not appreciated the full threat of this. Normally when you lost things in the army, a pair of socks or the oil bottle for your rifle or even your belt, you simply had to provide replacements out of your pay, and after all it was not my fault that my bayonet was now lying in an ooze of river mud west of Mersing.

It was only when we had returned to Nee Soon in Singapore that the unpleasant reality came to me. I was called to see the Adjutant, a brusque but decent man, who looked worried. He picked up a sheet of paper from the desk. 'They want to court-martial you, Thomas,' he announced.

'Who does, sir?' I asked shocked.

'General Headquarters,' he sighed. 'And they can too. Losing a weapon on active service is a serious offence. I've had a word with the Commanding Officer and we've been trying to think of ways to get you off. Up to now we've come up with nothing. It looks pretty serious.' He grinned good-naturedly. 'Perhaps you'd better make a run for it, son,' he suggested.

White-faced I returned to my desk. How long in the glasshouse would I get? The prospect was frightening. Military prisons were notorious. Mr Lee, the young Chinese clerk on our section who had given me the *Roget's Thesaurus*, shook his head and muttered, 'King's Legulations,' followed by a section and a paragraph number.

'What's that?' I asked hopefully. I had forgotten he was a wizard of military law. What he was doing posting off packets of accounts I never understood.

'Excuses,' he said. 'Leasons for no court martial.'

'What are they? I'll do them,' I said instantly.

'Mostry medical,' he said. He regarded me wisely. 'You said one day that you had leumatism?'

'After playing football I ache,' I agreed. 'I had rheumatic fever when I was about five, I think.'

'This crimate,' he continued eruditely. 'Bad for leumatism.'

'Swamps and steamy heat and all that,' I added hopefully. I rubbed my legs. 'I can feel them aching now.'

'And your arms?' he suggested. 'Leumatism often get in the arms.'

At a quick limp and holding my shoulder I went back to the Adjutant. He had already thought of the medical let-out. 'Been on sick parade much?' he asked before I could tell him why I had come.

'Prickly heat, sir,' I said not wishing to rush it. 'And I got a cricket ball on the head.' He regarded me in a prompting manner. 'Any rheumatism?' he asked.

'Arms and legs, sir.'

'Good. Let's get you to the medical officer and build up a bit of a case history for you. By rights you shouldn't be soldiering in this climate, at all.'

'Might they send me home, sir?' How my fortunes had changed in half an hour!

'I think we'd better concentrate on the court martial,' he cautioned.

That morning I went to the medical officer and he examined me, cocking his ear so that he could hear my joints creak. From somewhere the Adjutant had produced a whole sheaf of medical reports giving dates when I had needed to report sick with my aches, although I remembered none of them. The MO played along sportingly. 'Rusty,' he announced. 'You're all rusty, Thomas. Better send you to hospital.'

An ambulance was ordered and I was put on a stretcher and transported to the British military hospital in Singapore. If I felt a fraud, I felt a justified fraud until waiting in the entrance hall I saw two young soldiers carried in, eyes staring uncomprehendingly through smeared blood. Their faces were like putty. They were hurried away. I heard an orderly say to another: 'There's a third squaddie in the wagon. Stiff as a board.'

Chastened, I sat until the specialist could see me. He listened closely but he did not seem to be able to hear my joints creaking. He said I would be admitted for a few days for observation. I was taken into a ward and placed in a bed between a hairy Seaforth Highlander with malaria and a French sailor with appendicitis. It was more difficult understanding what the Seaforth Highlander said, even when he was not delirious, than it was the French sailor. No one else in the ward, however, even tried to converse with the matelot and he was despondent. My solitary and distant year's French, under the indomitable Miss Quick at Stow Hill School in Newport, was scraped together. I worked out convoluted sentences about the Frenchman's *maladie* and his *bateau* not to mention his *appellation* and his *ville*. When I tried them out on him his eyes widened with thanks and delight and he gabbled off fiercely until I stopped him. After that I used to converse, briefly, with him every hour before going away to put together some more painful sentences.

286

Twice a day I had to go to the physiotherapy department and, standing in pyjamas under the instruction of an attractively spruce nurse, I was required to turn a great wheel fixed to the wall, first with one arm and then the other, and then by means of a pedal attachment, with both legs, an occupation as tiring and boring as it was unproductive, but better than being court-martialled.

There were two soldiers in the ward who were in for circumcision. 'Great skive,' one informed me from behind his hand. 'Little snip here and there, and you 'ave a week in 'ospital, all mod cons and 'aving a decko up the nurses' skirts and that. Then you can get sick leave as well. Nothing to it.'

Unfortunately I had been given a precautionary snip as an infant. In the urinals at school I had often wondered why mine had a different end from so many others, and in my early teens I had indeed begun to wonder whether I was Jewish. Nevertheless this information seemed too good to waste. When I returned to Nee Soon, my medical dossier now complete (there was no court martial), I passed the idea on to several inmates of the barrack room. Three of them actually went to have the operation, having complained to the medical officer that the heavy climate was having nasty repercussions on their private bits. They returned furious. 'We ought to kill you, Thomas, you daft bastard,' observed one. 'It 'urt like bloody 'ell, especially when you got the 'orn wiv them nurses comin' and ticklin' your feet. *And* there's *no* bloody sick leave, neither!'

A lot of our thinking time was directed to those lower regions. Being up at Mersing, and indeed seeing those poor young soldiers carried into the hospital, made me realise how brief life could be. And yet I still did not know what it was like to be with a woman. Such were matters in those days that eighty-five per cent of my comrades were in similar uncertainty. We used to sit and debate what women were *really* like. 'I hope,' said one youth piously, 'I don't get a bullet before I get a shag.' In that moment the idea for *The Virgin Soldiers*, not written for many years, was born.

Such was our ignorance of what was required and *how it actually felt* that we were stunned with admiration when we learned that a mild, curly-haired, young lad, who lived quietly in the corner of the barrack room without bothering anyone, was being sent back to Britain *because his girlfriend was pregnant.* Here was one of the smallest and most innocent-looking soldiers in the garrison and he had not only got a lady up the stick, as was the expression – but he was being repatriated on the strength of it! As he sauntered off towards his four-day trip by plane, home and his wedding, we squatted disconsolately, jealous of his luck and his foresight.

'Leave,' decided a brightly browed youth called Harold Wilson from Manchester. 'That's what we need – leave.'

'Penang,' muttered Johnny Staton, who came from the same city, with a confirming sniff. We were like boys planning an unofficial outing from school.

'The City Lights,' I added, naming a legendary place of fun and filth. 'The Piccadilly,' I went on, naming a second. I was eager to make a start to my sex life. 'Get anything you want there, so they reckon.'

'And some things you don't want,' added a cautious lad called White.

'Got to take some risks,' pointed out a soldier called Smudge. He sat with both feet in the barrack room tea bucket.

The risks were not all sexual, however, for Penang, an island off the west coast of Malaya, was reached only after a long and perilous journey by rail through the length of the bandit-haunted country. Ambushing expresses was the easiest attrition the Communists could undertake. They simply lay in the darkness on the side of the line and fired through the windows or the roof of the train as it roared through the steamy night. One group of national servicemen had returned to Nee Soon from leave only two weeks earlier, white-faced and with the most terrible tale of an ambush when the train was almost at Johore Bahru where the causeway took the line across the strait to the safety of Singapore. Machine-gun fire had come from a high embankment. Two civilians had been struck dead in front of the eyes of the hapless British soldiers and the foot of a Chinese baby had been shot off. The conscripts returned, shaking and splattered with the child's blood. They did not want to go on leave again.

Nevertheless we voted to risk our lives in the pursuit of sexual initiation and six of us arrived at Singapore station on a rainy evening and boarded the express for Ipoh in the distant north. At the platform the scene was not encouraging. In front of the locomotive was another, smaller, engine, coupled to two flat trucks loaded down with concrete slabs. This, we knew from the tales of past travellers, was the pilot train which would run ahead of the main express. If the rails had been quietly removed by the Communists or they had dropped a tree across the track then the poor little pilot engine would bear the brunt. Understandably, driving the engine was not a popular job with the local railwaymen.

At the rear of the main train was another truck, mounted upon which was an armoured car. As we boarded the carriage, our rifles slung over our shoulders, we asked the crew of the armoured car who were sitting drinking tea on top of their vehicle, how often they had seen action. 'Never seen it at all, mucker,' replied one affably. 'Soon as there's trouble we get down inside and keep out of the bloody way.'

Thus reassured we boarded the express. There was a notice inside the carriage which said: 'In the event of firing from the lineside passengers are advised to put out all lights and lie on the floor.'

The rain continued and in a warm, watery sunset we left the sanctuary of the garrison island and trundled over the darkening Straits of Johore into dangerous country.

Had there not been the lurking threat of ambush the journey would have been wonderful. The rolling stock of the Malayan State Railways was elegantly pre-war, the Japanese having seen it was kept in trim during their occupation. There were many touches of luxury, velvet seats, ornate decoration, edges of gilt, and silently moving stewards in stiff white jackets. The accumulative effect was to make a very ordinary private soldier take on a touch of the sahib. We could neither afford the dining car nor a couchette but we ate our tough packed sandwiches, provided by the Nee Soon cookhouse, and opened some bottles of Tiger Beer before settling for the night. At two in the morning the train pulled up like a frightened horse, tumbling us about. The lights went out and we sat apprehensively for half an hour clutching our rifles. Then we did the stupidest thing possible; we left the train to have a look.

We were on a pitch-dark embankment, with the jungle piled almost to the track. Far up ahead were some bobbing lights. Crickets scraped metallically. Down below us beyond the first trees were other lights and presently we made out the roofs of a village. 'I could do with a beer,' said Smudge eerily. Yes, we agreed in low voices, we could all do with a beer. We jolted down the muddy embankment, six novice soldiers, and went into the street of the kampong. There was a rough, open-fronted bar and there, at three o'clock in the morning, sat half a dozen Chinese. Their eyes seemed even narrower than usual as they watched us. No one stirred as we foolishly stood at the bar. The Malay barman was shaking so much he could scarcely hand the beers over the counter. They spilled and the liquid fell in several small cataracts over the edge. We stood, armed but idiotically vulnerable, surrounded by what in all probability was a group of terrorists. I tried nodding affably at the small dim faces behind the bare tables. There was no response. We drank our beer nervously.

''Evening,' said Smudge to three of the Chinese.

''Evening, 'Evening, 'Evening,' we acknowledged the others.

'Chinese. No speak,' said the Malay behind the bar ambiguously.

'We can see that, mate,' said Harold Wilson. We were all eyeing each other. As if at a signal we gulped the rest of our beer and made to exit. 'Got to catch a train,' joked Smudge to the Chinese.

Almost falling over each other in our attempt at being casual we reached the door and then, all together, scrambled like fury up the embankment. As we reached the train it began to move off. Shouting, we pursued it along the track, stumbling over the railway sleepers. 'Stop! Stop! Stop the train!' we howled. As if it had heard it stopped. Panting and grateful we clattered aboard. There was another ten-minute wait during which we retold to other travellers how we had gone on a quick patrol in hostile territory. Then the engine puffed again and we jogged on. Looking from the window we saw that in the beam of our armoured car's searchlight, the little toy engine that had gone before us was lying pathetically on its side on the embankment. Our train, the driver of the pilot train aboard and scarcely bruised, pulled on. The quicker we were all out of that place the better.

But the night diminished, we left the train and the morning saw us crossing the glassy channel between the mainland and Penang, sampans, junks and large ships all around. The island rose beautifully into the paper sky. We could see its white buildings and the beaches embroidering the green bays, and behind them the hills rose lucidly. Spices, scents and sounds drifted from the land. I wondered what time the City Lights opened.

XII

It almost did not work this time either. There was I, eighteen and determined to lose, abandon, throw away my unwanted virginity, and the first night I was in Penang I fell in damned love again. Spruced, brushed, prepared for the wickedest of the world's women, we travelled into Georgetown and after some jovial beers climbed the stairs of a restaurant for chop, egg and chips. Sitting in the place were two young girls of film star loveliness, glowing and blonde. They were sisters, members of a Penang Eurasian family who liked to entertain young soldiers at their beach house. Breathlessly they talked with us, their fawn shoulders rippling, their bodices full, their eyes blatant. After the meal they invited us to their home to meet their parents and play some records. My comrades, still intent on the cheap thrills of the City Lights, were sidling towards the door. But I, the blind and ever-hopeful romantic, could see only what I imagined was a certain promise in the smile of the older sister. Her eyes were like pigeon's eggs. I was lost. Yes, of course, I would enjoy going to their house. The others were tugging me towards the door and a night of sin, but I told them nonchalantly that I would see them the next day. After all the City Lights would always be there; like a second parachute.

So my fellow adventurers left for the illuminations and the ladies, and I walked home with the two sisters to their house by the shore. As we strolled I held the hands of both. The parents, a handsome and wealthy couple, greeted me as they might greet some new stray to a house where strays were welcomed. We drank Cola-Cola and listened to Kay Starr and Frank Sinatra on the gramophone and at eleven o'clock the elder girl, whom I had decided to choose, walked to the gate with me and kissed me luxuriously on the lips. I could smell mimosa in her hair, or it might have been a shrub hanging over from the garden.

'We always attend the football matches,' she mentioned. Her voice was throbbing but strangely official. 'The boys from the leave centre play every week against the Penang team. I'll be there tomorrow. Will you?' Certainly I would. We kissed again and her heavily lounging bosom, under the embroidered blouse, pushed against my new cream sharkskin shirt. God, it was wonderful. Returning to the leave centre I did a whirling, romantic, waltz in the empty road. As I did so a lady, furtive and dark, slipped around a corner and asked me if I would like a good time. 'No thanks,' I said like the lofty prig I was, 'I've just had one.'

'Hope you didn't get the pox,' the dark lady warned. 'There's plenty of poxes around.'

They were not where I'd been, I thought blissfully. Jesus, I *had* to get in that football team tomorrow. There she would be on the touchline, beautiful tears of pride in her eyes, waving her silk scarf, jumping up and down in her summer dress, her bosom bouncing as I fooled the full backs and scored spectacularly. What a twerp!

To my gratification there was no difficulty about getting into the leave centre football team. The man who arranged it (when I got him out of bed that night) said sleepily that there were always places because so many men got drunk or ended up staying away with women. I went to bed and thought of Dolores, or whatever she was called. That scent, that smile, that promise. At four in the morning two of my comrades returned, one so drunk he could not climb into bed and so spent the night on the floor. The other, Smudge Smith, took off his clothes and lay groaning. 'Fuckin' 'ell,' he murmured in the dimness. 'My love muscle's like a lump of liver, Les.'

I informed him of the prevalence of various poxes and said I had to get my rest. ''Ow did you get on then?' he enquired. 'Get your leg across?'

Brusquely I told him that it was not like that. But it would be. 'It's there, all right, Smudge,' I breathed. 'But it has to be right for *her*, see. But it's *there*. She's coming to see me play football tomorrow.'

'Football?' he muttered. 'Gor blimey, football. I'm keeping away from that lark. If anybody kicked me in these balls they'd fall off.'

My participation in the soccer match the following day was brief and sordid. The game was scarcely in progress when a cubic Mongolian half-back kicked my legs from under me when I was glancing towards the touchline to see if my beloved had yet arrived. It was both blatant and vicious but no one else seemed to witness it, least of all the Chinese referee who was enthusiastically keeping up with the ball at the remote end of the field. The wryly named Sporting Club

295

scored and it was not until the teams were trooping back towards the centre of the field for the new kick-off that someone noted that I was curled like a wood-louse in the home penalty area. The moonlike Mongolian's expression never changed as I accused him of breaking my ankle. A faint cheer wimpered from the small crowd as I was carried off by two of the opposing side and it was only when this was happening that I saw the delectable Dolores, laughing and lolling on the arm of a second lieutenant in the Medical Corps. She seemed to have some difficulty in recalling who I was and the officer added injury to the insult by giving my swelling ankle a heavy prod and diagnosing that I would be lame for the rest of my leave.

Miserably I was transported to the hospital where the joint was embalmed. It was a bad sprain they said, but cheerfully confirmed that it would be better in time for me to get back to duty in Singapore. Hobbling about the leave centre, anger and despair mixing inside, I decided to tell Dolores what I thought of her perfidity. Smudge was lying on his bed in the room when I returned to get some coins for the telephone. I told him how my ankle was throbbing.

'Nowhere as much as my love muscle, mate,' he groaned.

'I'm fed up with hearing about your bloody love muscle,' I said nastily. 'You've got a dose, I expect.'

'Nah,' he retorted. 'It was 'er teef. She 'ad teef like a wood saw.'

Moaning slightly I went out into the mocking sunshine, dragging my parcelled leg. It was all damned well passing me by again. Christ, now I could not even dance. Furiously I dialled the number of the house on the beach. Yes, Dolores was in and she was expecting my call. My foolish heart began to beat harder at this and even more violently when she came on the telephone with honeyed condolences for my condition. No, that young officer was only a tennis friend. She would *love* me to go to her house again. Yes, that night. We could play some records and drink Cola-Cola. She had the new Rosemary Clooney.

As dusk drifted over Penang I dragged my lump of a foot up the gravel path of her home, making a track in the stones. They had a large and randy dog which throughout the evening kept trying to have sex with my ankle. I knew how he felt. When I was gaseous with Cola-Cola and weary of Sinatra, Clooney and the rest (although I did clumsily try to jive with her to 'Put another nickle in . . . in the nickelodeon . . .' sung by Teresa Brewer) she said she would walk me to the moonlit gate. Her eyes were dreamy, her lips wet, her breasts protruded with promise. We reached the gate, below the mimosa. I picked a blossom and she put it in her hair. We kissed, engulfing each other and, getting my balance on my uninjured leg, I slid my hand up to the flank of her bosom. She stopped kissing and drew back. 'Don't please,' she requested softly. 'Please don't spoil it. Not now.'

Spoil it! Spoil it! Spoil what? Seething, I punched the air as I hobbled away from the gate. I heard her swaying back down the gravel path and close the door of the house. Oh God, why did I have to drag romance wherever I went, even to the Orient? I was still cursing when the lurking lady I had met the first night crept from her private shadow and accosted me. Briskly I refused and dragged my leg on. 'You got poxes,' she called after me with a cackling laugh. 'That's what you got boy, poxes.'

When I reached the City Lights three sailors were coming out with six girls, every one giggling, the sailors with their hands on bottoms and other parts. In my anxiety to get in I dropped my entry fee and picked it up with much pain and difficulty. Then, like a thin monster, I dragged myself through the rosy smoke and into the wonderland of iniquity and fulfilment. My time for holding hands, for kissing at gates, was finished. Here, in all its tawdry hues and raucous noise was the real and certain world.

I stomped around the dim perimeter looking for my friends. The girls, Chinese, Eurasian, some Indian and Malay, sat primly at the edge of the huge dance floor, waiting for partners. Other swirled to the music in the sweating clutches of British servicemen. At the distant end, like rowdy ghosts, the band moaned through the haze.

Hobbling to the bar I discovered Smudge hanging onto the handle of a beer mug as if it were his sole means of support. 'Give 'er it tonight then, did you?' he asked, smugly certain of the truth.

'Shut up,' I said testily. 'Would I be here if I did?'

'Thought you was just coming to see what the real thing is like.'

'I am.'

'My gonga still hurts,' he confessed. 'I reckon your ankle will be better before my gonga is. I need a doctor.'

'From what you told me, son,' I said. 'You want a dentist.'

He was not upset. ''Er teef,' he repeated. 'Them teef.'

Decently he bought me a Tiger Beer and I had just leaned back on the bar giving the impression of an aficionado surveying the prospects when a small bow-legged woman waddled over to me.

'Big dick,' she began as if she had known me for years. 'You wanna buy a nice pussy cat?'

Smudge gave me an encouraging push and before I knew where I was I was performing a tango with this scrofulous creature. She was agile, like a circus tumbler, whisking this way and that while I towed my hurting leg after her. She tried to press the key to her house onto me and confidently promised a night that would not only be memorable but work out economically as well.

'My leg,' I pleaded. 'I can't because of my leg, see.'

'You no do it with your leg,' she said as though correcting a serious design fault. 'We lying down, you let leg hang from bed.'

I told her that I had been medically advised to give it a few days' rest and we parted less than amicably. While we had been dragging around the floor I was glancing around to see what the other girls were like; there was no denying they were a pretty poor crowd. 'Late, that's why,' judged Smudge. 'You ought to 'ave got in early. All the good 'uns 'ave gone.'

But not quite all. I saw her sitting near the corner of the room, wearing a white blouse and a tight black skirt, with her shining Chinese hair piled high, her face and her eyes reposed. In my anxiety to get to her before any of the other prowling squaddies I hit my ankle against a table and let out an agonised howl. Her eyes flicked towards me and she smiled.

'Dance?' She looked surprised at my enquiry. 'Me hat check girl.' She looked at her watch. 'But finished now. You got ticket?'

'Stay there,' I pleaded. 'Don't move. Don't go off, will you?'

'I wait,' she promised and she did. When I returned with a two-dollar book of tickets she was standing at the edge of the floor tapping her foot to the music. All the girls were taxi dancers and you had to have a ticket before you could travel around the floor with them. It was a little like getting on a bus.

There were four tickets in each book but she deftly plucked the whole lot from me and slid them down the front of her dress. 'You don't dance with no more girls tonight, all right?' she said.

'No. No, of course not. Mind my foot, please.'

'We dance slow,' she promised. 'No hurt foot then.'

We closed against each other and began to move through the cloying smoke, through the noise and the perfume and the sweat, the beery laughs and the raised retorts. A girl fell on the floor and another began to kick a drunken soldier on his shins. I hugged my partner protectively to me, felt her breasts indent against my shirt. Her lips went to my perspiring cheek and she rubbed the lipstick off with her nose. 'You come home with me,' she said quietly. 'I good girl and clean. I cost you fifteen dollars. Okay?'

'Okay,' I mumbled from the vicinity of her neck. My

heart was hammering. The feel and the smell of her filled me. True romance was here. The real thing at last.

Her name was sometimes Rita. It was also sometimes Doris and then sometimes Veronica. Much depended on the female star of the current film at the Georgetown cinema. Later, when she arrived in Singapore, she kept to the same simple system, Rita Hayworth, Doris Day, Veronica Lake (for whom, in addition, she attempted a hairstyle that hid one eye) and other beauties were honoured in their turn. Although I got to know her very well, on an amateur basis in addition to her normal professional life, I have never remembered her true name. One Wednesday afternoon, in Singapore, during the army's traditional and jealously guarded recreation half-day, I spent some time on her sunlit bed embroidered with a giggling dragon, reciting her Chinese name under her instruction. But soon it had slipped my mind again. In *The Virgin Soldiers* I called her Juicy Lucy. The story of our first fifteen-dollar night together is told as honestly as it will ever be in that novel:

> It was not so much a bedroom as a storeroom, Lucy was apparently a collector. Of anything. There were dolls, fans, and three stuffed poodles. Boxes and trinkets, books and comics, gramophone records, lubricant jelly, three sizes of contraceptives, a picture of Mao Tse-tung and a beautifully embroidered plaque saying: 'Happy New Year from the Gordon Highlanders'.
>
> . . . He had been standing, an enchanted spectator,

*and was about to move forward into what he imagined
must be the opening hold, when she rose coolly from the
bed and began flopping her hair about in front of the
mirror. Her blouse buttons were still free and as she raised
her hands to her black hair, in that most graceful of all
womanly movements, he could see her breasts attempting
escape like prisoners trying to climb a wall. She pushed
them back again with a pout. Then she smiled at him,
a full professional smile in the mirror, all eyes and teeth,
and simpered: 'You pay now. Then we have nice filthy
time. Please fifteen dollars.'*

*. . . After he had given her the dollars, he stood around
awkwardly wondering what to do next, like a man waiting
for casual labour. She looked at him peculiarly then moved
away from the mirror and sat on the edge of the bed.*

'How you like me?' she enquired sweetly.

*'Oh,' he stammered, thinking she was awaiting instruc-
tions for the position she should assume. 'Just the usual.'*

*'The usual?' she asked. 'What's usual? How you like
me? I am pretty, yes?'*

*'Yes, yes,' he hurried, annoyed at his mistake. 'You're
very beautiful, Lucy.'*

*. . . He fixed his starving, anxious gaze on her and
scrambled forward in the crawl that infantrymen use over
broken ground.*

*When he was near, or thought he was near, he stabbed
at her frantically and missed. It was painful. The second
time he all but fell from the bed.*

*. . . Brigg was sweating waterfalls. Where was it?
Where in hell was it? Fancy hiding the bloody thing under
there. He wiped the perspiration from his eyes so he could
see better. Then he made another huge lunge. This time he*

302

*did a fantastic pole vault, hurting himself, and landed
heavily on top of her. She was holding her breath expectantly and he knocked it all out of her.*

*She started to be angry, but looked and saw he was
crying. With a tender, involuntary movement, she brought
him close to her with his cheek against her breast and the
tears wetting both.*

*'You cry?' she whispered in wonder. 'Why so rough,
then cry?'*

'It's the first time,' he sniffed like a schoolboy.

'The very first . . .'

*Lucy emitted a round little whoop, sitting stark upright
as though she had a spring in the small of her back. Her
slant eyes were round and glistening with amazement.*

*'First time?' she repeated as though it were the Hidden
Name of God. 'Never have before?'*

*'Never,' he mumbled miserably, waiting to be tossed
with scorn from the bed.*

*'A virgin,' she breathed unbelievingly. 'A little virgin
soldier.'*

Juicy Lucy is, in fact, the name of an old American
jazz tune. Just after writing the novel I was appearing
on a television programme in New York when one of
the technicians enquired if I were a jazz historian. He
then told me the origin of the name. After the appearance of *The Virgin Soldiers* it surfaced in a number of
forms; there was a pop group called Juicy Lucy and a
number of restaurants adopted it, those dealing in
nature foods, fruit and vegetable juices found it particularly apt. It also appeared for several seasons on a
newsagent's board in Soho. It would have been pleasant

to think that it was the same lady, but the passing years and the width of oceans made me come to the logical conclusion that it was not, which was a pity.

She had told me that first night in Penang, when I was lying smug, triumphant, and at last wise, that she wanted to travel south to Singapore. Her story was that she had run away from home in the north of Malaya, near the Siamese border, because her father wanted to trade her off in an advantageous (for him) marriage. She had found her way to Penang and at nineteen had set herself up in business. On the girls' grapevine she now heard that the rates and conditions were better in Singapore and she wanted to get there. Would I take her with me?

After the first shock and the secondary confusion I explained that the army to which I was pledged might be unsympathetic. She argued she knew of several Chinese and Eurasian girls who had gone with soldiers to Singapore – and even *married* them. The thought took my breath away. Here was I, after all those worried years, at last rid of my virginity at a cost of fifteen Malay dollars – and she was talking of *marriage*. She must have thought my stunned attitude meant that I was considering the proposal because she offered to give me my money back. (The sequence in the book and in the film where Lucy actually does return Brigg's money is fiction. Some things have to be. Few hardworking Chinese girls, no matter how good-hearted, would have refunded the fee solely on account of it being the young soldier's initiation. The part about her offering cocoa is also made up. Although Lucy did have an opened packet of

Cadbury's on a tray at the side of her bed she never offered any to me.)

After that first night in Georgetown I remember how I got a bus back to the leave centre and strode in the gate like a Trojan, taking lungfuls of morning air. As I flung open the door of the room I shared with Smudge he turned dismally on his bed and muttered: ''Ere comes the night shift.'

'Smudge,' I intoned. 'Smudge, she was terrific. There's not many girls like that around.'

'Only a few million,' he commented acidly but truthfully. He turned rheumy-eyed. 'I've 'ad enough,' he said hoarsely. 'Enough for the rest of my working life, mate. I ain't going to abuse my body any more. I'm going to save the rest of it for going 'ome. For the girlfriend.'

As for me, the energetic companionship of that night had given me a taste for it. Before I went back from leave I expended a further fifteen dollars on Mitzi (as she was known during the second week. Mitzi Gaynor being named in lights above the cinema). Earlier that evening I was with the others in the restaurant we used for our steak, egg and chips, and Dolores, my unassailable Eurasian beauty, swayed in with her untouched sister. As I left she smiled and I coolly kissed her on the cheek, a touch of nonchalance, before sauntering off towards the evil and beckoning glow of the City Lights. Smudge it was who remained and in the morning he reported that they had enjoyed a wonderful conversation. 'Wiv them Chinese tarts,' he observed with disdainful wisdom. 'You can't 'ave a talk, only a shag. I like to 'ave a good talk sometimes.'

When I left Penang my Chinese girl who, for the

sake of clarity, I shall identify by her eventual fictional name, Juicy Lucy, promised that she would soon join me in Singapore. She had heard that the Liberty Club in that city was looking for girls.

I only half-believed her but, on our return and after a month of barrack room boredom, I took the Saturday-night bus and sought out this place which remains, deep as a murky pool, in my memory. It was a heavy stone building which appeared in some not-too-distant previous life to have been in ecclesiastical use. It had a tall ceiling, church-shaped windows which had been boarded up or otherwise covered as if to decently blind-fold them, and two long rows of stalwart stone columns. It was a curious edifice to find at the centre of an Oriental city, a sober relic of some British devotees I suppose. They would have been less than happy to witness its conversion. Viewed from the bandstand where, as it turned out, I spent some of my time, it presented a scene of desperate and unbridled sin. The band blared and in the wreathing smoke the dancers clutched each other, performing motions and actions that fell little short of the carnal act. Sometimes a quickstep would be played and the partners would work up a tremendous sweat to add to the gathering passion and would then sink soggily together for a sensual and insanitary embrace to the music of a waltz. Songs like 'My Foolish Heart', 'We'll Gather Lilac' and even 'Tumbling Tumbleweed', played by a Chinese band, had a lot for which to answer.

The girls who worked at the Liberty Club were unencumbered by shame and the soldiers, sailors and airmen were grateful for the simplicity. Not all the dancing partners were attractive but they knew their business. They freely entered a competition between themselves, observed to much Eastern female giggling from the floorside seats, to see who could provoke the most manifest erection in her partner during the dance, the results and the scores noted as the said partners limped away from the arena. Once I got my comb wedged sideways in my trouser pocket and my partner was adjudged the winner of that round. They were of all sad sorts (so were we, I suppose) making a living the only way they could. There was one poor speechless little tart called Dum-Dum, whose tongue, so the tale went, had been cut out by the Japanese. She laughed nearly all the time.

I was singing with the band one night (just how this stardom occurred I will later relate) and, looking down on the Hogarthian hell, I saw Juicy Lucy standing on one side, facing the floor fetchingly sipping a soft drink and looking up at me. She was taller than most Chinese, her face and shoulders white, her dress long and black. She wore elbow-length gloves. I tried to imagine that she did not belong in that place.

But Lucy was delighted with the situation. As we danced, very properly compared to the simulated sin going on around us, she told me that she had found a room and was now eager to make her fortune. We were both aware that she was not going to make it from me, but from that moment and for the next year we saw each other every week, sometimes once, sometimes twice. We went swimming together at Changi beach and to the pictures and rode about in a trishaw. When I could afford it we went to bed, but only then for it was understood that this was something separate; the

307

way she earned her difficult living. Up to that period of my life, she was the nearest thing I had ever had to a regular and active girlfriend. She was mine Saturday nights, Wednesday afternoons and sometimes Sundays, when I was not playing cricket. The rest of the time she was anybody's.

Someone with improving ideas decided to demonstrate to Lucy, and her many sisters-in-sin, the error of their ways and the rewarding alternatives life offered – in this case basket weaving. All the bar and dance-hall girls were rounded up and shown how to make baskets and other pastoral arts. There were so many attending these lectures (a rumour was abroad that the participants would be paid) that they were held, not inappropriately, in a wrestling stadium. Lucy enjoyed them greatly for, as she explained, it gave the assembled girls an unusual opportunity to compare notes and to work out current prices in the trade. She also found the weaving interesting and would sit at the side of the dance floor in the Liberty Club industriously working away at a flower or fruit basket while waiting for her real living to come along. She showed me how to do the weaving once as she lay in bed of a hot Wednesday afternoon. I can still see her sitting up, grave and naked, reciting 'This go through there, and pop out there, this go through there . . .' as she fingered the strips of bamboo. Another thing she taught me was to sing 'Jingle Bells' in Chinese, an attainment which, for subsequent lack of opportunity, has declined to disuse over the years. All I can recall now is that the first two lines went:

Ding, ding, ding,
Ding, ding, ding.

Another song she could sing in Chinese (and so for
some reason could many of her compatriots) was 'Auld
Lang Syne' which made her something of a favourite
with Scottish soldiers, two of whom, however, hastened
the closing down of her workplace, the Liberty Club,
by celebrating Hogmanay too strenuously. They tried
to kill each other and one succeeded. The next day
the authorities barred the doors for ever. It was well
named, for no place I have ever entered, and I've
entered a few, lent itself to more liberties, both taken
and accepted, although the enchantingly named
Crockford's Club in Colombo does run it quite close.

Throughout the happy time I knew Lucy, there
remained living within me a little prude who unend-
ingly nagged. In an attempt to satisfy this void and to
become legitimate again, I asked one of the Chinese
girl clerks at the office to go to the cinema with me
and she agreed. She looked like a melon but she was
not on the game, which to my personal internal
hypocrite seemed important at the time. Unfortunately
when I turned up for our date outside the Cathay
Cinema she was there accompanied by her entire
family. There was no escape; I had to take the girl,
her mother, father, grandmother and two small melon
babies into the pictures. Fortunately the seats were
cheap but I had a salutary lesson and a miserable time.
The grandmother, who kept cracking nuts and spit-
ting out the shells, and the mother sat on either side
of me so I could not even get my arm around the girl.

One of the children, who had just wet, climbed onto my lap, and then Gran, who had become overly excited by the film (which was about the Berlin air lift), poked me in the eye with her long black fingernail. After that night I remained faithful to Lucy.

She could rarely get my name right and when she did manage it, after some rehearsal, she had forgotten it by our next assignation. So I took a leaf from her book and adopted the names of film stars, Humphrey (as in Bogart), James (as in Cagney), and my mother's old heart-throb Edward G. (as in Robinson).

In my stupid young and romantic way I suppose she was my first true (in the sense of real) love. She had given me something no other woman had thought appropriate and with it her friendship. Over the years I have many times visited Singapore and I have wryly wondered if she is still there. One night she threw my trousers out of the window while I was asleep and I had much difficulty the following day in retrieving them. The incident was the one possibly recognisable part of our relationship portrayed in *The Virgin Soldiers*. If she, a dedicated cinema-goer, saw the film, perhaps some far-off chord might have been struck for her. Would she, in her thirties by then, have realised that she was Juicy Lucy?

Perhaps, perhaps not. All I know is that on the final night in Singapore, before the long-awaited troopship came to carry me back to England, I went to see her for the last time at the club where she had begun work when the Liberty closed its doors. I remember going up the familiar fetid stairs into the compressed room, the garish lights and the strained music, and seeing her at once sitting in her usual corner waiting for someone to hand her a ticket for a dance. She did not see me and I could not bring myself to go across the floor. A creased sergeant, whom I dimly recognised as a cook at Nee Soon, nodded towards her. 'Nice that one,' he observed. 'Calls herself Oliver. Funny name for a bint ain't it, Oliver?' I was so choked that I merely turned and walked down the stairs and out again. The air was dense, men sat in the gutters selling little bits of food from glowing stoves, I could hear the imperious voice of the Raffles Hotel doorman summoning chauffeurs by number, like a bingo caller. Tomorrow my dream of going home would be realised. I walked steadily towards the bus station. Yes, there it was, above the Cathay Cinema, Olivia de Havilland starring in so-and-so.

I could have meant only little to her and the art of forgetting was an integral part of her trade. But I was, and am, someone who needs someone to love and for a while it was her, Juicy Lucy, Rita, Doris, Veronica, and the rest. I have always been grateful. Whoever she was.

XIII

The troopship sailing out to take me back to England had proved to be a long time coming. Our original eighteen months' term of national service was summarily increased to two years on account of the war in Korea. Mr Attlee, the far-off Prime Minister, made a speech which was broadcast on Radio Malaya as we sat stunned on our beds, draped in the customary off-duty towels like men in an unhappy Turkish bath. The thin voice of the Labour Premier issued irresolutely from the loudspeaker set across one corner of the room where it had functioned perfectly well until Trooper Johns had got his hands on it. Johns, a large Welshman sprouting spider-red hair, had mysteriously appeared in our midst from up-country, and having made up his bed turned his attention to improving our general domestic situation, beginning by repairing the perfectly good radio set. He had several pieces left over when he had finished and the set had never worked properly since. Even now, at this trying moment, there were glares in his direction as the sounds crackled, faded and wobbled about, as if Trooper Johns and not the Government were responsible for the bad news.

'The increase in national service,' Atlee forecast

from his safe distance, 'is bound to cause disappoint-ment and hardship. It is bound to be unpopular . . .'

That was the understatement of the century. There we had been, marking our names, numbers and destin-ation on our energetically scrubbed kitbags ('UK ex-Malaya'). We had been measured for our last flimsy civilian suits from the Chinese village tailor and some, in an excess of vanity, had even had special and very unofficial uniforms made privately from smooth American-looking olive green material with all sorts of coloured flashes and insignia, mostly thought up by the tailor himself. One lance-corporal, short-sighted and with a hump on the left side of his back, was all prepared to go home looking like General Eisenhower. The show-off uniforms could, at the most, only be worn during the dreamed-of two weeks of disembarka-tion leave in England but it was judged that they would prove to be well worth their cost in just one evening at the Hammersmith Palais de Danse. ('Just come back from the jungle, see love, haven't seen a white woman in months.')

Now, after all this and ritual crossing off of calendar dates, the promising letters to females, friends and families, the imagining of English sunlight slanting across Southampton Water; now the dream was to be postponed, perhaps even indefinitely. We remained speechless after the faraway Attlee had faded. Then Trooper Johns, who was a regular on a seven-year term, proclaimed loudly, with the triumphant and certain fervour of a Welsh evangelist. 'Six months – never! Six years more like it. The next big war is coming, boys!'

We told him to shut up but he would not and he was bigger than any of us. 'Sign on, lads, you might as well. Get the extra money while you can. You're never going home now.'

According to our pipe-voiced premier we were going to get a rise in pay anyway, in consolation, but it was little to relieve our despond. It was the beginning of the week and nobody had any money. The skinny Mongo, our Tamil bearer who for a dollar a week used to make your bed, clean your boots and brasses, was always willing to lend the dollar back, at a small percentage, and on this night several of the young men in the barrack room availed themselves of this facility. Now, at least, they could afford a NAAFI beer. The rest of us sat moodily on our beds. Some hauled up their mosquito nets and dubiously retired to privacy.

The acute Cockney, Reg Wilcox, normally ebullient and cheerfully insubordinate (he saluted officers with a clenched fist), sat cloudily and picked at his guitar while his neighbour, an unparticular corporal, did likewise at his nose. Eventually Reg went to the centre of the barrack room, where the tea-bucket was located, and sat on one of the two wooden cross-benches, our only furniture apart from beds and lockers. He began to sing, like a dirge, a song intended for more jovial moments:

> She's a big fat cow,
> She's twice the size of me,
> She's got hairs on her belly
> Like the branches on a tree . . .

Some of us joined in. Then others, gathering around, made a sing-song of our woe. As we chorused through the crude repertoire, more and more soldiers appeared from other disconsolate barrack rooms. People started to do individual acts, somebody told worn jokes, and a nice young fellow who occupied the next bed to mine and was leader of a local Chinese Wolf Cub pack, demonstrated the wonders of knot-making and amazed us with Kim's Game, the Boy Scout memory technique to recall in sequence up to thirty different objects. We were all in this together. Reg and I harmonised in 'Moon above Malaya', a song composed by someone snugly back home about a boy and girl 'dreaming in a bamboo hut'. There was a raucous version of this and everyone heartily joined in. It was simple and innocent enough and we were astonished when a glowering sergeant and three armed and heavily booted men entered resoundingly into the room. The trio of strangers were transit troops from the camp next door, with a sergeant we recognised as being a resident misery. The singing faltered but, under Reg Wilcox's defiant leadership, gathered again until it was far louder and ruder than before. The sergeant, a thin wet-eyed individual, scowled. 'Stop it!' he squeaked. 'Stop this row!'

With slow obedience the song faded. We sat dumbly. The armed soldiers were standing nonplussed. They were newly out from Britain and they looked nervous. 'Find it!' ordered the sergeant in their direction. 'Search the place. Find it!'

Not one of us had said a word and now we looked askance at each other. Find it? Find what? Perhaps, I thought, they were searching for our secret dog, a wretched pooping pup which we had found and, against the regulations, were rearing in the barrack room. At that moment it was below somebody's bed. But it was not the dog. 'All right, smart alecs,' said the sergeant straightening up. 'Where's the booze?'

Booze! Reg looked everywhere as if searching. 'Booze, Sarge?' he said with half his usual grin. 'I wish we had some. Have you got any?'

'Less of your lip, lad, or I'll have you on a charge,' responded the man nastily. I wondered if he had a wife and family. 'There must be booze somewhere. Or you wouldn't be singing, would you?'

The remote logic of this was hard to grasp. The young fellow who ran the Wolf Cubs, and was respected everywhere except when he trooped them into the barrack room on a Sunday morning, said to the sergeant, 'Nobody here has had a drop of drink, sergeant, We're singing because we're unhappy.'

The watery NCO looked at us uncomprehendingly.

'Because you're what?'

'Browned off,' translated Reg.

'What for? What have you lot got to be browned off about?'

'Six months extra on our service,' Reg told him.

'Six months! Six bloody months!' He almost wept. 'I'm in for eighteen years!'

Reg Wilcox was never lost for a reply. 'You'd better sit down and join in, sarge,' he suggested politely. 'You'll like the next song. "Happy Days Are Here Again!"'

He gave a twang on his guitar.

*

If the new war and its resulting demands on our lives came as a shock to us, our annoyance was nothing compared to those who had served through the harsh years of the Second World War only to find themselves summarily pressed into the army again and hurriedly transported overseas to a place of which many had never heard.

A favourite legitimate and cheap haunt of conscripts in Singapore was the appropriately named Shackles Club, a bar and social centre where selected local girls, known for their decency and dancing, used to foxtrot with us for nothing. There was nothing to follow either for they were invariably escorted away from the corrugated iron building while we stood in a down-faced group like dogs who had suddenly seen a variety of tasty bones removed from under their noses. It was in the bamboo bar of this otherwise pleasant establishment, among the rattan chairs and yellow-covered wedges of the *Daily Mirror* overseas edition, that I met a man who looked almost too elderly to be in army uniform. He was drinking Tiger Beer in deep thought, every now and then pausing to peer about him in the manner of someone who has quite recently lost their memory.

'How did you get here then?' he asked us simply. 'All this way from home? Lads like you?'

I was with Smudge. We had been dancing with two sinuous Eurasian girls whose fat mother had just arrived to take them home because it was ten o'clock. In her sing-songy voice she was saying: 'It is past my girls' bedtime.'

'Not much it fucking ain't,' Smudge remarked,

taking a consoling swig of his beer as he watched the slight and slinky backsides retreat. It was left to me to tell the sad soldier that we were doing our national service, a condition of which he appeared to have no knowledge. I thought he might have come from somewhere remote for he had a wild accent; perhaps a place where the outside world did not greatly intrude.

'I thought,' he intoned, regarding us as if he were still unsure we were flesh and blood, 'that when the war was finished it was *finished*. All over and done with. We could all go home like they promised. I'm married now, I got two boys and I've just started a new farm job. All going nice. And then they come around and tell me that I've got to go back in the army because I'm a reservist. I never knew they could get you back just like that.' My heart felt very heavy for him. 'And,' he added almost like an accusation, 'I come out here and you're here already.'

'Well,' offered Smudge a little defensively, 'we don't want to be 'ere either, mate, and now we've got another six bleeding months.'

'As for this place, Korea,' said the soldier as if he had never heard Smudge, 'I'd never heard tell of it until now. And I've got to go and fight there. Nothing seems sensible, do it?'

We left him and returned thoughtfully on the bus to Nee Soon, our now familiar home, the smelly wooden village at the foot of the hill with its shops and houses spilling into the roadside monsoon drains, the cafés and the tailors' shops and the wooden cinema so flimsy it swayed when there was a wind. There we often sat rooting for the cowboys while, for some deep

318

reason, the local Chinese always identified with the Indians.

It was dull but it was safe and, after all, Mr Attlee had promised faithfully that after our new six months, provided no further war had cropped up, we could all go home. There were some, however, who deeply doubted this and for the first few days, following the imposition of the extended service, I was among them. Sitting at my desk sorting through the details of dead men, I realised that in all dread probability I was in the army for ever. I might as well sign on as a regular soldier and at least get a lance-corporal's stripe and extra money. The inevitability stared me in the face. At that moment I almost marched into the Adjutant's office and offered my body to my country. Fortunately I had to pass the latrines on the way and I paused there, as one might pause when troubled at a wayside church, sitting in the cubicle studying the map of Korea on the front page of the *Straits Times*. The forces of the north, the Communist Koreans and their Chinese allies, were pushing in fierce black arrows far down into the south of the peninsular country. As a military man myself I judged that it would not be long before they drove the United Nations Forces, mostly Americans, with ourselves and some Australians as helpmates, into the China Sea. (Actually they did not. When only a small pocket was left to our side the advance was stemmed and a clever amphibious landing at Inchon further north eventually resulted in the Communist forces retreating.)

It was while I was in the lavatory, studying the

strategy and becoming more convinced that I might as well face facts and throw in my lot with the army, that my eye was taken by a separate paragraph low on the page saying that a British swimmer, Roy Romain, was to take part in some events in Singapore. He was from Walthamstow and I had seen him swim a number of times when I worked for the local newspaper. Once I asked him how he was and he replied: 'Fine, thanks.' Now, miraculously, I saw myself transformed back again looking smooth, interviewing the grand and the great, attending receptions and crimes, writing in the late yellow light of some famous Fleet Street office. I rose from the bog with my mind changed and my ambitions relit. What, after all, was labouring in an army pay office compared to going to Cup Finals and economically meeting attractive women? On the following day it was announced that the Chinese advance had been halted.

A rumour went around as swiftly as rumours do in such enclosed societies, that some men from Nee Soon would be required to go to Korea, a prospect so unpleasing that there was a communal sigh of relief when it was decided that clerks from elsewhere would be sent. They, as it turned out, had very much the final laugh because they got no further to the front line than Tokyo, where the pay office was established, and enjoyed themselves immeasurably in that city of pleasure.

For other young soldiers, of course, the going was much more painful. The Gloucestershire Regiment, mainly conscripts like ourselves, had paused in Singapore on their way to Korea and they had been somewhat in awe of those of us who had been getting our knees brown, as the expression was, for a year or more. Later they fought in one of the fiercest battles of the Korean War, along the Imjin River, and earned themselves many honours and many deaths. They were the real soldiers.

Even in the blackest circumstances, however, there are those whose inborn optimism carries them on, and sometimes it is most oddly apparent. A friend in the West Country has the skeleton of a Chinese soldier on the sitting room piano at his home. In the middle of mud and death in Korea he began considering his future and decided he would like to qualify as a doctor when his national service was complete. A doctor, he was aware, needed a skeleton and even imitation skeletons were expensive. The real thing cost a fortune. And there he was in the front line of battle surrounded by potential skeletons. Why not take one home? He crept out and at considerable risk returned with a Chinese soldier who had been dead some time. The men under his command were not very taken with this addition to the unit and even less so when their officer proceeded to 'boil up' the body in a large cooking pot. Eventually, after much disgust, the bones were clean and he clattered about with them throughout his Korean war service. When he returned home he changed his mind about the life of medicine but he kept the skeleton. His children played at skipping with the threaded vertebrae.

I have also heard a story that when the Argentine prisoners were being evacuated from the Falklands they were told they could take as many of their belongings as they could carry personally. One fellow was humping a huge sack as he prepared to board the ship. He was stopped by a British officer and asked what it contained. 'It's my brother. He is dead,' said the soldier. And it was.

For us, for another six months, the fans continued to whirr in the heavy air of the office; the arrival of the tea trolley and a journey to the latrines every hour helped to push the time by but it was still slow. My task of burying the financial affairs of soldiers who were themselves by that time buried continued to be undemanding but depressing. My physical aspect was not out of keeping with the role for, stripped to the waist as we often were in the office, my ribs were easily visible and my shoulders were like a yoke. This cadaverous ensemble was topped with a head of sharp cheekbones and deeply saucered eyes. By crossing my thin arms below my chin I could do a fair imitation of a pirate flag. Once I took some documents to a sergeant in charge of a distant section. I was wearing my shorts, gaiters and boots and presumably a serious expression. 'Death cases, sarge,' I said as I put the folders on his desk.

He took in my skeletal frame. A wrinkle of a grin cracked the skin of his jaw. As I went away I heard the clerks in his section erupt with laughter. One of them told me later that as soon as my back was turned the sergeant said: 'Death cases! Blimey, he looks like a bloody death case himself. What an 'orrible thing, dying in a pay office.'

I had tried desperately to build up my frame by going to the garrison swimming pool each evening and crawling a laboured, lonely, mile. As a rule the only other occupant was the conscript who was trying to go blind by getting as much of the water's chemicals into his eyes as possible, thus gaining his passage home. Swimming opposite ways we would trudge up and down the pool although he could at least alleviate the tedium by merely sitting in the shallow end and ducking his eyes. After more than a month of this not a solitary enlarged muscle could be detected in my frame. My comrades used to count my ribs as the Chinese counted the abacus frames and our secret barrack room dog tried to gnaw my shinbone.

Even now, although the remainder of me has spread, my legs remain spidery. In those days I only wore shorts when I had to. I even refused to play cricket away from the garrison because someone said that in white shorts I looked like two surrender flags. It was very personal and distressing.

In my more optimistic moments, however, I believed that I bore some resemblance to the famished fledgling Frank Sinatra of a few years before. When I began to sing professionally I did my hair like him. This stardom had come because of that dejected evening when we had tried to sing to ourselves and the sergeant thought we were drunk.

The guitar-playing Reg Wilcox decided that we harmonised adeptly and we formed a quartet with a fellow called Chalky White from the next barrack block and a Women's Royal Army Corps girl who had a good voice and a bust nudging disturbingly at her shirt buttons when she breathed. We called ourselves Three

Boys, A Girl and A Guitar, and it was thus I made my
first broadcast crooning 'Tumbling Tumbleweed' and
'Mamoola Moon' (the popular version of a traditional
song that has since been elevated to Malaysia's national
anthem but in those days was a mere foxtrot).

Our career began with a performance in the
sergeants' mess at their Sunday beer night, and then
at a neighbouring camp, then for some officers and
their wives, and even at a children's party, where the
army brats bombarded us with sultanas and raisins.
We were paid a pound each for these recitals. Reg,
the cheerful anarchist, sometimes adapted the words
of a song (as at the children's party) so that 'My
Grandfather's Clock' was rendered:

My grandfather's *cock*
Was too tall for the shelf,
So it stood by itself in the hall.
It was taller by half than the old man himself . . .

Our delight when Radio Malaya invited us to
partake in a forces concert was only exceeded when
the compère announced us as coming 'Right off the
top shelf!' The top shelf must have been somewhat
dusty because my memory of the result, as broadcast later, is that it was not unlike the ragged harmonising outside a pub after closing time. Nonetheless we
continued to give performances, supplementing our
meagre army earnings. The girl went on to make
broadcasts on her own and Reg and I, together and
individually, crooned through the murk and garish
lights of many a Singapore dance hall. Our speciality

was 'My Foolish Heart', a ballad made popular by a band singer in Britain called Steve Conway who tragically died almost at the moment of his success. It was this song that I sang at the early apex of my career as a vocalist, standing one night on the stage of the ballroom at the fabled Raffles Hotel with a large orchestra behind me and the floor crammed with the quality of colonial Singapore, white dinner-jacketed, long-dressed, absently applauding, chattering and gin-slinging. That night, looking down on those select heads, the last generation of their sort, although no one knew it then, I thought how splendid it would be to be able to afford to buy a drink at the legendary long bar where Somerset Maugham and Noël Coward had sipped.

It was fifteen years later, on my way to Australia as a newspaperman assigned to a royal tour, that I entered the Raffles under my own auspices. But before I could realise the then attainable ambition I was stricken with a rapid case of appendicitis. All I could manage was a drink of water, brought to me nonetheless by a turbaned Sikh bearing a silver tray. When in 1977 I went with my wife Diana to Singapore to write and appear in a television commercial for Singapore Airlines, I set the final scene of the sixty-second drama in the Palm Court of the Raffles. There as we sat in evening dress, beneath the palms and the stars, with a Chinese string quartet playing Vivaldi, I lifted a glass of wine. That drink had been a long time coming.

To the small rewards gained by singing were added the occasional pounds I still earned from writing unimportant articles for provincial newspapers back home. (The RSM, to whom I continued to submit these pieces for censorship, remarked that it was amazing how easy it was to make good money from writing and that he was determined to enter the field when he finished his term of service – the first of many who have told me that they intend to start writing their best-seller tomorrow, or the day after, or as soon as they've finished their career or their drink.) Briefly I had become a lance-corporal, although I was ingloriously demoted following the incident when Juicy Lucy flung my trousers from her window in the middle of the night, causing me to report late at the barracks the following morning. My extramural activities resulted in the trebling of my pay, not a difficult achievement bearing in mind that the original amounted to less than two pounds a week. This largesse meant, however, that I could purchase further flimsy going-home suits from Fuk Yew, the village tailor. Others were doing the same and I even heard it said that the only advantage of the additional imposition of service was that it enabled the conscript to return better furnished with Chinese tailoring.

I now had several suits, one in peacock blue, as well as a fawn jacket and chocolate-brown trousers which I wore when I was singing. In the ensuing years Fuk Yew has paid me back many times for my custom because I involved him and his curious name (his family probably came from Fukien Province in China) in *The Virgin Soldiers*, although Columbia Pictures ducked the risk of having it spoken in the film. The name is not uncommon among Chinese. There was a shop in Hong Kong where it was blazoned over the façade and just along the street another trader, in hundred-year-old eggs and dried frogs, advertised himself as Fuk Yew Tew.

It was my fawn and brown ensemble that I chose to wear at the most lavish function I ever attended in my days as a soldier – the Annual St David's Day Dinner of the Singapore Welsh Society. My section officer, the good-humouredly languid Lieutenant Williams, was a member of this society and when the dinner was being arranged he insisted that 'private soldiers who are breathing the very fire of Wales' should be invited as well as those who owned their own white dinner jackets. He pressed his point with such vigour that not only were our tickets provided free but we were transported in military vehicles to the banqueting hall in the city, our arrival provoking only a little less attention than that of the General Officer Commanding, Field Marshal Sir John Harding. The group of us, six or eight, were wearing what was our version of formal clothes, me in my singing outfit, another Welsh lad in a chequered sports jacket with a naked girl painted on his tie, and another surrealistically hung with a kilt of the Seaforth Highlanders, borrowed from a Scottish soldier who owed him money and who guaranteed that it was approved formal wear, even on a Welsh night.

Many years later in London I interviewed Sir John Harding at the Naval and Military Club and he remembered that night. But since on this latter occasion I was more properly dressed, wearing a cricket club tie and arriving by taxi, he concluded that I must have been commissioned during my time in the army. He politely suggested that we might well have met up on service duties at that time and asked which unit 'did you have?'. I had to confess that the unit had me, rather than me it, after which he bought me a drink and said that the ordinary soldier, even those in the Pay Corps, had behaved magnificently when the emergency arose.

Indeed he had prophesied an emergency on that Singapore Welsh night while most guests were drinking liqueurs and I was sipping a Burton's bottled brown ale. It was, he said, important that such national societies should keep in close contact both with each other and with other like organisations in the colony. There might come an occasion when everybody would have to close ranks and if Welsh, Scots, Irish and English people knew each other well, that combining would be all the more effective. My instinct was to make notes of the speech and write it up for the *Straits Times* but Lieutenant Williams saw me starting to scribble and rolled his eyes to warn me off.

Sir John Harding was right. Within only a few days the emergency arose. While the two Singapore cinemas were proclaiming in lofty neon their current films: *Panic in the Streets* and *The Wicked City*, there was real drama down below.

On one Saturday morning each month at Nee Soon we rehearsed rioting. The practice was rarely short of farce but even so it fell well short of the real thing. For these drills the unit was divided into two sections, one designated British Army and the other local riff-raff. We took it in turns to be part of one or the other and the latter category was by far the most popular since you were allowed to dress up, hurl abuse at commissioned and non-commissioned officers and throw things. The two factions would face each other across the barrack square, under the silent and sardonic scrutiny of the Chinese waiters from the NAAFI who, when it came to it, would presumably be numbered among the riff-raff. Reg Wilcox made a natural riot leader, encouraging the shouting of obscene and obscure sentiments. For some reason, which I did not even understand at the time, a catch insult had gone around the garrison to be bellowed at odd moments, in the cookhouse, in the barrack room and – at considerable risk – on such occasions as drill periods and pay parades. The phrase was 'Old Boot!' and the object of the game was to shout it at a moment when it put the caller at most peril. Reg would march up for his pay, stamp in front of the bored paying officer at his table, thrust up his clenched-fist salute, stamp his feet and emit a muffled 'Old Boot!' before announcing his name and number.

Few officers ever even glanced up but one, perhaps more awake, did raise his eyes and asked Wilcox, 'What did you say?'

Reg's shining face spread to the cherubic, 'Me, sir? Nothing, sir. Just name and number, sir.'

'I could have sworn you said Old Boot.'

'Old Boot, sir? Me, sir? No, sir.'

'Very well. Carry on.'

The riff-raff section of the riot rehearsal adopted this pointless slogan as their war cry and a stranger might well have been puzzled at the sight of a phalanx of British soldiery confronting a rabble in fancy dress howling 'Old Boot!' at them.

The soldiers would then bring forward a banner, held aloft by two men holding its poles. This, in several languages, told the insurgents, somewhat unnecessarily, that we were British troops and, therefore, *in charge*. They must disperse and return to their homes, if they had any. The appearance of this banner was greeted with derision by the mob who stayed put and continued to throw objects.

When the real riot occurred it was for none of the reasons that might have been anticipated. There was no political motive, although doubtless such elements took due advantage of the situation. The outbreak was, in fact, caused by a twelve-year-old Dutch girl.

Her name was Bertha Hoertog and she had been left in the Dutch East Indies as a child when the Japanese invaded the islands in 1942. Her parents, depositing her with an amah, escaped to Europe. When they returned after the war both girl and amah had vanished. Eventually they were traced to a village in Malaya where the round-faced, pig-tailed, white girl had been brought up among the native children. She spoke their language, she ate their food, she washed in a stream and played in the shade below the stilts upon which her home and the other houses in the kampong were built.

The parents claimed the girl but the amah refused to give her up. Immediately the Dutch couple applied for a court order in Singapore and the Malays retaliated by 'marrying' the girl to the village schoolteacher, seeking to establish in this way that she was a Moslem.

The Singapore Supreme Court, sitting in its municipally domed, white building, decided that until the case was decided, Bertha was to be accommodated in a *convent*. It was that which so enraged the Moslem Malays. To put the girl in a Christian establishment was taken as the deepest affront. Within hours the whole city was in smoke and turmoil.

At Nee Soon there was the customary military mayhem. The order went out to form the riot squad, and thinking it was just a surprise practice (we were twelve miles from the city and knew nothing of the outbreaking violence) half of us appeared in our fancy dress ready to throw clods of earth and bellow 'Old Boot!'. We were hastily instructed to discard our costumes, to get into uniform, draw rifles and ammunition, and parade in battle order. Ashen-faced, an officer said he had heard that the pavilion of the cricket club had been blown up. Matters were patently serious.

Looking and feeling warlike we were convoyed to the city. Smoke was making a curtain over the sunset and peeping through the gap over the cab of the lorry we began to experience a few touches of apprehension. The riot was well under way by the time we arrived. People had been killed, buildings were toppled and cars were blazing in the gutters. A Chinese of prosperous proportions, stood outside his car showroom looking benignly at the crackling vehicles and rubbing his hands.

We disembarked from the lorries near the Happy World amusement park which, naturally, was under heavy guard. A national service officer, pink as a flamingo, was rushing about with a piece of paper sending platoons off in different directions to protect government offices, residences, junctions and bridges.

331

He appeared to have run out of locations when he reached us. He checked his list and his face was rose, the pink deepened to scarlet. He mumbled: 'Peculiar posting for you chaps, I'm afraid . . . It's the . . . you know . . . The VD Clinic.'

It did indeed seem an odd place to require protection but we obediently set off. When we reached it we found, in fact, that we were part of a larger force which was surrounding not only the clinic but the adjoining Shackles Services Club which was situated in convenient proximity.

'Never thought I'd have to guard this place,' sniffed Smudge, surveying the barred windows. 'Blimey, look at them bars. Do they reckon somebody's going to break in to pinch the bloody spoggies.'

Spoggies were contraceptives which the clinic dispensed to soldiers who felt desperate. A man, ominously several fingers short, and some fussy orderlies normally manned the station. Around the walls were warnings of what might happen to you if you dallied with wicked women, posters depicting little children of the future with no arms and legs, that sort of propaganda. One ex-soldier (he was wearing campaign medals and an old beret) was portrayed groping blind and lame along a gutter. Selling matches, naturally.

To prevent this sort of inconvenience in years to come soldiers who felt they *had to* could go to the building and there receive a protection kit not much smaller than the average picnic basket. There was a supply of French letters (several, presuming I suppose that you might lose one, or one might explode, or that you might not feel satisfied with the first time) and a selection of ointments and lotions which were supposed to be spread over the genital region before the illicit congress. Smudge swore he had been there once but that they would never inveigle him again. 'There was all these tubes of stuff,' he remarked in his graphic way. 'Creams and junk like that. You're supposed to spread them over the spoggie once you've got that on. By the time I'd done all that, and the bint was standing there, starkers, twiddling her thumbs, watching me . . . by the time I'd put that lot on, I'd forgot what I'd gone for.'

It occurred to me that perhaps that was the real object. Another former client of the clinic, an engineer who arrived in the night to test the telephone, confirmed the details. 'By the time I'd squeezed all that lot on me,' he said, 'I felt like a pastrycook.'

While we were guarding this essential installation there were plenty of explosions, smoke and other signs of trouble in the vicinity. An infantry officer came in and, disdainfully seeing we were desk soldiers, ordered us to try and appear fierce and follow him to the next street. None too bravely we obeyed and found ourselves around the back of St Andrew's Cathedral, a wedding cake church built to look like a corner of old England, where there was a commotion. There were shadowy figures and a car was blazing at one corner. On another, a calm crouching Chinese was still putting morsels of meat on skewers which he cooked over another, rather smaller, fire and sold to both rioters and troops.

We must have looked more businesslike than we felt

because the insurgents broke as soon as we appeared and vanished into the many alleys and cuts. We joined up with some more troops from Nee Soon who had heavily embarrassed their platoon officer by displaying the riot banner back to front. We spread along the street and six of us had just tentatively taken up position behind some ornamental shrubs when the door of the church-like building opposite burst open and out poured a frenzied gang of Orientals. They were shouting and gesticulating, several fell down the steps, and they were lucky we did not open fire without waiting for orders.

The leader, in a gorgeous blue and silver costume rushed towards us and exclaimed: 'Oh boys, so glad you're here! Hooray! Hooray!' Clearly this was no rioter.

The English upper-crust accent scarcely fitted the curly costume and the bells on his toes, or the painted pointed eyes. He was not only exotic, he was drunk. He was also more than a bit queer. He saw that we were staring. 'I'm Nankipoo!' he exclaimed.

'Nanki . . . who?'

'Nankipoo. You know, silly. Nankipoo – from *The Mikado*!' He turned to where the rest of the Orientals were sorting themselves out, doffing costumes and hats and revealing solid, if temporarily shaky, British citizens. 'This is the rest of the cast,' announced Nankipoo. 'It was our dress rehearsal tonight. Singapore Operatic Society, you know. And this wretched disturbance started. We've been shut in that hall for hours. I feel quite faint.'

*

After a few days of enthusiastic civil disorder, the appearance of a squadron of armoured cars from up-country, accompanied by a company of diminutive but businessless Ghurkas, quickly settled the city. We went back to Nee Soon, to the ledgers and the calculations, me to dead men's dockets and a short story I was busily composing in the army's time.

Others in the office were also busy at unrecognised occupations. There was a scandal when one of these was uncovered and everyone was thrilled at the arrest of the garrison's most popular young officer. He and a senior non-commissioned officer were charged and confined to barracks while army detectives from the Special Investigation Branch uncovered a unique and ingenious fraud. Sitting sweating in that humid pay office, the lieutenant had formulated a scheme which I am certain began as fancy but quickly solidified to fact once the possibilities were recognised. He simply *invented* a small army. He was in charge of a section dealing with Ghurka accounts, a specialised subject since the little warriors from Nepal had a different pay scale and different service arrangements from the rest of the army (if he so wished, so it was said, a Ghurka could go home and send his brother to replace him in the service). The young pay office lieutenant simply wrote down a list of concocted Ghurka names and invented home addresses in remote Nepal. He then proceeded to have his phantom troops posted up into the Malay jungle to fight the Communists. Up-country an accomplice would indent for money to pay these fictitious fighters. When the money arrived it was all properly accounted for and the records in Singapore were straight. Every now and then the two officers and their accomplices would meet up and share out the spare cash. It was ingenious.

How the plot was uncovered I do not know. But there was to be a court martial at Nee Soon and strict orders were given that on no account was the accused officer to be allowed in the vicinity of the pay office. He was under open arrest and wandered around amiably in much the same way as he had always done. His benign attitude had always made him popular with the other ranks; now he became the object of admiration. One evening I was on guard duty at the pay office, patrolling up and down, bayonet fixed on rifle, the crickets creaking, watching the dying day, and thinking about England. Up the path from the direction of the officers' mess came a figure with a familiar saunter.

'Halt, who goes there?' I challenged.

'Is that you, Thomas?'

'Yes, sir,' I replied, worried at the quick reversal of roles.

'Well this is me. You know me, Thomas.'

'Yes, sir. Of course, sir.'

He reached the head of the path and lit a cigarette, offering me one. 'No thanks, sir. Not on guard. I don't smoke anyway.' I was very worried about his presence.

He laughed languidly. 'Good chap.' He took a meditative puff towards the setting sun. 'Absolute shithouse place this, don't you think?'

Flattered by the familiarity I confirmed the assessment. 'Be glad to get home won't you, son?' he went on. 'How long now?'

'Three months, fourteen days, seven hours, sir. Before actually sailing that is.' Troopships always departed on the evening tide and with our demobilisation calendars, tide tables, sailing lists, names of vessels, duration of voyages and all other essential information, we knew to the moment.

'I'll probably be here for the next ten years,' he shrugged, conversationally. 'Hope they don't stick me in Changi jail.'

I seconded that and at that moment he patted me on the shoulder and said: 'Be a good chap, Thomas. How about letting me slip into the office for a couple of minutes? There's something I've left in my desk.'

My mouth sagged. I could feel it dangling. 'I . . . I . . . can't, sir,' I pleaded. 'There's special orders that you're not allowed in. I'd be court-martialled myself.'

He looked sorry he had asked. 'Right,' he said. 'Of course you would. Never mind, Thomas. I thought I'd give it a try. Have a good trip home, son.' To my overwhelming relief he strolled away down the path towards the sunset and the officers' mess. I seem to remember he got three years in the end. Whether it was in Changi I don't know.

Our excitements were generally more domestic. The arrival of a new intake of national servicemen from Britain invariably provided a measure of minor amusement. We would lean over the barrack room balcony like old sweats, making rude comments on the quality of the arriving troops, how pale their legs were and the eternity of service stretching ahead of them. This, as a measure of status, strangely mattered. 'Get some service in,' or more frequently, 'Get some in,' was no flippant phrase, but a method of showing seniority even if, like me, you were an unexalted private. One day Smudge and I were stopped in Singapore by two obvious, freshly arrived, military policemen. They said we were out of bounds and had our hands in our pockets, both accusations being true. We gave them a terrible lecture about the necessity of getting some service under their belts before accosting veterans like us and they went away suitably chastened.

Jokes were gleefully played on the newcomers, sending them out on bogus midnight patrols, putting giant beetles in their boots, telling them that it was their turn to sweep the barrack square and so on. The cost was occasionally heavy. Their retaliations were, in the main, unconscious and genuine mistakes, but dramatic for all that. In the middle of the barrack room was a large bucket which was used for what the army calls 'gunfire' – early morning tea. The overnight guard would bring in a couple of gallons of the thick brown liquid at first daylight and we would stagger from our beds and fill our enamel mugs, half for drinking, half for shaving because there was no hot water in the mornings.

On the night after the arrival of a fresh intake of conscripts, I woke to an ominous noise, realised what it was, and shot up in bed just as others were doing the same. On went the lights to reveal a long, white and nervous newcomer peeing into the tea bucket.

In the latrines were rows of what were poetically known as thunderboxes, wooden crates with a lavatory seat fashioned on the top. These were removed every day and scrubbed, being left on the balcony to dry in the sun. One of the newcomers was found squatting on a thunderbox on the balcony. 'It's too late – I've done it!' he howled miserably when we rushed towards him. 'I thought this was the proper place!'

Occasionally a novelty arrived with a new group. Such was Corporal Ankers, a breezy regular, who had occupied himself on the outgoing troopship by learning to be a hypnotist. A few nights after his arrival several men in the barrack room sprang upright at midnight and wished everyone a hearty goodnight. Half asleep, the rest of us took little heed. Then it happened again, and then again. It transpired that Corporal Ankers had hypnotised these men in the NAAFI that evening, leaving in their subconscious an instructions that at certain hours they were to rise in their beds and wish everyone goodnight.

He was encouraged to demonstrate further. Dangling a coin on a chain in front of the subject's eyes he would whisper, 'You're going into a deep sleep . . . deeper and deeper into a deep, deep sleep. Deeper and deeper into a deep . . . refreshing sleep.' Astonishingly the victim would keel over into the obedient unconscious. Then he could be made to do almost anything, from reciting rhymes to a striptease. Corporal Ankers seemed to be able to do it at will, to anyone and everyone. A sceptical NCO entered the barrack room one evening to witness this miracle and ended up making embarrassingly carnal love to a bolster which he firmly believed to be his wife back in England. When he came out of the trance he burst into tears. An ape-like potato wallah from the cookhouse, a mountainous fellow who sweated more than anyone else in Singapore, stood reciting 'Georgie-porgie, pudding and pie . . . kissed the girls and made them cry . . .' knees together, finger in mouth like the four-year-old he had once been and had suddenly become again. We had to stifle our hilarity in case we woke him up, but it proved impossible to suppress when he forgot one of the lines and stood, a huge infant, scratching his head, trying to remember.

Corporal Ankers was the star turn of the garrison concert although not in the way intended. He was worried that, in the spotlights, his powers might wane and he would not be able to entrance any and every volunteer who went up to the stage. So he asked six men, on the premise that if he failed with two or three, then others would be successes.

I was one of the six. He had successfully put me in a trance before and I had balanced, according to witnesses, supported only by my heels and the back of my head between two chairs. On the concert night volunteers were spaced across the stage and Ankers started at one end of the line and progressed to the other, putting each subject under the influence in a matter of moments. I was the first to be hypnotised, soon captured by the dangling coin and the repeated words. Apparently I stood there, at attention, while Corporal Ankers moved on to the next man, and, having put him under, to the next. When he reached number six, I suddenly toppled, still stiff as a pole, from the stage and into the lap of the Colonel's wife who was sitting beside her husband in the front row. All I know is I woke up looking into the startled eyes and flushed cheeks of the grey-haired lady, with the

340

Commanding Officer's voice beseeching me: 'Come on now, lad. Wake up. Wake up.'

Even after this debacle Corporal Ankers was permitted to continue with his performance, although while they were recovering me from the stalls the second standing soldier dropped likewise from the stage, this time narrowly missing the Adjutant. The climax of the display, however, went even more disastrously awry. The subject was persuaded, as I had been in the barrack room, to lie like a plank of wood between the slender backs of two chairs. The applause which greeted his feat provoked Ankers to overplay his hand. With a flourish he climbed up on the man's chest and stood there, feet apart, arms outstretched like a Cossack bareback rider. The clapping was immense but above it came two distinct cracks and the medical officer leapt to his feet and shouted: 'Now you've done it, Corporal! You've broken his ribs!'

He had too. The act finished in agony and confusion. Later, sitting chastened on his barrack room bed, Ankers snatched at a crumb of comfort: 'You'll notice,' he pointed out, 'that he didn't yelp until I'd brought him around, did he?'

XIV

There were still some weeks until May and our embarkation for home. The war in Korea seemed to be going better for our side and there were no alternative wars breaking out anywhere else, although each breach of the peace was followed anxiously in the newspapers. It seemed we might be getting on the boat after all. I was glad I had not signed on for life.

Roy Romain, the swimmer, who unknowingly had helped to save me from a military career, came to Singapore and swam in the international gala. He was a tall hairy man with long arms, who wore a skullcap in the water. I wrote a news story about his appearance and, since he was a personality in Walthamstow, I sent it back to my old newspaper. I was also sending reports of Nee Soon garrison rugby and soccer matches to the *Straits Times* and once caused some trouble when the newspaper sent a reporter to interview one of our conscripts who, so he said, had been secretly signed by Manchester United. The Chinese journalist walked past the garrison guardhouse and sat in the barrack room asking questions of the footballer and taking a picture of him sitting on his bed. Our colonel wanted to know how this civilian had penetrated the security. It was not very difficult. He merely walked through the gate. Indian taxi drivers, Chinese laundry boys, Tamil cleaners and Sew-Sew, the lady who used to sit on the balcony and mend our clothes for a dollar a time, all walked through the gate. Years later when I made a sentimental journey to Nee Soon, Australian troops were in the barracks and they had taken the gate off altogether. Then, on a further much later visit, I found the small alert soldiers of the Singapore army in occupation. They had replaced the gate and security was very tight.

Nee Soon does not appear in the film of *The Virgin Soldiers*. The barracks scenes were filmed at Tanglin, another almost identical garrison in Singapore. The army authorities, after initially being helpful, refused to let real soldiers appear as extras and the troops seen drilling in the picture are off-duty British sailors and airmen and Chinese troops of the Singapore army, all dressed up to look like we were. Since the latter bear no resemblance to British national servicemen, they were only filmed at a distance. Close-ups were confined to their boots.

To prepare myself for my assault on Fleet Street, I had obtained a complete, although antiquated, correspondence course on journalism. It included advice on the care and feeding of carrier pigeons taken by the reporter to wing his copy back to the office, but its general principles seemed, at the time, sound enough and I digested it avidly. I had already written to every British national newspaper giving them the good news that I was on my way home and ready to be employed. They responded with a great indifference. Only one, the *Daily Herald*, actually replied and that was to say

343

they did not want me. I was realistic enough to accept that Fleet Street might have to wait for a while so I then wrote to numerous provincial newspapers only to evoke from them a similar lack of enthusiasm. I heard that there might be a job on the *Essex Chronicle* at Chelmsford and the *Croydon Times* in south London so I wrote warning them to expect me as soon as I disembarked from the troopship. I could hardly wait to be a reporter again.

There were some soldiering duties first, however, one of these being an impressive parade to mark the King's birthday to be held on the Padang in the middle of Singapore city, an especially formidable one this year, apparently to show the flag and the guns to the natives who had so recently been insurrecting. The Padang was a famous setting, a great green alongside the harbour, with the Supreme Court on one side, the cricket club pavilion on another and St Andrew's Cathedral on the fourth – commerce, the law, cricket and the church, foundations upon which the British had built this and many other overseas possessions. On a Saturday or a Sunday I would sometimes watch the matches on the Padang where the leading teams came to play against the Singapore Cricket Club. It was all slow and pukka; hot afternoons punctuated by polite applause.

Travelling through, years later, I was there for only a few hours and I took a taxi from the airport to the Padang. The Indian driver was intrigued. 'Never, sir, have I been asked to go to Padang,' he said over his shoulder. 'Straight from airport, sir, unheard of. Unheard of. Which part of Padang, sir?'

'Fourth bong tree on the left,' I replied. He set me down. It was a Saturday and once more I sat below the deep tree-shade I had used years before and watched the batsman at the wicket. Years of shadows had filtered by but the cricket was unchanged. It could have quite easily been the same match, second innings.

Our King's birthday parade was to occupy all this sacred green, apart from the roped-off square of the cricket playing area. Even mass homage to His Majesty was excluded from that. Hundreds of us lined up in the sunshine while the General Officer Commanding walked along the heavy ranks. He was upright and only gently perspiring (they perspired; we sweated). Out of the corner of my eye I could see him approaching, progressing along the unending lines of jungle green topped by resolute expressions. The order came for our company to present arms and we all managed to do it at the same time. My rifle was vertical, directly in front of my nose, the sun was bouncing on my forehead. I was soaking inside my shirt. A large wasp settled on the rifle, then moved across to my nose before striding confidently up my nostril. I went cross-eyed trying to see this drama. The Field Marshal was nearly abreast of me. The wasp began to potter about inside my nose, buzzing busily in the cavity. If ever a soldier on parade had a good excuse for fainting, or at least sneezing, then it must have been me. But the Field Marshal was before us. The soldiers on each flank were tense. Our colonel shone with pride and the Regimental Sergeant-Major eyed us like steel. I dare not faint. The wasp continued investigating my nostril. The General Officer Commanding taking easy paces nodded amiably as he went along the ranks, solid with resolve and earnestness. As he reached me the wasp departed from my nose, crawling quite slowly out of the aperture and then zooming away. The great man stared at me. 'Good God,' he said before passing on.

There were still a few disappointments left in the days remaining at Nee Soon. In preparation for a renewed and, I sincerely hoped, improved love-life on my return to England I had been corresponding with a young lady I had known when I was attending the college in Walthamstow. Our letters had been transformed from the friendly to the endearing to the passionate as my time in Singapore neared its end. I refused to admit to myself that this ardour may have had something to do with the nylon stockings I sent to her (they were plentiful in Nee Soon village shops but unobtainable in Britain) and the promise of a bumper supply on my homecoming. Extra endearments appeared in each letter and there were more kisses at the conclusion as time went on. For some reason, I think to fool the Customs, I used to send the stockings singly, wrapped inside an airmail letter. To get a pair she had to reply to the letter promptly, so that the second nylon would be winged on its way (I was not such a fool as to send the second one without getting a further reassurance of love and endless devotion). Then the whole dream was dissolved by a coincidence that came my way as they have done, great and minor, over the years. Playing in my final cricket match, against a neighbouring RAF team, before boarding my homeward boat, I was sitting at the tea interval next to an airman who came from Ilford,

Essex, which was where my exclusive beloved lived. He produced a photograph of his girlfriend who turned out to be one and the same girl. Even the photographs were identical! I showed him mine and we sat drinking air force tea, watching the batsmen, and trying to calculate how many pairs of nylons we had sent her between us. My only consolation was that I was going home before him.

The final disaster occurred only a week before we were due to depart from Nee Soon. The ship, we knew, was at that moment crossing the Indian Ocean, Singapore just over its horizon. Marking off the days to embarkation had now become a ritual, something to be kept and savoured for a given moment. I used to regularly refrain from touching my calendar until the actual day I was to delete was almost over. Some cheated by crossing off in the early morning, some were even a couple of days in advance, but for me the ceremony took place only a moment before lights-out in the barracks room.

On this particular night the magic moment arrived and I rose from my habitual posture on the bed and opened the locker door. The calendar was pinned inside the door and I had crossed out the day and was about to happily close the locker when I noticed that the cupboard was bare – my suits had gone! All those wonderful, hard-paid-for, sleek, fashionably hued suits, that Mr Fuk Yew had sewn together for me. There were five altogether, each one meant for an occasion in England – a suit for the Palais, a suit for going for a job in Fleet Street, a suit to actually wear on newspaper assignments, and so on. Five! All vanished. Only my singing outfit, my brown trousers and fawn jacket were left.

It was no prank. They had been stolen. I never discovered by whom. The laundry man who called to carry away the sheets in a huge basket was the prime suspect, but although several Charlie Chans of the local Chinese CID were called in by our Adjutant, no clue was ever forthcoming. I was demolished. All I had in which to face England, and its waiting women, was my Frank Sinatra ensemble. (This, incidentally, I wore for a singing competition at a holiday camp after my return home. I thought I was bound to win until standing at the side of the stage I saw the next competitor, a dwarf, dressed in a smart fawn and brown suit like mine, but in miniature. He sang 'Don't Laugh At Me 'Cos I'm A Fool' and won by miles.)

These disasters, however, could in the end do nothing to dilute the joy of leaving. On the final afternoon in the office the documents of another poor devil killed 'aiding the civil power', as the subterfuge went, were delivered to my desk and I was glad to pass the job to someone else.

The army tried a final, crafty hand, however, because in the penultimate hour before quitting, I was offered a sergeant's stripes if I would sign on as a regular and continue to do the task which I had been doing as an ill-paid private for more than a year. I had no difficulty in refusing but there were others who, astonishingly, accepted such rewards and blandishments. On their very last day in Singapore they signed on for another three years in the army! They unpacked their kitbags, took down their calendars, and sewed on

348

their stripes. Two fey lads, who had always been friends, signed on because one was due to go home and the other was not. Since neither would come to the end of his service at the same time as the other they vowed to keep signing on for more years and then for more after that. It was love they said. Another barrack room friend, an outgoing Welshman called Barney Harris, remained in the Pay Corps for another twenty-five years, eventually becoming the most important man in the corps, the Regimental Sergeant-Major. I met him just after his retirement and he appeared scarcely changed from the nineteen-year-old I last saw waving from the barrack room balcony as we left. He said he had enjoyed the life.

So it was all done. The moment that we had lived so often in dreams we now experienced in reality. We humped our kitbags aboard the trucks and we drove through the gates for the last time. Even Reg Wilcox was speechless, merely raising two fingers as we departed. It seems odd now that we should have set so much store on going home and should have taken so little advantage of our visit to foreign parts at the expense of the British Government. But there it was. When we reached the docks the big white troopship was sitting there awaiting us. We thought she was the most beautiful sight we had ever seen.

A month later, early on a muslin morning, I went up onto the deck of the troopship and saw the lovely land of England on the port bow. It was Start Point in Devon; rising above it the fingers of some lofty radio masts that I remembered were rooted next to the field where we had played football in my brief schooldays in Kingsbridge. That was the moment I knew I was really home, nothing could recall me now. The land began to appear along the hem of the sea. Cliffs, beaches and docile hills, the white faces of houses, the towers of churches, and everywhere the June green of my home country.

'Can't wait for a good knees-up down the pub,' commented Reg, surveying the same scene. 'Take the old woman and my old man out for a few pints. Blimey, will we have a time!'

Others voiced their differing ambitions. To see their families, obviously; to take their girlfriend or the dog or both for a walk, to sleep in their own bed in a single room, to see how the people at the office, or the bank, or the building yard, were getting on, to enquire about a job. One fellow said he was anxious to ride his bike. It was hard for me to share some of these ambitions, certainly the family plans. (Although I determined to visit my brother who was in Wales, living now with the choral Kate and Uncle Jack) but, ever romantic, I was glad to see my homeland for its own sake. We turned half left, to cheers from all the decks, into Southampton Water; the Isle of Wight, which I planned to visit as soon as possible, rising temptingly on the other side. Singapore, Colombo, Aden and Port Said I had seen. Now I was eager to extend my travels to Cowes and Ventnor.

At Southampton there was, to me, a surprisingly large crowd on the quayside. I did not realise that people had so many relatives. As we tied up one of the soldiers shouted to a docker on a crane: 'Hey, mate, had any good strikes lately?' The taunt nearly caused one. The man glowered and then refused to swing the gangplank in, and it seemed as if setting foot on our native shore might be delayed as there was a summary union meeting to decide action. The man who had called the insult was under critical scrutiny on board. The stevedores decided that the disembarkation could go on provided the man who had shouted called out an apology in a similarly loud tone and that he would be the last to get off the ship. This was easily agreed, the caustic soldier's comrades leaning on him a trifle to obtain his acquiescence, and the joyful scenes continued.

'Oh, there he is!' called a mother from the dock-side seeing her boy at the rails. 'Oooo . . . isn't he thin! Haven't they been feeding you, Tommy?'

Few things are more embarrassing and ungainly than bawling a conversation up the side of a ship but most were undeterred. 'Big party tonight!' 'Got you some nice pork chops!' 'You're back in time to mow the lawn!' 'You're playing for the team on Saturday!' 'Auntie Mary died last week!' The soldiers remained relatively silent. A few remarks called back seemed the best they could manage. Some attempted, at that difficult distance, to introduce their comrades of the past two years but for the most part they merely stared at the flushed faces and the moving hands and handkerchiefs. Most, with nothing to say, retired below, calling down that they had received orders. They merely sat in the canteen, almost hiding. One young man had actually seen his welcome disintegrate into a terrible bawling row between himself and his father over some money that was owed. His mother had been so incensed at this crass intrusion on the occasion that she struck her husband with her handbag and in a moment there was a pitched fight on the dockside and the police had to be called. The boy sat morosely. 'Christ,' he muttered. 'They were scrapping when I went away and they're still scrapping when I get back. Wish I'd signed on, I do.'

From the ship those of us not delayed by tearful embraces were transported to a camp near Aldershot and that evening had the almost mystic experience of walking down a country lane for a beer at the local inn. There were rustics sitting outside on benches made from logs and we eventually fell into conversation with them. They were only vaguely interested in our tales from the distant side of the world, and not impressed in any way whatever by our shoulder flashes saying 'Singapore' or 'Malaya'. One of them told us a long story about a woman in the village who had been squashed to death by a horse and another reckoned that the fine weather was bound to break soon, probably at the change of the moon. The dusk deepened into a purple night and the honeysuckle smelled so fine in the hedgerows when we were having a pee on the way back to camp.

Most of us went on disembarkation leave although one unfortunate soul, having been cheeky to the local sergeant-major, was put on a spiteful seven days confined-to-barracks and when we left was pounding

352

up and down the square in the sun carrying full kit and rifle, something he had avoided all through his service overseas.

I was given a rail warrant to Barry, where my brother lived with our aunt and uncle, but on the train running westwards to Wales an unkindly inspector came to the compartment and said that there was an error in my ticket and I would have to pay extra. This so incensed a man seated by the door that he vehemently attacked the inspector. 'Can't you see?' he demanded. 'This boy's been overseas for his country. Look at that, mister.' He pointed to my shoulder flash. 'Know where that is – Singapore? Don't suppose you do.'

'There during the war,' replied the ticket man with a sniff. 'Taken prisoner. You should have had a bit of my medicine.'

'Well I was in Italy,' retorted the man. 'And that *was* bloody war, I can tell you. Mud everywhere and at Anzio . . .'

Nonplussed I watched this unfamiliar British confrontation developing before my eyes. Other passengers joined in. A woman said she had done her bit like for her country like everybody else and a man told her it was very hard in the Tank Corps. Everyone was arguing at once and there was an Irishman who kept modestly muttering: 'Well, who built the airfields, I ask you? I'll tell you, *we* built the airfields. The airfields . . . the Irish built the airfields . . .'

I was taking no part, just watching, astonished while the two main protagonists were getting heated. 'I *walked*,' asserted the passenger who had defended me.

'Walked, mate, from one end of Italy to the other!' He glared at the inspector as if it were his fault. 'In the end my boots were in tatters on my . . .'

'Boots?' echoed the ticket inspector scornfully. 'You had *boots*?'

The arguments ended in a great deal of animosity with the Irishman, presumably as a neutral, trying to mediate. The ticket inspector went off in a huff, slamming the door, but forgetting my faulty ticket which had begun it all.

I spent a week in Barry getting to know my brother again. He was no less unpredictable. He had gained, or had thrust upon him, a job in Cardiff, through the influence of our Uncle Chris, but his response had not been quite what the family hoped. He had to travel every day by train, the eight miles from Barry and, in order to conserve the money that should have been spent on fares, he used to leap from the slowing train into a convenient pile of sand just short of Cardiff Central Station and then scamper down the embankment. It was dark when he began this practice in the winter and he had become careless. He jumped one day only to find, suddenly and painfully, that the friendly sand had been replaced by stony rubble and sharp gravel. He was carried off to hospital to have his wounds stitched.

My Auntie Kate was still singing volubly, sometimes in the early hours, and occasionally in tune. She begged me never to 'go foreign' again. She could not appreciate how anyone could have ambition that stretched beyond the Great Western Railway, although she dolefully admitted that Roy was now unlikely to progress that far as 'The Company' was thought to be pressing criminal charges. Uncle Jack, silver head almost fluorescent, came in breezily each evening from driving his lorry for the Tubal Cain Iron Works, had his dinner and departed for the Institute. On Friday nights, when he opened his wage packet, he would recite sonorously in his fine voice: 'Tubal Cain was a man of might, in the days when the earth was young.' Kate used to crane her thin neck to ascertain how much was in the wage packet but he never let her see. That was no business for a woman. He referred amiably to their decent house as 'this crib', to his fat dog rolling like dough from the settee as 'this pup', and if a lady were visiting he would invariably offer to conduct her to the lavatory and hold her out. Kindly, this childless couple asked me if I would like to live with them but I declined. My ambitions were different and at some distance.

After my leave, when the final army day arrived our national service group was taken to a demobilisation centre at Hounslow where we gladly surrendered most of our kit. The practice of giving released soldiers civilian clothing had ceased but we were allowed to retain one uniform since we were on the reserve for three years and we were informed darkly that we might need it. It was just as well that they let us keep the uniform because apart from that I only had my singing suit.

I remember well those last few military moments. We came out of the demobilisation centre and stood in a bantering and awkward group on the pavement; all my comrades, my friends, Reg, Harold Wilson, Johnny Staton, Smudge, of the past two years. The

Virgin Soldiers had come home. There were hand-clasps, back slaps and good wishes, the exchanging of addresses and promise of reunions. Then they all went away. In a trice they were gone. Gone to different parts of London, to Manchester, to Glasgow, to unknown towns and villages. In that moment, and for the first time in years, I felt myself completely alone.

Standing there in khaki with a single suitcase containing, in the main, my fawn jacket and brown trousers, I knew that from that morning I was starting my life again. I was at liberty to go where I pleased, anywhere in the world; it would not matter. At twenty I was freer than most people are at any time in their lives. I could travel to any point of the compass; to Timbuctoo, New York, or even back to Singapore, provided I could find the fare. There was no one to stop me and I had nowhere special to go. I felt solitary but excited.

Along came a London bus and on the front it said simply 'Kingston'. The sign was good enough for me. I got aboard. It was not Timbuctoo, but it was the only place I felt I knew and belonged. So I got a ticket to Kingston. Back to Barnardo's.

PART FOUR

IN THE STREETS

XV

Even as I boarded that bus one part of my life reached out to touch the next. The conductor came along and I fumbled for the fare, taking from my pocket an assortment of change including some Malay one-cent pieces, which must be among the world's few square coins. The conductor spotted them at once.

'Just come back have you?'

'First day in civvy street,' I nodded.

'Out there in forty-two,' he said. 'Ended up on the Burma blinking railway.' He told me his regiment.

There was only one man I had ever met from that regiment, a character at Nee Soon who used to regale us to boredom with legends of deeds against the Japanese that no one could deny. The conductor smiled ruefully at the name. 'Knew him well,' he sniffed. 'Deserted when the Japs were coming. Ended up in a cell.'

The bus trundled towards Kingston. The conductor said he now lived in the Surrey suburb of Carshalton where my friend from my early army days, Kenneth West, also lived. I decided to go and see Ken as soon as I was settled. I would need to start collecting a few friends.

Dickies was outwardly much as I remembered. There was nothing that could alter or alleviate that grim façade. Years later, when they finally knocked it down and I watched the demolition men at work, it was with an oddly mixed sensation. There were piles of broken bricks and pyres of burning floorboards. The toppling of the tower was a climactic sight but somehow the intended cheer stuck in my throat. They had even unearthed the archaic golden letters, long removed from the front, 'The Dalziel of Wooler Memorial Home. Dr Barnardo's Homes'. They were lying randomly about like gigantic ingredients for alphabet soup.

On that previous day at the beginning of August, 1951, I trooped up the familiar hill and was once more confronted with my past and my immediate future. I knew they would give me a bed and they did. Vernon Paul had proved a decent and liberal superintendent and he and the hardworking Miss Blott, who had a swift laugh for the numerous oddities that occurred, had brought about a change in the comfort and well-being of the boys. I had brought Miss Blott a present from Singapore, an electric-blue Chinese dressing gown, crawling with red dragons. She seemed both pleased and taken aback. I do not know whether she ever wore it.

They gave me a small room and I arranged my few belongings and sat down on the bed with a sigh of relief. I was home.

There was another boy of my era staying there, who even in his young days had spoken with a rounded City businessman's voice. His name was Michael Earwaker, which although pronounced Erica was naturally translated as Ear-whacker. When I appeared on *This Is Your Life* a few years ago, Michael, splendid in a waistcoated suit and striped tie, with the same matching accent (which had never really fitted the

360

patched trousers and Dickie boy jersey), appeared on the programme as part of my past. A few weeks later I heard that he had died.

The new generation of Barnardo boys looked at me with some historical interest. I told them how it was in the old days before everyone was fed properly, had a bike, could play billiards or go to the pictures more or less when they liked. The amiable but firm Mr Paul patrolled the home with his golden retriever, a dog I had been sent to fetch as a pup from the kennels and which was gloriously sick on the bus. It had proved good-natured to the point of lethargy. Some boys had built a trolley and the dog was accustomed to sitting on it while being towed about the grounds.

My first need was to get a job. Initially I went to Chelmsford where there had been some faint response to one of my Singapore letters. The editor of the *Essex Chronicle*, however, did little to encourage me. They were really looking for a sports columnist, he said. They had found one, I asserted. I went back to Kingston and that evening composed a sharp specimen sports column. The editor wrote back and said they had miraculously filled the job during the few hours that I was writing it. The only other hopeful note had been sounded by the editor of the *Croydon Times*. It diminished every moment I sat in his office.

'You've got a boil on your nose,' he said perceptively.

Yes, I said I had noticed it.

'How old do you say you are?'

'Twenty.'

'You look much older than that,' he said.

A man as crushingly observant as this must, I

thought, be able to pick out a sharp-eyed reporter like me, so I swallowed my indignation.

'I've been out in Malaya,' I reminded him as if this might be an explanation both for the boil and my premature senility.

'Oh, really,' he said, picking up a page proof of his paper from the desk and reading it avidly, making small, pecking corrections as he did so. 'Whatever were you doing out there?'

'Fighting,' I answered desperately. 'In the jungle.'

'Croydon is a jungle,' he recited dreamily. He paused and wrote the words on a pad, presumably as a future headline. 'Perhaps we may have something for you,' he decided, looking over the top of the page. 'Why don't you come and see me again in a few months?'

All right, I said, I would. Perhaps when my boil was better. Miserably I walked out into the street. Carshalton was only a bus ride away and I went there and saw my friend Ken West, who had completed his national service two weeks before me. His posting had been to Richmond Park and he had gone home to sleep every night. He was, and remains, both handsome and humorous and his family welcomed me. There was his tiny, beautiful and regal mother Marie (in Australia, to which they eventually migrated, she was known as the Duchess of Dandenong), and his stepfather Ben who loved cricket and ballroom dancing. He and Marie were experts, and once I saw them perform a tango where *he* leapt into *her* arms at the climax. There was Ken's sister Barbara, a chatty schoolgirl, and a sturdy toddler called John. One day John, who was only three, crept up behind Ben, who was sitting reading a newspaper, and cracked him over the balding head with a cricket bat. The cricket bat broke and Ben slumped silently to the floor. They were an interesting family.

Very soon they had made me feel entirely at home. My feet were under the table and I was drinking tea and telling them of my adventures in Malaya. When they suggested that I should go and live with them I felt my smile travel across my face. It had not been such a bad day after all. So I had a boil on my nose, perhaps I looked considerably older than twenty, certainly I had not got a job, but I had found a family.

Since I had hoped for higher things, it was with some reluctance that I retraced my steps to the printing press at Voluntary Place, Wanstead. There it was, still pounding into the night, its wood and corrugated iron walls rattling and emitting blasts of heat and workers holding their faces as they staggered into the open air for a breather. Mr Harold was there also, his narrow face cleft with anxiety but able to smile wryly when he saw I had returned – as if I had fallen into a well-prepared trap. 'You can have a job any time you like, Thomas,' he announced. 'We haven't forgotten you sent us a story from Singapore about Roy Romain. Sorry you didn't get anything for it.'

There was a vacancy (there nearly always was on one of the group's more weedy journals) on the far north-west side of London, the *Willesden Citizen*. I was to start on Monday and at five pounds a week.

Although this was a good distance from my new home with the Wests at Carshalton there was a connecting bus, which took an hour at the huge fare of ten pence, and I decided that I need not sacrifice my novel and contented domesticity. Novel and contented it undoubt-edly was. It was my first adult experience of living in a house, having a room and family, going to dances, walking home, playing cricket, eating meals, discussing things and arguing others. It was a suburban living of which I fully approved. After all the uncertainties of the first part of my life I took pedantic delight in leaving the front door at eight every morning, buying the same news-paper (the *News Chronicle*) at the same corner shop, boarding the same bus with the same people, and returning the same way in the evening, reading the *Evening News* on the way home. For thirty shillings a week I was housed and fed, my washing was done, and I had companionship. On Fridays I came home with my pay packet and put at least a pound in the savings bank as a buttress against the future. On Saturday nights I would whirl around Wallington Public Hall or the Orchid Ballroom, Purley, and afterwards walk some girl home for a doorstep embrace; on Sundays there was cricket and a pint in the pub. It was as secure as Heaven.

I acquired my first enthusiastic girlfriend and several times a week we would become entwined in the alley at the rear of Merton underground station. As the chills of autumn drifted over Merton her mother insisted that she wore a vest. We were behind the tube station after going to the cinema one night, engulfed in passion, and I was pulling handfuls of the vest from her bloomers. It was the longest vest in the world; it came out in bales. My arms were full of it. She mumbled some apology for its length but her arms were busily about my neck (she was a real revo-lution in my love-life) and she was muttering enticements while I was hauling out her vest like a linen draper. When I had gathered all the slack over my elbow and was wondering what to do with it a door, previously unnoticed in an anonymous wall, opened and a troop of jolly London Transport workers about a dozen strong emerged. They wished us many jovial goodnights after realising the potency of the scene upon which they had intruded. In my shock I dropped the vest and it fell like a sail almost to her ankles. One of the men even made obligingly to gather it up for me. When they had gone we stood, me still the prig, mortified, her giggling into her hands. 'It's my mum's,' she confided. 'She's six-foot-one tall.'

On the Sunday before I began my first week's work on the *Willesden Citizen*, I conscientiously made a reconnoitring visit to my new territory. Outside a public house in the High Street were pools of blood, like red islands on the pavement. Brigades of Irishmen walked by on their way to Mass and some eyed the blood as if it evoked some indistinct memory. The publican came out with a woman carrying a bucket and broom. He rolled up his sleeves and then set her to work clearing the pavement. 'Be a busy day in the magistrates' court tomorrow,' he forecast. 'Biggest Saturday night for years.' Grateful for this complimentary information I enquired how the disturbance had begun. 'Two brothers,' he offered readily. 'Tom and Michael O'Farrell, from Kerry. Hadn't set eyes on each other in years. Their first drink together since they were boys. And . . . well, you know how it happens.' He surveyed the gore as it was washed into the gutter . . . 'They started on about old times and one thing led to another . . .'

It was apparently an area strong on news. The following day I went to the magistrates' court, my first assignment for my new paper, and the O'Farrell brothers, displaying both damage and remorse, appeared in the dock, arms on each other's shoulders. The magistrate was given the same explanation as the publican had offered me. 'Ah, it was a family reunion,' he said wisely and with no surprise.

'Oh, yes, sir, you could say that,' agreed one of the brothers gratefully.

'But it got out of hand,' prompted the magistrate.

''Twas the others,' interpolated the second brother. 'Not us. 'Twas the others. The boys from Cork.'

The magistrate appeared to find this completely reasonable. 'Fined five shillings each or one day in prison,' he intoned. They were familiar with the form. They chose to take the one day and were sat down next to the press bench to witness the rest of that morning's action, whereupon they were allowed to go. As I went out into the gritty industrial sunlight they were arguing with another man outside the first public house on the right. One of the brothers had him by the lapels of his coat. It was going to be an interesting place to work.

In its neighbourhood Willesden had a great number of illustrious persons, all dead. Kensal Green was to the south of the borough, eternalised by Chesterton ('before we go to Paradise by way of Kensal Green'). Most people went by way of a 662 trolley bus. From the top deck you could look, if you desired, over the grey wall to the mildewed city that housed the famous dead.

The large borough stretched up to Cricklewood in

with a cobbler's premises on one side and a car sales pitch, occupying a space cleared by a wartime bomb, on the other. The front of the shop was taken up with a counter for the important business of receiving small advertisements. The two ladies who handled this matter, as well as the general accounting and the making of tea, being accommodated in a cosy cubicle between the counter and the dank back room which housed the reporting staff. The squalor of this place would be hard to exaggerate. Linoleum on the floor was rotting and, when lifted, revealed not boards but bare clay. There was a single table and four chairs, a bench with a telephone and ragged piles of iodine-coloured past issues. There was a big single window, which looked out, or at least would have looked out if it had ever been cleaned, onto a dismally enclosed yard where a lavatory crouched guiltily in one corner. In summer, if you rubbed a portion of grime from the window, you could see a single, ashen dandelion protruding bravely from a crack in the boundary wall. In the winter there was no wild life to be seen at all.

During the two and a half years I worked on the *Citizen*, the reporting staff varied in strength from the luxury of four people to one, which was me. Since I did all the work on these latter occasions, everything from football to flower shows and Uncle Binkie's Kiddies Korner as well, I felt I could justifiably boast that, at twenty-one, I was the editor of a newspaper.

On the Monday morning I joined I found the office occupied by a cheerful young man of some size, who came from the upper-class part of Maida Vale, had been to a public school and was a member of the

MCC. His name was Richard Streeton and he was the sports staff, although he was only keen on cricket. He moved on to write with distinction about that game for *The Times*. There was a sweet red-haired girl called Paula, also from an upper-middle-class background, who used to have a cry when she was sent to funerals or when she was called to distant Voluntary Place to be admonished by the editor, Mr Cyril. 'It is not the way he tells me off,' she pleaded. 'It's the light shining through his ears. *I can't take my eyes off those ears!*'

It would be unjust to say that either of these amiable young people put less than their whole being into the job of reporting the dusty doings of Willesden, but there were afternoons when they quietly slipped off to the cinema at the other end of the High Street.

The chief reporter appeared equally out of place, but for other reasons. He was a brash and busy Scot, engulfed at any season in a thick-collared blue over-coat. He had a red face and wore spotted ties. He had experience on provincial and national newspapers and, when he was not drinking in the West End, or sleeping it off at his lodgings, he could find a story anywhere and sell it anywhere too.

Although the business of compiling a weekly news-paper, which came a poor second to the established journal of the area – the *Willesden Chronicle* – was marginally his main concern, our chief reporter was often engrossed in the study of greyhounds or horses running that day. To finance these investments he did a steady trade in filing linage stories to Fleet Street and it was he who properly taught me this art. One Friday night when I was going to a youth club dance, he bet me five shillings I could not come into the office the next morning with a story that would make the national papers. Having rashly accepted the wager I was relieved and delighted to be told during the first waltz that my partner's sister had become engaged that day to an internationally famous speedway rider.

At once I went to see the lucky girl, the daughter of a local shopkeeper. Yes, they were engaged. She was pretty, the speedway rider (absent abroad at that moment) was notoriously handsome. There would be a motorbike wedding in the spring. Happily I telephoned the story to the national newspapers.

On the Monday morning my chief reporter cheerfully paid up the wager, then the telephone rang and it was the famous motorbike man. 'Engaged!' he bawled. 'Who said I'm engaged? All I know is I'm in a whole lot of trouble because of *you*. I'm going to be sued for breach of promise by somebody else. It's all your fault!'

Inexperienced as I was, I was petrified. Visions of expensive libel actions hovered before me. In great anxiety I rang the alleged fiancée. Her mother, a no-nonsense London lady, answered. 'I don't know what he's playing at,' she said grimly. 'He proposed and my daughter accepted. He's accepted presents from us and he's put his motorbikes at the back of our shop. As far as I'm concerned they're engaged. So there.'

So there it was, indeed. They had a motorbike wedding in the spring.

It was in the magistrates' court I found a course of unending, small, but often touching and funny theatre. When I first went to the courtroom a wry man from the rival paper leaned over on the press bench and said: 'Ah, you're this week's reporter, are you?' The turnover in staff at the *Citizen* had become legendary.

Willesden was what the police called a 'good crime area' which meant there was a lot of it. Several CID men from Harlesden, Willesden Green and Harrow Road found their eventual way to the upper glories of Scotland Yard. There was a young and enthusiastic detective-constable who later rose to some eminence, but in those days was feeling his early way. We were two of a kind. 'How do I get my name in the paper?' he anxiously asked me one day. He said it was essential as a detective to get your name in the paper so that superiors noticed you.

He had, frankly, only been engaged in the sort of investigations that rarely evoke even local headlines. 'When you're in court giving evidence,' I advised him. 'If there's some unusual aspect of a case, some odd name or something a bit outlandish, then make sure you emphasise it. I'll take it down and write it up. I may even be able to get it in a national paper.'

A week or so later I was sitting in the juvenile court and my detective friend was giving evidence against two boys, the siblings of a well-known local clan, every member of which was occupied with crime of one sort or another. (It was alleged that even the grandfather had trapped sparrows, sprayed them yellow and sold them as canaries.) These two lawless juveniles, aged about seven and eight, were accused of stealing two bicycles. The chairman, a grim-looking lady with kindly ways, asked the policeman what the boys had told him. Cocking a speculative eye in my direction, my friend said: 'They said they wanted the cycles as *adventure bikes*, your honour.'

I groaned and shook my head. Adventure bikes! That would never do. I grimaced towards him. The magistrate looked puzzled. So did the two accused.

'Adventure bikes?' asked the justice. 'Whatever did they mean, adventure bikes?'

The young detective looked desperate. 'They . . .' he hesitated, glanced at the scowling little boys, then back towards me. He brightened with inspiration. 'They said,' he reported softly, 'that they wanted an adventure. They wanted to ride the bikes to *fairyland*.'

Horrified, the two tough children stared at the policeman. The magistrate smiled indulgently. 'Is that so?' she said beaming at them. 'To ride to fairyland?'

'Nah,' said the youngest. 'That's a lot of bollocks.'

Before going to the Willesden paper I had never been required to cover inquests, so often touched with a paltry sadness and at other times with a macabre fascination. It was astonishing how many women sat down and made a phlegmatic cup of tea after finding their husband with his head in the gas oven. One said she cooked the Sunday lunch in the same oven once they'd removed the body.

A retired policeman was being evicted from his house. He had apparently left and a bland estate agent was showing some prospective purchasers, newly weds, around the property. They reached an outhouse door. The agent, opening the door but not looking in, intoned, 'This is quite a useful shed. You can use it for all sorts of things.' Someone had. The evicted tenant was sitting in a chair with his throat cut.

A pathetic husband one morning went along the press bench offering 'all the money I can afford' if his dead wife's name could be kept out of the newspapers. His children did not know their mother had committed suicide. The tragedy had taken place outside my area and would not have appeared in my newspaper anyway. I was vastly relieved.

Among those tight streets there was drama every day. When I was first instructed to cover an inquest, on a Monday morning, I went by mistake to a little-used Coroner's Court in Kilburn instead of the normal venue at Ealing. No one seemed to be about, the door was locked, and eventually I enquired at the fire station next door. A fireman told me that I ought to find the coroner's officer 'down the yard' and I walked across a paved area and into what appeared to be an open garage. Stepping in, I found myself among the mangled but neatly sorted remains of three road accident victims. I had walked into the mortuary.

Years later, in Rio de Janeiro, I was researching an article about some men from a village in central Brazil who had been found dead after going out to 'keep a rendezvous with an Unidentified Flying Object'. After much difficulty I tracked down the pathologist who had performed the autopsies on the men to the Legal-Medical Institute in the humid centre of the city. The pathologist was friendly and offered to show me his reports if I would care to follow him to his office on a higher floor. One elevator was out of order so we stepped into another and went up in the company of a bleeding corpse on a trolley (the hair was standing on end in shock) and two young girl secretaries who chatted and filed their nails unconcernedly during the short and shocking journey. We left the elevator and then had to walk the length of a huge morgue to reach the pathologist's office. It was just after the Rio Carnival and there were bodies everywhere, as though some mad carnage had taken place in the room. Chatting idly, the pathologist led me on into his office. He got a file from a cabinet and when he turned around I had passed out cold in a chair.

Dealing with death becomes such an everyday thing for some people. I remember peeking over the shoulder of a famous pathologist who was waiting to give evidence at a London inquest. He was doodling colourfully on his folder – spleens and livers and curly intestines. And a heart with a dagger through it.

Winter came to Willesden and I was discovering that the daily journey from Surrey to the north-west edge of London and especially the return, after I had covered an evening assignment, was becoming difficult. It was necessary to leave the friendly West family and find somewhere locally to live. Outside a nearby newsagent's shop there was a frame of postcard advertisements, one offering a small, single, clean room in a nice house with breakfast and evening meal – one pound, fifteen shillings a week.

Inside the newsagent's I asked a fluffy, middle-aged lady about the advertisement. Yes, she could recommend it thoroughly, it was a good house in a decent road and it was owned by a conscientious lady who really looked after her lodgers. In fact it was herself.

Mrs Dyer was the widow of the manager of the local Odeon, who had passed on not long before, leaving her with the house and a black dog called 'Deon', named after the cinema. The house was in a road with trees, something of a rarity in that area; a red-brick front, with stairs going up and up inside. My room was at the very top of the house, adequate and clean, next to an Irishman who, I was forewarned, lobbed his empty Guinness bottles into the loft after finishing their contents while sitting up in bed. I said that did not bother me and we came to an agreement. I lived there for the next two and a half years.

Jimmie, the Irishman, worked on a car assembly line where his workmates used to weld his hammer to the metal bench at least three times a week. He would sit at the table and, halfway through the evening meal, suddenly put down his knife and fork and grin as though remembering something from long ago in Sligo. 'Those bhoys,' he would remark, shaking his head until his rimless glasses slithered sideways on his nose. 'Those bhoys, they did it again today, they did. Welded the hammer to the bench and, God help me, every time I fall for it! Every blessed time. I'm picking up the hammer and it's stuck to the bench and they all laugh and I think to myself, Jesu, they've done it again . . . and there's me falling for it . . . well . . . well . . .'

He was a goodly man of unalterable habit. He poetically called neighbouring Cricklewood *Crinklewood*. Every evening, whatever the season, he would retire to his narrow room immediately following the meal, after announcing to the other boarders that he was considering taking an early night. Up there he would read books, drink Guinness in bed, tossing the empties through the open loft trapdoor. When he went home to

Ireland to see his wife, an annual pilgrimage, Mrs Dyer would get a ladder and go into the loft and bring the bottles down. There were hundreds. His reading had filled him with lore about foreign places but with a margin of error that outdistanced even that of my father. 'Now, do your people still use the pysinned arrows?' he enquired gently of an Indian metallurgist who was briefly a guest. 'And do they extract the pysin from the trees of the jungle?'

Each Saturday at lunchtime, Jimmie would repair to the pub on the corner and stay until closing time, during which period he had backed several horses tipped by his workmates and which invariably lost. Apart from his work and the pub he rarely went anywhere. His wife paid him a surprise visit from Ireland once and he told her he would show her the sights of London, the like of which she had never seen, indicating that they were an everyday thing to him. They set out and walked down the Harrow Road towards London, several miles distant. It was only after they had gone halfway, and she saw a signpost, that she suggested that a bus might be, by chance, going in their direction.

His undemanding routine was such that he would wake at six-thirty each day, without an alarm clock and look across the street to ensure that a neighbouring work-mate's light was on. This meant that it was time for him to get up. One night I had been to a Chamber of Commerce ball or some other excitement and, arriving home at about one in the morning, was astonished to see Jimmie shaving in front of the bathroom mirror. 'Ah, young fellah!' he exclaimed. 'What would you be doing about so early in the day?' He stared at my black tie and dinner jacket. 'And dressed like that and all?'

I explained that I had not yet been to bed and it was one o'clock in the morning. 'But . . . but . . . but . . .' blustered Jimmie. Like a man betrayed he glared out of the window and across the street. The other man's light had gone out. He had apparently only got up to go to the lavatory. 'Who can you trust these days, I ask you?' muttered Jimmie, returning to bed.

His good nature was not even put out by the circumstances of his son's wedding. The son had been to university and lived separately next door. On the day of the wedding, Jimmie took over the responsibility of shepherding the guests from the house to the Roman Catholic church, and insisted that everything should be done with minute precision. Unfortunately his watch was wrong and the procession of highly dressed Irish folk arrived at the church doors just as the puzzled couple were emerging from the sparsely attended service.

At Mrs Dyer's, the other guests included a Dutch bus conductor who was a fast bowler, an Australian who ate only ice cream during the day and (so Mrs Dyer believed) was almost bald as a result, and Mr Turner, a wry Lancastrian who was stationmaster of Wembley Central and spent his weekends walking from public house to public house. He drank little, the object of the safaris being to collect pub names. He used to enter them in a little book and study them in the evenings. My room had previously been occupied by two Irishmen who had departed hurriedly after failing to put together the ingredients of a bomb. Although they were in a rush they remained long enough to settle the rent, which Mrs Dyer thought was pretty decent considering the police were on the way.

Our landlady was not so much shocked as amused by all that fuss. She was a genteel person with a nice voice and careful manners. I only once saw her lose her temper and that was with me. A staunch Tory, she was outraged when I brashly suggested that Winston Churchill was a warmonger and promptly cracked me over the head with a saucepan which dented as a result.

I was the youngest in the house and she was sufficiently understanding to light a fire in the front parlour on Sunday afternoons so that I could entertain a girlfriend. One night she appeared on the landing, a powdery figure in a long, ghostly nightie, and apprehended me carrying my blankets and pillow down to the same front room where I had planned to make a young lady (and myself) more comfortable.

Mrs Dyer missed her husband who had been the cinema manager and often talked romantically of their days at the pictures. She had one or two friends on the fringe of showbusiness; one old lady used to come to tea and talk about her career with a performing dogs act in a circus. The newsagent's shop where my landlady worked in the afternoons was owned by a grey, upright colonelish-looking man called Mr Rogers. They liked each other very much and sometimes he would be invited around to supper and at others they would go out for a ride on a bus.

They would have been married, I expect, but he was taken suddenly ill and I came downstairs one morning and found her weeping while cooking the breakfast. Her great tears were falling sizzling into the frying pan with the sausages. 'He's dead,' she sobbed to me. 'My Mr Rogers is dead.' My heart went out to her for, like me, she was one of the world's solitaries and we embraced while the fat splattered. She went to see him in his coffin at the undertakers'. 'They do make them look very nice,' she said, her sense of the theatre unwilling to be subdued. 'He looked quite in the pink.'

The theft of almost my entire wardrobe before I left Singapore had made dressing in style difficult in my new civilian life. It was difficult to wear my singing outfit all the time and the five pounds a week I was earning afforded little for replenishments. From somewhere I had obtained a pale blue hopsack suit, an unusual material that, like sacking, parted in holes like windows with the cross-fibres dividing the apertures into panes. I paid twenty-eight shillings for a pair of brown Oxford shoes and when winter came I dug out my long straight black overcoat which had come from Barnardo's. My body continued skinny (despite a diet of horsemeat steaks and chips at a café I used to frequent) and the overcoat hung on me like a pall. Topped by the white face and hollow eyes I presented an unhealthy spectacle. One day when I was sitting on a park bench, killing time before going to interview someone, a passer-by actually stopped and asked if I felt ill.

It seems, however, that I was not wholly unattractive. I had a very pretty girlfriend, who later became my wife, and I noticed older women considering me with longing expressions as if they were interested in fattening me up. One of these ladies, in her late twenties, always gave me a glass of sherry whenever I made a regular call at her flat in connection with the Kilburn Cacti and Succulent Society, not, you might think, an organisation which had a frequent output of news. Her husband was always out at work when I arrived and she eventually became quite skittish. One afternoon, with the sun streaming through her lace curtains, and the cacti and succulents lined up on the window sill, she grabbed me and threw me bodily to the floor. She was long and bony, like a horse-woman, and she proceeded to fling me about the carpet in the most frightful manner. I was both surprised and pleasured and we began laughing hysterically, although that was difficult when she was sitting across my stomach. I had not had a fight like this since the pink-faced assistant master at Kingsbridge had invited me to wrestle on the lawn.

This rough and tumble excited both the secretary of the Kilburn Cacti and Succulent Society and the local reporter but, through some naive blockage, I still did not appreciate the full import of it. We rolled, bumped and somersaulted and that was all. Furniture was knocked and scattered, a big cactus spilled and the pot broke, and it was while we were lying panting, perspiring and still trying to stop laughing that she picked up the clock from beneath the table and said, 'Good God, Henry will be back soon. We'll have to carry on next week.'

I looked forward to the next week like mad but, not for the first nor last time, I had failed to seize an opportunity. When I arrived on her doorstep she appeared almost frosty and said that the Society had no news that week, thank you. Then she shut the door. A few weeks later they moved away from the district.

It was my regular routine to do the rounds of the various organisations in the crowded borough. One of these was to the Conservative Club where a dear old boozer was the political agent. In that generally dingy area the party was very much in the minority. Labour members of the council outnumbered Tories by eight to one (which did not stop the Socialists electing a Tory mayor, in recognition of long service to the town, something that would be a little short of a miracle today).

One morning, making my customary call at the Conservative Club, I found the agent, a retired army officer, as usual affably at the bar. I asked if the forthcoming council elections had meant much additional work. He choked on his Scotch and, ashen-faced, asked me the date, then the time. When I told him he emitted a spectral howl and staggered towards his office, slamming the door. Noon that day was the deadline for the handing in of nomination papers for the forthcoming elections. It was now eleven-thirty and he had forgotten to send them. Nor were they signed and seconded.

Somehow a scrawl of somewhat instant signatures appeared on the hastily filled-out papers and there was a dash to the town hall. The town clerk looked at the clock and shrugged. It was three minutes past noon. The nominations were invalid. The next council had a vastly increased Labour majority and the Tory agent decided to retire.

One of the Labour councillors was a personable

young man called Reginald Freeson who rose to the higher levels of the party and who became, despite an attempted left-wing intrusion, Member of Parliament for Brent, of which Willesden forms part. Reg Freeson was a journalist who at one time worked for a series of children's comic papers. Once, years later at some sort of party, where *The Times* man introduced himself sonorously: 'Martin-Thompson-Billings, *The Times*,' and I said: 'Leslie Thomas, *Evening News*,' slightly less impressively, Reg Freeson added unselfconsciously: 'Reginald Freeson, *Mickey Mouse Weekly*.'

Social events, lunches, annual dinners and receptions in Willesden were usually my concern since most of the other reporters had homes to go to. I welcomed this because I was fed and watered rather better than my pocket would allow (I also went to the cinema free). One of the regular festivities was the social evening of the Anglo-German Friendship Club where Teutonic ladies and gentlemen and Willesden residents tried to forget the enmities of war, which had been over only six years. At these gatherings the waiters were uniformed members of the Royal Artillery Association who not long previously had been firing shells in the direction of the selfsame Germans they were now serving. I asked one of the former gunners how he felt about this: 'They're a very good crowd, the Krauts,' he said after thinking about it. 'During the war I must have killed quite a few of them but I'm sorry now.'

After Mrs Dyer had hit me on the head with the saucepan we decided that, with no further hard feelings, we should part company. I took my belongings a mile or so further into the centre of Willesden to the house of another widow, Mrs Bailey, where I had a room directly overlooking the cemetery.

Mrs Bailey was a splintery old dear whose concern was 'to feed you up for your wedding'. This agricultural ambition she attempted to achieve by shovelling fried and other food onto my plate in great quantities at all hours of the day and with what she considered to be apt commentary. 'Here's your belly lining!' she would proclaim, bringing in smoking porridge at seven in the morning. She was not a good cook. Her piles of chips often resembled a burnt-out log cabin and I saw many a baleful-eyed egg looking out of the charred wreckage. 'You won't notice it under this gunge,' she would enthuse, sloshing out the HP sauce. 'That'll keep you stoked up for the winter,' and 'Let this lot gurgle down inside you,' were other culinary phrases.

She was also magically untidy. Clothes, utensils and furniture were piled everywhere, only being moved to be piled elsewhere. It was really only a two-roomed flat with the bathroom also doubling as the kitchen. A small gas-cooking range was placed on top of the toilet cistern. 'It saves a lot of time,' was her unhappy joke, and there was a wooden board which could be placed on top of the bath to provide a surface for kitchen work and to support mountains of undone washing-up and dirty laundry. Both the crockery and the clothes were washed in the bath, sometimes together.

When I first arrived I immediately decided to make another move as soon as decently possible but I did not want to hurt my new landlady's feelings and I had to wait for a proper-looking opportunity. By the time that arrived, if it ever did, I had been so won over by her sweetness and eccentricity that I forgot to go. Her only son had gone off to France in 1939 with the British Expeditionary Force when he was about my age, and had been killed in the first trenches. She saw me as a sort of replacement.

The cemetery, its crosses and posturing angels almost beneath my window, was a constant source of interest. Drinking a cup of tea, I could watch the funerals. Their variety was infinite; masses of mourners and forests of flowers for one occasion down to a solitary matchstick man I once saw head hung over the open grave, with the white billowing clergyman and the idling grave-diggers. One night a young drunk climbed the iron gates and went to sleep on his mother's tombstone; one day the chapel in the middle of the cemetery caught fire during a service and everybody hurried out into the open air, the undertaker's men rushing through the flames to rescue the coffin and its occupant.

On the distant side of the cemetery was a park and I sometimes used to go over there on Friday, my day off, to kick a football around. There was rarely anyone else to join in and I would dribble the ball around the feet of trees and practice passing to non-existent team-mates. Often I was observed by an ancient man who sat unattended in the park shelter, and one day he asked me if he could play. It was impossible for him to run for he hobbled on a stick, but the park shelter was not unlike a goal and he suggested that I should kick the ball towards him and he would be the goalkeeper. He could continue sitting. I concurred, mainly to do him a favour but after trying this out a few times I found that it was quite useful practice in placing the ball carefully either side of his hopefully stretching hands. He enjoyed it greatly and kept waving his stick (which he often used as an elongation of his arm to stop me from scoring) and shouting, 'Shoot! Go on, lad, shoot!'

It was strange but good fun and I combined it with my serious practice by dribbling the ball around the tree roots and then kicking it at the goal with its seated custodian. The old man loved it and became more enthusiastic as time went on. Once I flattened him against the wooden boards at the back of the shelter by selfishly getting too excited and firing the ball in with some velocity. Even this did not deter him. Once I had picked him up and he had regained his breath he was keen to carry on with the game. One morning when I arrived with the ball he was sitting there grinning smugly in a green goalkeeper's jersey which he wore thereafter. God knows what the person who looked after him thought when he went out dressed like that and came back covered with sweat and odd bruises. Then, one day, he was not there and he never came to the park again. I never knew his name so I could not find out what had happened to him, but I suppose he had died. Not, I hope, through any overexertion at football. I really believed he looked forward to it and, as he once told me, it was a lot better that just staring at nothing.

Going to the park with the ball and returning to my lodgings meant a detour around the cemetery. One day it began to rain coldly while I was kicking around among the trees and I decided to risk a short cut through the tombstones. I was wearing old trousers, a jersey and muddy boots and I was carrying the ball. Although it was raining thickly I felt I should not run but, at the most, trot.

My route took me down the central path of the cemetery to where the chapel stood in the middle. As I was rounding the corner of the chapel I bounced the ball once, without thinking, and then turned the corner to be confronted by a funeral. At the same moment the ball struck my toe, bouncing away from me, alongside the procession of mourners, until it became horribly entangled in the legs of the men who were carrying the coffin. One of them trod on it, another sidestepped and the long box wobbled perilously. The pallbearers then played a close-passing game, each one trying to flick the ball clear, only to see it strike the shoes of another. Eventually, one fellow, with a firm clearance, sent the ball skidding along the path – *and into the prepared grave*! Oh my God, I thought, what now? Some of the mourners were beginning to cry, glaring in my direction while I stood stupefied. The coffin wobbled once more. What could I do? Ask: 'Could I have my ball back, please?' One of the gravediggers solved the crisis by jumping into the hole and retrieving the ball. The final terrible, farcical moment came when my football suddenly shot out of the open ground like a shell discharged from a mortar and bounced away between the tombstones with me following. I never went into the cemetery again.

*

My life's dream was still Fleet Street. Scarcely a week went by without my posting off another warning that the national newspaper world was missing a gem. In addition I was about to get married and I needed the money.

One Saturday, in the Willesden church where my marriage was shortly to take place, there was another wedding during which the bridegroom made a sudden dash from the altar and hopped over the boundary wall. It was not a case of cold feet. He was on the run from the army and the police were closing in. The ceremony was abandoned but the reception went on as planned and the couple afterwards met at a secret rendezvous and embarked on their honeymoon. A friendly local policeman tipped me off about this and I went to the church to investigate. There before me I found a reporter from the *Sunday Express* who asked me not to tell any of the other Fleet Street papers. He also hinted he had heard that Exchange Telegraph, the international news agency, was looking for a likely chap like me. He had a friend there and would put in a good word. A week later glory dawned. A letter from Philip Burn, the editor of Exchange Telegraph, arrived inviting me to go for an interview. I went and I got the job. It was not exactly Fleet Street, for the office was in Cannon Street in the City of London, but it was getting close.

XVI

In the early part of this century Philip Gibbs wrote *The Street of Adventure,* one of the few lasting novels to have been published about Fleet Street. In my local reporting days I read its archaic story many times, savouring the excitements of the high-collared correspondent dispatched to catch the first possible cross-Channel steamer by an early morning telegram delivered to his door; of reporters picking up their quill pens to record the latest trial at the Old Bailey; of writers returning to the office by hansom cab or on the open top of an omnibus; of gas lamps and coal fires burning late in the editorial room.

When I joined the Exchange Telegraph Company I realised almost at once that I was about to become part of one of the few remaining remnants of this ancient world. The building which housed the news agency in Cannon Street was tall and narrow with a lift that wheezed and squeezed between its floors (the company's doctor had a lift which you operated by pulling on a rope). The newsroom on the fourth floor had, not long before, been illuminated by gas and the odour lingered. Along its length and reaching into the teleprinter room next door, at just-below ceiling level, was a miniature cable-car contraption running on rails, into which written and edited copy could be clipped as the appropriate clamp travelled by. It was somewhat like the apparatus once to be found in department stores which hurried invoices and other dockets from one part of the building to another. The Exchange Telegraph contraption clanked and clattered as it ran, curled around corners and disappeared through holes in the wall to materialise miraculously elsewhere.

There was a legend that when the construction had been installed in the nineteen-twenties a maintenance engineer had arrived with it and had been taken onto the staff, but no one had ever been able to find him since. It was rumoured that he was bricked up in the basement. He was certainly never to be found when the railway broke down, which was frequently, and stories had to be run by relays of office lads in silver-buttoned uniforms from one part of the building to another.

The lift was also prone to fits. One Christmas Eve the distinguished reporter Mr Alan Whicker, before his fame on television an employee of Exchange Telegraph, was trapped in the lift between floors in the select company of Humphrey the office cat. At that season no one could be located who could unstick the cage and pieces of food for both man and cat were pushed through the gratings by other members of the staff who were happily indulging in the office revelries. That was possibly the same Christmas that a rotund sub-editor called Harold Taylor left the office for home and returned half an hour later criss-crossed with sticking plaster and bearing the exclusive news that he had been involved in a train crash. No one believed him and he was put in a corner with a drink and told what a very good prank it was. After several more drinks he stopped trying to tell anybody and it was not until someone bothered to pick up an irritating telephone that we realised about the train crash. By that time Harold had progressed so far into a bottle of Scotch that no eyewitness details could be extracted from him.

The very title the Exchange Telegraph Company had a Victorian resonance. Reporters complained that they were often mistaken for someone to do with the General Post Office. At the time I joined its staff in the early nineteen-fifties it was already a journalistic anachronism. It had an unwieldy corps of foreign correspondents, some harking back to the First World War. The Paris man, André Glarner, had been an Olympic cyclist and apparently it was thought in the office that he used his bicycle speed to reach the cable bureau before his rivals. On one occasion he filed an exclusive and sensational story with an embargo that it was not to be released for publication until he sent a coded signal which would read: 'Send More Expenses'. In the dust and disarray of the Exchange Telegraph newsroom the first dispatch was mislaid and the second message so much misunderstood that Monsieur Glarner was told sharply that he could have no further expenses that month since he had already used up his allowance.

Home news was covered by a group of reporters and local correspondents. There was one called East of Twickenham who was known as West of Zanzibar. Some were experienced but others worked with more enthusiasm or élan than expertise. The Court

Correspondent wafted around in a velvet-collared coat and composed short dullish stories about the doings of the Royal Family. When a different angle, or perhaps something a little more colourful, was suggested he waved it away with the words: 'Her Majesty would not like that one little bit.' There were people who went to police courts and others to conferences. There was an excellent industrial correspondent and a nice religious affairs chap who later became a naval correspondent. The chief sub-editor was tiny and worried. He had to jump from the floor to put copy in the travelling clamps. His night-time counterpart was a slow and urbane ex-army officer, who was writing a history of the Sudan when things were not too pressing in the office. The editor, Philip Burn, was a Will Hay character with an explosion of white hair but only one tooth. He was said to have been playing chess in the Sugar Loaf pub across the street when the news of the Edward the Eighth abdication crisis broke. Like Drake, he decided to complete the game before attending to the matter.

When I first went for my interview I told him that I hoped for a job as a reporter. 'I need good sub-editors,' he said sonorously as if making an ecclesiastical pronouncement. 'I can get a reporter by lifting my finger and can't get a first-rate sub-editor by lifting my whole arm.' I was impressed and so apparently was he. He repeated: 'A reporter by lifting my finger . . . a sub not my lifting my whole arm.' He smiled more with one tooth than most people do with a mouthful. 'What do you think of that?' he said. 'Not at all a bad phrase, eh?'

So I became a news agency sub-editor, a job far less exacting and exciting than its equivalent on a newspaper since no knowledge of typefaces or make-up was necessary. The copy had to be checked, rewritten or cut if necessary and passed on to be sent out on the teleprinter to newspapers and other clients. There was a special Club Tape which went to London Clubs upon which the Stock Exchange prices, other City news and the cricket and racing results were of paramount importance.

Disappointed by my failure to become a reporter, I consoled myself that at least it was half a step in the right direction and the office was a mere half a mile from the real Fleet Street. When I was working on the evening shift I would walk to Fleet Street during my break and sit, clutching a brown ale, in the corner of the newspaper bars, listening to men like gods talking about their journalistic adventures. If I saw a man running down the front steps of the *Daily Express* building or hailing a taxi outside the doors of the *Daily Telegraph*, I would catch my breath because I was sure he was off to Afghanistan or Hong Kong, whereas it was much more probably the bar at Auntie's or Waterloo station. The romance has never left me. I would think the same today.

The Exchange Telegraph Company offered little chance of a junior sub-editor entering those realms of adventure. We worked in shifts around the clock and on every day of the year. On the all-night shift the duty sub-editor, who arrived at eleven-thirty, was in command of the entire operation. Things used to quieten down about one in the morning, as a rule, although there was usually some unsleeping local correspondent who could find a fire somewhere. On quiet nights I used to carry a mattress from a wartime air raid store in the basement, spread it out on the desk, and go happily to sleep until five o'clock when the tapes would start chattering again and the telephone would wake up. On these occasions I was frequently joined by Humphrey, the tabby and tough office cat, who would stretch out on the mattress alongside me or even make himself comfortable on my chest, breathing mice into my face.

Mr Burn, the editor, lived out in the country and rarely visited London at night. One evening, however, entertaining some Americans, he took them to the theatre and later, with their encouragement, decided to show them how a great news agency worked on timelessly through the dark hours. He arrived in the newsroom with the telephone operator slumped at the switchboard and the one-man editorial staff snoring on a mattress surmounted by an equally sleepful tabby cat.

I roused to see him standing speechless, gesturing about the shadowy room to his American friends. Humphrey grumbled as I pushed him off my chest. 'Hello . . . Thomas . . .' mumbled the editor. 'Er . . . what's happening in the world?'

'Everything, sir,' I gasped, sizing up the situation. 'Absolutely *everything*.' Like a prophet I pointed to the ceiling, above which both he and I knew was the naked roof of the building. 'Don't go up to the main newsroom, sir. It's bedlam.'

He blinked and then understood. Relief crumpled

his annoyance. He hung gladly onto the subterfuge. 'Oh . . . oh . . . really, well no . . . perhaps we'd better not.'

'Oh,' said the American lady, clutching her husband, 'we wouldn't want to get in the way, would we, honey?'

'No, surely not,' he agreed.

'They've sent me down for a rest, sir,' I reported to Mr Burn. 'We're taking it in turns to get some sleep. It's been quite a night.'

As they left, the visitors turned their heads upwards as if they might catch some sound of the frantic night-work going on above. The editor gave me a half-and-half look and looked upwards also to where he and I knew only the London stars were shining. 'Better get your head down again, Thomas,' he nodded. 'Sorry we disturbed you. And . . . look after the cat.'

On the following day, a Sunday, I was playing in a football match against our deadly rivals, in all spheres, Reuters, and I managed to score a crucial goal. On the Monday I was called into the editor's office and fully expected to emerge with my career, such as it was, in ruins. 'Having a rest, were you?' Philip Burn enquired mildly. 'Getting ready for the big match?'

'Yes, sir, that was it,' I replied gratefully. 'I would not have been asleep otherwise, sir. Not me.'

'No, I'm sure not.' His oblong tooth gleamed. 'If you ever fail in journalism, Thomas, you ought to have a shot at being something like an actor.'

The enclosed and routine work of a news agency sub-editor was some distance from the romantic Fleet

Street about which I had dreamed. Bereft of the necessity for tailoring the stories to fit the page, having no call for presentation and where only the sketchiest of headlines was required, it was, in truth, merely a matter of dull processing. Sometimes I amused myself with the headlines and some of them appeared intact, with the stories when they eventually saw publication. Exchange Telegraph was, however, set in solid ways and I was censured for a headline which I appended to a report about a civil defence exercise which involved a simulated atom-bomb explosion on a Hampshire village. The words: 'Big Wallop Near Little Wallop' seemed both apt and reasonable to me, but others disapproved.

Several times I went to see the editor to ask about a reporter's job but he always forestalled me; before I had uttered a sentence he would perform his mime, lifting one finger representing a reporter, and then one arm denoting a sub-editor.

So I returned to cutting and paragraphing with occasional forays to a wooden telephone booth in one corner where it was a sub-editor's duty to sit and take down in shorthand interminable and often boring political and economic intelligence from overseas correspondents. We had on the desk a dear and gentlemanly old chap called Sidney, approaching retirement, who was stone deaf. He insisted, however, on taking his fair share of these overseas calls. One of the foreign correspondents was also deaf and to hear the pair of them trying to outshout each other over a continent was a treat that brought the entire newsroom to a standstill.

On rare and happy occasions I managed to get involved in the writing and reporting side of a story. Sometimes I even found them for myself. One spring evening, taking a walk over the almost deserted London Bridge during my meal break, I observed that a ship had become firmly jammed under one of the arches. The vessel had somehow taken a wrong turning and the incoming tide had put it in this embarrassing position. As the tide rose so the wood splintered. The Spanish captain was on the bridge wringing his hands and sobbing orders. I poked my head over and asked him what had happened. He pleaded with me to go and get someone. It was difficult to know whether to call out the fire brigade or the lifeboat but I solved the crisis by stopping a wandering policeman and taking him to what he described as the rummest traffic accident as ever he had set eyes upon. After getting some emotional quotes from the captain I hurried back to the office and wrote the story which was joyfully reported and much photographed in the next morning's papers.

Then, one dull night, we had a report of a gory double murder in a west London suburb. One of the victims was said to be 'Lady Menzies'. There were no reporters in the office so I looked up Lady Menzies in the telephone directory and dialled the number. I wondered what I should say. 'Please can you tell me if Lady Menzies has been murdered?' seemed unnecessarily brutal. 'I wonder if you can tell me how Lady Menzies is?' was obviously erring the other way.

In the event when my call was answered I merely

said: 'Could I please speak to Lady Menzies?' The voice at the other end replied briskly: 'Yes, speaking.'

My hair went slightly on end. It was not easy trying to explain that according to my information she was lying in a pool of blood in Ealing. Calmly she helped me out. There had been other enquirers. No, she was not murdered. She was perfectly well, thank you. It turned out that the killer's victim had been passing herself off with the title.

The majority of my spare-time reporting was less thrilling. Each early morning the agency would put out a series of minor items called 'overnights' which evening newspapers used as fillers in the first racing editions and which might occasionally find their way into feature pages or magazine sections. Each item was worth an extra ten shillings in my pay packet. I used to spend my lunch hours walking around the City of London, much of which was still scarred with wartime bombed sites, looking for stories. I found a family of wild cats living among the shut-off ruins and then realised that there were whole tribes of the fierce and skinny animals hunting the wide spaces in the centre of London. It was following these cats that finally led the police to discover the body of a murderer, a young man who had killed a housewife and, himself condemned by some disease, went to a bombed site to die. He was hunted for weeks until the cats, who had gruesomely eaten most of him, led the authorities to the place. It was directly opposite our office. While the police and the newspapers had been looking for him he had been there all the time.

The fencing off of large areas of the city, which

had been cleared of rubble but still remained void, resulted in colonies of wild flowers appearing, foxgloves, dog roses and honeysuckle, which had not been seen in those streets for years. I wrote one of my ten-shilling stories about that. Countryside birds appeared; there were rumours of foxes. Owls nested. I became an urban naturalist. Other stories I found by visiting City churches, by getting to know people at small museums and by simply walking by the Thames or through the streets and keeping my eyes open.

One of these quiet enquiries resulted, in fact, in a story which went sensationally around the world. On the large blitzed area opposite the office – where the dead murderer had been found – some archaeologists had been exploring the ground below what had once been the cellars of London offices. I had wandered over to watch them but they had been reticent about their work and promised that if they actually found anything of interest they would let me know. There came a quiet Sunday afternoon when, looking out from the window of Exchange Telegraph, I saw children digging enthusiastically at the site – and carrying away pots and dishes. One boy of about twelve was trotting away with a stone arm!

The archaeologist concerned was a Professor Grimes and I telephoned him and told him what was going on. At first he did not believe me, then he gurgled at the end of the phone and howled: 'For God's sake stop them! Get the police! Anybody! I am coming there right away . . . oh dear . . . oh dear . . .'

The site turned out to be the Temple of Mithras,

the most complete Roman shrine ever found in London. Within hours the whole area was roped off. Armies of archaeologists descended with their spades and even the contractors, who were about to lay the foundations of a new office block on the site, held up work until the entire temple and its contents could be removed. It is now displayed alongside that building. I often wondered whether the boy managed to keep his Roman arm.

The forty pounds a month which the Exchange Telegraph Company calculated to be my worth (and they were probably accurate) enabled me to wed. My wife, Maureen, after eighteen months of marriage, produced a round and laughing baby daughter on the same day as I passed my driving test. The examiner congratulated me on both achievements – although I was careful not to tell him about my fatherhood until after the test in case he thought I was trying to influence him. Elated that I had passed, I replied extravagantly that had the baby been a boy I would have called it after him. He grimaced and confided that he had never told any of his colleagues his real Christian name, but he would reveal it to me. It was Halibut.

We were broke, not an unusual affliction with young marrieds although we tended to take risks. We had a flat, soon to be followed by a house, a car, and nothing could deter us from holidays abroad.

We rented an apartment in the Italian resort of San Remo and one evening I went to the butcher's shop to purchase some steak. In giving me the change for a thousand-lira note the dastardly tradesman carefully passed on an Albanian coin, a lek, worth in those days about sixpence. An hour later when I discovered the fraud I went furiously back to the shop. It was not the amount – it scarcely could have been – it was the deliberate execution of the trick. The butcher denied he had ever seen me, or my lek, and a tremendous row ensued during the course of which I called him a 'ladro' – a thief (my knowledge of Italian was small but *Ali Baba and the Forty Lardroni* was showing at the cinema). This was apparently the worst insult I could have thrown. Enraged, the large butcher (are there any *small* butchers?) came around his counter with a meat cleaver. Customers tried to restrain him but he broke away and chased me around the shop in the best Abbott and Costello tradition. Death or not, there was no chance of me leaving. I ran and I dodged. A fresh set of customers pinned the puce-faced avenger against the wall and shouted for me to run. At that moment I saw a uniformed figure on the pavement outside. I rushed out and pulled him in. There was a lot of shouting and the butcher was still struggling. I demanded to know why the policeman was not taking any action. He was just staring. 'Policeman?' he said spreading his hands. 'Signor – me postman!'

As a practical father I was not very adept. Once I offered to rock the baby to sleep in front of the living room fire. I sang her a song from distant days, the only one my father ever knew to sing to me. He had, not surprisingly, made it up himself:

> Mummy's gone down the shops,
> To buy some bread and cheese . . .

Possibly it was not the ideal lullaby and although baby remained obstinately awake I went off to sleep, finally tipping forward and depositing my surprised and offended daughter on the hearthrug. We took her to Cornwall in the winter and to East Anglia in the spring. Returning to London on the latter occasion I saw a signpost 'Borley' and on impulse I turned the car in that direction. Borley Rectory had been called the Most Haunted House in England.

Books had been written about its ghosts – a sly nun, a coach and horses, an unexplained cold spot. There had been scientific investigations into its fierce poltergeist and Harry Price, the long-time secretary of the Society for Psychic Research, made it his life's work. Some even believed he had kept the story going. The house had been burned down in the late nineteenthirties but the place still looked haunted.

It was a fine, open, sunlit day when we reached Borley on the Essex-Suffolk border, but over the village there were chill and slinking shadows. We arrived at the Rectory, or what remained of it, just in time to see a bulldozer push a first load of earth into the cavities that had been its cellars. A man came over and obligingly muttered to me: 'Now perhaps we'll bury the damned ghost for ever.'

Returning home I sat down and wrote an article called: 'Can They Bury the Borley Ghost?' which I took along to the offices of my favourite paper the *News Chronicle* on my way to work the next day. They published it on the Saturday and paid me ten guineas. It was the first time anything I had written had appeared in a national newspaper.

Still fretting after being a full-time reporter, I continued to dispatch letters to editors informing them how lucky they were that I was available and they resiliently continued to ignore them. I had to be satisfied with occasional pieces I could write outside my normal duties (Exchange Telegraph did not seem to mind and the work appeared under my own name. Nor did they see fit to use my writing in their own operations). There was an article on cricket which *Reveille*, of all magazines, published, then came a piece about the Isles of Scilly, then little known, which was accepted to my great joy by the *Evening News*. Maureen and I had been to the islands on our honeymoon, returning in a bucking aeroplane (a de Haviland Rapide, the only aircraft ever to suffer woodworm in the airframe) loaded with fresh flowers from the Scilly Isles fields.

The *Evening News* was my heart's desire. From my boy's days at Kingston I had always read it and I knew the names of its writers like a litany: E.M. Wellings on cricket, Leslie Ayre on Radio and Television, Bill Bourne on the theatre, Harold Abrahams – of *Chariots of Fire* fame – on athletics, and the Courts Day by Day by a mysterious and wry man called J.A.J. It was a large paper in every sense of the word, it spread generously, a wide-sheeted journal, not one of your miserly tabloids (although, before its demise, it became one). It was the biggest-selling evening newspaper in the world.

402

Encouraged by the publication of the article about the Scilly Isles ('Eden Beyond Land's End') I submitted a succession of short stories, all of which were rejected. Then, one morning, I received a fifteen-guinea cheque with a slip which merely noted: 'Short Story'. No one had told me it had been accepted. The *Evening News* was famous for its short stories and I was in good company. It was published on a Saturday, it was called 'A Good Boy Griffith' and was adapted from a joke I had heard. It was also my first published piece of fiction.

All of this, however, was getting me no nearer Fleet Street. Physically, there was a definite move in the right direction because Exchange Telegraph moved from its cobwebbed premises in Cannon Street to a new building at East Harding Street, just behind Gough Square, one of the Georgian alleys behind Fleet Street. Gough Square is famous for the house of Dr Samuel Johnson and there is an arrow on the wall saying: 'To Dr Johnson's House'. Early one morning, emerging from the office after an all-night shift, I found a poor man lying on the pavement having had some sort of seizure. I opened his shirt collar and looked anxiously around for aid. A dawn charlady was coming up the street. 'Ooooh, dear me,' she said, looking down at the man's ashen face. ''Eee don't 'arf look poorly.'

After concurring with the diagnosis I asked her to get a doctor. To my amazement, instead of going into the building to telephone she trotted off down the pavement. At that moment a policeman arrived and took over. I peered through the alley where the char-lady had gone and saw her knocking briskly at the

403

door of Dr Johnson's house. After a while she came back disconsolate. 'There's nobody in,' she grumbled. 'Either that or he's still in bed asleep.'

My only lasting claim to fame at the Exchange Telegraph Company was the result of my final year there. The regional television and radio news and magazine programmes which are transmitted throughout the country today, including *Nationwide* and *Tonight*, had their infant roots at a desk in the agency building and I was the man behind the desk.

It had become obvious that Exchange Telegraph could not compete on a foreign news basis with Reuters and was frequently a poor second in the home news area to the powerful Press Association. First one service and eventually the other were abandoned and Extel – as it is now called – reconstituted itself on the foundation of its always successful racing and financial services. Before the fall there was an attempt to bring new life into the old machine. The BBC was to establish a local news programme to follow its six o'clock bulletin. It was to be called *Town and Around* and we were invited to provide news items for it.

It was not quite as simple as that, for the Press Association was also bidding for the contract and there was to be a six months' trial run on the part of both services. I had been on one of my periodic missions to the editor, asking for a reporter's job. This time Philip Burn did not raise the single finger followed by the whole arm, but announced: 'I've got something that is new, revolutionary, and I want you to handle it. It could change the fortunes of this company, Thomas. A lot depends on it.' He looked at me strongly, his tooth serious. 'We'll give you an extra pound a week,' he said.

Not only did I get the pound, I got a desk, a telephone, a typewriter, eventually an assistant, and a shared secretary. On the first day we operated the service there were one hundred and fifty news items on the tape, none of which were used because it was only a dummy run. The dummy run lasted for weeks. Sometimes if I wanted to go secretly to a mid-week afternoon football match I would leave a pile of news items to be fed into the teleprinter at timed intervals, go to the match, and get back in time to go home. No one looking at the tape would ever have known I was away.

At the end of the trial period the BBC gave us the contract and the board of Exchange Telegraph were so exhilarated that I discovered a further pound in my pay packet. The real rewards, however, were less tangible then. Mollie Lee, who was the editor of *Woman's Hour*, was looking for someone to speak for three minutes about reading newspapers and Maurice Ennals, who produced *Town and Around* at the Broadcasting House end, suggested that I might like to try my hand at broadcasting. A long interval had elapsed since my singing debut on Radio Malaya but now I managed to record my own script, receiving two pounds for it. It was also the beginning of a new facet in my life which, at a tangent, was to have great importance later for it was Mollie Lee who had the idea which changed my whole existence.

I was, however, still broke. Maureen and I had ambitions and we were quite brave. We bought a chalet-roofed house, and had a car and a mass of hire-purchase commitments. When I went to an insurance office in the City in connection with my mortgage, a dusty, middle-aged gentleman glanced at the papers and said: 'I see you are earning *thirteen* pounds a week. That's a lot of money for a young man, I don't earn that and I'm gone fifty.'

It may, indeed, have been a lot to him but it was not enough. We gradually dropped more into debt. When the bank balance showed us to be fifty pounds in the red I thought the abyss had opened. I sold the car but that was only temporary relief. At the end of one week it looked as though we would have to sell something to pay for the groceries. From somewhere I had obtained a thick old book, the size, shape and colour of the Bible. It was called *Haydn's Dictionary of Dates* and it was dated 1911. Thinking it might be worth enough money to pay the next week's bills, I tramped with this tome down Charing Cross Road, going into numerous second-hand bookshops and asking an optimistic fiver. The best offer I had was thirty shillings. So, dejectedly, I took it home again.

On the underground, on my homeward journey, I picked up a copy of the *Evening News* which someone had left behind on the seat. Contained in it was the first of a new series of articles called 'The World's Strangest Stories'. It was not a very original idea, each article retelling some fairly familiar mystery or oddity. The first article was about Borley Rectory and its ghosts. As I read it I thought: I could have written this.

The series was meant to continue for a week but it proved so popular that it was extended for a month, then for three months, and eventually ran for two years or more. It also saved my financial life.

When I reached home, Maureen's face fell when she saw I had not sold the book. But to us it was to prove a treasure chest. Each page was crammed with one-paragraph references to all manner of notable occurrences throughout the world – storms, earthquakes, explosions, assassinations, frauds, discoveries, sieges, wars, freaks and frauds. Picking out some obscure item about a revolution in Rio de Janeiro I went to the Guildhall Library, looked up the aged files of *The Times*, then to the Newspaper Library at Hendon for more information and finally into the British Museum for books on the history of Brazil. Then I sat down and wrote the piece and posted it off. It was published the following week and they sent me a cheque for twenty guineas. After that I wrote one of the 'World's Strangest Stories' every two weeks. It was financial salvation and another turning point.

There came a time, after I had written a number of these articles, when the *Evening News* announced a prize of a thousand pounds in a competition for the best 'World's Strangest Story'. There were to be ten other prizes. Something in the back of my memory kept nagging me about an oddity which I had heard connected with an early colony at Roanoke Island, Virginia, which had vanished without trace and about some clues written on stones and found two centuries later. My intention was to go to the Newspaper Library to dig out any references I could find. The deadline for the competition was nearing. A Saturday arrived when I could have gone to the Library. I also wanted to play football.

Football won and I arrived at the clubhouse of the team for which I played at Ruislip, Middlesex, at just after two in the afternoon. The captain of the club was a young man called Tony Williamson who became a director of Queen's Park Rangers Football Club. I turned up two or three minutes late and began to change. Tony came over and said: 'I'm sorry, but you're not playing. You're late. We've put somebody else in the team.'

Heartily disgruntled I walked out and, now having the afternoon free, went to Hendon to the Newspaper Library. I spent two hours going through the files and when I got home that evening I wrote my entry for the competition. It came fourth. I won a hundred pounds, went to the presentation lunch at the Savoy (where I met my first real author, H.E. Bates) and, eventually, my heart's desire – a job as a reporter on the London *Evening News*.

XVII

There was still something left of Philip Gibbs's *Street of Adventure* in the offices of the *Evening News*. There were small untidy rooms where specialist writers sat in front of glowing coal fires, there was a spiral iron staircase from the features department down to the compositors on the floor below. Reginald Willis, the editor, would sometimes return from lunch, red in the face, and looking for somebody's blood. He had a trumpeting voice which forewarned of his mood and as he approached there would be a comedy rush for the escape stairs, a clattering of sub-editors, reporters, writers and heads of departments, down the iron curl, a sound reminiscent of the escaping feet in *The Goon Show*.

Willis was an extraordinary man. He invariably wore a blue pin-striped suit and his black hair was brushed fiercely back from his often scarlet brow. He had a lyrical rural accent, part Yorkshire, part Somerset, and when he appeared on the editorial floor there was usually some action in the offing, especially if he had discarded his coat and was twanging his red braces. He believed fervently that we were producing a newspaper for London, not for Fleet Street, and his belief was borne out at that time by sales approaching a million and a half, unequalled by any evening newspaper in history. 'The London story is the important story!' was his clarion cry. The doings of the world were minor compared to Clapham or Hampstead Heath. One day there was a report of a house on fire in the Finchley region. 'Good! Good!' he exclaimed. 'Big readership area! Is it burning well? Any casualties? Any rescues? Which road is it in?' He was told. 'Good address! Live there myself.' He did too. The burning house was his.

When I went to see him for my first, job-hoping, interview he produced a cricket bat. 'Leonard Hutton used that to make his 365 at the Oval in 1938,' he said sonorously. 'World record that was.' He fondled the bat. Everyone who went into that office was shown that bat, especially if they were seeking a pay rise, or were bent on making a complaint. By the time the discussion on Hutton's world record had been accomplished, plus other cricketing matters, the visitor had frequently forgotten the details of his carefully rehearsed plea.

At my interview Willis said: 'Why do you want to be on the staff of the *Evening News*?'

'I've never wanted to do anything else,' I asserted truthfully.

'That's a good enough reason,' he approved. 'I'll pay you twenty a week.' He studied me challengingly. It was not as much as I had hoped. 'Pounds,' he added. 'Not guineas.' There was another interval while I nodded agreement. He patted me cheerfully. 'At least it's not shillings,' he said.

Thus I found myself entering on the following Monday morning at nine o'clock what had for so long

410

been my dream world. The news desk of a famous paper. Reporters were ranged down each side of a long table under the scrutiny of the news editor, Sam Jackett, a legendary crime reporter who wore suits like a rich detective. He was a tall, silver-haired man, of impressive carriage, who said things like: 'Walk down any London street and you will pass at least two unconvicted murderers.' From the outset he did not like me, and when the news editor does not like you only the difficult and unrewarding jobs come your way; and frequently the hardest-to-get stories are the ones that appear smallest on the page. Eager as I was to range at least London, if not the world, finding and writing sensations, he resolutely kept me shackled to the desk making enquiries on the telephone. Many of the other reporters also nursed this complaint. We thought it was the sign of an uncertain chief, needing to have his forces close at hand. There was a joke that some weeks previously a reporter had actually been sent to Trafalgar Square and had not been sure of where it was.

On the other hand, on that initial morning, my opening story for the paper came because I was sitting with the telephone in front of me. A London bus had swerved in the City and crashed into a small shop. I was told to telephone the shop and find out what had happened. The phone rang two or three times and then was picked up by a man who said, yes, he was the manager. Had the bus caused much damage? Yes, it had demolished the whole shop. In fact the bonnet of the driver's cab was at that moment wedged into the shop. No, there were no serious casualties, as far as he knew, although it was difficult for him to say because he, at that moment, was *trapped under the bus*. The telephone had rung right in front of his nose so he thought he might as well pick it up since he had nothing better to do. The counter had collapsed on top of him and the bus was wedged over that. He thought he might have broken a leg, but he was not sure. They had told him they would have him out in half an hour.

To interview a man trapped under a bus might seem to be a good start, but Sam Jackett's regard for me did not flourish. I think that his resentment stemmed from the fact that my appointment had not been made by him, as was usual. He also considered, rightly, that I was not an experienced reporter.

After two or three weeks of investigating trivia by telephone and raising his ire by suggesting that perhaps a bus ride to the scene of the story might not be un-rewarding, he called me to his desk. 'I don't think you've settled down very well,' he said darkly. 'The editor says I can get rid of you if I like. On the other hand I can send you down to Scotland Yard. Start down there on Monday.'

Scotland Yard, or more accurately the Yard Press Bureau, might sound to the outsider an exciting assignment but that would be far from the truth. It was a single malodorous room reached by a green door in the granite walls of the great turreted building on the Thames Embankment. On the Friday afternoon, before starting my vigil there on the Monday, I was sent down to acclimatise myself and to meet my fellow denizens from other newspapers, always providing that the pubs were closed.

I pushed open the heavy green door and stepped into a room of great squalor. There was a large central table ragged with newspapers. On the floor were further sprawling newspapers, some yellowing with age. Along one side of the room was a rank of telephone boxes above which, lined like targets in a shooting gallery, were dozens of empty beer bottles. There was an armchair of the style and condition that tramps in cartoons are often depicted as occupying, and the analogy is not too far adrift. Once, when I was doing an article about down-and-outs living below Charing Cross railway arches, I took one into the conveniently situated Yard Press Bureau, just to get him out of the rain. He looked around, sniffed and then said: 'I'm not staying in this place,' before making for the green exit.

On my initial visit, on that downcast Friday, I thought at first that the bureau was unoccupied but after detecting a groan, I investigated to find a tiny and hopelessly inebriated reporter, a man known as Tich, lying beneath some furniture in the corner. I thought the furniture had just been carelessly piled up like that but apparently it had fallen on him when he collapsed on his return from the saloon bar. After I had lifted some of the debris he opened tiny eyes set deep in his small mildewed face. He tugged a pork pie hat over his forehead and muttered: 'I'm going to tear this bloody place to shreds.'

To have torn the gargantuan Scottish baronial granite building (or even anything less, at that moment) to shreds was fortunately beyond him. It was just as well, since the wanton destruction would have not only disrupted the operations of the Metropolitan Police but deprived a group of reporters of their daily club. It was these men's function, in the main, to merely sit in that room and wait for something to happen. When it did, a crime or a major disaster, the Press Bureau men were not, as a rule, required to do anything further than report it to their offices, whereupon the star reporters would fly out and get all the credit. These stars would sometimes come into the bureau, like upper-crust relatives and, after a brief nod in the direction of the inhabitants of the single room, would be led mysteriously and portentously to the inner sanctum where the Yard's press officers lived behind locked doors. If the bureau reporter was required to make an enquiry he would have to press a button, wait for the press official to appear and then conduct his conversation through a crack in the door. Sometimes the door was loudly unlocked and one of the men from our room would be permitted to enter. When this happened it was performed like a ritual, with much secrecy and glancing over shoulders for, although we were all crammed in the dingy room together, there was still a farrago of confidential information and private tips to be maintained. Someone would sidle into the inner room and, watched cagily by the others, emerge some minutes later perhaps looking smugly confident. I never had cause to be allowed into that inner room.

The job, little more than that of a messenger boy, had given birth to a faded but attractive group of individuals. Most were past ambition and the position presented an opportunity for a decent living with little effort. Each morning one of the Yard press officers would appear from the inside door and tell us skeletal details of the various misdemeanours and misfortunes which had occurred throughout London in the hours of darkness. These were then transmitted to the newspaper offices from the line of scarred telephone boxes with their dusty coronet of beer bottles. After that there was nothing to do but read the papers and wait for something else to happen, whereupon the Yard man would emerge and tell us about it. Life in that room could be enclosed and cosy.

It was unofficially organised, to the point of being mothered, by a small and decent man called Nelson Sullivan who worked for the *Evening Standard*. He collected money for tea, retirement presents and wreaths. His lifetime's moment of glory came one Saturday night when, working an extra shift for the *Sunday Express*, he kept a murderer talking on the telephone for half an hour while the police traced the call and moved in on the criminal.

There was Cecil Catlin, a professor from the *Star*, a working-class evening newspaper which ran an annual ballroom-dancing championship about which he always talked with scorn. 'Everyone in the *Star* Dance Championship,' he would announce without prejudice, 'is a Jew. If you've got a foreskin they charge you corkage.'

He referred to the assembly of men at the Press Bureau, especially during the post-lunch sleep-off when the pubs had emptied as 'these quidnuncs' and he frequently went off into poetic regrets for lost youth, love, lust and opportunity. His hobby was photography and one day, while drunk, he attended an auction of

415

general goods intending to bid for a photographic enlarger. In his mazed state, however, he bid for the wrong lot and the following day half a ton of custard powder was delivered to his small house. It was summarily dumped in the garden. 'When it rains,' he said with a careful smugness, 'it ferments and it sends out yellow bubbles all over south London.'

Another of the inmates was a tall man called Pinky who worked for the Press Association and looked quite like General de Gaulle. He remembered the time, before the war, when the Prince of Wales, later the abdicating King Edward the Eighth, attended the annual dinner of a regimental association in London and became inebriated. Pinky, entering the gentlemen's lavatory, found the heir to the throne lying flat on his back with the royal winkle still protruding from the royal trousers. 'I put it back with my fountain pen,' mentioned Pinky modestly. 'It was a gold fountain pen.'

There was Stanley Gardiner, not the author of thrillers but the crime man of my old company Exchange Telegraph, seated with the eternal aplomb of Buddha at the end of the table, surveying the day's runners. The racing pages were digested before anything else, and there were startled shuttlings to and from a then illegal bookie's runner who used to position himself outside the neighbouring Cannon Row Police Station, either on the principle that the law would not notice what was happening right under its nose, or perhaps to collect the policemen's bets. Within the Yard Press Bureau there was also a serious poker school, although this was as illegal as anything uncovered in police raids on gaming dens in Soho. Pound

416

notes were sometimes to be seen piled like lettuce on the table and the games went on until long after both reporters and policemen should have been home in their suburban beds. When Premium Bonds were first issued a club was started to which everyone in the Press Bureau contributed a pound a week. I was never aware of any distribution of prize money and neither did I ever get my investment money returned. When I enquired about this, having left the Yard by that time, I was told that I was several months in arrears with my payments.

Life in that grimy room often resembled a cheery sort of bunk-house fellowship. Routine was everything. The morning visit of the police official with his tid-bits of information; a long perusal of the newspapers and the election of the day's horses before lunchtime opening; a couple of hours in the saloon bar (emblazoned in expense sheets as 'entertaining police contacts'), followed by a siesta before going home. Sometimes we would have visitors, the real crime reporters, who wandered in for a chat and some tea from Nelson Sullivan's huge teapot. One of these was a thin man with the smile of a gnome. His name was Arthur Tietgen and he was the crime correspondent of the *Daily Mail*. Once, at the Old Bailey, Arthur was attending the trial of a man accused of having sexual intercourse with an under-age girl. The accused was trembling in the dock while his counsel cross-examined the girl in the witness box.

'In your evidence,' intoned the defending counsel, 'you mentioned a "French letter". Do you *know* what a "French letter" is?'

The girl, not very bright, replied: 'Oh yes, sir. I know all right.' A glance went from the counsel towards the judge.

'How old do you say you are, young lady?'

'Sixteen in November, sir.'

'So you're fifteen – and you know the function of a "French letter"? You are familiar with its use?'

'I know what it's for, sir, yes.'

'Hmmm . . . When did you last see a "French letter"?'

'Yesterday, sir.'

'Yesterday!' Further glances darted in the direction of the judge. 'In what circumstances did you see this "French letter"?'

'What . . . what do you mean, sir?'

'Where? Where did you see this "French letter" *yesterday?*'

'At work, sir. I works in a "French letter" factory.'

Most of the time at the Press Bureau was less entertaining. I sought refuge from the boredom by arranging my day so that I spent periods sitting in the sun on the Thames Embankment, watching the boats go by, and also by writing my first novel. This was called *My Name Is Mudd* and was about a story-prone chap whose name was Mudd and who worked on a local newspaper.

When it was finished I sent it to various publishers who returned the manuscript with regret and patterned with tea-mug rings. No one accepted it and it is today interred somewhere in the laden tea chests that sit quiet and square in my loft. My agent, Desmond Elliott, has told me that if the book ever emerges he will have nothing to do with it. I am happy to let it rest unseen and unread there. If nothing else, it is probably the only novel ever written at Scotland Yard.

The danger of sitting watching the boats drift by on the Thames was that sometimes something sensational would break and I would not be in the bureau to hear it. On occasions I managed to avoid this sackable embarrassment by getting someone to cover for me, but more often it was by luck. Luck, which is always necessary for success but can be cultivated, had a hand once more in changing my life. Occasionally, at the Yard, I was nearer to the scene of some occurrence than any reporter starting out from Fleet Street, a mile away. Because of this I was sent rushing out one morning to Barclays Bank in Sloane Street where an armed robbery had taken place. This was in the days when armed robberies were the exception rather than the rule.

Hurrying from the Embankment green door, I found a taxi drawn up, as if it had been waiting for me and, within two or three minutes I was at the bank, arriving at the same time as the CID men. No one prevented me, so I walked in and joined the circle of detectives taking down statements from the shocked and robbed cashiers. My notebook in my hand, I recorded the intimate dramas, walked out and telephoned the story to the office. It made front page headlines and was the easiest job I ever did as a journalist.

Emboldened by this, I asked the news editor if perhaps I had not served enough time in exile at the Yard and might be brought back into the general fold.

Sam Jackett showed no inclination to agree, so I thought the time had come to force the change or resign, which would have been a great shame after all the dreams I had dreamed about working for this great newspaper.

I went to see Reginald Willis and he brought out the cricket bat. 'Leonard Hutton,' he began, 'used this bat at the Oval in 1938 . . .' This, of course, was not news to me. Those who had been puzzled by the same subterfuge, when comparing notes, had come to the conclusion that the bat was not the original at all; in fact that several differing bats were used in the act.

Once the record-breaking score had been disposed of the editor asked me what I wanted and I told him. He sat at his desk and picked up a letter. He sniffed as he read it and said: 'Wouldn't like to go to a nice refugee camp for a couple of weeks, would you?'

A refugee camp! Refugee camps were in Austria and Germany or, better still, in the Middle East. Refugee camps were abroad!

'Yes, sir,' I answered, trying to keep my voice steady. 'I'll go. Where is it?'

'South London,' he recited. 'Crystal Palace. You go there on Monday.'

As it turned out the Crystal Palace refugee camp was a notable public relations exercise that provoked much attention and afforded me my first appearance on television. I am fairly sure that *I* was only sent there to get me out of the way, perhaps as a cushion before I was given the sack, but for me it proved a profitable experience.

420

It was organised as part of the United Nations World Refugee Year. At that time, there were still camps spread throughout Europe and the Middle East - housing hundreds of thousands of war victims. To focus attention on their plight the Refugee Year was established and this 'camp' in suburban Crystal Palace, dreamed up by a public relations company, was part of the campaign. The notion was that a group of Fleet Street journalists would be literally dumped on an enclosed piece of wasteland, given a pile of odd wood, some basic tools and told to build themselves a house. Each 'refugee' was then permitted a shilling a day for food. We arrived on a chilly September morning with the London Transport buses standing outside our 'camp' like red wraiths in the mist. Some of the reporters arrived, took a few notes, especially of the living conditions, and went straight back to their offices. 'There's not a lot you can make on expenses, is there,' said one as he climbed back into his car.

A dozen of us stayed, plus three or four people connected with an East End church and led by a lively Cornish shipwright-turned-minister called John Pellow. There was only one woman, Diana Norman, the pretty wife of Barry Norman, the television presenter. She collected our shillings and went out into the outside world to purchase vegetables for our nightly cauldron of stew. She also did our sewing and organised the household tasks. By the end of the week there was not a man there who was not hopelessly in love with her. She handled the situation especially well and returned to her husband quite unperturbed by these devotions.

A resident psychiatrist might have found his time spent there worthwhile because, although we were within sight of Londoners and their homes and buses, we became absolutely insular. We lived and did our work within our compound, growing closer with each day, sitting around our campfire and its cauldron at night – and beginning to resent any interference from the outside world. It was as close to being on a desert island as I have experienced in half a lifetime of visiting and writing about islands.

Our mutually felt regard for Diana was such that we became incredibly over-protective. She slept among us in our hut. No one embarrassed her and if they had I swear the others would have fallen upon him like dogs. Once a visitor to the camp, one of the breed we already resented, smiled a little too much at her and we stood in a rough group and growled at him.

We had constructed the hut, under the Reverend Pellow's shipbuilding guidance, entirely of doors. In the pile of wood which was lying there when we arrived (some contractor's contribution to charity) were twenty or thirty old doors. After putting up the framework of the hut we built the walls of doors, most of them still having handles. It was a curious sight, like a line of adjacent bathing huts or latrines. In the night, if you needed to get out, it was sometimes necessary to try several handles before discovering the right one.

As the only evening newspaperman there, I was permitted each morning to go to the nearest telephone box to call my office and dictate my experiences. The daily paper men performed the same duty in the evening. Two magazine people said they did not need to go outside the compound and did not want to do so anyway. The only time I went any further than the telephone (before scurrying back 'home') was to drive one of the church volunteers in a van to the East End to draw his dole money.

What many people might have classified as a no-hope idea turned into a resounding public relations triumph, and did nothing to harm the reputations of the participants. The *Evening News* gave my dispatches as much prominence as if they had been filed from some far foreign corner and there were photographs of me looking hungrily through the barbed wire. Genuine refugees were brought in and told us of their experiences. They seemed puzzled that we should voluntarily live like that. Then the television cameras arrived. David Holmes, later a well-known political commentator for the BBC and one of our group, used to pace up and down inside the wire rehearsing his nightly pieces for radio. Everyone began to take interest. Crowds formed outside the wire to look at these curious people as spectators might do at the zoo. A team from the television programme *Tonight* came to interview us and I appeared on the film. When the intruders were gone, however, when the autumn night dropped on Crystal Palace and Sydenham, and we gathered around our stew and our fire, that was the time we enjoyed most. Everyone had stories and everyone could tell them. Baden Powell would have approved. At the end of the ten days we left our camp and each other a little sadly and returned to our families and our homes and the everyday stories of Fleet Street. It was a silly idea that had gone right.

XVIII

There was often as much drama within the office of the *Evening News* as there was outside. Pestilence and politics, wars and weather, sport and speeches occupied the pages, but while these were being written and transported to print, things also happened to those whose job it was to tell the world of them. I was now firmly established on the reporting staff – although the news editor still did not care for my style. One day he handed me a book to fillet. It was called *Thunder of the Guns – A History of the Battleship Era*. As he handed it over he murmured knowledgeably: 'Famous ship that, HMS *Era* . . .'

When it became legal to brew your own beer I went to the obliging Watneys Brewery to learn the secrets of the craft. Returning with what I was confident were the knowledge and the ingredients, I brewed the latter in the canteen kitchen and left them to gurgle. I had scarcely finished writing the story of how easy it was to make your own ale when there was a rattling explosion and I rushed upstairs to see the canteen manager covered in wet hops and two windows shattered.

Mistakes were far from unknown. An article encouraging readers to take to the open air and walk across several miles of wonderful English countryside also directed them over an army firing range and mine-field. After the War Office had pointed out the error, vans had to be sent out to block all approach roads and stop the hikers with the words: '*Evening News* Walk Cancelled. Danger Keep Out'. There were eight editions a day, a prodigious technical achievement, and sheer speed caused some things to be overlooked. It was difficult, however, since feature articles were normally subject to a slower gestation, to understand how the Children's Corner managed to tell the tale of 'A dear little fairy called Chinkleburyfuckpot'.

The sub-editor who handled the crossword was subject to forays to Auntie's, a public house whose door was temptingly adjacent, and knew that his days on the paper were numbered. He had resorted to a variety of ruses to sneak from desk to drink, one of which involved a fictitious person who was always calling (at opening time) and demanding to see the journalist concerned with a 'Personal Message from God'. When this excuse for being absent ran thin he dreamed up others but it was apparent that sooner rather than later the heavy hand of dismissal would drop on his shoulder. Standing at bay in the saloon bar he grin-ningly revealed to me his plan of revenge to be carried out at the moment of sacking. He had formulated an obscene crossword to be substituted at the last moment for the real thing. I cannot remember much about it now except that one of the clues was: 'A wrinkled old retainer'. The answer, he told me with a slicing smile, was 'Scrotum'.

The two largest men in the office were also the most widespread drinkers. One, a great fellow with a red beard, found himself one evening to his bemusement in Richmond upon Thames. Some impulse led him to leap over a wall and he fell feet first into the shallows of the river. At the same moment he crapped himself. The joint experience sobered him sufficiently to evolve a plan for getting back to London. He rid himself of his trousers by simply allowing them to float away. Then he put on his raincoat and wrapped it around his large stomach and with bare, red and hairy legs sat on the District Line train to London pretending he was a Scotsman with a kilt beneath his coat. To complete the disguise he muttered Highland songs.

Trains appeared to play an important part in the misadventures of those who found it impolite to refuse several final drinks. Ernie Behar, a huge jovial fellow, was famous for his adventures on the railway. Getting into the train in London one evening, intending to alight somewhere in Kent, he fell to sleep and aroused only when the train arrived at Dover. He had another drink or so and then reboarded to be taken to his destination but dozed off again and returned to London. After several further attempts he fell deeply to dreams and awoke in cold darkness. 'There was rain beating down outside, so I thought,' he told us in the office on his eventual return. 'It was three o'clock in the perishing morning. I put my head out of the window and got soaked.' The carriage was in the washing sheds.

On another evening, having been on holiday in Germany, in the Black Forest, he celebrated his return to work, missed his normal train and eventually awoke at the not inappropriately entitled Effingham Junction.

426

The steep banks alongside this station are ranked with pine trees and Ernie believed for some time that he was back in the Black Forest. A porter came along shouting, 'All change! All change, here!' Ernie caught his arm. 'You speak good English, my son,' he told him admiringly.

When he related this in the office (we would crowd around his desk to hear the latest misadventure and some said he ought to write a book) he said philosophically: 'Well, I didn't know what I was doing there, but there was a very decent pub outside the station so I went in and had a few. Not a thing did I remember after that until I woke up sitting in a yard. There were beer barrels piled up everywhere. Do you know, I thought I was in Heaven.'

He is in Heaven now but his stories remain. His interest in railways was not always fanciful for he was a member of the Fleet Street Railway Circle. One evening he went to a film show at the British Transport Commission headquarters in Mayfair and having partaken, as he used to admit, of a little sherbet he wandered through the streets afterwards, amiable and minding his own business. Then he heard a woman's cries. Gallantly he plodded around alleys and corners trying to trace the source of the distress and eventually mounted some concrete steps from a loading bay at the back of a massive grey building. 'I opened the door,' he told us. 'And there . . . what do you think? Rows of women behind bars. All screaming!' He had, as it happened, gone into Savile Row Police Station by a back door and had arrived just as the nightly round-up of street girls had been completed. He was ejected through the same door, he said, by a large and violent policewoman.

The classic Ernie Behar stories, however, concern his disorganised journeys to Boulogne as leader of a Fleet Street outing which took place several times a year. It is difficult to appreciate that much-travelled journalists looked forward so eagerly to the modest trip across the Channel, but there was no doubt they did. The club had its own emblazoned tie bearing its motto: 'Encore des Moules', and invitations strictly stipulated that there was to be no drinking before Denmark Hill, about five miles south of London.

It was in France, however, that real adventures took place. On the first trip the sound citizens of Boulogne turned out in some numbers to greet the English journalists, with the town band and beaming Maire as well. The travellers, however, had been heavily compensating for seasickness and descended in a terrible tumble down the gangplank on to the quay. Their efforts to stand when the band played the national anthems was a singular and unhappy sight.

Each day I would leave my house in the shrubbed suburbs wearing my Burton suit, my Dolcis shoes, my Tootal tie and my Rael Brook shirt and travel by Metropolitan Line to chronicle the history of the world.

I was present on some occasions of great note but it is not always those which lodge deeply in the memory. More often it was the diminutive dramas, some funny, others so tragic that the reporter, coming in from the outside, could only stand by with a lump in his throat.

It was impossible for me to become uncaring although I had a sneaking regard for those who could apparently bury all feeling, and sometimes all decency, in the cause of getting a story. Some were detached to the point of cruelty. My first view of national newspapermen was at the Harrow & Wealdstone train crash in 1952 when I was a local reporter. Sipping from a cup given to him by a lady from the Women's Voluntary Service, one of them remarked: 'I suppose you could say this is the first rail crash since tea came off the ration.' There were 112 dead.

I often wondered what motivated such men – loyalty to their newspaper or some driving ego that compelled them to come up with the desperately coveted scoop at whatever cost. There were reporters who were good companions, who gave to charity and who lived lawful private lives with their families, but who would filch a photograph from a dead man's mantelshelf or promise heaven and earth to a confused and weeping widow in return for some poignant quote. If she refused they frequently made it up. There was no room for pity; the story was all. One day I saw two huge journalists bodily drag a woman who had been a key witness at an inquest (she was suspecting of causing it) over gravestones so that they could keep her away from rival reporters. These men would loiter for days in great discomfort, hide, lie, steal, connive and bribe, all for the sake of a story. One carried a black tie in the glove compartment of his car in case he ever found it necessary to interpolate himself into a funeral.

There was a Press Council ruling on 'intrusion into private grief' but the hard men were unimpressed.

They even made up a derisory ditty about it which was sung in the bar of many a village inn invaded by the newsmen staking out a good story.

For all my eagerness to shine as a reporter I found these sardonic methods both repugnant and frightening. Only twice did I try them myself and on both occasions I was deeply ashamed. The first was a story about a teenage girl who had fallen, it appeared accidentally, under a London Underground train. She had miraculously survived and was in St Thomas's Hospital. In normal circumstances there would have been no opportunity for a reporter to reach that girl's bedside, an enquiry to the hospital secretary would have elicited nothing more than a terse statement about her condition. Through a series of misunderstandings, however, I found myself inside the hospital and being led to her bedside. The sister accompanying me apparently thought that I was a relative and I did not disillusion her. After all, the first-hand story of someone who had survived such a violent adventure seemed worth it. I was led into a ward and then to a private room. At once I knew I had done the wrong thing. The poor girl was black with bruises and covered with lacerations. She could scarcely speak. At that moment I knew I should have turned around and left but instead I still said: 'Tell me what happened?'

She apparently thought I was a plain-clothes policeman. Her whole terribly injured face trembled and she leaned forward beggingly, holding my sleeve and weeping. She was so bruised she could hardly utter the words. 'I'll never do it again,' she sobbed. 'Never. I promise.'

430

I patted her hand and, speechless, went out of the ward and down the stairs. I sat on a seat on the embankment for half an hour and wondered what sort of person I was. Then I telephoned in the story, in three lines.

Not infrequently a reporter would be on the scene of a crime or an accident as quickly as, sometimes even before, the emergency services, due to a tip-off from someone eavesdropping on the police radio wavelength.

It was illegal to pass on information gained in this way and there were a number of prosecutions. The tipsters continued to transmit their intelligence, however, and one, who was an insurance assessor and used the early warning to be at the scene of a fire sometimes in advance of the brigade, also had a side-line in providing information to newspapers. It was after one of these calls to the newsdesk that I was dispatched to Chelsea Flour Mills where there had been a sudden death. I was there within minutes and walked into a scene I shall never forget. A worker had fallen into a huge revolving vat of flour and was liter-ally drowned before anyone could help him. I arrived just as the terrible white body was being taken from the vat with the man's workmates standing crying with horror. One of them was frenziedly trying to revive him by emptying the flour from his mouth. I do not think I have ever seen such a dreadful scene nor have I ever felt more of an intruder.

Fortunately there were compensating moments of warmth and humour. There was the morning I was sent to a street in north London where there had been a massive battle between two rival gangs of robbers

431

and the police. Each gang had shopped the other to Scotland Yard and the climax came when all three interested parties turned up at a rendezvous. There was a tremendous fight involving fifty combatants wielding pick-axe handles, knuckle-dusters and truncheons (this being in a gentler age when neither villains nor the law resorted to firearms). When I reached the battlefield, at the junction of two rows of terraced houses in Tottenham, the main fighting was over but the place was littered with weapons and men holding their heads. Three cars had collided spectacularly and there were lakes of blood. A cat had sat on a sunny wall and, unperturbed, watched the entire affray. Approaching the pet's owner, an elderly Cockney lady, I asked her what she had seen. 'Well,' she hesitated. 'I was polishing me passage and I 'eard all this noise so I looked out of me front door and saw all these bobbies and all these other men.'

'What were they doing?' I urged.

'Boxing,' she replied thoughtfully. 'They was all boxing.'

Another call took me to Upper Thames Street, among the river warehouses, where a building had caught fire and there had been some adventurous escapes. When I arrived, the firemen were rolling up their hoses but one told me that the foreman of a warehouse had an interesting tale to relate. I sought him out. It was quickly apparent that here was a thwarted man of action condemned to live a quiet life among bales and boxes. 'In the war,' he said, determined to start at the beginning. 'We was heavily bombed in this area as you might know.'

I said I did. 'Well, we 'ad a good team in this ware-house. Me and Harry, and old Sam who's dead now, and George over there, and little Bill and Mr Thompson from the office. All air raid wardens we was. Best team on the docks. Night after night when the Jerries was bombing . . .'

Aware of the narrowing time to the next edition I prodded him for his more recent experiences and eventually he drew breath and said: 'So when we saw this building on fire we knew *exactly* what to do. There was this bloke standing on the third-floor window sill, smoke pouring out, and I shouted to 'im to 'old on while we got our sheet.'

The sheet was one left over from the war, the sort that firemen used to hold out so that people could jump to safety. Harry and George and little Bill and Mr Thompson from the office were eagerly mobilised and under the command of the warehouse foreman they hurried with the sheet to the pavement below the burning building.

'There 'e was, up there,' recorded the foreman.

'Smoke pouring out,' I put in. I was in a hurry.

'You're right, it was,' he agreed looking at me suspiciously as if I had already heard the story. 'Pouring, it was. Out.'

'What did you do?'

'We 'eld out the sheet, like we did in the blitz, and I shouted for 'im to jump.'

'And he did?' I urged. 'He jumped?'

'Yes sir, 'e did,' nodded the foreman sagely. 'Jumped. Went straight through the bleedin' sheet and broke 'is leg on the pavement.'

Londoners of that breed were quite wonderful. I once went to interview a couple who had been married seventy-five years. They had lived in the same low little house since the masts of sailing ships in the Thames docks could be seen over the opposite rooftops. They had produced a large family and they lovingly described each of their offspring until it came to the eldest (who was dead anyway) and then fell to a bitter dispute about this first-born's age. The wife hit the old man across the shins with her walking stick because he told me that the girl would have been seventy-six that year. The old lady was deeply embarrassed by the reminder of an ancient indiscretion.

James Green, who joined the *Evening News* when the *Star* (affectionately known to Londoners as the La-de-da) sadly folded along with the wonderful *News Chronicle*, was once sent to interview a centenarian in the East End. A young woman let him into the house and then departed, leaving Jimmy with the cobwebby dear who was perched like a bird in her chair. She was stone deaf and all Jimmy's shouting evoked nothing. Eventually she howled back at him, 'Wait till Dad comes in, will you!'

Dad? God, how old was Dad? Eventually there was a banging at the door and Jimmy answered it. There stood an incredibly feeble and folded man, so bent his head was almost at floor level. He tottered in. This was Dad, at ninety-six. We used to cry laughing when Jimmy repeated this story because he would go through the actions of trying to interview the old chap at floor level, actually lying down and shouting into the ancient fellow's face. Dad could not understand why the young man was there at all until eventually it dawned on him that his wife's hundredth birthday was something of significance. Not, however, to him. "Er?" he bellowed at Jimmy's face on the floorboards. "Er? Silly old cow. Time she was dead!'

Similarly, I was once told how the Old Comrades' Association of a famous London regiment had purchased a flat in Ealing as an investment and had installed a ninety-year-old sergeant there, on the reasonable view that he would only be occupying it for a limited period. The veteran, however, resolutely refused to fade away and remained as a tenant until he was beyond his hundredth birthday. One day the welfare officer called on him and was astonished to find that he had gone out. He waited and eventually saw the sergeant tottering blithely along the street. The sergeant had thought, as it was a nice day, he would take himself out for a walk. The welfare man enquired if he had enjoyed the experience and his reply was so worthwhile that I included it in my novel, *Dangerous Davies: The Last Detective*. 'Oh yes, indeed,' said the veteran who had fought in Zululand. 'But everything's changed so much. All these blackies about. Last time I saw a black man that close he was on the end of my lance.'

In journalism, as in the life with which it is concerned, you not only need luck you need the luck to *know* when you are lucky. As my time went on in Fleet Street, and I began to be assigned to bigger and more far-flung stories, I sometimes thought that sitting on my shoulder

435

was a small, wryly grinning god who nudged me in many fortuitous directions.

My first foreign assignment took me by surprise. I had gone into the office one morning arrayed in the designs of Burton, Dolcis, Tootal and Rael Brook, via the Metropolitan Line, when I was dramatically met by the editor in his exciting red braces.

'Thomas,' he said, pointing out of the window in a generally southerly direction. 'Go to Monte Carlo!'

Sir Winston Churchill, the elder hero, had fallen down the stairs of the Hotel de Paris and broken his leg, a serious matter for one now frail.

Not being accustomed to winging my way much further than Reigate, I was unprepared for this amazing change of direction, although my passport was in my desk since I was intending to take it one lunchtime to get a Spanish visa in preparation for a holiday in Majorca. Swiftly I found myself with a circus of journalists on the first possible flight to Nice. We arrived at three in the afternoon, in time for me to scratch together some sort of story for that evening's final edition.

Foreign Fred, a ubiquitous and cheerful non-journalist who ran the foreign desk brilliantly when higher executives were in the saloon bar or the lavatory, had booked me into the Hotel de Paris, where Churchill had fallen upon his accident. Never had I been in such a place; high curling ceilings and floating cherubs, gilt and gold, and blinds that descended not only majestically but automatically as the sun climbed in to the Mediterranean sky. My room cost ten pounds a day, which I thought was astronomical. I stayed in the same hostelry only days before writing this (as part of the first cricket team ever to perform in Monaco) and the ten pounds now scarcely buys a double gin and tonic.

On the evening of that first visit, I decided that since I had come without luggage, I would need to wash out my shirt, my underpants and my socks in preparation for an early start the next day. On later foreign assignments the reporter was permitted to spend up to twenty pounds on suitable clothing, but this had been an emergency.

After going out with the rest of Fleet Street to eat and drink I returned to the hotel and somewhat fuzzily began to wash the garments in the bathroom basin. There was a high window and it was a deeply warm night so I decided that they would dry nicely in a few hours. Looking out I had a splendid spread of lights before me, glittering along the coast. Nearer to hand was a piece of convenient rope hanging vertically in the night breeze. To this I tied, by the arms, my shirt and then tied on my pants and socks. In the morning they were flying high on the flagmast with the unfurled banner of the Principality of Monaco.

A porter, who seemed to find nothing amusing or even untoward in the situation, retrieved my belongings but I decided that if I was to remain for a few days (which I intended to do even if Churchill was flown home), then I would need some extra clothes. Everything in the shops seemed outrageous in price until I came to a place in the backstreets which sold workingmen's clothes, and here I purchased a cheap blue shirt and a pair of denim trousers.

The French authorities were to fly the great man

home to London, and since the airport was at Nice, I quit the expensive hotel and made for the resort intending to find some cheaper accommodation once I was footing my own bill. Time was tight and I arrived at the airport to find the press obediently clustered on the observation balcony waiting for the ambulance to bring Churchill from the hospital to the plane. I wandered down to the lower floors and out into the sunshine where I saw some airport employees in their blue dungarees standing around a forked-lift truck, one of the sort used to load baggage into aircraft holds. I forwarded an interesting banknote in the direction of a lively looking fellow who confirmed my suspicion that one of the world's most illustrous men was to be hoisted into an airliner like a suitcase.

Security was non-existent. In those happier days it was scarcely considered necessary. The ambulance arrived and went out onto the tarmac where the medical attendants unloaded the great old man, his leg thick with plaster below the blanket. To my intense delight I saw that he was stoically puffing a cigar, which he condescended to dispose of (by dropping it over the side of the stretcher) before he was manoeuvred onto the mechanical lifting truck. As he was transferred to the plane he grumbled loudly, 'Steady, steady. That's a leg.'

James Cameron, the veteran journalist, tells the story of how, after an illness, he was invited to convalesce at Lord Beaverbrook's house on the Cote d'Azur and sat at a dinner table opposite Churchill, then in his dotage, who slept through most of the meal but finally awoke sufficiently to call croakily up the table to Beaverbrook: 'Max, in 1942 I sent you on a mission of major importance to Moscow, didn't I?'

Beaverbrook replied: 'That's correct, Winston.'

Churchill, before going back to sleep, grunted: 'Did you ever go?'

On the morning of Sir Winston's death I went to Bladon in Oxfordshire, the small village where he was to be buried. Council workmen were feverishly re-tarring the road outside the churchyard, having undoubtedly been dragged from their beds by a suddenly panic-stricken county engineer. There was an infants' school where almost every child was familiar with the famous figure. Their parents worked on the Blenheim estate. The lady teacher decided that, on that morning, they should each draw a picture of Sir Winston as they remembered him. In most he was shown shooting pheasants.

I was assigned to cover his funeral, at least the first part of it. Every reporter had a set place from which he would not dare to stray. Mine was at a lancet window in the Houses of Parliament, overlooking the yard where the funeral cortège was forming. My view was unsatisfactory, oblique and restricted. Near the window was a door and, pushing this, I discovered a lavatory. It had a window with a far better outlook so I stood on the seat and described the solemn event from there.

Churchill's London house was later put up for sale and a friendly estate agent allowed me to look around it. In one corner was a sad little lift, like a child's playpen, by which the mighty man had been trans-ported in the days of his final infirmity. I was told that while half the world was waiting outside the front door as he lay dying, waiting for each bulletin relayed by his frail physician Lord Moran (it was half-expected that Churchill himself might appear and announce that Lord Moran had passed away), the great leader was in fact lying in the house next door – the adjoining servants' quarters. He had been finally transferred there so that the medical team and their equipment could be more easily accommodated and accessible. On that day, in the empty house just before its sale, I found a table covered with wine glasses speckled with sun and dust. Afterwards I was asked why I had not purloined one as a souvenir. For some reason it never occurred to me.

That first foreign assignment in Monte Carlo had an immediate and most astonishing sequel. My elder son Mark, who had been born the previous December, was to be christened on a Sunday in the parish church at Willesden where his mother and I had been married. I returned from Monaco on the Saturday evening and went, feeling rather ill, to the church the next morning. The service had scarcely begun when I began experiencing sharp stomach pains. Trembling, I went out into the churchyard and sat on a seat. In no time I was in an ambulance and being carried to Hillingdon Hospital where I was prodded and examined and finally given a sedative.

While I was drowsy a notorious spy, having tried to kill himself on an airliner over London, was wheeled into the hospital – the most adjacent to the airport – and conveniently placed in the small room directly opposite mine.

440

His name was Dr Soblen. He had been spying for Russia in the United States, and when he realised that he was about to be apprehended, he fled to Israel. He was Jewish and he imagined, faintly I should think, that the Israelis would provide him with asylum. This super-optimism was misplaced and he was soon aboard an El Al plane and heading back to retribution. When the aircraft was over London he cut his wrists.

My first suspicion of something unusual was when I saw a strangely uniformed guard (an Israeli policeman) emerge from the room opposite. Still dopey, I enquired of a nurse, a wonderfully gossipy West Indian, what was happening and she told me all she knew.

It was late at night. I was still in pain but now I was sniffing a story it had noticeably receded. A late-visiting doctor kindly told me how the other new patient was progressing. There was nothing to do but to wait until the next morning, a Monday, when the *Evening News* would again be on the streets. When I awoke there was a travelling newspaper seller going about the ward with the daily editions, each headlining the sensational story of the spy from the sky. Half of Fleet Street was chaffing outside the hospital gates, trying to pick up any scrap of news and with no hope of getting in. Only *I* was inside.

I had watched the comings and goings of the medical staff and the security people and every time the door opened I saw the big doomed man propped up in bed, already looking dead. Just as I was wondering where the nearest phone was located and just in time for the midday edition, a nice lady wheeled a trolley telephone into my room and asked me if I

441

would like to call anyone, a relative perhaps. Thanking her fervently I plugged in the phone and deftly dialled Fleet Street 6000.

My world scoop began, melodramatically: 'The man in the opposite hospital bed to mine is a spy and he is dying . . .'

Reporters clamoured outside the gates, and some managed to get in by bringing me fruit and flowers before asking the latest on the Soblen story. I found myself giving press conferences. John Freeman, the distinguished journalist, who ought to have known better, decided in his column that I had purposely had myself smuggled into the hospital, under the pretext of being ill, in order to spy on the spy.

As for the sad Soblen, he was undoubtedly doomed. He hurriedly speeded up the event, in the end, by taking a poisoned pill concealed in a peach and brought to the hospital by a friend.

himself and patently drinking too much. Owen's wife suggested that they should make a steak and kidney pie for the bereft fellow and Owen agreed enthusiastically. She was a splendid cook and produced her best. The problem was how to give it to the undernourished man, without causing offence, without making him feel he was the object of charity. They evolved a story of having had an argument about the merits of English pies and French pies. The pie was then divided into separate parcels and Owen took them to the Yard. 'We know you're a man of taste,' he said, putting a friendly arm around the lonely reporter. 'And we want you to settle the matter. We want you to take these slices of pie home, heat them, and eat them. Then tell us what you think.' Then, to ensure that all the sustenance was consumed, he added: 'And make sure you eat every bit. Otherwise you won't have given them a proper trial.' Away went the Yardman with the two parcels, promising to report next day. The verdict was disappointing. 'Horrible,' he announced. 'Don't know which was the worse, the English or the French. Even the dog wouldn't touch the stuff.'

Alfred Draper, an old friend from local newspaper days, once found himself taking the mother of a condemned murderer on her last visit to her son at Wandsworth Prison. The youth was to be hanged the next day. Uncomfortably Alf waited in the car for her return. Her report was phlegmatic. 'He's quite cheerful,' she said. 'But, of course, he's not looking forward to the morning. I just told him to keep his chin up.'

The studious Cyril Aynsley of the *Daily Express* was with a group of reporters undertaking a death watch outside the home of George Bernard Shaw at Ayot St

Lawrence. The white-bearded seer was certainly dying but was taking some days about it. They camped out in some discomfort, each one aware that the nearest public telephone was a mile away, downhill, and that the fittest runner would get the news to his paper, and the world, first. Each of them was armed with his own magnetic disc so removing the piece from the mouth-piece was rendered pointless.

If Shaw died during the time when the daily news-papers were printing then there would have been a cavalry charge down the hill; if he departed during the publishing time of the evening newspapers then the rush would be only slightly less. The news agency men would have to be on their toes all the time.

Each day, during his off-watch period, Cyril would walk down to the telephone and make a check call to his news editor. During one of these conversations he was told that *Time* magazine required a piece about G.B.S.'s death and wanted him to write it. Cyril agreed. He was walking back towards the house when he saw a rush of evening and news agency men heading towards him and he knew that the great man had gone. Being out of his time, he was in no great hurry and continued to walk up the hill. A car stopped. In it was Nancy, Lady Astor. 'How is he?' she enquired, guessing he was a newsman.

'He's dead, so I believe,' replied Cyril solemnly.

'I see. Which newspaper do you represent?'

Knowing she despised the *Daily Express* he compro-mised and answered '*Time*', since he was also now committed to that journal. Lady Astor apparently thought he said: '*The Times*', and invited him to get into the car.

Thus Cyril found himself to be the first outsider to view Shaw's body. 'What were his last words?' he carefully enquired of the nurse.

She seemed doubtful. For a man of so many words Shaw had apparently said very little worthwhile, or so the nurse judged. 'He just opened his eyes and said: "You know, nurse, all my life I've done everything I have wanted to do. And now I can't do the thing I want to do most. I want to die."' The nurse shrugged: Cyril's pencil was trembling. 'And then he died,' she said.

The man who showed me the greatest friendship, encouragement and regard was Vincent Mulchrone, a shining writer. He was a big broad man with silvery hair, a north-country voice and an Irish background. Over a distance of fifteen hundred words he was unbeatable, whether it was a magnificent occasion or some small odd story that caught his imagination. A record company once had the nice idea of producing a long-player of stirring orchestral music and providing, as an extra, a conductor's baton so that you could lock the door and conduct away to your heart's content. Vincent wrote a piece about this innovation in the *Daily Mail* which began: 'In all the years we three have been conducting, Beecham and Barbarolli have had one undeniable advantage over me. They have had orchestras.'

His kindness to me, once I had become part of the world-touring circus of Fleet Street, was overwhelming. He used to call me Kid. Every day he drank champagne in the back bar of the Harrow, almost outside the door of the *Mail*, or wherever he happened to be. He was a superb teller of tales whether spoken or written. He died far too young and I cried when he did.

In my own office there were also memorable men. Leslie Ayre was the gentlest of people, a small soft man like a tailor, with a spotted bow tie. He wrote about radio and later television until these functions were taken over by James Green on his arrival from the *Star*. After that Leslie was glad and free to concentrate on his most profound love – music. He was often thoughtfully sad and seemed pleased if you stopped him for a chat. His god was Tchaikovsky. 'Ah, Tchai,' he would smile, shaking his head. 'Ah, Tchai . . .' One day, short of a general writer, the features editor asked him to compose a weather story: Why were we having such a terrible summer? Why was it always raining? What could be done about it? 'This morning,' I remember he wrote, 'I tried an ancient rite. I hung a piece of seaweed outside my window. In no time it was soaking.'

Colin Frame arrived after the demise of the *Star*, another grey-haired gentleman of quiet demeanour and a charming wit. He bought himself a boat and delighted to chuff it up and down the little River Wey in Surrey. If anyone in the office wished to hire it for a week he was amenable. One of these borrowers was Felix Barker, the mysteriously cloaked theatre critic, who unfortunately found on sailing to the first lock that it was closed and could not be opened because of extensive repairs which involved the draining of the entire river on the other side. So Felix and his family spent their entire week cruising somewhat monotonously up and down one half-mile stretch of river. Then Julian Holland, a bespectacled feature writer, who later distinguished himself at Broadcasting House, borrowed the boat. Just as Colin was leaving the office on the first evening that

Julian was aboard, there came an anguished telephone call from the banks of the River Wey. 'How do you stop the engine?' Julian had leapt ashore while his wife frantically grappled with the boat they could not stop.

In the *Evening News* Features Department, of which I became part although I continued to write and travel on news stories, was a budding and ebullient young man who, even today, twenty-five years later, has not lost either his enthusiasm or his wayward grin. Bill Hall wrote on films and was a private pyromaniac. He had an affinity for fireworks. Once travelling on a London bus and having ignited the fuse of a particularly violent banger, he pushed it into the used ticket container on the platform and rang the bell to get off at the approaching stop. Unfortunately the bus did not stop. Other people crowded the platform, waiting to alight, and Bill could see his own time bomb smoking almost below his nose. Such a rush of passengers wanted to get off at the following stop that he was pressed up against the used ticket box and the banger exploded, blackening his face and all but blowing off his eyebrows.

From those lively days I have retained many acquaintances and real friendships. One of these is with David Eliades, now an executive of the *Daily Express*, whom I first knew in my Willesden local paper days. In his youth he wore petrol-blue suits, florid ties and was an expert on roller skates. Partnered by a sometimes incredible man called Robert Forrest Webb (explorer, sheep-keeper, motorcyclist, Japanese martial arts expert, antique dealer, artist, but above all raconteur), David wrote a funny and successful novel called *And to My Nephew Albert I Leave the Island What I Won off Fatty Hagan in a Poker Game*. A later book, about English nannies in New York, became a Disney film and another called *After Me the Deluge* was the basis for a musical which was first produced in Italy and seems always to be playing somewhere in the world. Bob took himself and his wife off to the hills of Wales, but David is, at heart, an unrepentant Fleet Street man. He talks about news stories and how they were obtained, of exclusives and bungles and excitements in a way I have long and regrettably forgotten. He also takes notes of some oddities nearer home. He tells the story of a *Daily Express* executive going into the lavatory and, seeing a black man there, concluding that he was one of the journalists from former colonial territories whom Beaverbrook Newspapers sought to encourage and frequently brought to London for experience.

'Been into the editor's conference yet?' enquired the executive of the black man, as they stood at the trough. The latter admitted he had not.

'Come tomorrow,' invited the executive breezily as he zipped up. 'Good experience for you. Open your eyes to a few things.'

The invitation was graciously accepted but several of those present at the conference wondered at the presence of a man who had hitherto only been known as a lavatory cleaner.

Brian Freemantle (after being a colleague at the *Evening News* he eventually became foreign editor of the *Daily Mail*) went to Vietnam several times (on the final swift and controversial occasion to snatch away some abandoned orphans) and then quit to work on his own excellent books. Brian, or Bruin as he is known, is the sort of person who makes you happy when you see him.

He believes that he is urbane, even suave, and a wide enough vote might well prove him right. He has high taste from which no one, even someone of greater taste, can dislodge him; the sort of man who would order a bottle of Chateau Lafite '63 with a hamburger, confident that its power, its courage, its mellowness and its touch of blown hills and southern sunshine will not spoil the taste of the chips.

Both these friends are good companions and I have encouraged, perhaps inveigled, each of them (once) to share my enjoyment of travelling in the varied land of Britain.

David suffered bravely on the little bouncing boat called *The Good Shepherd* on a stormy voyage to this country's most isolated inhabited place, Fair Isle, south of Shetland. For four hours, soaking wet and festooned with fish scales he clung to a tarpaulin, mumbling his way feebly through: 'Eternal Father Strong to Save'. Once ashore on the magic island his spirit lifted and he took great risks to take pictures for the first edition of my travel book *Some Lovely Islands*. Once he was hanging over an astounding cliff, photographing puffins, and I was hanging onto his feet when his boot came off. I managed to haul him up by the other.

His photography was eventually pin-pointed by an American critic of the book as 'pleasantly amateur'. He took an artistic picture from below a cow which resulted in what appeared to be a set of pornographic bagpipes. One day we ran ourselves breathless trying to reach a crashed plane in time to rescue the pilot. We arrived thirty-eight years late. It was a German fighter left over from the war. We consoled ourselves by observing that the metal was unrusted and it looked as if it might well be a brand-new crash.

Fair Isle is, of course, a place of migratory birds. There are no trees. To see an Arctic woodpecker in a frenzy, attempting to make an impression on a concrete post, is a pitiful experience. Each night the birdwatchers were expected to assemble in the fire-lit common room of the observatory and report their finds of the day. David and I had hilarious moments making up the names of unlikely and frequently obscene birds, like the bent-billed, puzzled-face, brown duck, which could fly as fast as the other ducks but could not brake as quickly. Sometimes we laughed so much we were told reproachfully we could be heard on the far side of the island and we were frightening the fulmars. When eventually I returned to Fair Isle with a BBC Television team to make a documentary of my book, the entire unit – writer, producer, camera and sound men – was told that it was our turn to wash up at the bird observatory and we could not continue about our work until we did. So we did.

The journey upon which I was accompanied by Bruin Freemantle was also north, to the Wester Ross coast of Scotland, when I was writing another travelogue called *The Hidden Places of Britain*:

I had chosen to make the journey to the remoteness of Ross and Cromarty with another writer, my long-time friend Brian Freemantle, a novelist of much talent whose mode of life, however, makes him singularly unsuited for anywhere that does not have – at least – a choice of luxury hotels; the sort of man who treats a label on a bottle of wine in a Scots ale bar to a disgruntled knitting of the

451

eyebrows. He has, in addition, a fastidiousness about his
clothes and personal appearance which scarcely fits him
for adventure in the wild open air . . .

We stopped eventually at a small but fine baronial hotel.
Freemantle, who looks for stars on hotels with much the
same diligence as an astronomer seeks them in the firma-
ment, mentioned that while it was not a patch on the
Georges Cinq in Paris, it did appear to be comfortable in
a primitive sort of way.

That night there was an unbelieving hush over the
land. At the World Cup Finals in South America,
Scotland had played lowly Peru – and lost. We
wandered to the village bar which was prostrate with
men full of drink and grief. Freemantle muttered: 'I
think this is our sort of place.'

One shining day we set out to walk the five miles
along a threadlike cliff path to a remote settlement at
the nose of the Loch Broom Peninsula:

I was frankly astonished that Freemantle had not only agreed
to accompany me on my projected arduous journey . . . but
had insisted on making the arrangements for provisioning the
adventure. This, I thought at the time, was much the same
as Beau Brummell offering to go in place of Stanley to find
Livingstone in Africa.

The lunch pack turned out to be a gourmet feast.
After we had trudged a difficult and dangerous mile
on the tight path with a sobering drop to the sea below,
Freemantle sat down and said he was dizzy. He was
amazed that we had only travelled a mile in an hour.

There were four more miles (and hours) to go and then we had to get back.

'Let's have the lunch and go home,' he suggested intrepidly. So we did.

XX

If I had initially been discouraged in Fleet Street by the lack of travel and adventure in the assignments I was afforded, then within a couple of years the situation had been completely reversed. Half of my working life then was spent either out of town, as it was called, or out of the country. While Maureen was bringing up our daughter and our son on the flat-roofed estate to which we had now moved (and which became the *Tropic of Ruislip* of my later novel), I was in Jerusalem, Paris, Sydney, Tokyo or Salisbury, the one that was in what was Rhodesia.

One of my early trips was to Paris where the young heir to the Peugeot car fortune had been kidnapped. In those days, the late nineteen-fifties, kidnapping and abduction were crimes which had only previously been connected with Chicago. Since then the habit has, of course, spread widely. My lack of French was a handicap but I managed pretty well with the help of the staff of our sister paper, the *Daily Mail*, at their office in the Rue de Sentier. I went down to St Cloud golf course, from which the lad had been spirited, and came to the conclusion that some of his acquaintances had perpetrated the crime, that they had kidnapped him for fun. This theory was somewhat borne out when the hostage was finally recovered and the culprits arrested. They were rich kids looking for amusement.

To work in a fabled foreign city was wonderful. Carefully I watched the other reporters so that, with their experience (not to mention their French), they did not steal a march on me. I followed up clues and viewed even the most sinless-faced nuns as suspects. One day I was sitting in a café and I spotted a journalist from a daily newspaper at a neighbouring table. Suddenly he half rose, then completely rose, having spotted something among the boulevard crowds. I heard him whistle softly and go out of the door. I was not going to be beaten like that. If he was the first to spot some clue, some lead, then I wanted to be second. At a cautious distance I followed him, threading through the people until I saw him going into a cinema. By the time I had reached the foyer he had paid at the box office and was walking through the curtain. Hurriedly I bought my ticket and went into the darkness. He was standing in the shadows surveying the people in the rows of seats. Then he saw me. He seemed more pleased than anything. 'Ah,' he said. 'It's you.' He selected a seat and motioned me to sit in the next one. The film was just starting on the screen. *Tarzan's Secret Treasure*, he whispered. 'Always wanted to see this.'

At the top of the Rue de Sentier was a bistro where the oldest prostitute in Paris used to hold court, regaling the journalists who assembled there with her memories of earlier and, she claimed, much naughtier days. Particularly exotic were her descriptions of the methods used at the end of the nineteenth century to take pornographic photographs. These T-shaped flashes were used in those times and, although these were safe enough at a distance, the capturing of erotic close-ups was riven with risks. Sometimes if the man holding the naked flash drew too near to the parts of the anatomy being immortalised and the explosion occurred, the participants frequently found themselves running around the room trying to extinguish fires in their pubic hair. A tantalising picture.

My sojourn in the odd refugee camp at Crystal Palace, with the London buses on the road outside, had resulted in an arranged trip, also by the World Refugee Year organisers, to the Middle East to visit some real camps for dispossessed people. We flew from the small Blackbushe Airport in a rattling Viking which took two days for the flight to Beirut. Luck was with me again because as the plane chugged over the Mediterranean coast of France we had an amazing view of a terrible disaster (other people's disasters are luck to journalists). The dam at Fréjus had burst and the water had swept into the sea taking people and houses with it. The bite out of the barrage was clearly visible in the mocking sunshine that now lit the landscape below, and the bright blue sea was stained a cocoa-brown for miles. In the bay French and American warships were helping with the rescue operations.

I had spent two weeks the previous summer in a village along that coast, so I was easily able to pick out places. We chugged on to Naples and landed there for the night. Early the next morning, in time for the first edition of the *Evening News*, I telephoned an eyewitness report of the tragedy which was occupying the world headlines. After what I considered to be some graphic aerial description, a bored-sounding sub-editor came on the phone and yawned: 'Did you manage to get any interviews?'

It was always difficult for those at large in the big moving world and those in the confined office to reconcile their outlooks. My days as a sub-editor were not so far behind that I did not appreciate the attitude. Vivid prose and exciting happenings frequently seem pretty poor meat in the murk of some early morning office. There were other desk-bound men who appeared to take a real delight in cutting my stories just before the carefully climaxed punchline so I took to devising alternative punchlines and distributing them throughout the story so that the cut could be made at any almost point. It was usually made *between* them.

The tour of the Middle East took us from Lebanon to Jordan and into Israel through the Mendelbaum Gate in Jerusalem. The first part was undertaken in a United Nations Dakota which made our ramshackle Viking look like Concorde. There were metal seats and no seat belts. On the side was reassuringly stencilled, 'Refurbished 1946'.

It was a good time to go to the Holy Land, for Christmas was nearing and I wrote a series of articles about the unhappy region from which so much hope was always expected. In Nazareth I stayed at a hotel where the foyer was thick with posters and pictures of Kew Gardens. The manager said it was his heart's desire to go to Kew. I also sat through a nativity play in Christ's own town. Not one of the children taking part was a Christian. They were all Arab Moslems attending the Nazareth Anglican School. Like all visitors to Jerusalem I wasted much time looking for the 'green hill far away' where Our Lord was crucified. There is no hill, not according to the official and accepted view. In fact the ugly Church of the Crucifixion lies at the foot of the Via Dolorosa, the Way of Tears, where Jesus carried His cross. We were solicited by the usual gabbling guides who tried to persuade us that the crucifixion, the tomb and the resurrection were all neatly packaged within the confines of the church. Much more convincing, but unacceptable to the variety of churches who squabble in that sacred city, to me at any rate, was the Garden of the Tomb, a simple and quiet place of olive trees and wine presses, with a sepulchre carved into the rock. Beyond the garden *is* a hill which, although not green, is *fashioned* in the shape of a skull, the Golgotha of the Bible, and is historically accepted as having been a place of criminal punishment. It overlooks the Jerusalem bus station.

Not long after this first visit to Israel, the Nazi war criminal Adolf Eichmann was spirited from his hideaway in Argentina and flown to Jerusalem to face charges of crimes against humanity. I attended the trial. The accusation, although seemingly large for one man, was not too much for Mr Eichmann. He was an entirely despicable figure, standing in his bullet-proof glass case as the evidence was piled up against him. Even when sentenced to death he stood like a man applying for a job.

The Israeli authorities had thoughtfully provided him with a blue suit for his public appearances and he sat, evil-faced, in this throughout the weeks of the trial. The Nazi ego had not died. When one particularly horrifying piece of material, filmed in a concentration camp, was being shown, it was decided to clear the courtroom. They brought Eichmann from the cells in his prison clothes and sat him in his glass booth while the terrible indictment contained in the film was presented to him. He figured in the action depicted on the screen but remained unperturbed. What concerned him most were his prison clothes, especially when photographers crept close to him and began to take pictures. 'Why are they taking photographs?' he asked crossly. 'And I am not wearing my suit.'

Fortunately, because of the time difference, there was no necessity for me to attend the hearings after the lunch adjournment each day. Any copy I filed would have reached London too late for the final edition. Any time I did not have to be in the courtroom was welcome. Some of the evidence was out-rageous and Eichmann's attitude was of studied indifference. One part of his testimony went something like this:

I had visited a place where they were going to shoot some Jews and when they were shooting them I was standing close and the blood from them spurted onto my uniform. I remember the place well because there was a fine railway station there, built in the reign of the Emperor Franz Josef, and my mother had always taught me to appreciate the good things of those times. After lunch we went back to where they had killed the Jews. By this time they were buried, but the grave was

459

*too shallow or there were too many bodies because the blood
was coming from the earth like a spring . . .*

Any man who could describe a scene like that, and
put a railway station (not to mention lunch) in the
middle, richly deserved everything that was to happen
to him. He was hanged and his body taken out to sea
on a plane, then dropped into the water. Amazingly
many of the younger people in Israel could see no
point in the trial. It was merely a show they said. How
could punishment of one man avenge the deaths of
six million? The older people, those with the death
camps still shadows in their eyes, and their camp identity number tattooed for ever on their wrists, understandably felt differently.

Even such a long-running horror as the Eichmann
trial, however, had its wry moments. Within the
compound of the Beit Ha'am, where the court was
sitting, was a restaurant for the use of the journalists,
the translators and other people connected with the
court. On the first day we sat down to lunch and *in
walked Adolf Eichmann.* He busily began rearranging the
trays on the self-service counter. It was not Eichmann
of course, but it needed more than a second glance to
realise this. The man was the restaurant manager. He
went about blissfully unaware of his evil double and was
bemused when people wanted to have their photographs
taken with him. He thought it was because of the food.

The timing of the trial made unusual demands on
the Jerusalem hotel trade. Not only was the city
crowded with journalists and television people, but it
was the Passover holiday and the independence

celebrations when there was to be a big military parade and dancing in the streets. I was staying in a hotel where the owner had overstretched his resources so much that he had three people booked for each room available. The British journalists were told by the Israeli Government Press Office that they would have to move out into private lodgings. None of us liked the idea but there was nothing for it. I was taken to a block of council flats (you don't think of Jerusalem having *council* flats, do you?) and introduced to a couple who I am certain were as reluctant to accommodate me as I was to be there. Their son was in the army and they had a small spare room. I left my belongings and went out.

It was Independence Day and the rejoicing went on long into the starlit night. Several hours I spent in a night club (you don't think of Jerusalem having *night clubs*, do you?) in the company of the American writer Meyer Levene, who lived on the shores of the Sea of Gallilee, and Stephen Ward, who committed suicide during the Profumo, Christine Keeler, Mandy Rice-Davies sex scandal (he was an artist and was sketching for the *Daily Telegraph*). By the time the dancing in the streets had finished it was dawn and Meyer and his wife drove me to the hotel. By this time I had consumed a liberal amount of local wine and I had forgotten that I had been transferred to a council flat. When I did remember the Levenes had gone, and I had to walk in the warm grey dawn to my correct lodging.

When I reached the place I was confronted with six identical blocks of flats and, I knew, within each of those blocks every flat was identical. As I fingered the

461

key I had been given I was aware that I had no idea where I lived. There followed a furtive and embarrassing sequence. I crept into the blocks one by one, hoping by some fluke to recognise *something*. The wine was not assisting matters. Like a felon up and down stairs I went, secretly trying the key in any door I thought might be likely. Eventually the key turned. Relieved, I went into the small hallway. Yes, that seemed right. I crept into a sitting room that, in the dawn light through the window, seemed to be vaguely familiar. Yes, there was a door at the end. The door to my room, surely. I opened it. Lying on the bed was a sleeping and beautiful girl, wearing nothing at all.

Just keeping panic at bay, I backed out towards the front door of the apartment. As I did so the biggest shadow I have ever seen loomed from a couch in the sitting room. The huge man sat up and leaned on his elbow, staring at me through the gloom.

'Shalom,' I muttered as I backed through the main door. 'Peace be with you.' Outside I tumbled down the stairs and hared out into the main road, not stopping running until I reached the foyer of the hotel. That is where I spent the rest of the night.

If it is true that the evil that men do lives after them, then they have, at least, the consolation of knowing that they are not available for retribution. During separate times in Israel I had two experiences that came home to roost many days after in England.

The first concerned two American girls who were standing in the Negev desert, under the boiling sun, at a bare crossroads with no habitation or inhabitant visible for many miles. Had Moses and his flock happened by it would have done nothing to disturb the scene. I was driving over the desert hills with a beserk Russian. He was a huge, emotional man with a Joe Stalin moustache and eyes like my dog's. When they played Russian songs at the End of the World, a hostelry on the Red Sea, he shed the largest tears I have ever seen from a man.

As we drove over those hot and flinty mountains, and came upon the prospect of the plain, spread out brown and baked before us, my friend at once spotted the two specks, far below, further away, at the cross-roads. 'Women,' he forecast, like a hunter saying 'Bison'. 'They have had a lift on a truck going to the kibbutz to the west. Now they are waiting for someone to take them down to Eilat.'

His forecast was perfect and after coming down onto the flatter desert we eventually arrived alongside the dusty young ladies, standing veiled with flies and with their thumbs held hopefully out. They came with us to Eilat, on the Red Sea, where they stayed at the youth hostel and we stayed at the Queen of Sheba hotel. During the course of the next few days, influenced no doubt by the warmth of both the local friendship and sunshine, I suggested to the girls that if they should ever arrive in London then they might telephone me at the *Evening News*.

At least two years went by and I was working in the garden of my flat-roofed house one Sunday when the telephone rang and my wife answered it. She appeared a little peevishly I thought, and said: 'It's Mimi.'

Mimi I did not know, but she had been given my number by one of the girls from Israel under that irritating system where every American's friend is everyone else's boon companion. She was visiting London and would just love to meet me. She had been given, against the strictest rules, my home number by an accommodating, if lax, telephone operator at the office.

She was very insistent and, after explaining that I could not rendezvous with her immediately since I was among the weeds, I agreed to have an innocuous tea the following afternoon.

We met at Lyon's Corner House, me and Mimi and forty-three of her teenage girlfriends. They were so flattering and so pleased to see me that I ended up showing them around London. In a long and noisy crocodile we trudged through the tourist spots, me in the van. Every now and then I would pause to answer some question about our architectural heritage, our history, what sort of trees grew in the parks, or whether we had ice cubes yet. There were some enquiries to which I did not know the answer so I made it up. When we were trooping along the Mall, a policeman at a crossing called out to me: 'Guide! Will you keep your party off the road, please.'

Naturally I was very fed up with the whole farrago. It was also extremely wearying. Eventually they demanded to go to Soho to see some sin and I agreed to lead them, with the proviso that it was to be the last call. I wanted to go home to my weeds.

Like some latter-day General Booth I marched this wholesome mob up and down Old Compton Street,

Greek Street, Romilly Street and all those nefarious by-ways that appear to change places every time you visit them. There was no sin visible and I had to assemble my team and confess that in all the years I had been familiar with Soho I had never seen a gangster. Soho's reputation was just a fable. At that moment a man began stabbing another man to death outside a green-grocer's. The victim was stabbing the assilant back and a box of plums was knocked onto the pavement. The American girls crowded around, thrilled to bits, while the two men rolled and stabbed each other. Blood was all over the pavement and the shopkeeper was howling somewhat surrealistically: 'My plums! My plums!' Eventually the police and the ambulancemen appeared and the protagonists were cleared up and carried away. The forty-four American girls were fizzing with excite-ment. Mimi kissed me violently and gushed: 'Oh, thank you, Leslie. Thank you. London is just wonderful!'

The second fall from grace concerned a young lady of extreme beauty and madness called Hannah. I met her one day in the California Bar in Tel Aviv, an estab-lishment run by one Abe Nathan who shortly after tried to bring about a one-man peace in the Middle East by flying to the Egyptians and asking them to be reasonable. I like to think it was Abe to whom they eventually listened. He has spent his life, since then, abandoning his former wine-women-and-song exis-tence, in trying to bring peace and understanding to all parts of the world most of which obstinately refuses to listen. He sails in a boat and broadcasts sanity. Sanity, unfortunately, is something not many people recognise when they see it. But Abe tries.

In his bar, this hot afternoon, I met Hannah who told me in the same breath as her name that her life's ambition was to visit England. During the time I knew her she remained the most dedicated and most voluptuous Anglophile I have ever met. She was also, as I have mentioned, impetuous to the point of being crazy.

Two years or more after our meeting when I was, so to speak, between marriages, she suddenly appeared in London, at Aldgate Pump to be precise, and announced that she had come to live with me. This would have been complicated in the extreme, but I was just going to Norwich to take part in a programme at Anglia Television and it occurred to me that, just for old time's sake, she might like to accompany me.

On the train she told me her story. She had taken part in a film and won a beauty contest in Israel and with the money she gained she had set out by sea to Greece and then overland to see the England she had loved so long from afar. Her English was limited (Hebrew being her natural language) but she graphically recounted her adventures across Europe and how she had arrived, with passport but no work permit or other documents, at Dover. It was raining and she was cold. She began to cry. A sympathetic, if predatory, dock policeman put his cloak about her and took her home with him. There she stayed for a week. Now she was with me again, overjoyed to be in England and eager to become famous.

We went to the dining car to have tea and there she produced a wad of her latest glamour photographs. She was deeply in love with herself. The pictures were by no means obscene but might have been considered

466

a trifle over-exposed. She had a great pack of them and she was very proud. Sitting opposite was a young man reading an evangelistic newspaper with good-news headlines: 'God's Word Proved'! and 'Jesus Lives Today'! I had been keeping an anxious eye on his prox-imity and I was not worried for nothing. Suddenly Hannah began distributing her naked photographs like a dealer in a poker school. One, and then another, slid beneath the religious young man's paper and I heard him gasp, then moan.

Hannah would have never understood anything complicated so while attempting to gather up her pictures I said: 'Stop. He is religious. He is . . . a . . .' Inspiration came. 'He is a rabbi.'

The young man, puce-faced, pushed the offending photographs back at us, folded his gospel news and scrambled from behind the table. When he had reached the aisle he turned and glared at me. 'And I'm *not* a rabbi either!' he squeaked.

Hannah was quite without restraint. A sort of madness came over her at, for me, the most inopor-tune moments. Another arrived early that evening. I was sitting in the interview chair at Anglia Television talking about my latest novel. The programme was going out live in the evening magazine. Suddenly I saw the interviewer's eyeballs begin to curl. To my left and slightly behind me there was an ominous crash. Still attempting to talk rationally I saw from the edge of my eye that the lovely Hannah was being pinned to the floor of the studio by four technicians who were patently enjoying every moment of it. One was sitting across her stomach, one had her legs and the third her arms. The fourth, most important, had his fortunately large hands across her mouth.

Somehow we got through the allotted four minutes of the interview; I do not know how. Afterwards they switched to some film item and we managed to man-handle her struggling from the studio. She recovered quickly. 'I am beautiful,' she announced to the massed technicians. 'It is *me* who must be on the television.'

There was one further incident before our merci-fully short reunion came to an end (she was eventu-ally deported, having entered the country illegally, I imagine to the relief of a good many frightened men in London and elsewhere). We sat at dinner in the County Hotel, Norwich. In the middle of the table was a large bowl of salad. The dining room was full. Along came a waiter and Hannah, typically, asked him if he knew where she came from. After several attempts he gave up and she proudly said: 'I am Hannah from Israel.'

'Oh, Palestine,' he said, realisation dawning. 'Out there myself just after the war. Shot quite a lot of your people.'

He passed on. But I could see she was boiling to do something outrageous. 'Steady, steady,' I warned. 'He was only joking.' Then she did it. Seizing the salad bowl, she shouted: 'What is this market!' and flung it violently at the ceiling. I closed my eyes and, conscious of being struck by falling cucumber slices, when I opened them I saw that our salad had been distrib-uted about the room. A woman was sitting shocked, with a lettuce leaf on her head while her husband scraped a squashy half tomato from the bridge of his spectacles. There were lumps of lettuce, spring onions, cucumber, and sloppy slices of tomato everywhere. The bowl itself had struck a child a resounding blow and the boy was holding it up and asking wonderingly: 'Where did it come from?' 'From *whence* did it come?' corrected his mother insistently. An onion had been added to another diner's soup and the crunch of radishes sounded below the feet of waiters. People began to wipe themselves down and a waitress collected the bits of salad and put them back in the bowl which she then pointedly replaced on our table. Eventually I looked up into the smoky and disgruntled eyes of the manager. 'Sorry,' I mumbled. 'It was an accident.'

XXI

In my final three years at the *Evening News* I was involved in a bewildering diversity of assignments. I travelled with the Queen to Australia and to Germany; I arrived in Rhodesia on the day the truculent Ian Smith declared UDI and began a revolution; I drove around half the United States; I taught some Japanese in the Shega Kogan mountains to sing 'Old Uncle Tom Cobbly and All' (not an easy achievement for people who cannot pronounce the letter 'L'); I fell into freezing Holy Loch while manoeuvring for a better view of the first Polaris nuclear submarine to arrive in Britain, and I played Prime Minister Harold Wilson at bar billiards. Any regular reader of the newspaper might have been forgiven for wondering who this busy bee was. In one edition I had a front page story on the consecration of Coventry Cathedral, an article on the prospects for the Old Trafford Test Match (as told to me by Sir Leonard Hutton), a book review and a column on pop music which firmly forecast that the Beatles would flop spectacularly in America.

On the other hand I had no ambitions in newspapers for all my wants had been, almost miraculously, realised. There was never a moment when I desired either to work for another, perhaps grander, newspaper or to change my function within my own office. I never yearned to be an editor or even an assistant or associate editor. There were those who coveted that power and lay in waiting, eating their egg-and-chips lunches at their desks, fearing that some opportunity for glory might arrive when they were absent from the office. Neither, however, was I making much money. When I eventually left the paper I was, I suppose, its leading writer and I was making forty-two pounds ten shillings a week before deductions. Even in 1965 this was not a large salary. My second wife, Diana, was making more managing a ladies' health club. There were, of course, always expenses.

Fleet Street stories concerning expenses are legion, usually beginning with the legend of the reporter running towards the Strand who, on passing his news editor going the other way, shouted to him that he could not stop as he was in a taxi.

On the *News* we had an amiable and gifted reporter called Cyril who had a long history of crises involving his expenses sheets. Once he was sent on a flood story and entered the purchase of a pair of wellington boots on his charges. Sam Jackett, the news editor, cynically told Cyril that before he would sanction the item he wanted to see the boots. 'I had to go out and buy a pair,' grumbled Cyril.

He had assembled a fictitious family, members of which appeared in many of the stories he covered as eyewitnesses of various happenings, always ready with a quote, later to be entered on the expenses sheet as: 'Entertaining Mr Robinson, Re: smash and grab. Holborn – three shillings and sixpence'. Members of the family Robinson (they were known in the office as the Swizz Family Robinson) materialised in all manner of situations. Mrs Mary Robinson would be interviewed on the poor quality of school meals in Dagenham, Essex; then James Robinson would appear as witness to a gas explosion in Twickenham, Middlesex ('Went off like a bomb, it did'). Little Billy Robinson, for the consideration of an icecream, would give his views on Santa Claus, while teenage Mary, a distant cousin, would press for more youth facilities at Hemel Hempstead. Old greybeard Jasper Robinson was always good for a quote about the price of tobacco after each succeeding Budget, while their West Indian kinsman Jeremiah had a pungent word or two to say about race relations in Brixton. An Anglo-Indian, Jellubee Robinson was interviewed about his memories of the Raj. The whole family façade almost came tumbling down, however, when Cyril had recorded Mr Steven Robinson's graphic reconstruction of a bank robbery at Marble Arch. This was worth several Scotches because Mr Robinson had to be calmed before he could give his account and the items duly appeared on the expenses sheet. At about the same time as Cyril was computing the charges, however, he received a telephone call from Scotland Yard requesting Mr Steven Robinson's address since they lacked an essential witness to the robbery. He was obviously their man. Fortunately Cyril always gave his fabled family nebulous addresses. In this case the address was Edgware Road, London, a thoroughfare that runs from Marble Arch to Edgware, a distance of several miles. 'He didn't give me the number of the house,' said Cyril lamely.

On my forty-two pounds ten shillings a week, plus expenses, I went to some of the world's most exotic places and met the occasional important man. On an airliner going to Beirut I sat across the aisle from Harold Wilson, who had just become leader of the Labour Party. Over a certain mileage Fleet Street reporters travelled first class (although some used to cash the tickets in and fly economy, keeping the difference for their holidays) and we were the only two occupants of the elite compartment. We conversed a little, mostly about parliamentary journalists, and at Beirut we went our separate ways.

Several years later, when he was Prime Minister, Mr Wilson went on holiday with his wife Mary to their cottage in the Isles of Scilly, and all Fleet Street went with them. It was a planned operation, the reasonable idea of getting all the interviews, all the photographs and all the filming done in one weekend and then leaving the Wilsons to enjoy their vacation. Through someone who knew the family well, I found myself one evening playing bar billiards with the premier at the St Mary's fishermen's club. ''Arold', as he was universally known in the islands, was well liked and the fishermen treated him as a familiar. He was, naturally, quite adept at bar billiards and reacted to the friendly plaudits of the Penders, the Penhaligons and the Hicks boys. He was about to make a crucial shot and was lining up cue and ball ready to fire the latter at the assembly of wooden toadstools which are the target of the game. Since I was his opponent I thought it astute enough, as he was about to make his stroke, to remind him of our previous meeting, several years before on the plane to Beirut. Hardly pausing in his cue action he muttered from the corner of his mouth: 'It was 1961. December tenth.' He then knocked all the toadstools down with a single stroke. I was deeply impressed.

The following day it was announced that the Prime Minister was to give a press conference on one of the uninhabited islands. Appropriately, a touch of the master's hand here, the isle called Samson was chosen, and we all chugged out there on a convoy of boats. Once landed, Harold sat like a patriarch on a rock and expounded his views on the world situation. St Mary's, the main island, was misty across the water and I wondered what would happen if the ever expected Third World War was to break out while the British leader was thus marooned on an uninhabited speck in the Atlantic Ocean. I asked the premier what his views were on this and, for once, he was put out of his stride. 'Well,' he said, giving the pipe a fierce puff. 'We do have a telephone link of course from the mainland to the house on St Mary's. If I were needed urgently the RAF would send a plane for me.'

'But you're not on St Mary's,' I pressed. 'It's taken twenty-five minutes to get here by boat.'

'Peter Thompson, the boatman,' answered Wilson, a little tersely but not to be beaten, 'is a very good lad. He could be over here in no time to pick me up.'

Not 'no time', but twenty-five minutes, I thought. In that space the world could be ashes. I interviewed Peter Thompson and wrote a story about him – Peter the Boatman, the Last Link in the Hot Line. This, I thought, was pretty worthwhile stuff. It never appeared in my newspaper or any other, however. A hurried government 'D' notice was slapped on the matter even before I had finished dictating it into the telephone. The following year Mr Wilson was equipped with the most powerful walkie-talkie radio ever devised. There was an item on the television news where he was talking to his foreign secretary, Mr George Brown, who was holidaying in far-off Ireland.

One Sunday in the winter of 1963 the whole of Britain was covered with snow and I was sledging down a hill near my house on the Hertfordshire housing estate. It was a run rarely attainable in this country, thick, hard-pressed snow, with a glossy frozen surface. The hill was steep and there was a leap over a small, solid stream at its foot, before the moment of hard braking in an area where some new houses were being built. It was one of those afternoons that you remember all your life. Lois, my young daughter and Mark, my son, with the children and the fathers of the neighbourhood, shared the thrilling toboggan run. The air was like steel and an outrageous vermilion sunset spilled across the sky over Watford. The following day I was going to Australia and at that moment I did not really want to go. It was my turn for a solo run on the sledge and, flat out on my belly (and wearing no headgear), I began the descent and was soon accelerating down the steep white slope. To the stream I came and the toboggan took off like a salmon, clearing the gap easily. Then I forgot to brake, I careered over the broken surface towards the housing site, tried to swerve to avoid a hard-looking pile of bricks and crashed spectacularly through the door of a shaky wooden lavatory erected for the convenience of workmen. The toboggan hit the bucket and my head followed it. The entire little building collapsed on top of me. By the time rescuers had arrived and pulled away the timbers I was nearly dead through laughing. Everybody was holding their ribs. My children sat in the snow and wiped their eyes. At that moment I decided not to go to Australia.

Nevertheless I went, of course, to follow the Queen and the Duke of Edinburgh across the world. It had been a matter of great delight to be picked for such an assignment, and it was almost as big a moment to be invited to Buckingham Palace for the pre-tour cocktail party where the accredited correspondents were to meet members of the royal household who were making the journey.

Everywhere in London there was deep snow. I set out from Fleet Street very early because I wanted to be at the Palace on time and, in that weather, I thought it would be difficult to get a taxi. As it happened one came along at once, creeping through the white landscape, and we arrived outside the Palace gates a good hour too early for the reception. 'You can't go in yet,' said the gate policeman solemnly. 'There's nobody at home.' There was nothing for it but to dismiss the cab and try to keep myself warm for an hour. I walked around in the cold for a while and my feet began to freeze. I went into Victoria Station but a Siberian wind blew through its spaces. Then I saw a workman's caff, a wonderfully steamed-up window, and the magic letters: 'Tea and Snacks'. Within, it was crammed and warm. Porters from the station and bus and lorry drivers were thick around the tables drinking tea from powerful cups and munching into doorstep slices of bread and beef dripping. I joined the queue to the counter. While I waited I eavesdropped on the special language: 'Two o' drip and one medium, please, love.' 'One 'arry Lauder with two babies 'eads.' This latter order was for boiled beef and carrots (an old Harry Lauder song) and two boiled potatoes. When my turn came I asked modestly for a cup of tea, please, love.

'Strong or medium?' enquired Love.

'Er . . . medium, please, love.'

'ONE MEDIUM!' bawled Love deafeningly. She returned to me. Her round face was rosy with sweat. 'Any drip?'

It was years since I had eaten bread and dripping. In Barnardo's in fact. 'Two of drip,' I answered.

'TWO O' DRIP WIV THAT MEDIUM!' she bellowed.

The tea was in a mug as thick as a washbasin, the two of drip shimmered like grey mud under the neon lights. I sat down and warmed my hands on the cup, in the approved manner, and ate the two of drip with great enjoyment.

Twenty minutes later I was having sherry with the Queen.

From the outset my visit to Australia in 1963 was adventurous. Intending to go to the Australia versus England Test at the Sydney cricket ground I had departed a week early but I never actually got to the match. When the plane reached Singapore, where I planned to spend one day, I was again taken violently ill, the symptoms the same as those which had erupted in the church at Mark's christening. On that occasion they had subsided. This time I knew it was serious.

Instead of sensibly calling a doctor to the hotel, I staggered out at two in the morning, hailed a taxi and asked the driver to take me to a hospital. When we got there I was confronted with a long line of sick and injured Chinese, Indians and Malays, holding bones, rubbing bumps and complaining in their various languages. I got on the end of the line. Several times I collapsed and some of the Chinese and Indians helped me to my feet again. A kind Malay man went to get a wheelchair and I sat in this, turning the wheels painfully as the queue gradually moved towards the distant doctor.

When eventually I reached the head of the line I was in severe pain. The doctor was a Chinese lady. 'Who is wrong?' she enquired. Thinking she had just told me her name I told her mine and we curiously shook hands. 'I'm dying,' I said. She looked doubtful. 'We all die,' she said. 'From the moment of birth.' Oriental wisdom may be all very fine, but I was in agony. She rolled up my sleeve, injected something into me and I knew nothing more until I woke up on a wooden bed with a coolie picking my pocket. Having been caught in the act, he very contritely offered to go and get a taxi for me and this he did. I went to the Raffles Hotel, where all those years before I had sung with the band, and asked for a glass of water. My promise made to myself on that long-ago occasion, that

I would one day be able to buy a drink at the famous long bar, had to be postponed. A profound Sikh brought me the water on a silver tray. Then I went back to the airport, feeling now in less discomfort, and boarded the British Airways flight for Sydney. During the journey the pain returned viciously and the pilot radioed ahead for an ambulance to meet us on arrival. Even this had its moment of comedy. In those days any book even suspected of being mildly erotic was enthusiastically seized by the Australian Customs. I had with me a copy of *Lady Chatterley's Lover* which I had borrowed from the bookshelf of a friend in Beirut during my overnight stop there. While I was borne away on a stretcher, clutching my stomach and moaning, a Customs man spotted the book and impounded it.

I had not been in Australia more than a couple of hours when I was on the operating table. They had taken me to the Scottish Hospital at Paddington, Sydney, five minutes from the cricket ground which had been the object of my early journey. I was put into a bed in a general ward. Across the room was a man who had survived a fight with a crocodile. His face was a cobweb of stitches and I was warned that I must not make him laugh. At that time I could not think of anything funny to say. They had given me a sedative but then came a sudden onrush of agony and I shot up in bed, holding my stomach. The crocodile fighter tried to call the nurse but his stitches prevented him opening his mouth properly. Eventually he *whistled* for her. I was given another injection and then carried off to the operating table.

It was appendicitis, probably activated by flying.

The previous onset had come immediately after returning by plane from Monte Carlo. It was only by fortune that my appendix had not ruptured at 30,000 feet.

I was in hospital only five days – the five days of the Test Match, which I could plainly hear being played a few hundred yards away. The crowd would roar when a wicket fell or a boundary was scored but I still had to listen to the commentary by Brian Johnson in much the same way as I would have done if I had been at home in England. My friend, Ian Wooldridge, the notable sports columnist of the *Daily Mail,* came to see me, so did a stream of absolute strangers who had read of my misadventure in a Sydney daily newspaper. Several of them asked me about *Lady Chatterley's Lover.* My fame had spread through the hospital and I cheered considerably when a pretty young nurse arrived and enquired: 'Are you the Queen's reporter?'

I said I certainly was one of them. 'Can I rub some oil in your bum?' she asked.

After the five days in hospital I allowed myself a two-day convalescence at the beachside home of a kind but odd lady well-wisher. It was an unusual house. The furniture kept collapsing, water shot from holes in pipes. The chairs and tables on the terrace had gone rusty. There were many telephones, all of which had been cut off. Most of the lights would not work and while I was there a man arrived to take back a gigantic tank of tropical fish which, he alleged, had not been paid for. The tank was set in the wall between two rooms and he tried to manoeuvre it out while all the coloured fish, congregating in one corner, were staring at him in fear. In the end he gave up and left. The lady, who spent my entire visit walking about in a baby-doll nightie (she even went shopping in it), meant well but apparently found life difficult to handle. Her husband had died and she had no money to spend on anything until his financial affairs were worked out. There were three expensive cars in the overgrown drive and she could not make up her mind which one to sell. It was a curious convalescence.

One week after my eventful arrival in Australia I caught up with the royal tour. I flew to Hobart and was there on the quay on a cool dove-like morning that might have been in Sussex, when the royal yacht sailed into the harbour and Her Majesty and the Duke of Edinburgh stepped ashore. There had been a last minute of drama because the men laying the red carpet had started unrolling it from the wrong end. When they reached the quayside it was too short to reach the gangway of the ship so they had to roll it up and start again.

In the following two weeks I was in Sydney, in Melbourne, in Brisbane, under a hot sun, and trying to keep up with the royal party's vigorous schedule. I was still far from fit (I had lost fifteen pounds in weight) and although I managed to keep going, the office in London was anxious and eventually a disappointed and despondent reporter was instructed to return home. I took my time going back through the Pacific and I spent a couple of days on the beach in Honolulu. On the morning I left for Los Angeles I failed to pay for my breakfast and the bill (almost three dollars) followed me around the world for months, years even.

481

It haunted me, that breakfast, nudging my conscience at the most inconvenient times. In the end I paid it. It made no difference; the bills turned up regularly for years. When I returned to Honolulu two years ago I stayed at the same hotel and asked them to stop sending the bill because I had now paid it. They promised to do so. But when I returned home there was that breakfast again.

The year following the unfortunate Australian experience I was again sent abroad with the Queen. This time the visit was to Germany, the first tour by a British monarch since the beginning of the century. When Her Majesty met a grand and elderly duchess, a survivor of old German royalty to which, of course, our royal family are related, she murmured: 'It *has* been a long time.'

Of course I had my own misadventures. On the opening day of the tour I lost my car and had to get a hurried lift into Bonn on the back of a lorry before going to the royal press reception in a castle above the Rhine. It was very hot and there had been some cement on the back of the truck which blew in clouds over my clothes as we travelled. Since I was so late there was no time to shower and change, so I had to attend the function as I stood. Up to the castle I went and into a huge chamber crowded with the world's correspondents, all shining and clean, hundreds of them. Trying to brush myself down, I joined the long line of people being presented to Her Majesty, and to the Duke of Edinburgh. There was no doubt that I appeared most threadbare and there was still a lot of cement dust hanging about me. Each time I tried to brush it off it went up in clouds and people started sneezing. When I reached the Queen she looked at me quizzically before holding out her hand. The Duke was more forthright. 'Which newspaper do you represent?' he asked.

'The *Evening News*, sir,' I replied reluctantly, thinking he might be considering mentioning my appearance to the editor.

'The *News*, hey?' he said. 'You look as if you're from the *Farmers Weekly*.'

Covering a tour in Germany was far more exacting than in Australia where the time difference gave a comfortable amount of leeway to an evening news-paper correspondent. In Germany there was no such latitude and to keep in step with the busy progress of the tour, to write the stories and to telephone them, caused many problems to both myself and to Anne Sharpley of the *Evening Standard*. Once, with only minutes to go before filing time, we had to leap ashore from a vessel sailing down the Rhine, scamper up to a village and telephone our impressions, me from a grocer's shop and Anne from the establishment of an undertaker. In those days, before direct dialling, it was often a laborious and frustrating business getting through to London. I dictated my copy and emerged into the German village street to find Anne fuming. After a monumental amount of trouble she had finally been connected to the wrong number. Instead of Fleet Street 3000 she had Finchley 3000. 'Is that the *Evening Standard*?' she had enquired suspiciously.

'No,' said a lady with an operatic accent. 'This is Mrs Nissenbaum.'

When Prince Charles was proclaimed Prince of

Wales, I was sent to Anglesey to witness the first time he set foot in his principality. The young boy and his sister were to step ashore on an unscheduled visit from the royal yacht anchored in the harbour. I travelled to Holyhead by train on the previous evening and arrived in deep fog. Never having been there before I had no idea where anything was located. The taxi driver shook his head ponderously when I gave him the name of the hotel. 'Never get there tonight, boy,' he said, thickly Welsh. 'Not in this fog. It's miles.'

'But I *have* to get there,' I insisted. 'I'll pay double fare. How about that?'

Thoughtfully he said he would try and we set out on a terrifying journey along what, by the bumps and manoeuvrings, seemed like little more than a track. It was impossible to see more than a yard ahead of the vehicle and at one point the driver stopped and suggested dramatically that I should turn down my window and listen. I did. 'That's the sea you can hear,' he said morosely. 'Two hundred feet down. Sheer drop.'

After what seemed like hours we came across a shepherd, his dog and a single sheep. The two men conversed animatedly in Welsh, after which the driver turned to me. 'You won't mind a bit of company, will you?' he said casually. Without waiting for an answer the shepherd opened the door and pushed the sheep in. It was smelly as hell and steaming wet. The dog climbed in beside the driver as though he had spent all his life in taxis and the shepherd got in with the sheep and me. I felt I ought to protest, or at least argue, but I got the impression I would have been the one to get out, not the sheep.

'Sick ewe,' said the shepherd, holding the animal by the ear. It sat down placidly but emitted a large smell. After about ten minutes the car stopped and with many a parting benediction the other three passengers got out. Thoroughly disgruntled I sat in the back, unspeaking, until at last we arrived at a rosy light shining through the fog. It was the hotel.

I paid the driver his double fare, although I was inclined in the circumstances to dispute it, and went into the hotel. When I awoke in the morning I heard a distinct loudspeaker making announcements. Opening the curtains I found that the fog had cleared. The hotel was almost opposite the station where I had arrived the previous night.

On the following day, when the royal party had come ashore, the Queen and the Duke of Edinburgh went to Beaumaris for lunch, passing through the place with the longest name in Britain, Llanfairpwllgwngyll-lgogerychwyrndrobwillilantysillogogogoch.

I had purchased a local guide book, but when it came to telephoning my story I discovered that I had left it in a bar. In the middle of dictating the piece I could not, of course, remember how to spell Llanfairpwllgwngyllgogerychwyrndrobwillilanty-sillogogogoch. There was a young woman standing outside the box, waiting to use the phone, and with delight I spotted that she had the name embroidered around her skirt. After explaining my dilemma I persuaded her to stand with her skirt spread out while I repeated the letters from it. As I dictated so she obligingly revolved.

By the time, years later, of the investiture of Prince

Charles at Caernarfon Castle I had left Fleet Street but the *Evening News* commissioned me to write about the event for them as they also did at the wedding of Princess Anne. At the investiture the press were put up on the battlements of the castle, like so many gargoyles. This afforded an unequalled view of the ceremony below but posed problems for those of us who had to compose the story as it was taking place and somehow get our copy to an assistant who would telephone it to London. A system was devised by some official who may have been a relative of Heath Robinson. The written pages, clearly marked, were to be put in envelopes and *placed in a bucket* which was then lowered on a rope and pulley arrangement over the battlements to the back of the castle. There a Boy Scout runner would collect it and carry it to the man waiting by the telephone. The block and tackle worked all right and the Boy Scout was dutifully at his post. Unfortunately, when he was carrying my first few profound paragraphs – my introduction to the whole dramatic scene – he was detained by a policeman and told he could not be allowed to cross the road. At this the child burst into tears and ran home to his mother. My deathless sentences were never delivered nor were they ever found. At the *Evening News* office they had to write the introduction from what they could see on television.

XXII

One evening in August 1961, a fifteen-year-old girl went to visit a travelling fairground in Birmingham and failed to return home. Her body was later found in some disused allotments. She had been strangled with her own tights.

A tragic, but not altogether unfamiliar story. The cuttings from that morning's papers were placed on my desk with the features editor's suggestion that it might be worth a background article. After reading the material, I rang the police in Birmingham, but I do not believe I ever wrote the feature because I recall that something more important came up and I was diverted to that story. The murdered girl was named Jacqueline Thomas and it was not until ten years later that I realised she was my brother's daughter, one of the little girls I had taken to see Santa Claus in Birmingham in 1949 before I sailed for Singapore with the army.

Considering the matter now, it seems perhaps odd that I should have missed the clues. After all, the girl had the same surname as me. Thomas, however, is the sixth most common name in this country. After all those years I had forgotten the Christian names of my nieces. In addition I firmly believed that my brother was dead (my Uncle Chris had told me so years before) and in the newspaper stories the victim's father was quoted and there was mention of several brothers. My brother never had sons. The district of Birmingham where the family lived was also entirely different.

In the early nineteen-seventies I went to Birmingham as part of a promotion campaign for a book. At a cocktail party a reporter from the *Birmingham Post* asked if I had any connections in the city. I told him that I once had a brother who had lived there but who was now dead and, I said, his family had moved elsewhere. I described my journey to Birmingham many years before (leaving out, of course, the reason for it – seeing my brother in the mental hospital) and related the visit to Father Christmas in army uniform with a civilian overcoat. An item appeared in the newspaper's gossip column and a few days later I had a letter from my long-lost niece, Angela, the eldest girl. It said very little and I wrote asking what had happened to the family. Her reply shocked me.

Far from having died years before, my brother Harold had been alive until the previous year. He had never left the hospital but had worked for many years in the gardens. Angela, his daughter, had herself been employed in the hospital as a maid, and had got to know Harold, *without realising he was her own father*. She had taken racing bets to a bookmaker for him and had talked to him while he worked in the hospital greenhouses.

Her mother was also dead. 'She never got over the death of our Jackie,' wrote my niece, adding: 'Who was murdered.'

I had to sit down. Murdered? I began to remember. The following day I went to Birmingham and met my niece, by now in her late twenties and married. She told me the story. Her sister had gone to the fairground and vanished. Eventually the police called at the family's house and said to her mother: 'We've found your Jackie.' Believing that her daughter had just wandered away, the vastly relieved woman got into the patrol car thinking she was going to the police station to pick up the missing girl. Instead they took her to the mortuary and showed her the body.

The police and many other people know who committed the crime (and so do I) but the murderer had an alibi and was never arrested. He went free and on one occasion coolly stopped his car and asked the victim's sister, Angela, if she would like a lift. Years later he committed another crime and this time was charged and went to prison for life. This means that he is free today. If he had been convicted of the killing of Jackie, the penalty, in those days, was death.

Returning to London I went to the offices of the *Daily Mail* and read through the cuttings of the case. There it all was. The misleading items that had not aroused my suspicions. The man quoted as the girl's father was, in fact, a man with whom my sister-in-law had gone to live (in a different district) once she knew that her husband would never leave the mental hospital. This man had sons, which would account for the mention of the victim's brothers. Why my uncle had told me so categorically that Harold was dead I do not know. He must have thought so himself. Anyway he was wrong. After seeing my niece I wrote to her

489

several times and she replied. (I also received a letter from one of her sisters demanding to know why I had done nothing 'to help our mum when Jackie died'.) Then, just as it happened long ago, the letters ceased and I have not heard from her since.

Throughout my time on the *Evening News*, with all its travelling and its daily excitements, I was always trying to write something else. The manuscript of my first novel had been thrown from the window in disgust after the final publisher had rejected it. Never being one to abandon something which might one day come in useful, I retrieved it and wiped away the mud (it was, you may recall, called *My Name Is Mudd*) and put it away.

Then I wrote a television play which, to my joy and astonishment, the BBC decided to buy. It was called *A Piece Of Ribbon*, a sort of army detective story set in Malaya, very much the forerunner of *The Virgin Soldiers*. Luck came along again in time because in the cast was a Chinese actress Jacqui Chan who had been the girlfriend of Antony Armstrong-Jones. This young man was very much in the news as he had just become engaged to Princess Margaret. As the press homed in on Miss Chan, although she was commendably discreet, my play which she was rehearsing came in for a large amount of publicity.

When it was transmitted the reviews and reactions were encouraging and I thought that the door was open. From now on all I had to do was to write scripts and the BBC would be pleased to present them. It did

to start a literary section. I went to their offices in Soho and there I met this ebullient small man in a sharp blue suit; fair-haired and grinning in a way which indicated he was the recipient of secrets, itching to tell the latest gossip or the newest true story from the world of books. He bounced around the desk, held out his hand and said: 'What are you going to write for me?'

It turned out to be called *This Time Next Week*. Following Mollie Lee's words I had gone home and, after sitting in the back garden for half an hour to think it over, I sat down and typed the first ten pages. It began: '*One thing about living on a hill, there was always lots of sky to see and when you weren't busy you could study it. Sometimes the clouds would race along like lean, white lions; like heraldic lions on the shields of knights I used to think . . .*' Today I am sure I would write it differently. But they were the most important words I ever set on paper.

Constable commissioned the book on the evidence of those first pages. I was going to publish a book! When I left their office I almost floated down Orange Street. Working in the evenings, from nine to midnight (although many old Fleet Street hands insist that the book was written in the time I should have been dedicating to the *Evening News*), I finished *This Time Next Week* in six months. It was published in 1963 and had the best and most widespread reviews I shall ever have, even if I write until I'm a hundred. Even today, twenty-one years later, it continues as strongly as ever in hardback, in paperback, and in numerous other editions. It is and has been for many years required reading for people in the childcare departments of the social services, it is a set book for schools examinations (my own

492

sons have been obliged to read it!) and there is a splendid teenage edition published by Blackies with sets of questions at the end. One of these suggests, as the subject for a short essay: 'Describe Leslie's relationship with girls.'

All this time I was, of course, married. If I have failed to dwell long on this aspect of my life, it is because my important world was my professional world, selfish as that was. In addition there is, I think, an amnesia that mercifully webs over the details of a married life that is now a few years gone; perhaps the natural result of a divorce, the traumas, hurts and unhappiness it brings.

We had gone to live on the hilltop of a smart young housing estate at Carpenders Park in Hertfordshire. It became Plummers Park in my novel *Tropic of Ruislip* and I think the description afforded to it in that book is as adequate as any:

Plummers Park was thirty miles from Central London, in the latitude of Ruislip, in the country but not of it. The fields seemed almost touchable and yet remote. Wild roses bloomed and blew in seclusion just out of reach; rooks and flashing magpies in elm and rowan were merely distant birds in distant trees; the fox and the rabbit went unseen from the human windows. On Sundays the people had to drive out in their cars to witness a pig. The estate was the strangest crop ever to grow on that old Hertfordshire farming land. When it was built some trees were permitted to remain like unhappy captives spared because they are old. They remained in clusters, sometimes embedded in

493

garden walls as selling points for house-buyers desiring fresh air, twigs, greenness, and autumn acorns for their children. It was rumoured that the builders had a mechanical squirrel which ran up trees to delight, deceive and decide prospective purchasers.

The streets had, with commercial coyness, retained the sometimes embarrassing names of the various pastures and fields that now lay beneath concrete, crazy paving and statutory roses. Cowacre, Upmeadow, Rising Field, Sheep-Dip, The Sluice, and Bucket Way. Some of the new people said they found it embarrassing to give their address as Sows Hole Lane – provided for a policeman it always provoked suspicion – but others liked the rustic sound.

This was the home of Flat-Roof Man, and Flat-Roof Man had topped the agrarian names with his own fancies. As Andrew walked that morning he passed gates labelled 'Ponderosa', 'Khartoum' and 'High Sierra'. One, called 'Dobermann Lodge', was both a name and a dog warning, while his own uncompromising cube bore the name 'Bennunikin', old Navajo Indian for 'the wigwam on the hill'. In these houses lived men who played patience and others who played fast and loose; women who wanted love and others who desired only an automatic dishwasher. Dreams were regularly dreamed, ambitions thwarted, folded away or modestly attained. Love visited and sex sniffed around. Pottery and French classes were popular in winter; people booked their summer holidays as an antidote to the cold terrors of each New Year. Husbands polished cars; wives polished windows or fingernails. On summer and autumn evenings sunset gardeners burned leaves and rubbish, the smoke climbing like a silent plea for deliverance that forever went unanswered.

494

In writing this I was in no way sneering at the place and the life; I lived there and I was flat-roof man. We had carpets everywhere, a telephone stool, two cars and a copper fireplace like a great bell. In a hospital near Watford, in a theatrical thunderstorm, my second son Gareth was born. It was such an electric night – and forked lightning through picture windows in a bedroom is awesome – that I awoke the other two children who were sleeping quite soundly, and took them under the stairs, telling them whispered stories of how we used to crouch like this during the war. I am sure they were relieved when the thunder, the lightning and the anecdotes had finished and they could get back to the beds from which they had been so abruptly aroused.

Maureen took on a job for the builders of the estate, showing people around the showhouse and an apartment that had been furnished in the local style. Neighbours were friendly and young, all making their way, they hoped, upwards. Living and doing things seemed to leave little time, for me anyway, to read or to think carefully about anything. I took up golf to find space and solitude if not prizes. Parties took place at weekends and although I never knew personally of a single case of wife-swapping (with which readers associated my novel, *Tropic of Ruislip*, although there was no instance in the book either) there were romances and affairs. One lady so desired a young man who lived a short distance away that she called him on the telephone and said that she was terrified of a mouse running about her house. When he arrived to help she told him that the mouse had just run up the leg of her silk pyjamas.

My novel about the housing estate was written seven years after I had left it. It was prompted by two things. One was a hen-dinner of wives from a similar estate in Hampshire who were discussing their lives and their neighbours in the lounge of a hotel at Romsey when I was sitting in a nearby chair. The gossip, the aspirations, the comedy, tragedy and the philosophy, were all plainly to be heard. A few weeks later, because my car had broken down, I stayed overnight at the house of friends who still lived at Carpenders Park. In the morning I stood outside their house and looked across the early sunlight of the valley, over the rank on rank of flat roofs like rafts on the river. No person was to be seen, only a distant milkman whose tinkling bottles could be clearly heard, and an infant on a red tricycle who pursued a lonely track along a pavement and under the trees below. Reflectively I turned away, knowing that I had a story.

A great deal of suburban controversy was provoked by *Tropic of Ruislip* (this aided by a television series). Some of the reactions were quite remarkable. At Ruislip itself (some miles to the west – tropic being a line of latitude and only intended to indicate an environment) a public meeting was called to discuss the book. I attended and faced a crowded audience in the fine old barn that serves as the local library. One uncontrolled woman jumped to her feet and shouted: 'This book has blackened Ruislip in the eyes of the world!' (An exaggerated criticism, I felt, particularly as the Krogers, the infamous spies, had been resident just down the road and the local police had one or two murders on their books.) Later I heard that one lady resident was so ashamed that she might be associated with a book about suburban fornication that she ceased asking for a ticket to Ruislip when she returned by train from London each evening. She asked for a ticket to Eastcote and paid the extra on arrival.

But, when I lived in the 'Tropic'; when *I* was Andrew Maiby, the flat-roof man, who heard the warning of death approaching like the sound of distant thunder at a summer picnic, all those events were some years into the future. As a newspaperman I continued to travel to many parts of the world. In Tokyo I stayed for a week during which my elder brother Lindon, whom I had not met since childhood, died in a hospital all but next door to my hotel. In true Thomas tradition I did not know of his death for a year or more.

Constable, who had published *This Time Next Week*, confidently expected, I believe, that this was somebody's one-off book and that nothing more would be forthcoming from the same source. Desmond Elliott, I think, was also doubtful of the longer-term prospects of my writing. Although I desperately wanted to write a novel and I instinctively realised that the moment was right, I shied away from the obvious notion of using my national service time as the basis of the story. After all there had been an abundance of war stories, too many in fact. What would make this better, or indeed any different? For some time I dithered and thought. The final decision was made because I could not pay my rates.

My income from the *Evening News*, as I have said, continued modest despite the onerous, even regal, journeys and stories upon which I was sent. *This Time Next*

Week, although critically successful, serialised, and purchased for paperback, was not the sort of book to make an author a fortune (the paperback rights were sold to Pan – an act of faith on their part – for three hundred and fifty pounds). Expenditure continued to be tantalisingly ahead of income and when the rates bill came I did not have the money. I had lunch with Desmond at the Carvery at the Regent Palace Hotel in London, from which both of us graduated later, but fairly quickly, to the Connaught. The Regent Palace has important connotations for me because my then wife and the lady with whom I was hopelessly in love once had dinner there together to discuss what they should do about me. The earlier occasion was also to prove something of a catalyst.

Throughout lunch I told my new agent of my financial problems. Needing the rates money was not unusual – the rating officer at my previous address had been called Mr B. Quick. Now the Watford and District Council was demanding its just pound of flesh and I had no money.

As we parted outside Swan and Edgar's now-closed store, Desmond, whom I suspect feared that I might be trying to borrow the rates cash from him, said without any conviction: 'Well, I suppose you had better have a try at writing that novel.'

Thus it was the surburban householder's requirement to pay his due towards refuse collections, tree-lopping and the resurfacing of the roads, that set me on my way to write *The Virgin Soldiers* which went to the top of the bestseller list and sold millions. By the same token, when eventually I began to collect the royalties, I was politely and admiringly informed by the power board that I had paid my electricity bill twice.

I wrote my first novel in the evenings on my return from work, a conscientious nine until midnight routine. For several months I was not called on to make prolonged absences, although I was due to go to Russia for the trial of Gary Powers, the U–2 spy-plane pilot. For reasons known only to themselves the Russians refused me a visa. Other correspondents were granted immediate entry but after going through a tangle of literally red tape (and spending a lot of time in the public house opposite the Soviet Consulate in Kensington) I was confronted with a cartoonist's Russian: a square, bear man behind a desk, who announced simply, 'The Consulate of the Union of Soviet Socialist Republics is closed.' To reinforce his point he put up a sign in English which said: 'Closed', just like a tobacconist.

It is difficult for me to remember how long it took to write *The Virgin Soldiers*. It was published early in 1966, two years after my first book. Something I do remember, however, is that until it was almost in the hands of the printer it was called *The Little Soldiers*. The word 'Virgin', with its connotations, had crossed my mind but it seemed a touch blatant; catchpenny. The eventual Dutch title had the best of both worlds. It translated as *The Little Green Ones*.

When I had finished the manuscript and delivered it to Constable, who then began to become doubtfully excited, I was travelling on the Metropolitan Line, returning from work, when I met John Millard, a studious man, who, as fiction editor of the *Evening News*, had bought my first, and many subsequent, short stories. When I told him of my indecision with the title he frowned. 'I don't like the sound of *The Little Soldiers*,' he said. 'It sounds too much like a children's book.' He smiled wisely. 'Virgin has a better ring, don't you think.'

And so it was. It was not a difficult book to write. It was almost an extension of *This Time Next Week*, a chapter or two on. The single word 'Virgin' gave it a spurious reputation as a novel of sexual explicitness. Two elderly ladies who ran a bookshop in Chichester told me with charming bluntness: 'We did not *want* to stock it – but we simply *had* to.' Considering that it is of the same vintage as such American novels as *Last Exit to Brooklyn* and *The Naked Lunch* I think it is the mildest of love stories. On the other hand it was an exceptionally lucky novel. For all my inhibitions, the fact was that no one had written a novel about national service, as distinct from *wartime* military experience. Since hundreds of thousands of young men underwent that nominally peacetime obligation in all parts of the world, it has always surprised me that no other successful novel has appeared. It was, I truly believe, a beginner's book that arrived at the right moment. It was written from the heart, without subtlety, and perhaps that was the very reason for its success.

It also had a hand from that wry little god of luck who had been so amenable to me throughout my life as a journalist. On publication day I went to Alexandra Palace which, in those times, was used by BBC Television. In the magazine programme after the six

500

o'clock news, one of those I had helped to establish in my Exchange Telegraph days, I was interviewed by Michael Aspel. There was nothing very unusual about the interview but, when I had departed, the rules and worries of Auntie BBC surfaced and someone voiced doubt about transmitting – at six in the evening – an item about a book with 'Virgin' in the title, and with a story about failed virgins between the covers. Rather than scrap the interview, however, they decided that Aspel should record a rider, a warning. 'The book,' he said solemnly, 'is called *The Virgin Soldiers* by Leslie Thomas, and it is published by Constable at twenty-one shillings. *Don't leave it around where the children can pick it up.*'

Human curiosity being what it is, the publishers were sold out by the next afternoon. They had to empty their own window display to provide emergency copies for the bookstall at Waterloo Station. I had a bestseller.

Carl Foreman, the great producer and film writer, responsible for *High Noon*, *The Guns of Navarone*, and *The Victors*, bought the film rights of *The Virgin Soldiers* immediately upon reading the book. He then bludgeoned the dithering executives of Columbia Pictures into making the film which is still a success today. Carl became a friend and a mentor and we saw each other when I was in Hollywood or he and his English wife Eve were staying at their quiet thatched house in Hampshire. As I write this I have just heard of his death.

The film version of my novel was directed by John Dexter and produced by Ned Sherrin, who describes its making hilariously in his autobiography *A Small Thing Like an Explosion*. It had a fine cast. Brigg, the young conscript, was played by Hywell Bennett, who got so close to the part that I could see myself when young; T'sai Chin, who played Juicy Lucy, Lynn Redgrave and her mother Rachel Kempson, who played her mother in the film. At the première Lynn introduced me to her famous father, Sir Michael, with, I felt, exaggerated enthusiasm. 'Daddy,' she exclaimed. 'Here is the Creator!' For once I felt slightly inadequate.

Wayne Sleep, who has revolutionised ballet, and Christopher Timothy, who became James Herriott's television vet, were also in the film with Nigel Davenport and Nigel Patrick. The actor who, when *The Virgin Soldiers* is now shown on television, attracts most attention occupies less than thirty seconds on the screen.

This story goes back to Barnardo days. A Mr Jones was the publicity man for the Homes and, when I reached Fleet Street, he would sometimes call me with some item of news about Barnardo's. One day he had something different to offer: 'My son, David,' he said, 'is a pop singer.'

In those days most young people were. 'I think he sounds terrible,' confessed Mr Jones, 'but he must be some good because he's made a record. Do you think you could give it a mention in your column?' Those were the days of my incompetent record reviewing and I agreed to listen to it, which I did and, I believe, wrote a couple of paragraphs about it. Some time, perhaps three years, went by and one day I went to the auditions for *The Virgin Soldiers* film and there was young David Jones waiting to read for a part. He did not get the role but he was offered another, a brief appearance, and he accepted.

It was not until some years after the film had appeared that I realised who our bit-part actor was . . . David Bowie. Young people now watch the film just to catch the most shadowy glimpse of the man who has grown into a great international star. Recently a youthful lady said to me: 'You're the chap who wrote David Bowie's film, aren't you?'

On a hot August night in 1966 I was alone in my house at Carpenders Park. Recently, I had bought a second house, a neat place with bow windows at West Wittering on the Sussex coast, near Chichester. My wife and three children were down there that night.

I had only returned to London for twenty-four hours, intending to go back to the coast for the whole of August. The object of the brief visit was to see the preview of the film *Georgie Girl*; it could easily have cost me my life. Otto Plaskes, who produced the film, had asked me to see it. There were plans that I might write a script for a project he had in mind. That evening I returned to my house in Hertfordshire and went to my in-laws' home nearby to make the final arrangements for taking them down to West Wittering the following morning.

It was a close evening and I went to a public house

and then a restaurant where I ate alone. At midnight I was in bed in my son Mark's room since the bed in the main bedroom had not been made up. I opened the big swinging window and went to sleep. An hour later I awoke and smelled smoke. Going downstairs and into the other rooms I could see nothing amiss and I thought it must be the scent of somebody's garden fire which had smouldered on into the night. I closed my eyes and then heard breaking glass followed by a deep thump. Hurrying to the window I saw that a house about a hundred yards away was on fire.

What happened over the next few minutes is starkly clear to me, even though it was eighteen years ago. My actions seem to be like those of someone in a slowed-up dream. Wearing pyjamas (Marks and Spencer, non-flammable) I ran down the stairs and around the garden wall of my own house. I had nothing on my feet and the grass was dewy. For some reason I imagined that someone *must* have already telephoned the fire brigade and, indeed, that a crowd of neighbours would already be at the house. When I arrived I found myself alone, with a naked and dead man lying face down on the paved patio. Smoke was pouring from the upper window through which he had jumped or fallen. I had no idea who he might be.

The blaze seemed to be confined to the top floor. Almost casually the lady who lived there, undoubtedly in shock, approached me. She was wearing her dressing gown and she said calmly, 'I've telephoned the fire brigade.'

Knowing that she had three small children I asked where they were. 'They're still inside,' she answered.

At that moment the little girl, about seven or eight, appeared at the upper window. Her hair seemed to be on fire. She was crying with fear.

Her mother and I moved below her, by the body lying on the ground. Quite composedly her mother told the girl to jump. She did and we caught her safely and put her on the ground.

Another man had appeared, a neighbour who was walking his dog, a languid Great Dane. Everything seemed to be happening so naturally and slowly, as if were were going carefully through a rehearsal of some play. 'Where are the twins?' I asked the mother. She had twin boys, about four years of age.

'They're inside too,' she answered.

I went into the house with the man who had been walking the dog. The ground floor was wraithed in smoke but there was no fire down there. Even the electric lights were working. We looked up the stairs; oily smoke was billowing on the landing. I picked up a tea-towel, put it under the tap and held it across my mouth. Then, stupidly still bare-footed, I ran up the stairs.

Even now I don't know how long I was up there. Probably less than thirty seconds. I screamed the boys' names and barged into the bedrooms. There was no reply. Thick smoke was enveloping me, filling my lungs. Then a red glow loomed up in front of my eyes and I realised I was on fire.

Turning, I shouted and ran across the landing. I fell all the way down the stairs and rushed out of the house, to the front, where I rolled over and over in the wet grass. When eventually I sat up I realised I was naked, my pyjamas had shrivelled from me. My hair was gone and skin was hanging from my hands and arms like chewing gum. There was a strong smell of hamburger. The Great Dane came up and gave me a few exploratory licks.

While all this drama was going on people two houses away slept undisturbed. Indeed some did not wake until the firemen had finally put out the blaze. One neighbour had a telephone call from another and thought the caller was joking. He went to his window and saw all the evidence of the drama spread outside.

The twins, it appears, were not in the house at all. They had gone out of the back door and into another neighbour's house. This I did not know until months later at the inquest on the dead man, whose identity – like that of the other participants in this tragic matter – does not concern this story. The boys' mother truly believed they were inside because after I had come out of the blaze she went upstairs and tried to find them. She was badly burned also.

We were taken to a local hospital which, fortuitiously, had a special unit for treating burns. In the ambulance the mother and I, stretched out, conversed and decided that we would never again be able to face roast beef.

My injuries were widespread but not deep. The burns of the children's mother, and indeed of the little girl who had jumped from the window, were more serious but happily they recovered without noticeable scars. When we were able to move about in the hospital we used to visit each other in the wards and laugh about the state we were in. We wondered if we might audition for parts in a horror film.

My burns covered about half of my body. I looked a dreadful mess. Maureen, summoned from Sussex and not told the extent of the injuries, almost fainted when she came into my room at the hospital. A policewoman, who accompanied a male colleague when he came to get a statement, did faint. She apparently took one look at this swollen (even more than usual!) head and passed out cold on the floor. I had no lasting injuries, although I still have the marks of the seams of my pyjamas on my shoulders and scars on my hands, with which I must have covered my face. My main problem was the large amount of fumes I had consumed – enough, as one doctor cheerfully told me, for me – who had never smoked – to have got through twenty cigarettes a day for the whole of my life. This, however, had its compensations because an extremely attractive lady physiotherapist was given the three times daily task of rubbing and pushing my chest, even to the extent of sitting upon it, in an effort to get rid of the foul phlegm that was the result of the smoke. I wish I had been in a fit enough state to appreciate the treatment. A more unpleasant episode was when several students appeared and began to strip the skin from my already tender feet and legs. A doctor ordered a team of them to do it – to get the painful business over as quickly as possible.

For several days I could not see. I knew I was not blind and that it was merely the burned skin covering my eyes. Someone brought me a radio and I listened to more music than I had done for years. There was also a Morecambe and Wise radio programme where Eric said he had obtained a job in a zoo, feeding the pelicans. It did not pay much but it filled the bill. That

507

of land! Then, of course, my father died at sea, so she is there by herself. It is probably just as well. They would only quarrel.

One matter I feel, however, must be added to this chronicle. On a June day in 1966 I was going to a cricket match at Lords and there, sitting on the Metropolitan Line train, was a beautiful and composed young lady. We began a conversation which has continued to the present day. Diana is a remarkable person who is, as someone else once said of her, lovely and lovely with it. She is both busy and serene, a difficult achievement. She has calmed my life. In the fourteen years of our marriage we have lived in many places and produced one son, Matthew.

My other children are now grown. My daughter Lois was married on a sunlit day we will always remember when the horse and trap refused to go down the hill and the bride and groom had to walk; and the village band played on our lawn beside the stream. Maureen, my former wife, was of course there that day with her husband Bill, a sincere and funny man who has been my friend for many years.

When I told Diana that I was going to embark on writing this account of my early life she smiled and said in her apt way: 'Just mention me in passing.' And that is what I have done.

Perhaps one day, when the events described herein have become even further removed and more misty, I will write about the next part – my life with books. But that is another story. Or, possibly, several.

Dover Beach

Leslie Thomas

Summer 1940. Dunkirk has been evacuated. Dover is inundated with young soldiers, who wearily wander its streets, wondering what the future holds in store for them.

Toby Hendry, a fighter pilot, is awaiting orders when he meets Giselle, a young Frenchwoman who has fled occupied France. Can their love affair withstand the forces of war?

Reserve naval commander Paul Instow has been called up to fight in a war for which he feels too old. Distracting him from his worries is Molly, a young prostitute. Their relationship is tender and happy, but is this true love?

In *Dover Beach* Thomas chronicles the lives and loves of ordinary people in besieged Britain during these tense, but curiously elated days.

arrow books

Waiting for the Day

Leslie Thomas

Midwinter, 1943. Britain is gripped by intense cold and in the darkest days of the war. It is six months before D-Day and the battle to liberate Nazi-occupied Europe.

RAF officer Paget is heading home for Christmas, back to the resurrection of a passion he thought was long over.

In a freezing hut on Salisbury Plain, Sergeant Harris is training his troops for landing on the shores of Normandy, but his mind is occupied by thought of just how his young wife is coping with his absence.

Lieutenant Miller has arrived at an all-but-derelict mansion in Somerset where his American division has set up its head-quarters. His affair with an Englishwoman is both bittersweet and potentially dangerous.

Cook Sergeant Fred Weber is enjoying fishing off the coast of occupied Jersey. His calm is soon to be shattered as his war takes on a violent twist.

Each man is heading inexorably towards the beaches of France, where the great battle will commence . . .

The Magic Army

Leslie Thomas

The war, they said, would be over by Christmas. That was in 1939, and it is now January 1944. An exhausted Britain faces another year of conflict.

Meanwhile, small coastal villages in Devon are facing an invasion from an army just as foreign as that of the Germans. The Americans are smart, well-fed and well-equipped, and they have swept the bewildered citizens of South Devon from their homes in deadly earnest rehearsal for D-Day.

As the beaches echo to the sound of bullets and the local church to the sound of Glenn Miller, Americans and English are thrown together with sometimes hilarious, sometimes painful and puzzling results.

arrow books

The Virgin Soldiers

Leslie Thomas

'It rained a lot, and steamed when the sun shone. It was always hot. But it was safe . . .'

One way or another the Communist guerilla war in Malaya kept a whole British army occupied from 1948 until 1952. They were the virgin soldiers. Idle, homesick, afraid, bored, oversexed and undersatisfied.

A young virgin like Brigg had to grab his fun while and where he could – in the Liberty Club, in Juicy Lucy's flat or up in Phillipa's room – in one frantic attempt at living before he died or got demobbed . . .

'Scenes rivalling the best of D. H. Lawrence' *Daily Telegraphy*

'Truly exciting' *Daily Mail*

arrow books

Stand Up Virgin Soldiers

Leslie Thomas

The worst has happened. On the eve of their return to Blighty, Brigg and his fellow National Servicemen find themselves sentenced to another six months in Panglin Barracks . . .

Many of the surviving characters from *The Virgin Soldiers* live again in these pages: dogged Tasker, the odious Sergeant Wellbeloved, the vulnerable Colonel Bromley Pickering and the comically touching Juicy Lucy.

But we encounter new characters too: the fanatical and demented Lieutenant Grainger; the endearing Welshman, Morris Morris – strong as a horse but vagglingly buxom; US private Clay – mysteriously lost in transit by the American Army; and last, but not least, Bernice Harrison, the sporting nurse who threatens to replace the wayward Lucy in Brigg's affections . . .

'Ribald and rich in comic invention' *Daily Mail*

'Splendidly conveys . . . compassion, excitement, entertainment' *Evening Standard*

arrow books

Onward Virgin Soldiers

Leslie Thomas

The hero of *The Virgin Soldiers*, National Serviceman Brigg, is back. But now, instead of being stationed in his customary barracks at Panglin, he's a Regular Army sergeant, defending the Empire in the beds and bars of Hong Kong.

Peacetime diversions are numerous and distracting and include sensual fireworks with a pair of delicious Chinese twins and a tender, erotic affair with the lonely wife of an American serviceman.

Bursting with life and bawdy humour, *Onward Virgin Soldiers* is the second in Leslie Thomas's classic trilogy and an outstanding novel in its own right about the pleasures and privations of a soldier in the British army.

arrow books

Dangerous in Love

Leslie Thomas

A walk through Kensal Green Cemetery, a meat pie in the greasy spoon, a weekend away complete with flannel pyjamas – Dangerous Davies knows how to treat the woman he loves.

Detective Constable Davies has two things on his mind: Jemma Duval, the beautiful, black, hymn-singing social worker and 'Lofty' Brock, the harmless old eccentric who drowned in the canal. To prove that Lofty's death was no accident, our hero sets out to do some undercover detective work on his own. He soon discovers that something sinister is going on. Something that requires intuition, dedication, brilliant deduction – and a timely blow with a blunt instrument.